Heritage, Labour and the Working Classes

Heritage, Labour and the Working Classes is both a celebration and commemoration of working class culture. It contains sometimes inspiring accounts of working class communities and people telling their own stories, and weaves together examples of tangible and intangible heritage, place, history, memory, music and literature.

Rather than being framed in a 'social inclusion' framework, which sees working class culture as a deficit, this book addresses the question 'What is labour and working class heritage, how does it differ or stand in opposition to dominant ways of understanding heritage and history, and in what ways is it used as a contemporary resource?' It also explores how heritage is used in working class communities and by labour organisations, and considers what meanings and significance this heritage may have, while also identifying how and why communities and their heritage have been excluded. Drawing on new scholarship in heritage studies, social memory, the public history of labour and new working class studies, this volume highlights the heritage of working people, communities and organisations. Contributions are drawn from a number of Western countries including the USA, UK, Spain, Sweden, Australia and New Zealand, and from a range of disciplines including heritage and museum studies, history, sociology, politics, archaeology and anthropology.

Heritage, Labour and the Working Classes represents an innovative and useful resource for heritage and museum practitioners, students and academics concerned with understanding community heritage and the debate on social inclusion/exclusion. It offers new ways of understanding heritage, its values and consequences, and presents a challenge to dominant and traditional frameworks for understanding and identifying heritage and heritage making.

Laurajane Smith is ARC Future Fellow, School of Archaeology and Anthropology, Research School of Humanities and the Arts, the Australian National University, Canberra. Her previous publications include *Archaeological Theory and the Politics of Cultural Heritage* (2004); *Uses of Heritage* (2006) and *Intangible Heritage* (with Natsuko Akagawa, 2008). She is editor of the *International Journal of Heritage Studies*.

Paul A. Shackel is Professor and Chair of the Department of Anthropology at the University of Maryland. He has written several articles and books on labour, including *The Archaeology of American Labor and Working Class Life* (2009) and *Culture Change and the New Technology: An Archaeology of the Early American Industrial Era* (1996).

Gary Campbell is an independent researcher. He has worked and published with Laurajane Smith on working class heritage, and has a background in industrial sociology and political science. He has worked as a researcher for the Australian Manufacturing Workers Union.

Key Issues in Cultural Heritage
Series Editors:
William Logan and Laurajane Smith

Also in the series:

Heritage and Globalisation
Sophia Labadi and Colin Long

Intangible Heritage
Laurajane Smith and Natsuko Akagawa

Places of Pain and Shame
William Logan and Keir Reeves

Cultural Diversity, Heritage and Human Rights
Michele Langfield, William Logan and Máiréad Nic Craith

New in 2011:

The Heritage of War
Martin Gegner and Bart Ziino

Heritage, Labour and the Working Classes

Edited by
Laurajane Smith, Paul A. Shackel and
Gary Campbell

 Routledge
Taylor & Francis Group
LONDON AND NEW YORK

First published 2011
by Routledge
2 Park Square, Milton Park, Abingdon, Oxon OX14 4RN

Simultaneously published in the USA and Canada
by Routledge
711 Third Avenue, New York, NY 10017

Routledge is an imprint of the Taylor & Francis Group, an informa business

© 2011 Laurajane Smith, Paul Shackel and Gary Campbell for selection and editorial matter; individual contributions, the contributors.

The right of Laurajane Smith, Paul Shackel and Gary Campbell to be identified as the authors of the editorial material, and of the authors for their individual chapters, has been asserted in accordance with sections 77 and 78 of the Copyright, Designs and Patents Act 1988.

All rights reserved. No part of this book may be reprinted or reproduced or utilised in any form or by any electronic, mechanical, or other means, now known or hereafter invented, including photocopying and recording, or in any information storage or retrieval system, without permission in writing from the publishers.

Trademark notice: Product or corporate names may be trademarks or registered trademarks, and are used only for identification and explanation without intent to infringe.

British Library Cataloguing in Publication Data
A catalogue record for this book is available from the British Library

Library of Congress Cataloging in Publication Data
Heritage, labour, and the working classes / edited by Laurajane Smith, Paul A. Shackel and Gary Campbell. – 1st ed.
   p. cm.
   Includes index.
   1. Labor–History. 2. Working class–History. 3. Labor movement–History. I. Smith, Laurajane. II. Shackel, Paul A. III. Campbell, Gary.
   HD4841.H47 2011
   331.88–dc22
                  2010052683

ISBN: 978-0-415-61810-6 (hbk)
ISBN: 978-0-415-61811-3 (pbk)
ISBN: 978-0-203-81323-2 (ebk)

Typeset in Garamond
by Taylor and Francis Books

Printed and bound in Great Britain by
CPI Antony Rowe, Chippenham, Wiltshire

Contents

List of illustrations		viii
List of contributors		x
Series general co-editors' forward		xiv

1 Introduction: class still matters 1
   LAURAJANE SMITH, PAUL A. SHACKEL AND GARY CAMPBELL

PART I
Class, Commemoration and Conflict   17

2 The 1984/85 Miners' Strike: re-claiming cultural heritage 19
   MICHAEL BAILEY AND SIMON POPPLE

3 Remembering Haymarket and the control for public memory 34
   PAUL A. SHACKEL

4 The social and environmental upheaval of Blair Mountain: a working class struggle for unionisation and historic preservation 52
   BRANDON NIDA AND MICHAEL JESSEE ADKINS

5 This is our island: multiple class heritage or ethnic solidarities? 69
   RICHARD COURTNEY

PART II
Recognising and Commemorating Communities 83

6 Don't mourn organise: heritage, recognition and memory in Castleford, West Yorkshire 85
   LAURAJANE SMITH AND GARY CAMPBELL

vi Contents

7 Images, icons and artefacts: maintaining an industrial culture
   in a post-industrial environment ... 106
   DAVID WRAY

8 A working town empowered: retelling textile history at
   Cooleemee, North Carolina ... 119
   TAMASIN WEDGWOOD

9 The silencing of Blackball working class heritage,
   New Zealand ... 136
   PAUL MAUNDER

PART III
Working Class Self-Representation and
Intangible Heritage ... 145

10 Working class autobiography as cultural heritage ... 147
    TIM STRANGLEMAN

11 You say 'po' boy', I say poor boy: New Orleans culinary and
    labour history sandwiched together ... 160
    MICHAEL MIZELL-NELSON

12 Swedish working class literature and the class politics
    of heritage ... 178
    MAGNUS NILSSON

13 Singing for socialism ... 192
    KATE BOWAN AND PAUL A. PICKERING

14 'Faces in the Street': the Australian poetic working class heritage ... 216
    SARAH ATTFIELD

15 Industrial folk song in our time ... 231
    MARK GREGORY

PART IV
Case Studies in Commemoration, Remembrance
and Forgetting ... 247

16 'The world's most perfect town' reconsidered: negotiating class,
    labour and heritage in the Pullman community of Chicago ... 249
    JANE EVA BAXTER AND ANDREW H. BULLEN

17 Tolpuddle, Burston and Levellers: the making of radical and
national heritages at English labour movement festivals 266
HILDA KEAN

18 Working class heritage without the working class:
an ethnography on gentrification in Ciutat (Mallorca) 283
MARC MORELL

Index 303

Illustrations

3.1 The Anarchist Riot in Chicago: a dynamite bomb exploding among the police (Courtesy of the Chicago History Museum, ICHi-03665)   37
3.2 Memorial marking the graves of the martyrs of Haymarket (Photograph by Paul A. Shackel)   41
3.3 National Historic Landmark plaque with the added inscription that reads 'the United States of America's oppression of dissidents' (Photograph by Paul A. Shackel)   44
3.4 The Haymarket Memorial erected in 2004 (Photograph by Mary Brogger)   45
3.5 Protectors of Chicago Memorial in Haymarket Square (Courtesy of the Chicago History Museum, ICHi-14452)   47
3.6 Veterans gather for the twenty-second anniversary of the Haymarket Riot at Union Park (Courtesy of the Chicago History Museum, ICHi-2878)   48
3.7 Protectors of Chicago Memorial in the courtyard of the Police Academy (Photograph by Paul D. Rettig)   49
4.1 State of West Virginia. The distance from Charleston to Blair Mountain was roughly 50 miles. The miners' ultimate goal was to reach Matewan and liberate Mingo County from martial law that was enacted by the state to break an ongoing strike in the county   54
4.2 Unscaled map of the Blair Mountain Battlefield, redrawn and modified from Meador 1991:60. The defensive lines from Blair Gap to Mill Creek extended over ten miles, with the gaps fortified the heaviest   57
7.1 The Durham Gala, 2009. Photo David Wray   113
7.2 The memorial garden on the former site of New Herrington colliery. Photo David Wray   113
16.1 Pullman Panorama circa 1885. This photograph shows the remote and almost rural setting of the Pullman Community when it was still an area detached from the city of Chicago. This

view is looking east and shows the factory works to the left, and on the opposite side of the unpaved road the Hotel Florence, the Arcade and the Greenstone Church. Several of the more central executive and skilled worker homes can also be glimpsed between the hotel and arcade structures. (Photo courtesy of the Industrial Heritage Archives Collection, Pullman State Historic Site) 250

16.2 Visiting Pullman in 2009. Bike riders line up for the Annual Labor Day Bike Ride through the industrial landscapes of south Chicago and northwest Indiana, while others explore the veranda of the Hotel Florence and read surrounding signage. Events like these are one of the many ways the community opens itself up to outside visitors so they can engage with the local history of Pullman. (Photo courtesy of the Bertha Ludlam Library, Pullman State Historic Site) 252

Contributors

Michael Jessee Adkins holds a BA in Humanities and MA in Sociology from Marshall University. He is a military combat veteran, scholar and member of the National Anthropology Honour Society (Lambda Alpha, Beta Chapter). His research interests include social conflict theory, archaeology, Appalachian studies and working class social movements.

Sarah Attfield grew up in a working class family on a high-rise public housing estate in London. She now lives in Australia and completed a PhD in Australian working class poetry in 2007. She is currently working as a casual academic at the University of Technology, Sydney.

Michael Bailey teaches in the Sociology Department at the University of Essex. He is the author or editor of *The Uses of Richard Hoggart* (with Ben Clarke and John K. Walton), *Mediating Faiths* (with Guy Redden), *Richard Hoggart: Culture & Critique* (with Mary Eagleton), *Narrating Media History*. His next book is provisionally titled, *Beyond Cultural Studies*. He has held visiting fellowships at Goldsmiths, University of London; the London School of Economics and Political Science; Wolfson College and the Centre for the Arts, Social Sciences and Humanities, University of Cambridge.

Jane Eva Baxter is an Associate Professor of Anthropology at DePaul University in Chicago. She is a historical archaeologist who does community-based archaeology in the Pullman neighbourhood, where she also bought her first home, a skilled worker's cottage, in 2007. She volunteers as a docent and tour guide for the Pullman State Historic Site.

Kate Bowan is a Postdoctoral Fellow in the Research School of Humanities and the Arts, The Australian National University. She has published on early twentieth-century Australian music, and nineteenth-century music and politics. Her current project is with historian, Paul Pickering, on popular politics and music in the nineteenth-century British World, to be published by Manchester University Press.

List of contributors

Andrew H. Bullen has lived in the Pullman neighbourhood for over a decade. He writes a monthly column on Pullman History for the local newspaper and has developed the Virtual Pullman Museum http://www.pullman-museum.org/.

Gary Campbell is an independent researcher. He has worked and published with Laurajane Smith on working class heritage, and has a background in industrial sociology and political science. He has worked as a researcher for the Australian Manufacturing Workers Union.

Richard Courtney is the Knowledge Exchange Post-Doctoral Fellow for the College of Arts, Humanities, & Law at the University of Leicester. His current project on English heritage and the canal networks is based in the Centre for Urban History and the School of Museum Studies. His research interests are trans-disciplinary across Sociology, Geography and Politics. His substantive interests are social class, ethnicity and racism, gender and particularly masculinity and political and sociological theory.

Mark Gregory has been a union activist for about 40 years. He has written articles about union songs and organised workshops and concerts for folk festivals and labour history conferences. He has delivered papers on union songs to conferences of IASPM and MSA. His 2007 MA thesis by research is titled '*60 years of Australian union songs*'.

Hilda Kean is Dean of Ruskin College, Oxford and Director of its Public History programme. She sits on the advisory board of *Public History Review* (UTS Australia). She has published widely on public and cultural history and including articles in *Women's History Review*, *Public History Review*, and *The Public Historian*. Her books include: *People and their Pasts: Public History Today* (ed with Paul Ashton, Palgrave Macmillan, 2009); *London Stories, Personal Lives, Public Histories*, (Rivers Oram, 2004); *Seeing History: Public History in Britain Now* (ed with Paul Martin & Sally J Morgan, Francis Boutle, 1999).

Paul Maunder holds an MA, University of Canterbury, and is a member of the Blackball Working Class History Project. He is a film director, cultural activist and playwright, and is best known for the film *Sons for the Return Home* (1979) and his work with Amamus Theatre Group (1971–1978), Theatre of the Eighth Day (1981–1988) and Pou Mahi a Iwi – Cultural Work Centre (1989–present). His plays deal with issues of politics, class, activism or the history of the labour movement.

Michael Mizell-Nelson is an assistant professor of history at the University of New Orleans whose research interests centre upon the social history of New Orleans, twentieth-century US labour history and public history. He first interpreted New Orleans' cultural history as a video documentary producer.

Marc Morell is a PhD candidate at the Universitat de Barcelona and is a member of the 'Politics, Labour and Sustainability' research team at the Universitat de les Illes Balears. Drawing on political anthropology, he inquires into tourism and urban issues by focusing on the production of space in market society. He has conducted field research in Mallorca and Malta. For more information please visit http://www.uib.es/depart/dfl/pts/morell_eng.htm.

Brandon Nida is a native West Virginian, a graduate of Marshall University at Huntington, West Virginia, and is currently a doctoral student in archaeology at UC Berkeley. His interests are in social inequality, political economy, archaeology of labour conflict and hunter-gatherer archaeology.

Magnus Nilsson is Associate Professor in comparative literature at Malmö University. His research interests include working class literature, and Marxist theory.

Paul A. Pickering is Deputy Director of the Research School of Humanities and the Arts, The Australian National University. He has published extensively on Australian, British and Irish social, political and cultural history and public memory and commemoration. His current project is a study of music and politics in the nineteenth-century British world (with musicologist Kate Bowan) that will be published by Manchester University Press.

Simon Popple teaches cinema and photography at the University of Leeds, is Director of the Louis Le Prince Centre for Film, Photography and Television and founding editor of *Early Popular Visual Culture*. He is currently working on a book *The Last Hurrah! The Popular Visual Culture of the Anglo Boer-War* for I.B.Tauris. He has just finished a major collaboration with the BBC under the AHRC's KEP scheme which examined the role of the BBC's archive of the 1984/5 miners' strike and is currently conducting a follow-on project which is bringing former miners and police officers together to produce responses to archival sources and to create contextual resources.

Paul A. Shackel is Professor and Chair of the Department of Anthropology at the University of Maryland. He has written several articles and books on labour, including *Culture Change and the New Technology: An Archaeology of the Early American Industria Era* (Plenum 1996), *'They Worked Regular': Craft, Labor, Family and the Archaeology of an Industrial Community* (with Matthew Palus, Tennessee, 2006) and *An Archaeology of American Labor and Working Class Life* (Florida, 2009).

Laurajane Smith is Australian Research Council Future Fellow in the School of Archaeology and Anthropology, Research School of Humanities and the Arts, the Australian National University, Canberra. She has authored *Archaeological Theory and the Politics of Cultural Heritage* (2004); *Uses of Heritage* (2006) and edited *Cultural Heritage: Critical concepts in Media and Cultural Studies* (2007) and co-edited *Intangible Heritage* (with Natsuko Akagawa), all with Routledge, and she has co-authored *Heritage, Communities and Archaeology* (with Emma Waterton) Duckworth, 2009. She is editor of the *International Journal of Heritage Studies*.

Tim Strangleman is interested in a wide range of areas around the sociology of work and economic life. He has carried out research in the railway, engineering, mining, construction, brewing, banking, health and teaching sectors. These studies examine questions of work meaning and identity, de-industrialisation and the experience of industrial change, oral history, auto/biography, visual methods and approaches and nostalgia. He is author of two books *Work Identity at the End of the Line*, Palgrave (2004) and *Work and Society: Sociological approaches, themes and methods*, (with Tracey Waren) Routledge (2008). He is Reader in Sociology, School of Social Policy, Sociology and Social Research, University of Kent, UK.

Tamasin Wedgwood was born in Stoke-on-Trent, and has a Special Honours Degree in American Studies (Hull, 1990), and an MA (Distinction) in Museum Studies (Leicester, 2007). She is the author of 'History in 2-dimensions or three? Working class uses of History' published in the *International Journal of Heritage Studies* and of 'Partner or Pariah – Are some community partners in museum projects more "acceptable" than others?' published in Museum and Society. After five years living amid the declining mill towns of North Carolina, she has recently moved to the Isle of Man, where she continues as a freelance writer.

David Wray is a Senior Lecturer in the School of Arts and Social Sciences at the University of Northumbria. As an ex-miner himself, his main research interests are the consequences of post-industrialism in mining communities. His research is mainly located in Co. Durham, but includes the post-industrial mining communities of Cape Breton in Canada.

Series general co-editors' forward

The interdisciplinary field of Heritage Studies is now well established in many parts of the world. It differs from earlier scholarly and professional activities that focused narrowly on the architectural or archaeological preservation of monuments and sites. Such activities remain important, especially as modernisation and globalisation lead to new developments that threaten natural environments, archaeological sites, traditional buildings and arts and crafts. But they are subsumed within the new field that sees 'heritage' as a social and political construct encompassing all those places, artefacts and cultural expressions inherited from the past which, because they are seen to reflect and validate our identity as nations, communities, families and even individuals, are worthy of some form of respect and protection.

Heritage results from a selection process, often government-initiated and supported by official regulation; it is not the same as history, although this, too, has its own elements of selectivity. Heritage can be used in positive ways to give a sense of community to disparate groups and individuals or to create jobs on the basis of cultural tourism. It can be actively used by governments and communities to foster respect for cultural and social diversity, and to challenge prejudice and misrecognition. But it can also be used by governments in less benign ways, to reshape public attitudes in line with undemocratic political agendas or even to rally people against their neighbours in civil and international wars, ethnic cleansing and genocide. In this way there is a real connection between heritage and human rights.

This is the time for a new and unique series of books canvassing the key issues dealt with in the new Heritage Studies. The series seeks to address the deficiency facing the field identified by the Smithsonian in 2005 – that it is 'vastly under-theorized'. It is time to look again at the contestation that inevitably surrounds the identification and evaluation of heritage and to find new ways to elucidate the many layers of meaning that heritage places and intangible cultural expressions have acquired. Heritage conservation and safeguarding in such circumstances can only be understood as a form of cultural politics and that this needs to be reflected in heritage practice, be that in educational institutions or in the field.

It is time, too, to recognise more fully that heritage protection does not depend alone on top-down interventions by governments or the expert actions of heritage industry professionals, but must involve local communities and communities of interest. It is imperative that the values and practices of communities, together with traditional management systems, are fully understood, respected, encouraged and accommodated in management plans and policy documents if heritage resources are to be sustained into the future. Communities need to have a sense of 'ownership' of their heritage; this reaffirms their worth as a community, their ways of going about things, their 'culture'.

This series of books aims then to identify interdisciplinary debates within Heritage Studies and to explore how they impact on the practices not only of heritage management and conservation, but also the processes of production, consumption and engagement with heritage in its many and varied forms.

William S. Logan
Laurajane Smith

Chapter 1

Introduction
Class Still Matters
Laurajane Smith, Paul A. Shackel and Gary Campbell

This volume offers an international celebration of the heritage of the working class in its many and diverse forms. The focus is not so much on working class history – though that is discussed in various ways in the articles – but on the positive uses that heritage is being put to by working class people, communities and organisations in the present. By 'heritage' we mean not only tangible artefacts, buildings, places, sites and monuments, but also intangible traditions, commemorations, festivals, artwork, song and literature. We believe that it is important to stress the capacity for self-expression of working class people and communities, and the ways in which they draw on the past, and senses of place and tradition, to re-interpret and re-work contemporary identity, especially in the face of economic, social and political changes that have eroded long-standing bonds of class solidarity. These chapters show that working class people have a remarkable ability to avoid reactionary nostalgia and self-pity, and can build on their history, traditions and sense of place and community in novel ways. This leads us to reject the recent intellectual fashion of considering class a defunct, almost boorish interest, as it is a political position that is just that, a political position, but not one that captures the reality of modern working class life and culture.

The question that often arises in any community is 'which heritage is best to preserve, and will the promotion of heritage have an impact on the local cultural resources, the community, and the environment?' In his recent monograph that focuses on heritage development in the Chesapeake region, Erve Chambers writes that, 'heritage has largely become an instrument that defines the disturbances, irregularities, and uncertainties of the present much more than it truly represents the past' (Chambers 2006: 2). These disturbances and irregularities in the present are an opportunity for stakeholders to address current inequities, and it also leaves the door open to address the difficult pasts.

We would like to stress, for all those who hold an interest in forms of heritage, be they material or intangible, that there is a moral imperative to address issues of class and economic and social inequality (Sayer 2005) and its hidden injuries to self-respect and self-worth (Cobb and Sennett

1973). By revealing these inequalities it becomes easier to see how they were developed and are sustained, and we can choose whether we want to challenge these situations. Uncovering hidden injuries can set the tone for some form of justice and reconciliation within communities (Colwell-Chanthaphonh 2007).

We would also like to make it clear, to those who think that any heritage site or museum that references issues of class, work and de-industrialisation is anathema, that there are complex, authentic and genuine examples of working class heritage informing assertive reflexive projects of social memory-making. There are two misinterpretations of the moral imperative of addressing class and heritage. The first is the simple fact that the Authorized Heritage Discourse (see Smith 2006; Smith and Waterton 2011; Waterton 2010a) that animates what is chosen as 'heritage' in the West, deifies the great and the good, the beautiful and the old, the comfortable and the consensual. It also ignores or distains people, places, artefacts and traditions that are not associated with the economic and cultural elite, or recall uncomfortable or dissonant heritage. Industrial heritage makes some appearances, especially in Europe, and particularly in the UK and Scandinavia, and to some extent in the US, but the people, communities, events and places that constitute working class heritage are underrepresented in national and international heritage efforts. Its interpretation also tends to stress physical fabric and technology over the social relations of production, labour process and class conflict. For instance, while UNESCO's World Heritage List recognises over 900 sites, only 33 are related to industrial heritage (UNESCO 2010). In these few instances, working class heritage is often only indirectly commemorated, as the focus on industrial heritage is often void of people and class struggle. Nonetheless, these places have the potential to remember the human component of industry – working class life. England, known as the cradle of the industrial revolution, has more industrial-related sites designated by UNESCO than any other country. While European countries have the majority of UNESCO's industrial sites, they are also found in China, India, Bolivia, Brazil and Mexico. The United States, known as an industrial power for about a century, has none. While the United States has several national parks that celebrate industrial heritage, many interpretations are void of working class histories.

The second misinterpretation of the moral imperative is the tendency, often informed by the 'heritage industry' critique of Hewison (1987), Wright (1985) and Lowenthal (1985), to construe any heritage or museum attempt to present working class issues, in the face of de-industrialisation and attacks on organised labour, as conservative triumphalism, commercialisation and trivialisation of working class life and experience. Indeed, Debary (2004:123) for example, argues that 'wilful amnesia lies at the heart' of attempts to remember lost industries. This sense of amnesia is often linked to critiques of 'nostalgia', which is characterised as an insatiable yearning that, in regard to the working class, 'cherishes the romantic memory of a time when the working class could more easily produce its own meaningful world-view: the unproblematic community of the "general interest"' (Wright 1985: 22). As Smith (2006: 195f) argues, 'nostalgia' is often misidentified as being simply expressive of the ethos 'it was better back then', and fails to understand that nostalgic recollections can also involve critical and mindful memory work that recognises and engages with the emotionally painful. Discourses of 'nostalgia' and the 'heritage industry' critique work, as Robertson (2008) notes, to not only de-legitimise what he terms 'heritage from below', but also to obscure its inherently dissonant nature and the links it maintains to social protest.

The chapters in this volume show that, contrary to assumptions embedded in the 'heritage industry' critique, working class people, communities and organisations can speak for themselves. This is not to sweep the damage done to working class people, communities, organisations and political parties under the metaphorical carpet – they are real and profound – but to maintain Gramsci's lively pessimism of the intellect allied with an optimism of the will in the face of adversity. There are numerous examples of more positive accounts of working class life and culture that inform the position we take. The influential work of Raphael Samuel (1994) shows that heritage, rather than being a commercial misrepresentation or simulacra that dishonestly stands in for a 'real' history, can be a theatre of memory where active, complex and nuanced representations of working class life have contemporary resonance. Likewise the international network of labour and working class museums Worklab (http://www.worklab.info/) also demonstrates that there are, in the heritage sector, attempts to display working class heritage in all its messy detail, complete with industrial and class conflict. One example in the United States is the Museum of Work and Culture in Woonsocket, Rhode Island, which provides exhibits that are narrated by former factory workers. The stories of exploitation and oppression are prevalent throughout the museum. The work of Shackel (1996, 2009), Hayden (1997), Bruno (1999), Strangleman (1999, 2005, 2010), Dicks (2000), Linkon and Russo (2002), Bagnall (2003), Nadal-Klein (2003), Smith (2006), Rogaly and Taylor (2009) and West (2010) and the special edition of the journal *International Labour and Working Class History* (2009) amongst others, are at the forefront of what seems to be a re-awakening of interest in working class heritage.

The chapters in this book are either informed by, or echo, the 'new working class studies', which, according to Russo and Linkon (2005: 14–15) has:

A clear focus on the lived experiences and voices of working-class people; critical engagement with the complex intersections that link class with race, gender, ethnicity, and place; attention to how class is shaped by place and how the local is connected to the global ... new working class studies is multidisciplinary as well as interdisciplinary; it provides a site for conversation and opportunities for collaboration among scholars, artists, activists, and workers representing a wide range of approaches. New working class studies is about working-class people, but it also involves working-class people as full participants.

The new working class studies also shares territory with what has recently been referred to as 'critical heritage studies' (Harrison 2010). Critical heritage studies is a reaction against the AHD, and argues for a broadening of heritage analysis which takes as its starting point the understanding that heritage 'does' things in societies. It requires embracing the dissonant, and not simply acknowledging the multiplicity of values and cultural meanings that heritage places and practices may have, but also understanding their wider social consequences and ideological significance. For Smith (2006, 2010) heritage is redefined not simply as a thing or place, or even intangible event, but rather as a cultural process involved in the performance and negotiation of cultural values, narratives, memories and meanings. Heritage is one of the cultural tools used in the processes of individual and collective remembering and commemoration, while it is also a performance involved in 'working out' and asserting identity and sense of place and the various cultural, social and political values that underpin these. This emerging viewpoint challenges not just the assumptions but the practices of heritage, which we argue open up the entire heritage sector to more meaningful relations with subaltern groups, and demand that the unquestioned assumptions about class and national narratives are vigorously interrogated. It also implies a democratisation of heritage practice, as the power of the 'expert' is questioned, which creates openings for new heritage narratives and presentations that are shaped by people and communities rather than experts and traditional institutions.

The issue of social inclusion/exclusion has exercised much of national and international debate within the cultural sector. Museums and heritage agencies in a number of Western countries have been tasked with addressing ways of ensuring that traditionally excluded audiences and communities are encouraged to participate in cultural activities. Working class communities are one of the key groups identified among the socially 'excluded'. Cultural institutions are now faced with the difficult undertaking of how to ensure excluded groups participate in democratic and genuinely inclusive ways. All too often inclusion policies have been criticised for being little more than cynical attempts to increase visitor numbers or as practices designed to assimilate excluded audiences into dominant cultural values and understandings of history and heritage (see for instance chapters in Littler & Naidoo 2005; Smith 2006; Tlili 2008; Smith & Waterton 2009a). One of the key issues faced by museums, heritage institutions and those academics concerned with such debates is that there is often a misunderstanding or lack

Introduction 5

of knowledge about alternative forms of heritage that may sit outside of or are excluded and obscured by the Authorized Heritage Discourse. This volume explores various forms of tangible and intangible heritage and offers a way forward in these debates by addressing the questions what is labour and working class heritage, how does it differ or stand in opposition to dominant ways of understanding heritage and history? The book explores how heritage is used in working class communities and by labour organisations, and considers what meanings and significance this heritage may have, while also identifying how and why communities and their heritage have been excluded.

Chapters in this volume draw from a number of Western countries including the USA, UK, Spain, Sweden, Australia and New Zealand. Contributors are from a range of disciplines including heritage and museum studies, history, musicology, sociology, politics, archaeology and anthropology. This volume represents an innovative and useful resource for heritage and museum practitioners, students and academics concerned with understanding community heritage and the debate on social inclusion/exclusion. The volume offers new ways of understanding labour and working class heritage, its values and consequences, and it presents a challenge to dominant and traditional frameworks for understanding and identifying heritage and heritage making.

Class, Commemoration and Conflict

The studies in Part 1 of the book highlight issues related to either race conflict, or remembering the conflict between labour and capital. The authors acknowledge that versions of heritage can be communicated through various institutions, including schools, amusements, art and literature, government ceremonies, families and friends, as well as commemorative landscape features. The articles show the conflict about remembering how a working class past can be physical and violent, and/or racialised and exclusive.

Commemorating and remembering working class heritage is connected to how individual and collective memories develop through dialogue. In the case of Bailey and Popple's article, remembering the 1984/5 Miners' Strike in Great Britain has developed only after considerable effort to rethink the event as part of the community and national heritage. Post-industrial mining communities are beginning to claim the memory of the 1984/5 strike. The process of cultural reclamation helps to create meaning for communities, the veterans of the strike as well as working class life. The authors show that the mediation and commemoration of the strike is predominately negotiated through popular culture and via heritage-based discourses. However, museums, archives and dramatisations of events increasingly threaten to remove the history of these important events from the communities in which they unfolded and the people who bore the brunt of defeat and subsequent social and economic dislocation.

Race conflict is a form of symbolic violence. The conflict is about the political construction of race to create a situation of power over a subordinate group. Overt violence can be part of race conflict, although in these case studies the conflict is about the control over heritage. Subordinate groups who were successfully erased from the official memory or were portrayed in a negative light by the dominant group, struggle to be represented and become part of the official memory.

In the case of remembering class heritage in Thurrock, Essex, Richard Courtney shows that folk heritage is and has always been represented in constructions of Englishness, which is the construction of whiteness. This construction is opposed to Britishness, which is associated with multiculturalism. Scholarship shows that the social construction of whiteness and the connection to class and status frames the construction of racial identities. White equals good, pure, rich; and black, defined in opposition to white, equals defeated, ruined, bad, backwards and poor (see for instance Dyer 1997; Lipsitz 1998; Roediger 1998). Courtney demonstrates that the white communities predominantly recognised class as rooted in civic, rural and industrial heritage. This resulted in an insular, paranoid and reactive form of class identity that shared interests with far right and nationalist politics. He compares this to the narratives of minority groups whose class identity was future orientated, civic minded and structured within relations of global capitalism, and trans-national migration.

In the case studies about armed conflict, groups with opposing ideals confront each other in acts of aggression, often leaving physical traces of these events on the landscape or beneath the ground. While the event occurred many years ago, groups continue to battle over control of the meaning of the event. For instance, Paul Shackel shows how the events at Haymarket in May 1886 have had a lasting effect on how we remember the labour movement. Today, most of the world celebrates May Day, an event originally created to remember the labour movement martyrs at Haymarket. On the other hand, capital views the Haymarket event as a defeat of anarchists and socialists who confronted capitalism. The struggle between labour and capital to remember the events of Haymarket has resulted in an uneasy co-existence on the landscape and in the public memory. Recently, the City of Chicago reached out to both labour and law enforcement to help develop a compromise memorial at Haymarket.

The struggle to commemorate the memory of Blair Mountain also continues today. Like Haymarket, capital and labour are at odds on how to preserve and remember this important place in labour history. Brandon Nida and Michael Jessee Adkins describe the battle of Blair Mountain as the largest armed labour insurrection in US history. In 1921, approximately 10,000 coal miners participated in a battle against law enforcement officers and Baldwin-Felts Detectives, resulting in the US military suppressing the uprising. This conflict was pivotal in shifting narratives of the time about the labour movement from 'Bolsheviks fomenting social unrest' to 'quintessential Americans fighting for basic labour rights'. Because of the archaeology performed at the battle site portions of Blair Mountain were listed on the National Register of Historic Places; however recently, it was delisted. The Massey Energy Company is planning to conduct Mountain Top Removal operations on Blair Mountain. Preservationists and the coal company are at odds on how to treat this landscape that is important to the labour movement.

These studies in race, conflict and commemoration demonstrate how the past can be obscured in order to control the historical narrative. They show the struggle to recover a past to make a heritage part of the dominant discourse. The success of each case study varies and the struggle to remember continues.

Recognising and Commemorating Communities

Part 2 presents four assertive, direct and lively accounts of working class communities' attempts to directly, and in their own words, frame and present their own histories. Maunder's chapter shares some of the disquiet that Morel's chapter in Part 4 shows when working class and trade union issues are sidelined, or get a Walt Disney style make over to render their stories less contentious. However, the picture that emerges here shows that working class people and communities are able to eloquently present their own histories and heritage, often in uncompromising and challenging ways, that question dominant ways of conceptualising the history and heritage of the working class, and challenge or sidestep the authority of expert opinion. All of the chapters show the authors' commitment to working with communities, and taking their sense of agency and authorship seriously. Maunder himself is a community activist intimately involved in the events he writes about, and the other chapters all reveal the author's willingness to work with communities replete with the sorts of organic intellectuals Gramsci saw as the true intellectuals of the working class. Rather than being examples of active individuals leading initiatives, these chapters show dense networks of working class people taking an active role in shaping social memory of class, industry, unionism, race, gender and region.

Smith and Campbell's chapter documents the interplay of heritage, memory and class in Castleford, an ex-mining town near Leeds in Northern England. The chapter reveals the ways in which heritage is used to socialise and organise community members and the way it is held up within the community to reflect back to that community not only a sense of shared identity and place, but also the social and political values that inform community identity and experiences. The ways in which heritage is used in

Castleford have been informed by trade union legacies, rather than simply being a celebration of the past; heritage is actively and self-consciously used to help the community negotiate and navigate continuing economic and cultural change.

David Wray, an ex-miner himself, details another initiative in the North of England that shares many of the concerns of the activists in Castleford. County Durham is another ex-mining area, and the keen sense of independence that the New Herrington Miners Banner Partnership participants show is another example of the unwillingness of some working class organisations to be written out of history. The refusal of the activists involved in this project to be defined and explained by 'expert' opinion is a wonderful counter-example to the point of view that all heritage must be anodyne and devoid of tension and authenticity.

Similar themes can be found in Wedgwood's account of an ex-textile mill town in North Carolina. Again, we see expert opinion and comfortable stories sidelined, and activists, and an active community, telling a story in a unique way, and promoting their process of community research to other similar communities, and teaching lessons to academic historians along the way. The depth of commitment to creating social memory, that interweaves material and intangible heritage, is obvious in Cooleemee, as is the depth and subtlety of the sense of history and heritage that the local community evinces.

Working Class Self-Representation and Intangible Heritage

The concept of 'intangible heritage' has been given increasing credence since the drafting of the UNESCO Convention for the *Safeguarding of the Intangible Cultural Heritage*, 2003. This Convention came about following sustained criticism of the World Heritage Convention and its failure to engage with concepts of heritage understood in non-Western cultures (Aikawa-Faure 2009; Skounti 2009). Although this concept has been met with some bemusement in certain Western contexts (Smith and Waterton 2009b), it not only challenges aspects of the AHD, but also opens up debate about the idea and nature of 'heritage'. The chapters in Part 3 document and explore the significance of aspects of working class heritage that may be defined as 'intangible', and in doing so challenge normative assumptions not only about the nature of Western heritage, but also advance understanding about the role of heritage in community and individual self-representation and recognition.

Tim Strangleman's chapter offers a useful framework for the other chapters in this section. It centres on an apparently straightforward argument that working class autobiographies are a form of intangible heritage that not only should be understood and acknowledged as heritage in their own right, but that also have the potential to enrich and give nuance to the material markers and heritage centre interpretations of lost industries. In developing this argument, however, the chapter reveals how autobiography provides often profound and inevitably multiple and layered glimpses of 'captured experience'. Examples from a range of working class autobiographies are provided that reveal not only the importance of everyday life, but how particular work experiences are given social meaning, and how memories of these are used to represent, define and explore sense of place and the processes of socialisation both in the past and the present. One of the things that the concept of 'intangible heritage' has offered to debates in critical heritage studies is the realisation that heritage is about lived experiences that are not always adequately represented by the material forms that have been the focus of traditional heritage preservation and conservation concerns. The glimpses of autobiographical detail offered by Strangleman expose the impoverishment of traditional interpretive strategies of industrial heritage that focus on the technological and architectural achievements of such places and reinforce Munjeri's (2004:13) point that 'the tangible can only be understood and interpreted thorough the intangible'. Moreover, viewed as heritage, autobiography reinforces the dynamic and contested nature of heritage, and illustrates the ways in which remembering and recalling the past is part of the processes through which meaning is given to contemporary values and experiences.

This aspect of heritage is revealed in Mizell-Nelson's chapter which examines the animated debates over the name of the po' boy/poor boy sandwich of New Orleans. Although debate over the sandwich may be dismissed by some as an 'entertaining sidelight about quickly New Orleanians', as Mizell-Nelson reveals, the debate is intricately tied into the ways in which working class history in New Orleans is being both remembered and forgotten. In telling the story of the sandwich, the complexities and layers of meaning and value that are being negotiated in debates about the name reveal both the way class and race are understood and defined in New Orleans, and the way the past is recalled to validate or invalidate contemporary experiences of class and race. This chapter also reveals the complexities of meaning, as Strangleman argues, that can lie under everyday life experiences. The banality of ordering a po' boy or poor boy sandwich is an 'everyday event', which carries performative assertions of social and cultural alliances, while also socialising the sandwich patron into a range of cultural and social values.

Nilsson's chapter on Swedish working class literature examines another aspect of intangible heritage that confronts the AHD's focus on national heritage. This chapter also challenges the primary assumption in heritage studies that heritage is often 'magically', and certainly unproblematically, 'linked' to identity. As Nilsson reveals, attempts to recognise working class literary heritage in Sweden have tended to depoliticise accounts of class, as unproblematised ideas of the heritage/identity dyad work to obscure or subsume class politics that seek social justice and the end of exploitation. This chapter reveals the complexity of the links between heritage and identity, and echoes the arguments by Andrew Sayer (2007) that class politics cannot be reduced to identity politics or the politics of recognition.

The final three chapters in this section develop the insights offered by Strangleman in the form of autobiography through the medium of song and poetry. Bowan and Pickering provide a lively examination of socialist songbooks from Britain's colonies of settlement as both sites and sounds of memory. As with the previous chapters, they make the case for the intangible as heritage, but also reveal the complexities of commemoration, meaning and history that are transmitted in this form of heritage. Indeed, as a form of heritage the songbooks reveal the ways in which working class peoples have communicated with each other not only within specific places and time periods, but also internationally across national and cultural boundaries and, most importantly, through time.

Attfield calls on the history of Australian working class poetry to reveal the nature and intent of this form of heritage. Like the songs identified by Bowan and Pickering, and the autobiographies highlighted by Strangleman, the poetry Attfield explores offers insights into the lived experiences of working people. As she notes, working class poetry can be a celebration of identity and culture and, like all forms of working class heritage explored in this volume, a form of protest and call for social justice. Gregory, also concerned with song and poetry, documents the history of 'industrial folk song' and illustrates how websites have become 'a fifth estate in today's world' and how the Internet is facilitating the preservation, collection and transmission of this form of working class heritage. 'Digital heritage' has become a significant area of heritage concern in recent years, with a burgeoning of literature concerned primarily with the practices and technical aspects of digitising heritage records (see Richards 2010). As Waterton (2010b) points out, what much of this literature misses is the ways communities are using the Internet to redefine and express themselves, to communicate and to define and redefine their own sense of heritage. Gregory's chapter is a case in point, as he demonstrates how the Internet is facilitating the working class project of communication, celebration and protest through song and poetry.

Case Studies in Commemoration, Remembrance and Forgetting

Part 4, Case Studies in Commemoration, Remembrance and Forgetting highlights some of the strategies used to control the memory of a place. Shackel (2001) has outlined elsewhere the different strategies for creating a memory of the past. First, people can create an exclusionary past. Elements of the past remembered in common, as well as elements of the past forgotten in common create a form of group cohesion (Glassberg 1996: 13). A second method is to develop a public memory that commemorates a patriotic or nationalistic past. The official expression sponsored by the state government is concerned with promoting and preserving the ideals of cultural leaders and authorities, developing social unity and maintaining the status quo. They interpret the past and present reality in a way that helps to reduce competing interests (Bodner 1992: 13). A third way to construct a memory of the past that creates a useable heritage is the generation of precedence that serves our present needs. The political uses of heritage have been made very explicit within Western culture (Lowenthal 1997: xv).

Jane Baxter and Andrew Bullen's work in the Pullman community examines the growth and development of a late nineteenth-century modern industrial community on the south side of Chicago. Today, thousands of people visit the community, either because they want to see the place that was dubbed 'The World's Most Perfect Town' for 14 years straight, or because they want to experience the place of one of America's most notable strikes. The Pullman Strike occurred in 1894 during the height of an economic depression. Wages were cut by Pullman, while rents in the company-owned houses remained the same. The strike devastated the model community and the paternalistic relationship between Pullman and his workers deteriorated. After the Pullman Company closed in the 1950s, the community worked together to save their community from urban renewal projects. Working class history is now found in visitor centre films, tour presentations, docent training guides and museum exhibits. Class has been an integral part of the Pullman story from its inception as a model town designed to better the working classes, to its role as the epicentre of an important event in labour history, and later as one of many working class neighbourhoods on Chicago's industrial south side.

In another case study, Hilda Kean describes how every July trade unionists make a pilgrimage to a small Dorset village near Dorchester to remember the Tolpuddle Martyrs. Thousands commemorate the six local agricultural labourers who were deported to New South Wales and Tasmania, Australia, in the spring of 1834, after being found guilty of taking an 'illegal' oath in their bid to create a union. In her chapter, Kean explains this commemoration as well as other small labour movement festivals. Working class radical organisations and individuals have created a commemorative heritage separate from the official public memory that can be found throughout Great Britain. The emphasis on melodrama and political defeat has long origins in nineteenth-century labour movement motifs of martyrdom and suffering. The radical interpretation of the past is reinforced with these annual gatherings as a way of renewing the political hope and emotional strength of the participants. The labour movement festivals are also a way of validating a past to provide an inspirational connection with the present.

12 Introduction

In his chapter, Marc Morrell examines the relationship between heritage and gentrification. He explains that gentrification is the middle-class colonisation of working class neighbourhoods, as the presence of the working class vanishes from the community. He explains that when developers use past working class neighbourhoods for the development of heritage tourism they often omit the working class. The heritage of the working class therefore becomes controlled by the middle class. Morell describes this process as the working class being stripped of its social being. In Ciuta de Mallorca, he questions where the present working class is to be found, and whether its past actually matches that of the working class portrayed through heritage.

Traditions, meanings and memories are invented and they become legitimate through repetition or a process of formalisation and ritualisation characterised by reference to the past. By implying continuity with the past, and sometimes that is a matter of forgetting a past, or by reinventing a collective memory, these traditions reinforce values and behaviour (Hobsbawm 1983: 1–5). The repetition of the interpreting of working class history at Pullman makes the story part of the community's official discourse. The yearly labour movement festivals are a form of ritualisation that helps to make this local history prominent on the rural landscape. On the other hand, the removal of the working class during urban renewal in Mallorca transforms the memory of the place. Absence creates a type of reality of its non-existence.

Conclusion

The transformation of the world's political economy over the past century has endangered many communities and has threatened tangible and intangible forms of heritage that are important for providing a sense of place and identity. Heritage creates a useable past and it generates a precedent that serves our present needs. We know that people have used heritage for the control of the past and the present for at least as long as there has been writing (Harvey 2001). More recently, the political uses of heritage have been made very explicit within Western culture. While 'history explores and explains pasts grown ever more opaque over time; heritage clarifies pasts so as to infuse them with present purposes' (Lowenthal 1997: xv). Moreover, heritage is a discourse concerned with 'a certain way of knowing' the past (Byrne 2009: 230, 1996) and of mediating that past so that it can do 'work' in the present. The 'work' that heritage discourses do is, as this volume demonstrates, highly variable and can include the validation and celebration of identities and memories, the forging and re-forging of social and cultural networks, to the forgetting and remaking of class identities. Whatever heritage does, however, it will always be highly political as heritage is itself a resource of power. The ability to control your collective memory and the processes involved in its remembering and representation are important resources in struggles for political legitimacy (Teski & Climo 1995: 2; Taylor 1994 Fraser 1995).

As chapters in this volume reveal, the heritage of working class people is not only often advanced in the context of attempts to forget it or obscure its political and cultural significance, working class heritage, whatever its form, is also intrinsically linked to projects of protest and social justice. Remembering working class heritage, and understanding its links to social justice agendas, is given moral urgency in the face of ongoing attempts to forget and suppress labour history. Meanwhile, the moral imperative is given further imperatives as discourses of social justice in the US are ridiculed and international debates about immigration and class become increasingly reactionary in the context of the current global economic crisis.

One reaction to this in the heritage field, particularly in the UK, has been to press for cultural policies of 'social inclusion' of marginalised groups, often defined in terms of class and ethnicity. All too often these initiatives, though superficially worthy, if overly earnest, do not work to democratise heritage. Rather they work in an assimilationist fashion, where members of marginalised groups are urged to emulate the forms of cultural consumption of the middle classes. Initiatives of this sort do not attempt to promote cosmopolitan attendance, in the sense that sites, places and events that are seen as important by subaltern communities are not promoted as attractions for members of elite groups, or given any serious priority in heritage policy.

Yet, as the articles in this volume show, there is a great degree of interest in heritage and history by working class people, and as Bennett et al (2009) illustrate, working class people's modes of cultural consumption are simply different from those of the middle classes, which does not make them deficient. As Bennett et al (2009) demonstrate working class people see community, family and local historical memory as important resources, and this sense of memory and heritage has been under-researched.

Drawing on new scholarship in heritage studies, social memory, the public history of labour and new working class studies, this volume highlights the heritage of working people, communities and organisations. Many communities and labour organisations are actively using working class heritage as a resource to reflect on the past, reassess the present and plan for the future. At the beginning of the twenty-first century, there is a growing tendency for the heritage of working class people to be interpreted and presented to the public in museums and heritage sites. Working class communities and organisations are also playing an active role in creating a memory of their own past. Moreover, this is a global phenomenon in which heritage is becoming an increasingly significant resource for communities as they seek to remake themselves and represent themselves in the wake of de-industrialisation. In this volume, the authors theorise and document this phenomenon as an under-represented form of cultural heritage.

References

Aikawa-Faure, N. (2009) 'From the Proclamation of Masterpieces to the Convention for the Safeguarding of Intangible Cultural Heritage', in L. Smith and N. Akagawa (eds) *Intangible Heritage,* London: Routledge.

Bagnall, G. (2003) 'Performance and performativity at heritage sites', *Museum and Society,* 1 (2): 87–103.

Bennett, T., Savage, M. Silva, E., Warde, A., Gayo-Cal, M., and Wright, D. (2009) *Culture, Class, Distinction*, London: Routledge.

Bodner, J. (1992) *Remaking America: Public Memory, Commemoration, and Patriotism in the Twentieth Century*, Princeton: Princeton University Press.

Bourdieu, P. (1977) *Outline of a Theory of Practice*, New York: Cambridge University Press.

Bruno, R. (1999) *Steelworker Alley: How Class Works in Youngstown*, Ithaca: Cornell University Press.

Byrne, D. (1996) 'Deep nation: Australia's acquisition of an Indigenous past', *Aboriginal History* 20: 82–107.

——(2009) 'A critique of unfeeling heritage', in L. Smith and N. Akagawa (eds) *Intangible Heritage.* London: Routledge.

Chambers, E. (2006) *Heritage Matters: Heritage, Culture, History and Chesapeake Bay*, College Park: Maryland Sea Grant College.

Colwell-Chanthaphonh, C. (2007) 'History, Justice, and Reconciliation' in B. Little and P. Shackel (eds) *Archaeology as a Tool of Civic Engagement*, Lanham: AltaMira Press.

Cobb, R and Sennett, J. (1973) *The Hidden Injuries of Class*, New York: W. W. Norton & Company.

Debary, O. (2004) 'Deindustrialisation and museumification: From exhibited memory to forgotten history', *Annals of the American Academy of Political and Social Science,* 595 (1): 122–33.

Dicks, B. (2000) *Heritage, Place and Community*, Cardiff: University of Wales Press.

Dyer, R. (1997) *White*, London: Routledge.

Fraser, N. (1995) 'From redistribution to recognition? Dilemmas of justice in a "post-socialist" age', *New Left Review* 212: 68–93.

Glassberg, D. (1996) 'Public History and the Study of Memory', *The Public Historian* 18 (2): 7–23.

Harrison, R. (2010) 'Introduction', in R. Harrison (ed) *Understanding the Politics of Heritage,* Manchester: Manchester University Press in association with the Open University.

Harvey, D.C. (2001) 'Heritage pasts and heritage presents: Temporality, meaning and the scope of heritage studies', *International Journal of Heritage Studies,* 7 (4): 319–38.

Hayden, D. (1997) *The Power of Place*, Cambridge, Mass.: The MIT Press.

Hewison, R. (1987) *The Heritage Industry: Britain in a Climate of Decline*, London: Methuen London Ltd.

Hobsbawm, E. (1983) 'Introduction: Inventing traditions', in E. Hobsbawm and T. Ranger (eds), *The Invention of Tradition*, Cambridge: Cambridge University Press.

Lowenthal, D. (1985) *The Past is a Foreign Country*, Cambridge: Cambridge University Press.

——(1997) *The Heritage Crusade and the Spoils of History*, 2nd edn. Cambridge: Cambridge University Press.

Linkon, S. L. and Russo, J. (2002) *Steeltown U.S.A.: Work and memory in Youngstown*, Lawrence: University of Press of Kansas.

Lipsitz, G. (1998) *The Possessive Investment in Whiteness: From Identity Politics*, Philadelphia: Temple University Press.

Littler, J. and Naidoo, R. (2005) (eds) *The Politics of Heritage: The Legacies of 'Race'*, London: Routledge.

Munjeri, D. (2004) 'Tangible and intangible heritage: from difference to convergence', *Museum International*, 56 (1–2): 12–20.

Nadel-Klein, J. (2003) *Fishing for Heritage: Modernity and Loss Along the Scottish Coast*, Oxford: Berg.

Oliver-Smith, A. (2006) 'Communities after Catastophe: Reconstructing the Material, Reconstituting the Social' in S. Hyland (ed) *Community Building in the Twenty-First Century*, Santa Fe: School of American Research Press.

Putnam, R. D. (2000) *Bowling Alone: The Collapse and Revival of American Community*, New York, NY: Simon & Schuster.

Richards, J. (2010) 'Book reviews: digital heritage', *International Journal of Heritage Studies*, 16 (6): 527–29.

Robertson, I.J.M. (2008) 'Heritage from below: Class, social protest and resistance', in B. Graham and P. Howard (eds) *Heritage and Identity*, Aldershot: Ashgate.

Roediger, D. R. (1998) *The Wages of Whiteness: Race and the Making of the American Working Class*, London: Verso.

Rogaly, B. and Taylor, B. (2009) *Moving Histories of Class and Community: Identity, Place and Belonging in Contemporary England*, Basingstoke: Palgrave Macmillan.

Russo, J. and Linkon, S. L. (2005) 'Introduction: what's new about new working-class studies?', in J. Russo and S.L. Linkon (eds) *New Working-Class Studies*, Ithaca: Cornell University Press.

Samuel, R. (1994) *Theatres of Memory. Volume 1: Past and Present in Contemporary Culture*. London: Verso.

Sayer, A. (2005) *The Moral Significance of Class*, Cambridge: Cambridge University Press.

——(2007) 'Class, moral worth and recognition', in T. Lovell (ed.) *(Mis)recognition, Social Inequality and Social Justice Nancy Fraser and Pierre Bourdieu*, London: Routledge.

Shackel, P. (2001) *Myth, Memory and The Making of The American Landscape*, Gainesville: University Press of Florida.

——(1996) *Culture Change and the New Technology: An Archaeology of the Early American Industrial Era*, New York: Plenum Publishing Corp.

——(2009) *An Archaeology of American Labor and Working Class Life*, Gainesville: University of Florida Press.

Skounti, A. (2009) 'The authentic illusion: humanity's intangible cultural heritage, the Moroccan experience', in L. Smith and N. Akagawa (eds) *Intangible Heritage*, London: Routledge.

Smith, L. (2006) *Uses of Heritage*, London: Routledge.

——(2010) 'The 'doing' of heritage: heritage as performance, in A. Jackson and J. Kidd (eds) *Performing Heritage: Research, practice and development in museum theatre and live interpretation*, Manchester: Manchester University Press.

Smith, L. and Waterton, E. (2009) *Heritage, Communities and Archaeology*, London: Duckworth.

——(2009b) '"The envy of the world?": Intangible heritage in England', in L. Smith and N. Akagawa (eds) *Intangible Heritage*, London: Routledge.

——(2011, in press) 'Constrained by common sense: the Authorized Heritage Discourse in contemporary debates', in J. Carman, R. Skeats and C. McDavid (eds) *The Oxford Handbook of Public Archaeology*, Oxford University Press.

Strangleman, T. (1999) 'The nostalgia of organisations and the organisation of nostalgia: Past and present in the contemporary railway industry', *Sociology*, 33 (4): 725–46.

——(2005) 'Class memory: Autobiography and the art of forgetting', in J. Russo and S.L. Linkon (eds) *New Working-Class Studies,* Ithaca: Cornell University Press.

——(2010) 'Food, drink and the cultures of work: consumption in the life and death of an English factory', *Food, Culture and Society: An International Journal of Multidisciplinary Research,* 13 (2): 257–78.

Taylor, C. (1994) 'The politics of recognition', in A. Gutmann (ed) *Multiculturalism: Examining the Politics of Recognition,* Princeton: Princeton University Press.

Teski, M. C. and Climo J. J. (1995) 'Introduction', in M.C. Teski and J.J. Climo (eds) *The Labyrinth of Memory: Ethnographic Journeys,* Westport: Bergin & Garvey.

Tlili A. (2008) 'Behind the policy mantra of the inclusive museum: receptions of social exclusion and inclusion in museums and science centres', *Cultural Sociology,* 2 (1): 123–47.

Waterton, E. (2010a) *Politics, Policy and the Discourses of Heritage in Britain*, Basingstoke: Palgrave Macmillan.

——(2010b) 'Commentary article: the advent of new digital technologies', *Museum Management and Curatorship,* 25 (1): 5–11.

West, S. (2010) 'Heritage and class', in R. Harrison (ed) *Understanding the Politics of Heritage,* Manchester: Manchester University Press in association with the Open University.

Wright, P. (1985) *On Living in an Old Country,* London: Verso.

UNESCO (2010) 'World Heritage List', Electronic document, http://whc.unesco.org/en/list/ (accessed December 11, 2010).

Part I

Class, Commemoration and Conflict

Chapter 2

The 1984/85 Miners' Strike
Re-claiming cultural heritage

Michael Bailey and Simon Popple

> It may seem a paradox that the only radical politics left to us should be based upon resistance, recuperation and remembering. But in a social and economic system which requires the reverse of all these things, to oppose means to conserve.
> (Blackwell and Seabrook 1993: 4)

> This is our history. History that we, the strikers and our supporters made. We need to reclaim the strike as our event. People need to be able to see real people trying to take on the power of the state to understand the forces that stand in the way.
> (Miner questionnaire, 2008)

The making of working class heritage

In the *Eighteenth Brumaire* Karl Marx (1852) famously noted that, though 'men make their own history ... they do not make it just as they please', that is 'they do not make it under circumstances chosen by themselves, but under circumstances directly encountered, given and transmitted from the past'. Whilst it could be argued that Marx's statement on the relationship between structure and agency is an essentially negative one, there is another way of interpreting the above comment. Following Walter Benjamin's (1940) idea of *Jetztzeit* and his politics of *redemption*, a more optimistic reading of this Marxian dialectic is to argue that, though the present is certainly shaped by historical conditions, the past itself is always incomplete insofar as it is in a constant – and potentially volatile – relationship with 'the presence of the now'. In other words, the past and present are precariously intertwined, hence Benjamin's emphasis upon historical materialism as a form of remembering bygone generations and political struggles, in the hope that they may yet 'blast open the continuum of history', as the past and future converge in the present instant.

Of course, Marx warns us of the inherent dangers of conjuring up 'the spirits of the past', and how 'the tradition of dead generations weighs like a nightmare on the brain of the living'. If the working class are to ever create a new society, it must leave behind its forebears. In short, 'let the dead bury their dead'. For Marx, to do otherwise would be backward-looking, reactionary, even. However, there is a risk here, as noted by E. P. Thompson (1966: 12), of leaving the past and its spoils to the 'enormous condescension of posterity'. Worse still, there is the possibility that the hopes and struggles of 'the oppressed' are appropriated by 'the victors', which is why Benjamin was right to underline the importance of *political remembrance*, or what Jacques Derrida (1994) thought of as a *spectral solidarity* between life and death, matter and spirit. Both believed that the conjuration of past spirits can provide an occasion for exorcising *retrograde ghosts* so that we are left with the true spirit (*Geist*) of freedom rather than its counter-revolutionary spectre (*Gespenst*).[1]

The implications of this hypothesis, and there is much to be said in its favour, is that history matters, in particular the histories of working class people. More crucially, those histories need to be made accessible for present and future generations of working class people if they are to redeem and make good the hopes of their own past. It is in recognition of this Marxian imperative that socialist historians have long sought to democratise history by taking it back from elites ('the great and the good') and retelling it in and through the lived experiences of ordinary people ('the good and the many'). In the context of British history, this has taken the form of various intellectual movements, for example, the Communist Party of Great Britain's Historians Group, the Society for the Study of Labour History, so-called 'culturalism' and the New Left, the History Workshops at Ruskin College, Oxford, among others. It was in these forums that historians and cultural sociologists such as Christopher Hill, Eric Hobsbawn, Dorothy and Edward Thompson, Raphael Samuel, John Saville, Richard Hoggart, Raymond Williams and Sheila Rowbotham put class analysis firmly on the historical map.

Yet, in spite of the steady growth of 'history from below', especially in relation to gender, race and postcolonial studies, histories of the working class have in fact waned over the last two decades. This decline is partly due to the changing political climate and the current unpopularity of class politics: gone are the old collective solidarities and antagonisms, now that we live in a 'post-industrial society'. In fact, if we are to believe a current trend in sociological studies (for example, Skeggs 1997), being working class is a stigmatised social position, something to be refused. The contemporary working class no longer see themselves as a class apart. This turn against working class identity and working class consciousness can also be explained in terms of the epistemological challenges posed by the turn to post-structuralist theories of language and the attendant rise in historical revisionism (for example, Joyce 1991; Stedman Jones 1983), according to which, class is best understood as a reductionist concept, indeed, a figment of the historian's imagination. Consequently, there has been a turn away from the study of social class, prompting some social and political commentators to even pronounce the death of class.² This being the case, it would seem that the dead have indeed been left to bury their dead.

Thankfully, not all scholars have endorsed this approach to history and the related question of class.³ Whilst the majority of mainstream historians have been busying away rethinking class or concentrating on other tropes of analysis, working class history has been taken up by a relatively new interdisciplinary field of academic inquiry, commonly referred to as 'Heritage Studies' (see, for example, Brett 1996; Harvey and Corner 1991; Hewinson 1987; Lowenthal 1985; Samuel 1994; Wright 1985).⁴ Though initially preoccupied with the conservation of ancient monuments, sites of famous battle scenes, country houses, churches and the like, the idea of heritage has greatly expanded in recent years to include an array of everyday artefacts, landscapes and lived experiences. Almost every town and city has a 'cultural industrial quarters' where the public can relive a-day-in-the-life of the Victorian or Edwardian working class, for example. And whilst there are those who have argued *inter alia* that urban and industrial heritage is reactionary chic, a sanitised version of the past that turns the social relations of economic production into a depoliticised spectacle, a form of nostalgic false-consciousness concocted by the ruling elites, or yet another example of neo-liberal enterprise which commodifies the past, we want to argue, following Benjamin's example, that not all cultural heritage is necessarily conservative or tourist kitsch (see also Samuel 1994).⁵ On the contrary, heritage can be a highly contestable discourse that is continually modified by dissonant cultural relations and processes that challenge received wisdoms about past events and particular ways of life.⁶

'Here we go, here we go, here we go'

It is with the above in mind that we now turn to what is the main focus of this chapter: the 1984/85 miners' strike. Though there is evidence to suggest that the then Tory government, under the leadership of Margaret Thatcher, had been preparing for a confrontation with the National Union of Mineworkers (NUM) well before the dispute came to a head (see Milne 1994), the strike officially started in March 1984 and came to an end in March 1985, making it one of the most bitter and protracted industrial disputes in British history. The catalyst for the strike was the announced closure of Cortonwood Colliery in South Yorkshire without any offer of consultation, and the subsequent announcement of the government's intention to close a further twenty pits which would result in 20,000 redundancies. The response from the NUM and the miners was immediate. In no time at all, the traditionally militant coalfields of Yorkshire, Kent, South Wales and Scotland came to a standstill. And whilst about 30,000 miners decided to work the mines in Nottinghamshire and formed the break-away Union of Democratic Mineworkers, and in spite of the NUM not allowing a national ballot, over 165,000 miners decided to strike nationwide. In short, 80% of Britain's miners downed tools and the majority would remain on strike for the next twelve months.

The rest, as they say, is history. Following an unprecedented harnessing of the state's various functionaries (the judiciary, the police, the intelligence services, the armed forces even) and at an estimated cost of £4.8 billion to the taxpayer (Beckett and Hencke 2009: 212), the strike effort was eventually undermined and defeated. The consequence of this, apart from the immediate effect on the country's GDP, is that the number of deep-mine collieries has dramatically declined from 170 in 1984 to just six in 2008. Whereas the mining industry employed about 196,000 miners at the start of the strike, that number now stands at approximately 4000 (Williams 2009). More crucially, the subsequent closure of pits has resulted in the gradual demise of whole communities, a particular way of life known to generations of mining families up and down the country (see Wray of this volume). Many of the pit villages became some of the poorest in the European Union, let alone the UK, abandoned and forgotten. Destitute and impoverished, families broke up and children faced an uncertain future. What were once bedrocks of communitarian values and radical conservatism[7] (for example, strong familial relations, a sense of neighbourliness, a respect for one's elders, a deep-rooted commitment to civic pride, etc.) have been reduced, in some cases, to ruinous lumpenproletariat outlands, a disintegrated people cut off from the rest of society.[8]

The media's sustained attack on mining communities, both during and after the strike, has not helped matters either. With the odd exception, the press, radio and television routinely denigrated miners, their families and the union in a concerted effort to damage the reputation of the strike action (see Jones et al 1985; Williams 2009). Hence much of the media coverage at the time was completely lacking in objectivity and impartiality, deliberately portraying the miners as the aggressors, and thereby reinforcing Margaret Thatcher's depiction of the miners as the 'enemy within' (see Masterson 1985; Bailey 2009). Some commentators have even suggested that the media coverage was 'a war of propaganda' (for example, Douglas 1985). This is all the more salient in light of recent evidence which would suggest that hostilities towards the miners and the mining industry continued well into the 1990s: for example, the investigative journalist, Seumas Milne (1994), has written a riveting exposé of the state's continuing efforts to annihilate what little was left of the coal industry and to politically manipulate the strike's legacy, particularly the reputation of the then NUM's president, Arthur Scargill.

The Miners Strike Back

In spite of widespread social exclusion, economic hardship and ongoing political prejudice, the 1984/85 strike has since taken on a life of its own within many former mining communities, one that is not necessarily as defeatist as we might think it is. Though blighted by high levels of unemployment, poverty and anti-social crime, lots of post-industrial mining communities have started to rethink the strike as cultural heritage, in an effort to regenerate – economically and culturally – the localities in which they live. Rather than being ashamed of what happened in the strike, colliery towns are beginning to reclaim the history of the strike as a badge of honour, something to be proud of. In some localities, there is even evidence of social reconciliation, that is, a rapprochement between former pickets and those who returned to work before the strike action was brought to an end. Though the scars left by the strike still run deep, veterans of the original conflict have started to place greater emphasis on mining history more generally, that is mining as a way of life that goes back hundreds of years.[9] In so doing, an increasing number of miners and their families are starting to assert an element of control over their social history by means of the rediscovery and revitalisation of past traditions and social rituals.

By re-conceptualising the strike in this way, it has been possible for such communities to secure national and regional funding with which to organise social networks and events, thus enabling them to revalue their collective history in and through the recovery of 'popular memory'. For example, ethnographic research done by Carol Stephenson and David Wray (2005), in the Durham mining communities on community activism and what they call 'emotional regeneration', demonstrates that such communities are capable of 'giving meaning back to their lives' through 'culturally determined participatory socialization'. That is to say, though many of the miners they interviewed described the intervening years since the strike as a period of mourning, in the last few years many of the original veterans still living in the mining communities have started to revalue their collective identity and to rethink what happened during and after the strike as part of their working class heritage, as something to be celebrated so as to provide some kind of community engagement and social solidarity for present and future generations (cf. Benyon and Austin 1994). The reinvigoration of the Durham Miners' Gala (see Wray this volume) as the major political rally in the country has been central to this active process of remaking former mining towns and villages into sites of unofficial heritage. And in some cases, the Gala has also facilitated the repoliticisation of former mining communities by re-establishing links with the wider labour and trade union movement. Below are two such testimonies from two adults living in New Herrington, a former colliery village, just south of Sunderland:

> We want a proper history written, a people's history, the truth. We have to keep alive ourselves because no one else will tell the kids what our lives were about and how those lives have changed. The banner and the Gala are just representations of what our lives, our heritage if you like, is

all about. We are talking about educating the kids, so that they will know what it was like to live in a mining community.

Part of what we do is about letting Thatcher and her like know we are still here. They closed the pits and took the jobs, but every time we take that banner out, we are saying to them, we're still here, and we are still fighting for our communities.

(cited in Stephenson and Wray 2005: 191–92)

Similarly, in a notable book by Laurajane Smith (2006), we see how remembering and commemoration are integral to residents living in Castleford (a small mining town in West Yorkshire) and their struggle to maintain a sense of community pride in the aftermath of the 1984/85 strike (which resulted in the gradual loss of 3,000 jobs) and de-industrialization more generally; a struggle exacerbated by the failure of subsequent governments to invest public money – until very recently – in the town's regeneration, economic or otherwise. This and the town's changing landscape (viz. the demise of industrial buildings and working class neighbourhoods) have resulted in a widespread sense of loss. However, Smith (2006: 237–75) rightly argues that this collective lament has very little to do with 'reactionary nostalgia' or 'sentimentality'; rather, it is more to do with what she calls 'intangible heritage', that is an emphasis on such things as 'family', 'friends', 'looking out for one another', 'social spirit' and so on. Above all, Castleford's residents are deeply concerned about the future prospects for local children and upcoming generations. In other words, heritage for the residents of Castleford is as much about the present as it is backward looking, which is why local activists launched an annual, week-long festival in 2001, in an effort to rekindle some sort of community spirit by creating new memorable experiences associated with 'community cohesion', 'friendliness' and 'cooperation'.

Castleford's considerable efforts at community regeneration, and its residents wanting other communities in the UK to know something about the town and its heritage, were the subject of a Channel 4 series, *Kevin McCloud And The Big Town Plan*, broadcast in 2008.[10] Filmed over five years, the series was conceived as part of a much larger regeneration project in partnership with the Commission for Architecture and the Built Environment, English Partnerships, Arts Council England, The Environment Agency, The European Regional Development Fund, Groundwork UK, The Coalfields Regeneration Trust, Yorkshire Forward and Wakefield Metropolitan District Council. After lengthy consultation with the local community and civic groups, work began on a series of different projects across the town, including the design of a new footbridge across the River Aire, a new town square and several new recreational facilities for younger residents. In total, the project generated over £200 million in public funding and private investment.

Commenting on the success of the project on the programme's website, Kevin McCloud notes that, the 'big lesson to learn from the series is that we ... need to feel that we own, that we can change. That change can be effected by communities ...' Interestingly, he also notes how one of the projects – a sculpture park designed by American architect, Martha Schwartz – failed to galvanise the local community due to it being 'parachuted in by English Partnerships':

> ... there was little community involvement ... A £1 million play centre and garden came but they weren't interested – the community don't want it or look after it. No kids play on it. It's like a ghost project. English Partnerships, to be fair to them, have learnt a lot – community consultation isn't something that councils do or regeneration agencies generally do as part of a scheme ... Trying to do things top down doesn't work. Trying to do things bottom up, using Gandhian optics, that's where the power is, that's where the energy is – in society. Reading reports in newspapers about 'another initiative, another government programme' fills my heart with dread. It's great that the money is available, of course; it's great to know your way around the grant system, but social change happens from the bottom up.
> (McCloud 2008; cf. Holland 2009: 115)

To put it another way, governmental attempts to regenerate post-industrial communities, such as Castleford, must also bear some relation to the public they constitute if they are to be effective. Rather than merely imposing their own ideas about heritage and regeneration, cultural agencies such as the aforementioned also need to acknowledge actually existing social relations and thus be representative of the public they seek to regenerate. Indeed, a number of Castleford's residents articulated this point of view when filmed for a community media project that ran alongside the regeneration project.[11] More crucially, this dialectic opens up a space for ordinary citizens to challenge the 'authorized heritage discourse' (see Smith 2006). In so doing, it has the potential to radically alter the intention and efficacy of regeneration and heritage partnerships that might otherwise impose a discourse of their own making, which brings us to our concluding case study.

The BBC *Open Archive* and associated projects

Between autumn 2007 and summer 2009 two AHRC/BBC funded projects were undertaken by a small team from the Institute of Communications Studies, University of Leeds.[12] Both the initial *Open Archive* project, and its follow-up *Fusion* project were concerned with a range of issues which impacted on the debate concerning the cultural ownership of heritage and in particular the role played by the BBC's archive of the miners' strike. The projects set out to explore how regional BBC audiences, especially mining communities, could access a potent and often contested set of representations of the dispute, their broader communities, social and industrial heritage and cultural traditions. As a major public institution the BBC is the guardian of a vast 'heritage' archive which has traditionally only been the domain of academics and programme makers. However, in recent years, the BBC has become increasingly sensitive to these questions of ownership and audience engagement and through these projects has been helping to develop models in which audiences can interact and gain access to these heritage texts, contextualise and critique them. From the BBC's perspective the initial impetus came from its former Director General, Greg Dyke, who, at the 2003 Edinburgh Television Conference made a commitment to open up the BBCs archives to the general public as they had effectively paid for it via the licence fee. This was a bold move as the archive has an estimated 400,000 TV and Radio programmes and an estimated 900,000 hours of content. These sentiments were strongly echoed by a number of respondents in the following statements: 'History belongs to us all and if such items exist then everyone should have access to them. After all, we paid for it' (Miner: Questionnaire, 2008) and 'I think that everything that the BBC has should be in the public domain. All of us have paid for it in the first instance' (Miner Focus group, 4 August 2008).

The team worked with groups of miners and police officers who had been in conflict during this period and used BBC materials as the basis for developing alternative histories of the strike and explored the potential of these materials as sources of media and communications history, heritage and the best means by which they could be disseminated. The team wanted to know if audiences should have defined points of interaction with the archive? How audiences could make sense of what they were seeing? Should they be able to interact, comment and contextualise these materials? How they could use them to construct their own histories, mobilise memory and engage with the BBC in a period of exciting change and innovation? Through a series of focus groups and questionnaires the team gathered a strong set of commentaries relating to the idea of heritage, and specifically the ways in which uncorrected representations would create a historically distorted picture both of the strike and the broader communities and traditions which are increasingly dissipated and under threat.

The key findings from all participant groups suggested that there was a strong sense that the broadcast material was partial and that they, as a group or as individuals, had been misrepresented and that the complex and detailed social, political and historical issues associated with the strike had tended to be simplified and stereotyped in the past.[13] The role of the archive as a repository for memories was also a strong theme and participants commonly raised the importance of these films as a means of educating future generations and of continuing memories of events, people and communities which are rapidly disappearing. This again raised a central theme in relation to the need to supplement BBC holdings with their recorded memories to ensure the longevity and importance of the archive and to provide added value to materials. As one respondent noted:

> ... the footage needs also to be balanced by personal input ... by witness accounts. By the voice of people and the opinions of people who were involved. And also things like personal footage ... some people must have had video recorders, camcorders ... and their home movies ... and all this sort of stuff could make a valuable audio and visual archive ... I think the BBC stuff would be enormously valuable but I think on its own it's going to be very one-sided.
>
> (Miner: Focus group, 2008)

The question of how to target regional audiences beyond original participants and those living through or affected by the strike was more problematic. In the group work that we did many saw this as a problem relating directly to their own children and the difficulty in engaging them in what was seen as their heritage. Many spoke of the problems of interesting this generation and of the lack of comprehension of the significance of this event upon their own lives. For example, one miner described in detail the experiences of talking to schoolchildren in former mining communities and their lack of knowledge about their own family's recent history and the dismay he felt that the only thing the children wanted to ask him about mining was what miners ate and where they went to the toilet underground. Hence themes relating to the destruction of community, societal cohesion and mining culture were at the heart of the focus group discussions. Solutions often centred on the role the archive materials could play in schools and further education, and the need to package selections with a great deal of contextual material.

As a consequence of this first project the team identified a number of key enhancement activities in relation to the access and usage which both involved the general public and programme/content providers.[14] Some of the strongest evidence drawn from participants was a desire to engage with these holdings via a number of interfaces which went beyond the basic ability to view and search online materials. People expressed the desire to be able to interact, comment on and contextualise archival sources and to directly shape how these materials could become heritage texts for their own communities. As a means of exploring this, and of testing the value of these interactive activities the team undertook a follow-on project in conjunction with BBC Leeds to work with an audience group to create new contextual content to be published via regional BBC websites.[15] During the four months of this project, a group of original participants from the *Open Archive Project* worked to test the potential of some of the key findings from that report. Namely to assess, through practice, the range of ways in which public audiences and communities could interact, contextualise and deepen the value of the BBC's Archive and frame archival heritage texts. The group were keen to investigate this through the creation of a range of web and broadcast materials that were based on their original work with BBC archival materials.

The team recruited twelve original members drawn from a representative sample of people involved in the strike – this group included striking miners, union officials, political activists from Women Against Pit Closures, regionally based police officers and an industrial correspondent. The group worked together as a single group over a number of weeks to develop the project and took collective ownership of the materials that they wanted to develop. Following a series of preliminary discussions participants decided that they wanted to produce a range of materials, including films, written testimony, poems and to collect ephemera and photographs that would present a more rounded view of the strike that, crucially for them, would provide depth and context for the BBC's archive. Indeed, much of the second phase of the project has primarily involved the production and editing of a series of short films which were all shot on location in Manchester and in and around South Yorkshire.[16]

The films which were produced by the group clearly staked out many of the heritage and memory-based concerns expressed in the preceding study and focused on key tropes such as landscape, environment, the loss of historical identity and misrepresentation. The role of landscape was particularly evident in many of the films and Paul Winter's film *The Year We Saw the Light* (2009) strongly relates to the consequences of the changing landscape and the societal cohesion that changed with it. The film skilfully uses the remains of a pithead, a new faceless executive estate on demolished miners' houses and the re-use of a former mine-owner's stately home as an adult education college to chart not only the destruction of a community and a way of life but also as a springboard for optimism and enlightenment through the celebration of these traditions and the importance of education and history.

Similar themes run through Maurice Kent and Ian Oxley's *Rubble* (2009), a poignant meditation on the loss of Maurice's community, and Barbara Jackson's *Sheffield: Forgotten Buildings* (2009). However, Jackson's film shifts the focus away from the traditional habitus of the mining village or pithead to the antithesis of the city of Sheffield which formed the centre of the NUM's management of the strike. She revisits many of the key sites with which she was associated during the strike and uses historical photographs to mark the changes in use and the almost total disappearance of trade unionism from the landscape, drawing clear parallels with the cleansing process which has taken place elsewhere. In many respects these photographs and her film are the only mark of remembrance, there are no plaques or signs of commemoration.

Another form of antithesis deployed by some of the filmmakers was not to focus on the traditional or even clichéd cultural icons of mining like brass music or the pit itself but to mobilise debates about the practice of the strike and the positive and liberating effects on some of its participants. In this way the strike was not packaged as a tragic defeat but as a watershed event with elements of positivism. For example, Ian Oxley's film *In the Coal Board's Hands* (2009) gives a detailed account of how pickets organised themselves, the nature of picketing and how striking miners identified and tracked strike breakers, avoiding and outwitting the police. It shows the self-reliance and confidence of the strikers and their ability to counteract the authorities and retain a strong sense of community throughout this period. Barbara Jackson's second film *We Are Women, We are Strong* (2009) marks a similar sense of self realisation and strength.

The same approach was chosen by the group of former regional police officers involved in the second project. They produced a single film as a group entitled *Maggie's Boot Boys* (2009) which examined the media's portrayal of them as a group of thugs whose own perspectives on the strike and empathy for mining communities had been similarly ignored. Their film, although perhaps less cohesive than the individual films, also stresses the importance of looking beyond the obvious constructions of the strike and the need to seek multiple perspectives in relation to its historical representation and cultural heritage.

The ability to use these films as a means of contextualising their own heritage was seen as crucial by the group, and was clearly stated by many to be the key rationale for their involvement in the project. They spoke passionately about the need to preserve memories, which were only partially reflected in the original sources and which they felt would, over time, disappear. The films themselves are now part of an evolving, self generated heritage and clearly mark the possibilities for similar approaches.

Conclusions

Shortly after the 1984/85 miners' strike had come to an end, the socialist historian Raphael Samuel (1986: ix) noted that the meaning of the strike would be determined not 'by the terms of settlement ... or even by the events of the past year but by the way in which it is assimilated in popular memory, by ... retrospective understanding both in the pit villages themselves and in the country at large'. The significance of Samuel's remark is that, though the 1984/85 strike was a decisive defeat for mining communities, it is imperative that such communities are encouraged to participate in the creation of new representations and social rituals that seek to democratize the mediation of the strike. Not only because such texts hold out the promise of raising public awareness of what *actually* happened 25 years ago but because they also provide affirmation for those miners and families most affected by the strike-action and the subsequent closure of pits.

What the above also demonstrates is that the process of remembering can be a performative experience, that is, an active process that reworks existing memories so that they are made relevant and meaningful for the present day, thus enabling community renewal and growth.[17] What's more, such activities provide an occasion for commemorating a whole way of working class life, thus engendering a real sense of cultural empowerment for the working class more generally. This type of engagement also opens up possibilities for intersections with other 'working class' lives involved in the strike, not least those that were on the opposing side of the conflict. Hence, whilst some of the participants in the *Open Archive* project retained a strong position of hostility and resistance, the majority recognized that some form of reconciliation was possible, indeed, necessary, if only for the benefit of their grandchildren:

> Well, my abiding memory of the strike really is respect for the mining community in that I don't think that there is another group of people in this country who would stick to their guns with regard to the strike as they did.
> (Police Commander: Interview 2008)

> ... I believe in reconciliation, I really do believe in reconciliation ... and it's got to happen if communities are ... ever going to be communities again.
> (Miner: Focus Group 2008)

Other positive signs that a cultural re-evaluation of events and indeed a celebration of industrial working class life in general are now on the agenda of other major cultural organisations come in the form of the British Film Institute's major three-year retrospective on films that depict Britain's industrial heritage, *This Working Life*. The first subject is the coal industry under the title *King Coal* and much focus has been placed on representations of the strike including a première screening of the films produced as part of the *Open Archive* project.[18] Future subjects include the decline of the shipping and steel industries, both of which were similarly affected by the politics of Thatcherism, particularly the consequences of de-industrialisation.

Doubtless, there will be cynics who dismiss such activities as mundane, romanticised and backward looking, that the celebration of labourism has outlived its usefulness. However, what this scepticism fails to grasp is that such depictions keep alive a common culture and a tradition of working class heritage that was in many ways richer and more humane than the one many of us currently inhabit. They also provide an opportunity to rethink and expand the meaning of cultural heritage to include the lived experiences of ordinary people, a socio-cultural process that is still a site of contestation when it comes to such things as policy-making about the allocation of public and private funding. Above all, they bestow a resource of hope on those that are still determined to maintain an attachment to such things as community and collectivism; the alternative is a world dominated by narcissism and defeatism, in short, the loss of social hope and self-worth. Heritage-based initiatives such as those outlined above offer these communities, in genuine partnership with cultural organisations, the opportunity to revise Marx's dictum and to make their own history through heritage on their own terms. The loss of this potent collective memory would be a terrible tragedy for future generations.

Notes

1 See Neocleous (2004) for a more intelligent and sophisticated rendering of this thesis.
2 Of course, the proclamation that the working class have ceased to exist can be traced back to the post-war settlement of the 1950/60s and the emergence of a social democratic politics and so-called working class embourgeoisement, which, as noted by Clarke *et al.* (1979), was deeply paradoxical given it coincided with the publication of all kinds of seminal working class studies (for example, Dennis *et al.* (1956); Young and Wilmott (1957); Hoggart (1957); Williams (1958); Jackson and Marsden (1962), Thompson (1968), among others).
3 One of the most notable studies of working class culture in recent years is Simon Charlesworth's (2000) phenomenological study of working class life in Rotherham, a relatively small town in South Yorkshire.
4 Robert Hewison (1987) dates the 'historicist turn' to British heritage from the mid 1970s onwards, a period when both Britain's aristocracy and key industries were in serious decline. In other words heritage becomes a symbol for national decline.
5 Raphael Samuel (1994) is much the best when it comes to debunking the various anti-heritage arguments raised in, for example, Brett (1996), Harvey and Corner (1991), Hewinson (1987), Lowenthal (1985) and Wright (1985).
6 For other positive takes on heritage, working class heritage in particular, see Smith (2006) and de Groot (2009), among others.
7 See Blackwell and Seabrook (1993) for a more in-depth discussion on redefining conservatism vis-à-vis the revival of radicalism.
8 Among the many analyses of the aftermath of the 1985/85 miners' strike, see Coalfields Taskforce (1998); Waddington (2003), Waddington *et al.* (2001); Waddington *et al.* (1991). There are also a handful of televisual documentaries that critically investigate the socio-economic consequences of the strike; see, for example, *Real life: Children of the Miner's Strike* (ITV 2004).
9 Though published over 50 years ago, Dennis, *et al.*'s *Coal is Our* Life (1956) is still a seminal study of a typical mining community and the socio-cultural relations that characterise their lives. For a history of miners' collective identity and political struggle, see Richards (1996).
10 Further details about the series can be found at: http://www.channel4.com/4homes/on-tv/kevin-s-big-town-plan/castleford-regeneration-an-overview-08–07–31_p_1.html
11 The resulting films – *Making it Work*, *Spray Down Your Way* and *Cutting it at Cutsyke* – can be seen on the Community Channel: http://www.communitychannel.org/index.php?option=com_rnvideoarchive&task=view&vidclip=447&Itemid=139
12 The team was led by Simon Popple with the help of researcher Fiona Blair. The team worked closely with internal BBC sponsors Heather Powell – head of BBC information and Archives North and Helen Thomas – head of BBC North.

13 This was identified as a problem across most mainstream media, but the BBC was signalled out for particular criticism, e.g. 'I wouldn't trust t' BBC to tell me it were five to five.' (Miner Focus Group 2008).
14 The BBC are currently evaluating the recommendations of the project and looking at developing further case studies.
15 The idea was to target regional stories on region-specific websites to engage local audiences as well as providing links which would allow the public to view material from other regions as well.
16 The films that were produced as part of the second project: *What Did You Do In The Strike, Daddy?* – Stephen Brunt, *The Year We Saw The Light* – Paul Winter, *If You Didn't Know You Wouldn't Know* – Tony Fletcher, *Rubble* – Maurice Kent and Ian Oxley, *Sheffield: Forgotten Buildings* – Barbara Jackson, *In The Coal Board's Hands* – Ian Oxley, *We Are Women, We Are Strong* – Barbara Jackson, *Maggie's Boot Boys* – Bob Dunbar, Les, Derek Munday, Harry Shaw and Joe Walsh.
17 It is precisely this definition of community that Raymond Williams (1989: 124) had in mind when he reflected on community as one of the key words that characterised the miners' strike: 'What the miners, like most of us, mean by their communities is the places where they have lived and want to go on living, where generations not only of economic but of social effort and human care have been invested, and which new generations will inherit. Without that kind of strong whole attachment, there can be no meaningful community.'
18 For details see: http://www.bfi.org.uk/about/news/2009-07-02-coal.html

References

Bailey, M. (2009) 'Unfinished Business: Demythologising the Battle of Orgreave', in Granville Williams (ed.), *Shafted: The Media, the Miners' Strike and the Aftermath*, London: Campaign for Press and Broadcasting Freedom.
Beckett, F. and Hencke, D. (2009) *Marching to the Fault Line*, Constable.
Benjamin, W. (1940/2003) 'On the Concept of History', in Harry Zohn (trans.), H. Eiland and M. W. Jennings (eds), *Selected Writings, Vol. 4: 1938–1940*, Cambridge MA: Harvard University Press.
Benyon, H. and Austin, T. (1994) *Masters and Servants*, London: Rivers Oram Press.
Blackwell, T. and Seabrook, J. (1993) *The Revolt Against Change: Towards a Conserving Radicalism*, London: Vintage.
Brett, D. (1996) *The Construction of Heritage*, Cork: Cork University Press.
Charlesworth, S. J. (2000) *A Phenomenology of Working-Class Experience*, Cambridge: Cambridge University Press.
Clarke, J., Critcher, C. and Johnson, R. (eds.) (1979) *Working Class Culture*, London: Hutchinson.
Coalfields Taskforce (1998) *Making a Difference: A New Start for England's Coalfield Communities*, London: DETR.
Corner, J. and Harvey, S. (eds.) (1991) *Enterprise and Heritage: Crosscurrents of National Culture*, London: Routledge.
Dennis, N., Henriques, F. and Slaughter, C. (1956) *Coal is Our Life*, Tavistock.
Derrida, J. (1994) *The Specters of Marx*, London: Routledge.
Douglas, D. (1985) *Tell Us Lies About the Miners*, Aldgate Press.
de Groot, J. (2009) *Consuming History: Historians and Heritage in Contemporary Popular Culture*, London: Routledge.
Hewinson, R. (1987) *The Heritage Industry*, London: Methuen.
Hoggart, R. (1957) *The Uses of Literacy*, London: Chatto and Windus.

Holland, P. (2009) 'After memory: documentary films and the aftermath of the miners' strike', in *Shafted: The Media, the Miners' Strike and the Aftermath*, London: Campaign for Press and Broadcasting Freedom.

Jackson, D. and Marsden, B. (1962) *Education and the Working Class*, London: Routledge and Kegan Paul.

Jones, D., Petley, J., Power, M. and Wood, L. (1985) *Media Hits the Pits*, London: The Campaign for Press and Broadcasting Freedom.

Joyce, P. (1991) *Visions of the People: Industrial England and the Question of Class, 1840–1914*, Cambridge: Cambridge University Press.

Lowenthal, D. (1985) *The Past is a Foreign Country*, Cambridge: Cambridge University Press.

Marx, K. (1852/1977) 'The Eighteenth Brumaire of Louis Napoleon I', in David McLellan (ed.) *Karl Marx: Selected Writings*, Oxford: Oxford University Press.

Masterman, L. (1984) *Television Mythologies: Stars, Shows and Signs*, London: Comedia.

Milne, S. (1994) *The Enemy Within: the Secret War Against the Miners*, London and New York: Verso.

McCloud, K. (2008) 'The Big Town Plan: Kevin's View', Online interview. Available HTTP: <http://www.channel4.com/4homes/on-tv/kevin-s-big-town-plan/kevin-mccloud-and-the-big-town-plan-kevin-s-view-08-08-07_p_3.html> (last accessed 8 October 2009).

Neocleous, M. (2004) 'Let the Dead Bury Their Dead: Marxism and the Politics of Redemption', *Radical Philosophy*, 128: 23–32.

Richards, A. J. (1996) *Miners on Strike: Class Solidarity and Division in Britain*, Oxford: Berg.

Samuel, R. (1994) *Theatres of Memory*, London: Verso.

Samuel, R., Bloomfield, B. and Boanas, G. (1986) *The Enemy Within: Pit Villages and the Miners' Strike of 1984–5*, London: Routledge.

Skeggs, B. (1997) *Formations of Class and Gender*, London: Sage.

Smith, L. (2006) *Uses of Heritage*, London: Routledge.

Stedman Jones, G. (1983) *Languages of Class: Studies in English Working Class History, 1832–1982*, Cambridge: Cambridge University Press.

Stephenson, C. and Wray, D. 'Emotional Regeneration Through Community Action in Post-Industrial Mining Communities: The New Herrington Miners' Banner Partnership', *Capital and Class*, 2005 (87): 175–99.

Thompson, E. P. (1968) *The Making of the English Working-class*, Harmondsworth: Penguin Books.

Waddington, D. (2003) *Developing Coalfields Communities: Breathing New Life into Worksop Vale*, Bristol: The Policy Press.

Waddington, D., Critcher, C., Dicks, B. and Parry, D. (2001) *Out of the Ashes? The Social Impact of Industrial Contraction and Regeneration on Britain's Mining Communities*, Norwich: The Stationary Office.

Waddington, D., Wykes, M. and Critcher, C. (1991) *Split at The Seams: Community, Continuity and Change after the 1984–5 Coal Dispute*, Milton Keynes: Open University Press.

Williams, G. (2009) 'Look Back in Anger', in Granville Williams (ed.) *Shafted: The Media, the Miners' Strike and the Aftermath*, London: Campaign for Press and Broadcasting Freedom.

Williams, R. (1989) 'Mining the Meaning: Key Words in the Miners' Strike', *Resources of Hope*, London: Verso.

——(1958) *Culture and Society, 1780–1950*, London: Chatto and Windus.

Wright, P. (1985) *On Living in an Old Country*, London: Verso.

Young, M. and Wilmott, P. (1957) *Family and Kinship in East London*, London: Penguin.

Chapter 3

Remembering Haymarket and the control for public memory

Paul A. Shackel

The historical memory of any transforming or controversial event emerges from cultural and political competition, and issues related to the memory of labour are no different. Since the beginning of the industrial revolution, capital and labour have clashed over wages, length of the working day and safety conditions in the workplace. These differences sometimes have been expressed through covert acts of resistance such as sabotage, work slowdowns or absenteeism. Other times labour and capital have had public demonstrations of their disagreements and they have played out in the form of strikes and strike-breaking. Those who have the power to control the public memory of these events can command the historical consciousness. While labour and capital have been often at odds when interpreting the labour movement, the recent phenomenon to memorialise these contentious events through dialogue has muted some perspectives. As a result, the struggle for an inclusive official memory continues.

The Haymarket Riot in Chicago in 1886 is a fascinating story whereby capital and law enforcement tried unsuccessfully for over a century to mute the voices of labour. In fact, national and international labour rallied around the memory of the labour martyrs. Through ceremonial events, literature and memorials on the landscape, labour's perspective of the event is prominent. Those who were unjustly hanged for being associated with the riot have been transformed into martyrs around the globe. The events associated with the Haymarket riot and the competing versions for the memory of the incident are continually being negotiated today.

Haymarket

By the last quarter of the nineteenth century capitalists had invested substantial resources to develop industries and their large-scale enterprises thrived during what is now called the Gilded Age. From the 1860s, Chicago's industrial production grew dramatically. It became a centre for the production of steel, iron, men's clothing, farm machinery and meatpacking. Most workers laboured long hours with low wages and few privileges. A large immigrant community from central and Eastern Europe supplied the labour for these growing industries and they brought with them radical labour perspectives (Green 2006: 29–30, 63–64, 70).

Socialism was prominent in Chicago and the community could often find a socialist lecture, socialist Sunday schools for children, socialist picnics and saloons. Chicago supported English, Czech and three German anarchist newspapers. One of the anarchist newspapers was controlled by August Spies, a radicalised upholsterer. Spies wrote editorials while Michael Schwab, a bookbinder, reported on the conditions of working class neighbourhoods, including the slums. Albert Parsons edited the anarchist's English paper (Crain 2006: 84).

By the 1880s, the labour movement in the United States developed with three main organisations. One was the Knights of Labor, a large and loosely organised group that emphasised land reform and cooperatives. Second was the Federation of Organized Trades and Labor Unions, which eventually became the American Federation of Labor (AF of L). Third was the International Working Peoples Association, an anarchist organisation. While it had a small membership, it provided the most militant leadership in the labour movement. All three groups demanded an eight-hour workday, and the Federation acted on it with concrete demands. At the Federation's 1884 convention under the leadership of Samuel Gompers, they passed a resolution that read 'Resolved, that eight hours shall constitute a legal day's labour, from and after 1 May 1886, and that we recommend to labour organisations that they so direct their laws' (quoted in Goldway 2005: 219). The resolution was reaffirmed during the 1885 convention.

As 1 May 1886 approached, circulars were distributed to workers throughout the industrial cities in the United States. One circular read:

> Arouse ye toilers of America! Lay down your tools on May 1, 1886. Cease your labor. Close the factories, mills and mines, for one day in the year. One day of revolt, not of rest. A day not ordained by the bragging spokesmen of institutions holding the world of labor in bondage. A day on which labor makes its own cause, and has the power to execute them. A day of protest against oppression and tyranny, against ignorance and war of any kind. A day on which to enjoy eight hours for work, eight hours for rest, eight hours for what we will.
>
> (Goldway 2005: 219–20)

On 1 May 1886, in what many call the first May Day parade, between 30,000 and 40,000 Chicago workers struck, and Albert Parsons and his wife Lucy led 80,000 people through the streets in protest for an eight-hour work day. On 3 May, Spies spoke to German and Czech striking workers. A few blocks away, the workday ended at the McCormick Reaper Works. The company locked out striking workers and hired strikebreakers. As the strikebreakers left the company compound, a few hundred men peeled off from

Spies' group and threw stones at the strikebreakers. The police fired on the protesters, killing at least one and wounding several others (Crain 2006).

Outraged by the event, Spies, in one of the German-language anarchist papers, denounced the police as trained 'bloodhounds' and scolded the strikers for not being better prepared with dynamite to fight the police. Anarchists decided to protest against these killings by gathering at Haymarket the following day, on 4 May. Adolph Fischer printed a flyer with the headline in boldface declaring 'REVENGE'. The flyer also included the phrase: 'rise in your might, Hercules, and destroy the hideous monster that seeks to destroy you' (Avrich 1984: 190). The announcement confirmed that 'Good speakers will be present to denounce the latest atrocious act of the police, the shooting of our fellow workmen yesterday afternoon' (quoted in Green: 2006: 179). The first run of several hundred flyers included the phrase 'Working-men Arm Yourselves and Appear in Full Force'. Spies objected to this wording, fearing that it would reduce the protest crowd at Haymarket. He refused to participate in the rally, unless the words were struck from the leaflet. The second run of the flyer omitted this phrase although by the beginning of the rally 176 policemen had assembled a half block away at the Desplaines Street Station (Green 2006: 180). At the protest anarchists addressed the crowd at the Haymarket and throughout the day 3,000 people heard speeches decrying the murders of the workers at the McCormick factory. Even the mayor of Chicago attended for a while. Spies spoke and later Parsons addressed the crowd. It began to rain, so Parsons, his family, as well as Fischer took shelter in a nearby saloon. Spies and Fielden remained at the protest (Green 2006: 183–85).

The demonstration began to fade during the damp evening and Fielden harshened his tone: 'The law is your enemy', he said. 'Keep your eye upon it, throttle it, kill it, stab it, do everything you can do to wound it – to impede its progress' (quoted in David 1963:175). While he was finishing his words, about 200 policemen marched on the dwindling crowd and ordered them to disperse. Fielden replied: 'We are peaceable' and he began to step down from the wagon (quoted in David 1963:175). At that moment, one of the demonstrators threw a bomb into the police formation, wounding many (Figure 3.1; Dubofsky and Dulles 1999; Foote 1997).

The Chicago *Tribune*, which was owned by Cyrus McCormick, reported:

> It rose about twenty feet in the air, describing a curve, and fell right in the middle of the street and among the marching police. It gave a red glare while in the air. The bomb lay on the ground a few seconds, then a loud explosion occurred, and the crowd took to their heels, scattering in all directions. Immediately after the explosion the police pulled their revolvers and fired on the crowd. An incessant fire was kept up for nearly two minutes, and at least 250 shots were fired.
>
> (Crain 2006: 87)

Remembering Haymarket and the control for public memory 37

Figure 3.1 The Anarchist Riot in Chicago: a dynamite bomb exploding among the police (Courtesy of the Chicago History Museum, ICHi-03665).

Avrich's (1984) analysis of the event shows that there was not a pitched battle between workers and police. However, at the end of the riot, four demonstrators were killed and many injured. A total of seven police died and 60 were injured, many from crossfire (Dubofsky and Dulles 1999: 112–15; Foote 1997: 134–35).

The regional newspapers immediately called for justice and the end of the anarchist movement. The police arrested eight of the strike leaders, even though they had not been associated with the bombing, and placed them on trial. Three of the men arrested, August Spies, Albert Parsons and Samuel Fielden, had been speakers at the Haymarket meeting. However, when it began to rain Parsons and Fischer took refuge in a nearby saloon. Only Spies and Fielden were at the protest. Two of Spies' co-workers were also arrested, Michael Schwab and Adolph Fischer. Schwab was not in the vicinity of Haymarket when the bomb exploded, as he had left to speak at another meeting. Two other defendants were socialists, George Engel and Oscar Neebe, although they had no other connection to the Haymarket Riot that was ever proved. Neebe did not know about the meeting and Engel stayed home with his family. Louis Lingg, an anarchist who made crude explosives, had no connection to the violence at Haymarket, although he was delivering bombs to a saloon on the North side during the riot (Boudreau 2005; Crain 2006: 86; Dubofsky and Dulles 1999: 112–15; Foote 1997: 134–35).

The defence easily found holes in the testimonies of the government's star witnesses. One witness said that he saw the bomb thrower, and described him as having a moustache and stood at about 5ft 9in; but he did not resemble any of the defendants. The prosecution asserted that they did not have to prove that any of these men threw the bomb, but rather they were guilty of murder based on what they had said and written about anarchism and the use of violence. They all were known to have believed, and sometimes had written, that violence was a way to achieve socioeconomic justice (Avrich 1984).

The prosecutor closed his argument by stating that it was up to the jury to decide, 'whether the day of civilization shall go down into the night of barbarism' (Crain 2006: 88). Probably the major weakness of the anarchists was their support of the use of violence to promote a revolution, and their humanitarian goals, such as endorsing better working conditions, was overshadowed. Within three hours of deliberation, the jury found all eight men guilty in what many historians see as one of the great miscarriages of law in the United States. The judge sentenced seven men to death and the other received a 15-year jail sentence. They were not guilty of killing, but they were made an example to 'save our institutions, [and] our society' (Adelman 1976: 21; Avrich 1984).

The Illinois Supreme Court upheld the verdict and the US Supreme Court refused to hear the case since there were no federal questions involved. In November 1887, Parsons, Spies, Engel and Fischer were hanged. Fielden, Schwab and Neebe had their sentence commuted to life in prison by the governor. Lingg killed himself the morning of the executions by placing a cigar-sized bomb in his mouth and lighting it. The prosecution never proved that the eight convicted men had ever known about, planned or committed the bombing (Avrich 1984; Crain 2006: 88).

When August Spies was about to be hanged, he called out, 'There will come a time when our silence will be more powerful than the voices you strangle today!' (quoted in McKinley 1987: 386). Albert Parsons, who appealed to the English-speaking audiences, became the most popular martyr because of the post-death crusade of his wife to keep his struggle in the memory of the American people. But also for his 'noble spirit', freely surrendering himself to authorities after escaping the scene. He could have asked for clemency, but he refused, choosing martyrdom instead (McKinley 1987: 393).

Remembering Haymarket and the Labour Movement

Usually the victors control the dominant narrative of an event, and in this case, capital and labour are at odds over the control of the memory of Haymarket. The events at Haymarket, 'unleashed and licensed the first U.S. red scare; the 1886 proceedings were the most blatant use of judicial terror employed in the country up to that time' (Palmer 2006: 28). Anti-union businesses mounted the 'Red Scare' campaign that reached a national audience. They linked trade unions with anarchy. As a result, the movement towards the eight-hour day lost momentum and unions and militant workers lost considerable power. Cyrus McCormick used the *Chicago Tribune* to vilify labour organisations and the influence of the newspaper outweighed the influence of the several local anarchist papers (Green 2006).

For labour, those who died as a result of the Haymarket mistrial were transformed into martyrs. While the city prevented labour from memorialising their martyrs within the city limits, many thousands came to the funeral procession, which led to Waldheim Cemetery, across the city line. Many thousands viewed the funeral procession, more in numbers than had viewed the Lincoln funeral procession through Chicago (Dabakis 1998; Foote 1997).

The campaign to create martyrs of the Haymarket labour leaders began soon after the trial ended. The pamphlet, *August Spies' Autobiography; His Speech in Court, and General Notes*, was published by Nina Van Zandt in Chicago (with no date). She married Spies by proxy in the course of the trial. In an effort to save her husband, the pamphlet provides an emotional account of the trial. At about the same time Dyer D. Lum, a journalist in Chicago and activist in the radical movement, published *A Concise History of the Great Trial of the Chicago Anarchists in 1886, Condensed from the Official Record* (no date) (Kirk and Kirk 1969: 487–89).

A few weeks after the death of the martyrs, Rev. John Kimball preached to a Hartford Congregation: '[T]he newspapers may try to belittle [the anarchists] and laugh them down', but they 'are the very ore out of which the poets and balladists of all ages have wrought the lines of song which have shaped the world's onward way' (quoted in Boudreau 2005: 321). Many of the radical orators of the time, including Eugene Debs, Lucy Parsons, William Owens and Emma Goldman linked the Civil War and Haymarket with the idea that both were struggles to end slavery. They fought for the abolition of wage slavery. They often used the violent actions of John Brown, the famous American abolitionist, as an example to justify their cause. John Brown was executed by the state of Virginia, and his martyrdom ignited the cause for emancipation. They believed that the execution of the Haymarket martyrs would also help their struggle and alter existing practices in labour and property (Streeby 2007: 406–9).

In 1890, Samuel Gompers, president of the AF of L, urged the newly formed Socialist International to campaign for a worldwide eight-hour workday and to make 1 May the rallying day. European labour, knowing the events of Haymarket and the American May Day, enthusiastically supported the practice of laying down tools and demonstrating on 1 May (Goldway 2005: 223).

Lucy Parsons worked tirelessly to keep alive the spirit and memory of the Haymarket incident, as well as the writings of the martyrs as part of the public memory. Lucy and Albert Parsons published the newspaper *Alarm*, and after the martyrs' death, Lucy printed an article titled 'The Trial a Farce'. She wrote about the great injustices of the trial and explained, 'Our comrades sleep the sleep which knows no awakening, but the grand cause for which they died is not asleep nor dead!' (quoted in Streeby 2007: 412). Lucy Parsons compiled and published *The Life of Albert R. Parsons* in 1889, which was republished in a slightly different form in 1903. It included writings by Albert, Lucy and others about the history of the labour movement. The letters and articles of Albert's travels through the Midwest to organise labour also included various speeches made by Albert Parsons as he alluded to the war on wage slavery (Streeby 2007: 408). The capitalist and the state were at odds with the working class and therefore the workers needed to defend themselves, and liberate themselves from bondage.

Lucy Parsons also published *The Famous Speeches of the Eight Chicago Anarchists* in 1886, which went through several editions. She sold *The Life of Albert R. Parsons* and *The Famous Speeches* on the streets and through mail order, as well at labour events. She contributed to, or edited a variety of other radical periodicals, including the *Alarm, Freedom,* the *Rebel, Free Society,* the *Liberator, Industrial Worker*, the *Agitator,* the *Syndicalist*, to name a few. These periodicals tended to be short lived, closing because of a lack of funds, or being suppressed by the government. The Chicago police destroyed the *Free Society* after President McKinley's assassination in 1901 (Streeby 2007: 413).

Despite the Red Scare and the repression of free speech that followed the martyrs' execution, the memory of the events lived on in various forms of print culture. Along with the efforts of Lucy Parsons, others used newspapers, pamphlets, books, plays, poems, images, speeches and commemorations, which enabled radicals and working class people to make sense of the events and provide meaning for the present (Streeby 2007: 406). These populist forms of poetry were important for developing class solidarity. (Boudreau 2005: 325).

Labour and Law Engage Dialogue and Compromise

On 25 June 1893, about 8,000 people came to the unveiling of a large memorial that marked the martyrs' grave. The monument depicts a woman symbolising justice, placing a crown of laurels on the head of a fallen worker, while preparing to draw a sword (see Figure 3.2; see also Averich 1984; Foote 1997: 136; Kelland 2005: 33). The day after the unveiling Governor Altgeld pardoned the three imprisoned martyrs – Fielded, Schwab and Neebe (Kellard 2005: 33). Altgeld read the trial transcripts and he became enraged by the results of the trial. He was convinced that the men should not have been convicted because the trial could not prove who threw the bomb (Crain 2006: 88).

Figure 3.2 Memorial marking the graves of the martyrs of Haymarket (Photograph by Paul A. Shackel).

For several decades 'November 11 meetings' were held on the anniversary of the hanging of the martyrs. Accounts of 'November 11 meetings' in Chicago indicate that between 2,000 to 3,000 people attended these events to listen to speeches in English, German, and later Italian and Yiddish. A German orchestra usually opened the session, music and choral offerings punctuated the ceremonies. Floral tributes and banners decorated the halls, and these yearly rituals served to reaffirm labour's commitment to justice. While anarchists did not believe in religion, the five martyrs became the saints of the labour movement. In many of the anarchists' speeches, they made analogies to Christianity. In one 'November 11 meeting' in Boston, speakers compared the Chicago anarchists to Jesus Christ, who had been crucified for teaching human equality. In 1915, a noted militant communist-anarchist, Alexander Berkman said, 'When you think of the Nazarene and Golgotha, remember also Chicago and the 11th of November, 1887' (quoted in McKinley 1987: 389).

Haymarket took on international meaning. Activists in the 1930s reclaimed the place, and insisted on social justice in labour practices. In 1936, Lucy Parsons, on the 50th anniversary of the event, led communists, socialists and trade unionists in a parade through Chicago's loop during the May Day celebration. They commemorated the revolutionary and labour rights legacy of the riot. However, during World War II the American Communist Party collapsed, and along with the mounting tensions of the Cold War, the memory of martyrs faded from the national public memory (Kelland 2005: 33).

While the radical movement led by communists and anarchists went underground, organised labour began to take an active interest once again in 1969. Labour activist Les Orear and historian Bill Alderman developed a ceremony at the site on 4 May 1969. Studs Terkel gave a speech on a wagon; much like the speakers did 83 years prior. The Red Squad of the Chicago Police Department (CPD) monitored these activities. Orear and Alderman incorporated the Illinois Labor History Society (ILHS) that same year, and in 1986 they collaborated with the Chicago Historical Society (CHS) to create a centennial celebration. The CPD held commemorative events too; however, their ceremonies focused on all of the police officers who died in the line of duty (Kelland 2005: 33–34). The ILHS and CHS partnered and placed a plaque on the square, attaching it to the wall of the Catholic Charities building. However, vandals stole the plaque a few weeks later. It became difficult for the centennial committee to gain civic support to mark and commemorate the space (Kelland 2005: 34–35). Law enforcement and the labour heritage groups were not working collaboratively and could not find a common theme or message to help interpret the events of Haymarket.

Labour tried other channels to commemorate the events of Haymarket. This time they worked with the city's landmarks programme and in 1992, the Chicago Council approved Haymarket Square worthy of landmark status. That same year the site of the speakers' wagon was marked by a bronze plaque set into the sidewalk, reading:

> A decade of strife between labor and industry culminated here in a confrontation that resulted in the tragic death of both workers and

policemen. On May 4, 1886, spectators at a labor rally had gathered around the mouth of Crane's Alley. A contingent of police approaching on Des Plaines Street were met by a bomb thrown from just south of the alley. The resultant trial of eight activists gained worldwide attention for the labor movement, and initiated the tradition of 'May Day' labor rallies in many cities.

(Designated on 25 March 1992. Richard M. Daley, Mayor)

However, tensions exist between the anarchists and the ILHS. The ILHS mission is to emphasise the legacy of labour, while the anarchists want to remember the revolutionary aspects of the labour movement. Haymarket to the anarchists is the attempt to dismantle capitalism and government. As a result, the anarchists have been antagonistic towards the ILHS and they often appear at the Waldheim cemetery and try to interrupt ILHS commemorative events. The anarchists are also reputed to have placed phone threats prior to ILHS events. Before the centennial event they draped the Waldheim Cemetery memorial with a black flag, and when Les Orear tried to remove it, he was wrestled to the ground (Kelland 2005: 35).

The anarchists protested against the Landmark celebration at Waldheim and declared in a flyer handed out that day:

> From the Haymarket martyrs [:] The events of May 3 were a disgraceful sham. It maddens us and saddens us greatly. We were Anarchists. We fought for Revolution. They killed us for it. But today these lying hypocrites are associating us with the US government we so greatly hated. In no way do we wish to be connected to a system responsible for tens of millions of murders. Truly honor us by reading 'Anarchism' ed. Parsons & our 'Autobiographies. Amerikkka [sic] murdered us in 1887 but the truth about our lives lives on & our Movement still exists. Join us in protesting this terrible perversion of our ideas. 'Hurrah for Anarchy'.
>
> (quoted in Kelland 1998: 35).

The cemetery memorial was later designated a National Historic Landmark by the Secretary of the Interior in 1997. The inscription on the bronze plaque states: 'This monument represents the labor movement's struggle for workers' rights and possesses national significance in commemorating the history of the United States of America.' After the plaque was mounted on the monument the anarchist symbol was added by hand as well as a hand written phrase that made the last line read 'the United States of America's oppression of dissidents' (Figure 3.3).

A tension remained between the police, labour and anarchists into the late twentieth century. However, in the early twenty-first century, funding from the Illinois State legislature became available for a commemorative park

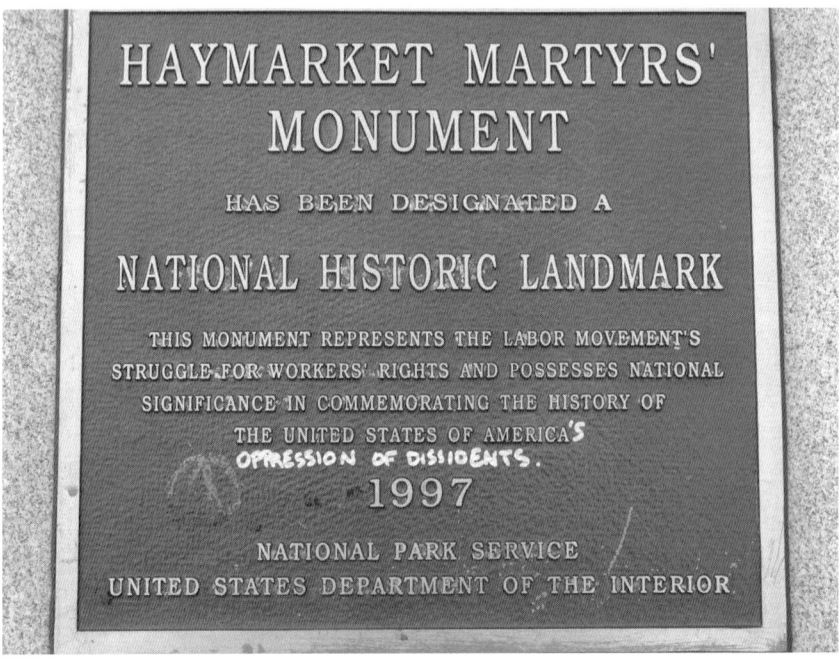

Figure 3.3 National Historic Landmark plaque with the added inscription that reads 'the United States of America's oppression of dissidents' (Photograph by Paul A. Shackel).

dedicated to the right for free speech. In order to create some sort of reconciliation between labour and the police a panel of stakeholders was created that consisted of representatives from the CPD and the ILHS. Together, along with representatives from other city organisations, in 2002 they began planning for a common memorial at the Haymarket site. Reconciliation is important to the police since they are now unionised and part of organised labour. However, it is unclear, but doubtful, that the opinions of anarchists and their views and critique on capitalism and industry were solicited, even though it was the anarchists who led the Haymarket strike (Kelland 2005: 36).

The cooperation between the police and labour, these once confrontational groups, was remarkable, reaching a consensus on how to remember the Haymarket events. The president of the Chicago Fraternal Order of Police stated, 'We are part of the labour movement now and glad to be there' (Kelland 2005: 36). The monument, erected in 2004, depicts workers – constructing a wagon and an anonymous figure is on the platform. It's a symbol of the platform where the workers gave speeches on the day of the riot. For many, the statue conveys the message of free assembly and free speech, something that is palpable for all involved in the project. The

Remembering Haymarket and the control for public memory 45

Figure 3.4 The Haymarket Memorial erected in 2004 (Photograph by Mary Brogger).

labour of anonymous agents as well as the collectivity of labourers is represented. However, the monument does not represent the martyrs (Figure 3.4).

Mary Brogger, the Haymarket memorial artist was given the stipulation that she had to depict in some way, a wagon. In a recent interview Brogger describes that the faceless characters in the sculpture do not represent the specific event or characters of Haymarket, but rather the memorial represents a greater meaning about power and responsibility. She explains that in her sculpture are:

> Some figures that appear to either be constructing or deconstructing a wagon. And I was thinking about the nature of anarchy, how you have to destroy something to build something, and I was thinking about the nature of truth and how faceted it is. So [in the] composition you can see the figures at the bottom working to create a platform on which the figures on the top can rise up and express themselves. But it seems to be that therein lies a responsibility, that your expression can dismantle the whole construction. So, you have a responsibility, in that, where power lies there is responsibility, so, it could be the undoing of the whole composition. So it's a cautionary tale about how power is wielded.
>
> (Interview, Marry Brogger 13 November 2009)

At the unveiling ceremony of the new monument Dennis Gannon, president of the Chicago Federation of Labor, spoke about the victory of organised labour. He stated:

> Today's memorial dedication must serve as an important lesson to all of us. A lesson for healing our emotional wounds; a lesson of solidarity, justice, and peace; a lesson of protecting our civil and human rights, and a lesson that at the end of the day, we are all workers, union and non-union alike.
> (quoted in Kelland 2005: 37).

Mark Donahue, the president of the Chicago Fraternal Order of Police also took the stage, as he did so anarchists, armed with their black flags, booed. One anarchist yelled out: 'They're trying to whitewash the whole thing, take it from the anarchists and make it a free speech issue.' Donahue proceeded with his speech:

> Organized labor and law enforcement have both come a long way in the past 118 years. Law enforcement is now part of the labor movement. The efforts of the pioneers of the labor movement and the sacrifices of those eight police officers who were killed have not gone unanswered. Organized labor has enjoyed and our country has reaped the rewards of those efforts.
> (Kelland 2005: 37–38).

One anarchist was invited to join in the development of the official wording in a bronze plaque for the monument, although he refused to be part of the process. He did, however, speak at the unveiling ceremony. Brogger also noted that her memorial is about the humanity of the event rather than the politics of Haymarket. There is an open invitation for groups to add plaques to the monument. So far, three countries have added plaques to the monument (Interview, Marry Brogger, 13 November 2009).

The protectors of Chicago

The business community also claimed the police were martyrs, calling them 'Protectors of Chicago'. In 1888 anti-union business leaders, led by a *Tribune* sponsored committee, raised $10,000 for a monument in Haymarket Square to commemorate the efforts of the policemen (Figure 3.5). The protectors of Chicago were also defenders of capitalism, and business leaders used the policeman's statue to keep the memory of the police as defenders of modern civilisation alive in the memory of the general public. In 1895, the police held a parade and carried a banner that designated them as 'Veterans of the Haymarket Riot'. In 1901, they incorporated themselves under this

Remembering Haymarket and the control for public memory   47

Figure 3.5 Protectors of Chicago Memorial in Haymarket Square (Courtesy of the Chicago History Museum, ICHi-14452).

name and annual celebrations were held that included a site visit, recreating pulling the alarm and retelling stories of the event (Figure 3.6). These festivities were carried on until the 1960s, even though the last surviving member of the 'veterans' died in 1947 (Kelland 2005: 32).

The police monument moved to several locations throughout the city. It serves as a symbol that in some way measures public sentiment about the

48 Remembering Haymarket and the control for public memory

Figure 3.6 Veterans gather for the twenty-second anniversary of the Haymarket Riot at Union Park (Courtesy of the Chicago History Museum, ICHi-2878).

role of law, and in other ways, it serves as a symbol that counters the labour movement's claim to public space and the public memory of the event. From the turn of the twentieth century, the policemen's monument has been annually vandalised on the anniversary of the riot. In 1900, it was declared a traffic hazard, sitting in the middle of Haymarket Square, and the city moved it to Union Park. On 4 May 1903, someone stole the crest of the city and the state from the memorial. On the anniversary day in 1927, a streetcar driver drove his vehicle into the monument, toppling and damaging it. The following year the city moved it again (on 4 May), father away from vehicle traffic. In 1958 (4 May), the statue was moved about 200 ft. from its original location to Randolph Street. On 4 May in 1969, black paint was sprayed on the monument. On 6 October 1969, a bomb demolished the statue and blew out nearby windows. Mayor Richard Daley ensured that the statue was repaired; however, one year later the statue was once again blown up. Daley funded the repairs of the statue and a 24-hour patrol of the statue was undertaken until February 1972. Daley ordered the statue be moved to police headquarters and four years later the city moved it to the courtyard of the Police Academy, making it inaccessible to the public (see Figure 3.7; Eisler 2007; Gallagher 2007; Kelland 2005: 32).

Remembering Haymarket and the control for public memory 49

Figure 3.7 Protectors of Chicago Memorial in the courtyard of the Police Academy (Photograph by Paul D. Rettig).

After 30 years of being out of public sight, the statue was rededicated on 1 June 2007. It was moved to a place outside of the Police Headquarters at 3510 S. Michigan Street and Superintendent Philip Cline of the Chicago Police Department, along with dignitaries, oversaw the rededication of the Policemen's monument. At the ceremony Geraldine Docekal, great-granddaughter of Officer Degan, the first officer to die at the Haymarket Riot, assisted with the unveiling of the statue (Cline 2007).

The claim for control over the memory of the Haymarket event is telling. For over a hundred years the monument has always been referred to as the Policemen's monument; however, a news release from the Chicago Police Department identifies the monument as the 'Haymarket Memorial Statue' (Cline 2007). This statement and naming of the monument claims Haymarket for the police. It is also interesting that after the compromise memorial was erected at Haymarket Square, which symbolises freedom to assemble and freedom of speech, the police reasserted their message on the public landscape. The base of the statue is loaded with symbolism that honours the fallen policemen. The pedestal has eight columns that represent the eight officers killed at Haymarket Square. There is a soft blue light shining within the columns representing the police force today, 'who currently serve and protect the city' (Cline 2007).

Conclusion

The struggle for control of the memory of labour's heritage is often contentious and regularly countered by capitalist enterprises. In the nineteenth century, Cyrus McCormick and others used the power of the *Tribune* and other media to incite the Red Scare and counter organised labour. However, grass roots efforts by the labouring class used the media to create martyrs of the Haymarket labour leaders. Today, the events at Haymarket are remembered around the world as millions of workers celebrate May Day, and remember the martyrs and events of Haymarket.

Joint efforts by the Illinois Labor History Society and the Chicago Police have created a new monument that has been erected at Haymarket Square. However, the radical social critique of government and industry is absent from this new public display. Instead, the monument is a compromise between labour and law enforcement and it symbolises values that both groups can agree upon – free speech. Clearly, the changing meaning of Haymarket and the new memorial that sits on the place of the Haymarket Riot is imposed by a new partnership, which has created a compromised heritage that is considered safe for both labour and law enforcement.

While the memory reflected in the new memorial at Haymarket appears to be a compromise, the chess game for the control of the memory of the place continues. The Chicago police have once again reasserted their memory and message of the events at Haymarket as protectors of law and freedom, and they have recently claimed the name 'Haymarket Memorial Statue' for what has always been known publicly as the Policemen's Memorial. While the current memorial at Haymarket will be antagonistic to the anarchists, although acceptable to organised labour, the inference that the Policemen's Memorial is now the Haymarket Memorial Statue will probably lay the foundation for additional commemoration events by organised labour in order to reassert their claim to the events at Haymarket.

References

Adelman, W. J. (1976) *Haymarket Revisited: a tour guide of labor history sites and ethnic neighborhoods connected with the Haymarket Affair*, Chicago, IL: Illinois Labor History Society.

Avrich, P. (1984) *The Haymarket Tragedy*, Princeton, NJ, Princeton University Press.

Boudreau, Kristin (2005) 'Elegies for the Haymarket Anarchists', *American Literature*, 77(2): 319–47.

Brogger, M. (2009) Interview, 13 November with Kristin Sullivan. On file, Department of Anthropology, University of Maryland, College Park, MD.

Cline, P. J. (2007) 'Haymarket Memorial Statue Rededicated at Chicago Police Headquarters: Memorial Placed at New Home after Six Previous Moves', News Release, Chicago Police Department. Philip J. Cline, Superintendent of Police. 3510 South Michigan Ave., Chicago, IL 60653.

Crain, C. (2006) 'Terror Last Time: What Happened at Haymarket', *The New Yorker* 13 March 82–89.

Dabakis, M. (1998) *Visualizing Labor in American Sculpture: Monuments, Manliness, and the Work Ethic, 1880–1935*, NY: Cambridge University Press.

Dubofsky, M. and Rhea Dulles, F. (1999) *Labor in America: A History*, Wheeling, IL: Harlan Davidson, Inc.

Eisler, G. (2007) 'Police Rededicate Haymarket Memorial Statue', ABC7 Chicago.com. HTTP: <www.abclocal.go.com/wls/story?section=news/local&id=5360296> (accessed 6 April 2009).

Foote, K. E. (1997) *Shadowed Ground: America's Landscapes of Violence and Tragedy*, Austin, TX: University of Texas Press.

Gallagher, R. (2007) 'Haymarket Monument Makes Comeback', Medill Reports – Chicago, Northwestern University. May 3, 2007. HTTP: <www.news.medill.northwestern.edu/chicago/news.aspx?id=35677> (accessed 6 April 2009).

Goldway, D. (2005) 'A Neglected page of History: The Story of May Day', *Science and Society*, 59(2): 218–24.

Green, J. (2006) *Death in the Haymarket: A Story of Chicago, the First Labor Movement and the Bombing That Divided Gilded Age America*, New York, NY: Pantheon Books.

Kelland, L. (2005) 'Putting Haymarket to Rest?', *Labor: Studies in Working-Class History of the Americas*, 2(2): 21–38.

McKinley, B. (1987) 'A Religion of the New Time': Anarchist Memorials to the Haymarket Martyrs, 1888–1917', *Labor History*, 28(3): 386–400.

Kirk, C. and Kirk, R. (1969) William Dean Howells, George William Curtis, and the 'Haymarket Affair', *American Literature*, 40(4): 487–98.

Palmer, B. D. (2006) 'CSI Labor History: Haymarket and the Forensics of Forgetting', *Labor: Studies in Working-Class History of the Americas*, 3(1): 25–36.

Streeby, S. (2007) 'Labor, memory, and the Boundaries of Print Culture: From Haymarket to the Mexican Revolution', *American Literary History*, 19(2): 406–33.

Chapter 4

The social and environmental upheaval of Blair Mountain

A working class struggle for unionisation and historic preservation

Brandon Nida and Michael Jessee Adkins

Armed miners gathered by the thousands in the late autumn of 1921, streaming out of the hills and hollows of West Virginia. Many wore blue overalls and tied red bandanas around their necks as a uniform, while others were dressed in their military gear from the recently ended First World War. They were a mixture of Appalachian hill folk from Scots-Irish ancestry, African-Americans who had migrated out of the Deep South, and emigrants from Italy, Wales, Poland and other European countries. This coal-miner army was assembling to confront a severely oppressive social and economic system maintained by coal operators in the region. After a generation of labour conflict in the West Virginia coalfields, mining communities erupted in the largest open class war in US history (Savage 1990: 3–6). Their struggle culminated on the ridges surrounding Blair Mountain in a fierce five-day battle against a private army backed by coal-mine owners.

This conflict occurred in a larger international context where labour movements were gaining momentum worldwide. Workers' councils in Germany seemed on the cusp of obtaining political control during 1917–18. The 1919 General Strikes in Barcelona, Winnipeg, Seattle and Belfast symbolised a growing solidarity and militancy among the industrial world's workers. In Britain, a general strike originating with coal miners brought the United Kingdom to a halt for ten days in May 1926. Most significantly, the Bolshevik Revolution installed a socialist government in Russia through violent revolution. Labour struggles in the US were no less significant, although this heritage is often marginalised in American historical discourse (Durrenburger 2006; McGuire 2008: 107). The history of violent labour struggles such as the Ludlow Massacre and the Haymarket Affair contradict Americanist narratives of enterprise, individuality and a classless society that help maintain, reinforce and mask power structures and inequalities (Foote 2003: 7, 134; Hamilakis and Duke 2007; McGuire and Reckner 2003: 84; McGuire and Walker 1999: 159; Shackel 2001: 657; Smith 2006).

Blair Mountain is one such episode of violent labour conflict that raises discomforting issues about the industrialisation of America. The coal industry was central to the growth of American prosperity in that it supplied the 'cheap energy' essential for the foundries and factories that propelled the industrial revolution. But the workers often toiled in poverty and brutal conditions, and they paid the true cost of this prosperity while receiving the least of its benefits. The insurrection was an attempt to gain basic human rights, and it was open class warfare at the heart of American state capitalism. It is where the collective might of unionised power struck hardest, and only the federal government could halt it. The miners seized territory and property, at one point controlling and managing over 500 square miles (Savage 1990: 130). Although this conflict was the second largest rebellion in America, next to the Civil War, this battle has been largely forgotten.

Today, a different conflict is being waged at Blair Mountain, and this time it is for the life of the mountain itself. Coal companies are attempting to conduct an extremely destructive form of coal extraction called mountaintop removal (MTR) at the site. This process would literally 'obliterate' the mountain and all traces of the miners' rebellion from the surrounding landscape (Foote 2004: 7). Archaeology has been an important tool in the efforts to preserve the battlefield, through both research and political action. Surveys undertaken by Dr Harvard Ayers of Appalachian State University highlighted the archaeological significance and integrity of the site, which was crucial in the site's nomination to the National Register of Historic Places (NRHP). Although being listed on the register does not entirely protect the battlefield, it was a significant step in securing the mountain's future. Unfortunately, the site was recently delisted due to a coal-operator-backed opposition, a decision that a group of concerned citizens and academics are currently challenging.

Since the story of Blair Mountain is largely unknown, our purposes in writing this chapter are to introduce the topic and raise awareness of the site's threatened status. To accomplish these goals, we focus on four elements of our research at the site. First, we describe the historical context of the labour insurrection in order to deconstruct narratives that have served to marginalise the battle in national discourse. Second, we discuss the actual battle while incorporating initial archaeological analysis of the battlefield. The third section examines the way in which the heritage of Blair Mountain is currently being reinterpreted and asserted in the contemporary struggle against mountaintop removal. Finally we explore the ways in which an engaged archaeology can be utilised in contemporary political struggles such as labour and environmental justice movements.

Historical background

The Battle of Blair Mountain was the culmination of more than 40 years of class struggle and social transformation within West Virginia. It is best understood within this context, although traditional narratives have often constructed it within negative stereotypes associated with central Appalachia.

The region gained notoriety when the Hatfield-McCoy feud broke out in Mingo County along the West Virginia and Kentucky border during the 1870s and 1890s. This conflict quickly became fodder for national newspapers and pulp fiction of the day, which caricaturised it as a blood feud between two fierce and backward mountain clans. In reality, the 'feud' was a political and economic contest between two competitors in the lumber trade (Bailey 2001: 25). Regardless, the sensational stories sold print and the negative stereotypes were perpetuated.

Accounts of labour struggle in the West Virginia coalfields are usually constructed from similar stereotypical conceptions of Appalachian culture. Labour strikes were seen as being violent because the people were backwards, irrational, lawless and militant (Corbin 1981: xiv; Wheeler 1976: 83). Blair Mountain was largely portrayed in the national press as that of a feud between hotheaded mountaineers, instead of an economic or class conflict (Blizzard 2004: 115; Bailey 2001: 25). Rather than relying on stereotypes, we will explore the historical context in order to deconstruct these narratives.

Why the miners marched

While the coal industry as a whole was notorious for its dangerous work conditions and problematic labour relations in the early twentieth century,

Figure 4.1 State of West Virginia. The distance from Charleston to Blair Mountain was roughly 50 miles. The miners' ultimate goal was to reach Matewan and liberate Mingo County from martial law that was enacted by the state to break an ongoing strike in the county.

these issues were often at their worst in the southern coalfields of West Virginia (Shogan 2004: 32–38). The coal industry operated with near impunity in the southern coalfields, under a system where local and state government officials were either in the pay or influence of coal operators (Blizzard 2004; Savage 1990; Wheeler 1976). One primary mechanism of operator control was through the company-town system (Shogan 2004: 9; Wheeler 1976: 85). These towns were justified by operators as providing basic necessities to their workers in an isolated region. But the company-owned towns allowed coal operators to exert an immense degree of control over the miners' social, political, economic and personal lives (Wheeler 1976: 84).

The company store was a major instrument through which coal operators maintained these feudal conditions. Miners were paid in company money called 'scrip' which was redeemable only at the company store, allowing the operators to have an enormous degree of economic leverage. When wages rose, so would the prices at the company store. The operators' influence also reached beyond the economic sphere – children attended company schools, company doctors provided medical care, and company preachers preached the gospel of the coal-mine owners. Most significantly, the company owned the houses in which the mining families lived. If a miner was injured, killed or joined the union, the company would force the family out, often at gunpoint (Fishback 1992: 348; Wheeler 1976: 81). In addition, mining families lived under constant threat from Baldwin-Felts detectives and other coal company agents who used terror, murder and espionage to thwart pro-union activity. Continual harassment and violence by the detective agents created an atmosphere of fear and charged emotions (Wheeler 1976: 81–82). Complete disregard by the state and federal government of their grievances frustrated the miners even further (Blizzard 2004: 161; Fishback 1995: 439).

The gathering storm

In the midst of these conditions, The United Mine Workers (UMW or UMWA) gained a foothold within the southern coalfields in Mingo County beginning in the spring of 1920. The UMW's organising effort promptly led to a bitter 28-month-long strike of which the Blair Mountain battle was part. Coal operators used every means available to block unionisation, and leading the coal operators' offensive were the Baldwin-Felts detectives (Blizzard 204: 109; Savage 1990: 18). This inflammatory situation set the stage for a gunfight in the town of Matewan on 19 May 1920. When a group of Baldwin-Felts agents arrived in Matewan and evicted striking miner families from their company houses, the pro-union sheriff and mayor questioned the legality of the evictions. After a few tense moments, gunfire erupted between the two groups. The mayor was shot first, and then Sheriff Sid Hatfield killed Albert Felts, the brother of the agency's founder, Thomas Felts. Seven detectives in all were killed including Albert and Lee Felts in what became known as 'The

Matewan Massacre' (Savage 1990: 21). This episode garnered national attention, and with a Hatfield from West Virginia involved the press once again cast the story as that of feuding mountaineers (Blizzard 2004: 116).

In the coalfields, Sid Hatfield gained heroic status among the miners and provided momentum for the organising efforts. Throughout 1920 and into 1921 the union gained strength in Mingo County, as did the resistance of the coal operators. Each side bolstered their arsenals, and miners began waging guerrilla warfare after the mines were reopened with armed guards and replacement workers (Blizzard 2004: 135; Shogan 2004: 114). On 1 August 1921, Sid Hatfield was called to the McDowell County Courthouse to answer an indictment for allegedly dynamiting a coal tipple the previous spring. As Hatfield, his friend Ed Chambers and their wives walked up the courthouse steps, a group of Baldwin-Felts agents gunned down the two unarmed men.

Word of the slayings spread quickly as Sid and Ed's bodies returned to Matewan. The news outraged the miners and they began to pour out of the mountains to take arms (Savage 1990: 73; Blizzard 2004: 239). Talk began to spread of a march to Mingo County to end the martial law that had been declared in the area, free imprisoned miners and organise the county. However, the anti-union Sheriff Don Chafin of Logan County, his private army and Blair Mountain stood directly in the miners' way (Shogan 2004: 166). Logan County was a major coal-operator stronghold, and Don Chafin was the main agent of operator control in the county. Operators paid Chafin fees for his deputies, and the Logan County law enforcement in turn prevented union organisers from entering the county through intimidation, beatings and murder (Wheeler 1976: 79; Blizzard 2004: 226).

Miners began gathering near the state capitol of Charleston around 7 August 1921, and by 24 August had grown into a force of roughly 10,000 (Blizzard 2004: 200). The type of march that the miners planned to engage in had a long tradition in Appalachian labour movements (Blizzard 2004: 208). Miners would congregate and hold rallies and speeches for a number of days. They would then march through the countryside proselytising about the union, much in the same manner as the great tent revivals in frontier America during the 1800s. But with the coal operators' increasing use of violence, these marches became militarised. By 1921, both sides had accumulated a large store of weaponry including machine guns and high-powered rifles (Blizzard 2004: 208).

The miners moved out from Charleston on 24 August toward Mingo County (Savage 1990: 79). Before the marchers travelled very far, the leaders of the regional UMW District 17 overtook the advancing army. They persuaded the miners to stop the march after conveying messages from Washington that the repercussions would be harsh if the insurrection continued (Wheeler 1976: 80). The miners grudgingly turned back and waited for trains that had been arranged to move them out of the area (Savage 1990: 86–89). But the trains arrived late, and in the meantime the shaky truce was

The social and environmental upheaval of Blair Mountain 57

shattered by a deadly night incursion of Sheriff Chafin's men into union territory (Blizzard 2004: 256). The march was back on, and the miners were even more determined to break Don Chafin's defences and reach Mingo (Savage 1990: 107).

The battle

On to Mingo

By 28 August, skirmishes between scouting parties of the enclosing forces began to break out in the area around Blair Mountain (Associated Press 29 Aug. 1921:1). The first day of open war began on the morning of 31 August, with the miners starting their assault on the entrenched defences of Don Chafin's army (Wheeler 1976: 81). The most intense fighting was reported to be concentrated at Blair Gap, Crooked Creek Gap and Beech Creek Gap (Savage 1990: 117). An Associated Press correspondent observed some of the action at the centre of the three-mile defensive line at Crooked Creek (AP 1 Sept. 1921:1). This line was linked to other defensive positions stretched over ten miles along the ridges, with machine guns overlooking the hollows that rose to the gaps (see Figure 4.2) (Ayers *et al.* 2006:13).

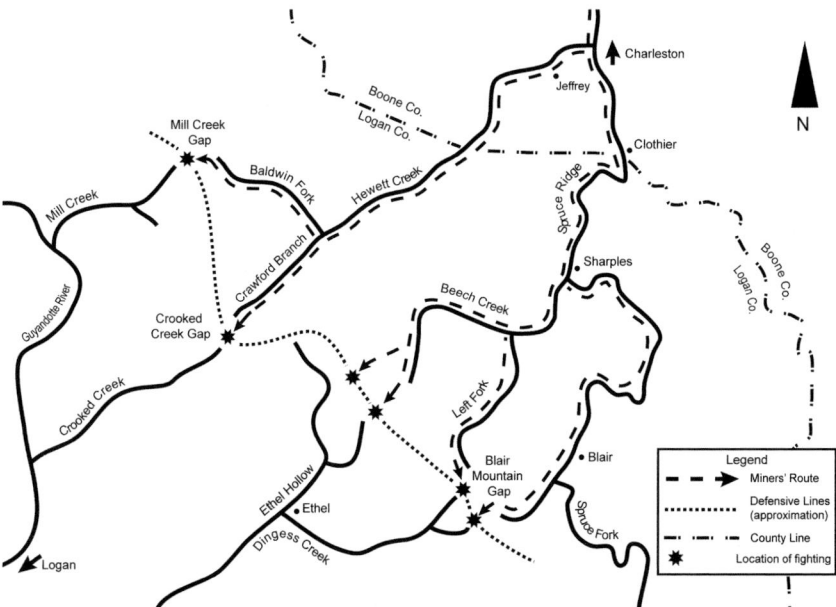

Figure 4.2 Unscaled map of the Blair Mountain Battlefield, redrawn and modified from Meador 1991:60. The defensive lines from Blair Gap to Mill Creek extended over ten miles, with the gaps fortified the heaviest.

Miners attempted numerous times to assault these strongholds, but heavy machine gun fire held them back (AP 1 Sept. 1921:1).

On 1 September, a force of roughly 500 miners assaulted Craddock Fork, a hollow that runs to Crooked Creek Gap. Three hours of constant fire resulted in one of the Logan defender's machine guns jamming. With this lull, the miners rushed and broke through the lines (Shogan 2004: 197). Before sunrise on 2 September it was reported that the miners were less than a mile from Logan (Savage 1990: 137). This crucial part of the battle remains murky due to the fact that until recently the only evidence about the battle was historical documents, which had inherent biases within them. The miners would not speak to reporters or allow them into the territory they controlled. This meant that the Logan defenders controlled information coming out of the region, and they heavily censored it to downplay the miners' success (Savage 1990: 137).

On 2 September, federal troops were mobilised into West Virginia and began moving into position behind both armies (Wheeler 1976: 81). By 5 September, the whole warfront was quiet (Associated Press 6 Sept. 1921: 13). During the roughly five days of fighting, it is estimated that over one million rounds were fired (Ayers *et al.* 2006: 2). A search for bodies and cached weapons began soon after the shooting ceased, but these efforts were fruitless because the miners had carried away all their casualties. Estimates put the number of miners killed during the battle at an exceptionally low number of around 20 people. The true number of casualties remains unknown due to the miners' continued silence regarding their dead and wounded (Blizzard 2004: 269).

In the aftermath of the insurrection, the UMW was severely weakened in West Virginia. Coal operators and the state of West Virginia felt they could deal a deathblow to the union, and they took advantage of the situation (Blizzard 2004: 288). Leaders of the strike were tried on charges of treason against the state, and the lengthy trial drained the UMW's funds (Blizzard 2004: 300). By the end of the 1920s only 512 union miners remained in West Virginia, a drop that was part of an overall nationwide decline in labour (Blizzard 2004: 343). But after the passage of the National Industrial Recovery Act in 1933, the southern coalfields rapidly organised and became a stronghold of union working class culture throughout the twentieth century.

Contemporary conflicts in the coalfields

Today, the Blair Mountain battlefield is the site of new conflicts due to proposed mountaintop removal operations (MTR) at the site. Because of the imminent threat from MTR, Blair Mountain's historical significance as a place of resistance is being reinterpreted in the contemporary struggle against MTR. The red bandanas worn by the union miners in 1921 have re-emerged, this time tied around the necks of anti-MTR activists. With this 'rediscovery' of Blair Mountain, community activists are transforming their understanding of their own struggle and its historical contextualization. In the process, they layer new meaning and remembrance onto the site, and are involved in 'active placemaking' through the creation of a 'rallying point' in the fight against MTR (Badcock and Johnson 2009: 139; Foote 2003: 32). Archaeological work has been a crucial part of the preservation and reinterpretation of the mountain.

Blair Mountain's nomination to the National Register

Until recently there has been a relative lack of archaeological interest in Blair Mountain except for Kenneth King – a local resident, self-trained archaeologist, and grandson of a union miner who fought in the battle. King has spearheaded the preservation efforts since 1991, and has initiated and participated in most of the archaeological research undertaken at Blair Mountain. In 2006 Dr Harvard Ayers conducted an archaeological survey at the site in cooperation with King. The survey has served to clarify the historic record, promote awareness of the site, and advance the movement for preservation. Fifteen sites were located in the survey and the investigators concluded that the overall battlefield has a high degree of integrity for 14 out of the 15 sites surveyed (Ayers *et al.* 2006: 14). Ayers and King, along with Dr Barbara Rasmussen from West Virginia University, led the effort to nominate Blair Mountain to the National Register of Historic Places (NHRP) in 2005. Their efforts resulted in the mountain's placement on the NHRP on 30 March 2009.

This victory was shattered on 7 July 2009 when local newspapers announced that Massey Energy Company was challenging the nomination to the National Register. On 10 January 2010, the site was officially taken off the list. The coal operators' opposition was based on objections of property owners to the listing, for which a simple majority was needed for the site to be removed. The initial vote was 35 owners in favour of listing and 22 objectors. But immediately after the listing the West Virginia State Historic Preservation Officer found that eight letters had been miscounted. After the changes were made, the final count became 30 objectors against the listing to only 27 in favour. This resulted in the process of delisting beginning in July of 2009. Dr Harvard Ayers and an attorney investigated these objector claims and discovered that five were not legal objectors (Ayers pers. comm. 10 Jan. 2010). In fact, Ayers and his attorney found that two of the objectors were dead – one person for over 27 years!

Even with these findings, the WV SHPO refused to re-evaluate the listing on grounds that it fell outside of their duties as pertained to federal code 36 CFR 60, which regulates the NHRP. The National Park Service and Keeper of the Register strongly recommended the WV SHPO to investigate Ayers' claims and resubmit the listing, but could not force the state agency to do so. On 30 December 2009, the site was delisted and returned to eligible status on Section 106 regulation. While this affords the battlefield certain protections, in the southern coalfields of West Virginia where coal owners still wield enormous influence, Blair Mountain's future is now precarious. This next part discusses in more detail the threat to both the mountain and the heritage it embodies, as well as its reinterpretation in the context of a grass-roots social movement.

Mountaintop removal

Mountaintop removal is an extremely destructive form of coal extraction employed primarily in impoverished regions of central Appalachia. Large swathes of forest are cleared, and the entire soil surface is stripped to the bedrock (House and Howard 2009:1). Explosives are then used to blast the rock until a coal seam is exposed, and the mountain overburden is pushed into surrounding valleys, known as valley fill (Palmer 2010:148). The entire coal extraction process, including washing the coal to make it 'clean', creates a large amount of toxic residue that is disposed of throughout the Appalachian landscape in large earthen dams or abandoned mines. As a result, serious health issues linked to the toxicity of the groundwater are prevalent throughout the region (Palmer 2010: 148). The scale of MTR operations is huge; the EPA calculates that over 1.4 million acres of land will be destroyed by the end of 2010 (House and Howard 2009: 2).

The largest conductor of MTR mining, Massey Energy Company, is also the primary foe of the UMWA due to the company's vehement anti-union position (Burns 2007: 27; UMW Journal May/June 2009: 12). Overall the southern coalfields of West Virginia, which were bastions of union solidarity from the 1930s to the 1990s, are turning anti-union with the increase in MTR operations (Burns 2007: 27). The majority of mountaintop removal operations are non-union; many union deep-shaft miners grumble about losing jobs to what they consider the 'heavy equipment operators' on surface mines. MTR, coupled with increasing mechanisation of the coal industry, has caused a precipitous drop in mine employment in West Virginia. In 1970, there were 45,261 miners employed in the state. In 2002, that number was 15,377 and declining (Burns 2007: 13). All the while, coal production during this time increased from 143 million tons to 163 million tons of coal mined annually (13).

The impact of MTR on Appalachian life and culture is one of the most important aspects of the MTR issue. There is a strong tie of Appalachian people to the land – the mountains are the backbone of our culture. Denise Giardinia, a writer of Appalachian life, best expresses what the mountains and their destruction mean to many of us:

> In the hundred odd years since the coal industry came to this part of West Virginia, land has been taken, miners have been worked to death,

streams have been polluted, piles of waste have accumulated, children have grown up in poverty. But throughout all the hardships ... the mountains have essentially remained. They were symbols of permanence, strength, hope. No more. Nothing worse can be taken from mountain people than mountains. The resulting loss is destroying the soul of the people.

(Giardinia 2005)

This statement expresses the sense that many local residents, some of whose families have lived in the area for up to ten generations, feel about the destruction of a landscape that is richly embedded with history and meaning (Anschuetz *et al.* 2001: 173; Ballard 2002: 19–22; Foote 2003: 32; Johnson 2007; Wilson and David 2002). The important interrelationships between memory, identity and place in Appalachian social construction are being unravelled with the destruction of the mountains.

Placemaking and resistance at Blair Mountain

Kenneth Foote notes that four modes of commemoration exist for sites of tragedy or violence – sanctification, designation, rectification and obliteration (2003: 7). While the dynamics of the Blair Mountain site contains elements of all four of these modes, the most significant is that of 'obliteration'. For in a very literal and irreversible sense MTR operations would completely erase the landscape of Blair Mountain and its inscribed meaning. The threat from MTR at Blair Mountain has caused the site and its historical significance to be thrust back into remembrance in a context where community activists are once again contending against the power of the coal industry. As Foote notes, this 'emergence often spurs extensive public debate over the meaning and significance of the original tragedy and, as a consequence, lends insight into the sentiments and social forces that shape landscape' (Foote 2003: 32–33). Although West Virginia has a long and rich tradition of activist movements, this history is mostly absent in West Virginian education and discourse. Appalachians' activist streak may be one of our most valuable hidden treasures, and we intend our work at Blair Mountain to expose this aspect.

An interesting example of how Blair Mountain is drawn upon by the activist community is seen in an article from the Ohio Valley Environmental Coalition's newsletter *Winds of Change*. Terry and Wilma Steele, a union mining family who are prominent activists in the anti-MTR movement, wrote a recent article titled 'United against MTR: red bandanas, dreadlocks, clean-cut, old folks and young' (2009:25). In this piece, the Steeles explain how Blair Mountain intersects environmental and labour issues (Steele and Steel 2009: 25). The Steeles discuss two Labor Day events from the summer of 2009 – one sponsored by the UMW near Racine, WV (to the east of Blair

Mountain), and the second held by Massey in Logan County (just west of Blair Mountain). Terry and Wilma state that directly between stands Blair Mountain, both spatially and metaphorically.

In the article, the authors use the name Don interchangeably to discuss both Don Blankenship (CEO of Massey Energy Company) and Don Chafin in the context of past and present conflicts,

> On the right is Don standing at Logan ... with his bought judges, DEP [Department of Environmental Protection] agents and many misled souls. Don stands with promises of jobs and security. In one hand, is a new mining permit, and in the other is dynamite. In his heart and mind is power to put down the UMWA, the environmentalists, and to mine coal his way: nonunion, unregulated, any way he wants! (25)

They continue:

> Eighty-eight years ago in the months of August and September another Don, backed by big coal and Gov. Morgan, rained down explosives on Blair Mountain and the union miners. There were many red bandanas streaked with blood and sweat but redeemed by honor and courage. ... Now, another Don, backed by big coal and Gov. Manchin, is trying to remove Blair Mountain from the Historic Register. Don has it in his crosshairs and armed with explosives, he plans to blast it away. (25)

Terry and Wilma then go on to directly call upon the history of Blair Mountain, describing the anti-MTR movement in a merging of past and present, 'Standing up to these giants is a ragtag, multicultural, red bandana army made up of old UMWA miners, their families and environmentalists ... Their mission: stop MTR!' In all this, concerned citizens such as the Steeles are drawing on and adding to a rich history of activism in Appalachian culture. They are producing their own conceptions of their history that is prideful and meaningful to them based upon traditional themes important in Appalachian life, and containing information about the past that can be used in today's struggles. In this process they layer new meaning onto Blair Mountain and are involved in 'active placemaking' (Badcock and Johnson 2009).

Archaeology and *political* action

Don't spend time mourning ... organise!

It may seem that the situation in West Virginia is overly bleak, but there is much to be optimistic about. Communities are fighting back, coalitions are being formed and attention is beginning to be drawn to the situation in the coalfields regarding MTR. Blair Mountain is starting to move from obscurity into potentially transformative historical remembrance. We intend our research to advance both causes, because we see them as interlinked. Our overall research is not limited to investigating the archaeology of Blair Mountain; it also involves community engagement and political action. For us it is necessary to stand on the picket lines, attend the meetings and work closely with communities to best address their concerns. These actions are not undertaken just for academic purposes, but rather because issues such as MTR affect ourselves and people we care about.

Emancipatory archaeology

Research for our archaeological work at Blair Mountain is framed by 'an emancipatory theory for the working class' (Duke and Saitta 1998; McGuire and Reckner 2003; McGuire and Walker 2003; Wood 2002). This activist theory builds upon innovations from feminist, Indigenous, African-American and Marxist standpoints to construct archaeological research that engages working or lower class families (Blakey and LaRoche 1997; Conkey and Spector 1984; Conkey 2005; Franklin 2001; Harding 2004; McGuire 1992, 2008; Watkins 2000; Zimmerman 2005). The overarching concerns of a working class archaeology are to analyse, illustrate and discuss the experiences of workers in the past in order to facilitate social change and understanding in the lives of workers today (Duke and Saitta 1998:1). It is at the core collaborative and seeks to engage community members and other stakeholders in the process of knowing and writing their history (Duke and Saitta 1998: 6).

Emancipatory archaeology begins from the understanding that knowledge production, such as the construction of historical narratives, is itself a process of social construction (Conkey and Spector 1984; Fowler 1987; Hamilakis and Duke 2007: 25; Harding 2004: 1; McGuire 2008: 14; Shackel 2001: 656–57). Archaeology is political, and archaeological methods and interpretations have often bolstered inequalities and asymmetrical social relationships (Conkey and Spector 1984; Trigger 2006; McGuire and Walker 1999: 159; Smith 2004: 1; Wobst 2005: 18). But archaeology also has the power to be transformative or emancipatory for marginalised people around the world. In recent years, many scholars have worked to realise this potential by building an engaged archaeology (Blakey 1997; Colwell-Chanthaphonh and Ferguson 2006; Conkey 2005; Faulkner 2000; Green *et al.* 2003; Hamilakis 2005; McGuire 2008; Shackel 2004; Smith 2007: 160). Part of this shift is to look at the practical applications of archaeology to the lives of subordinate peoples and constructing alternative ways of engaging with various communities.

The base of our activist research is long-term commitment to local communities, and our research at Blair Mountain is being developed with short- and long-term goals in mind (Harris 2005; Zimmerman 2005; Wobst

2005). These objectives are drawn from engagement with multiple groups including descendants of combatants, labour organisations, local residents and community organisations. From our initial discussions, we have identified three goals that various stakeholders have expressed interest in – preservation of the battlefield, building a museum or centre at the site (as per McGuire and Reckner 2003) and developing it in a commemorative way such as an interpretive hiking trail (as per Gonzalez 2007).

Tied into these goals are research questions drawn from the various stakeholders. Some questions relate to the military movements of the combatants and the locations where heavy fighting occurred. Other local residents have expressed interest in the common, everyday aspects of mining life – the 'what was it like back then for my grandma or grandpa' question. This is something which historical archaeology is well suited to answer due to its ability to combine documentary evidence with material culture studies. Another area of interest for local community members and activists is the larger political context of the miners' struggles and its relation to contemporary social problems in Appalachia. For this concern, we utilise the materialist dialectic as a metaphor to explain social change and to link the historical processes between past and present struggles. In addition we utilise a Gramscian-style (1971) analysis of hegemony in order to examine the way in which the power of the coal operators was maintained and contested. By understanding the above three areas of interest as a nestled hierarchy, we can move from the particulars of the battle to the everyday conditions of the mining families, and then to the larger process and institutions underlying the labour conflict. Tracing these institutions and structures historically through time in a dialectic framework will allow us to situate the political struggles in the coalfields today.

The process of building an emancipatory archaeological programme at Blair Mountain is still in its initial stages. The primary focus of this beginning phase is identifying and engaging possible stakeholders. Because we are native West Virginians and activists within the anti-MTR movement, certain social networks are open to us that we can draw upon in our organising efforts. This has enabled us to meet and collaborate with key community members in the immediate locale of Blair Mountain, as well as local historians, descendants of the combatants, modern day union members and environmental groups.

We are currently developing networks between various stakeholders to establish a base of support for preservation and commemoration efforts. This summer (2010), we will begin giving informal tours of the site to UMW miners and local community members. Additional commemorative and educational events are being planned such as a march and rally for the 90th anniversary of Blair Mountain in 2011. This event will involve a variety of academic, labour, community, environmental and historical preservation groups. Blair Mountain is particular in this aspect in that it is a major labour heritage site that has become significant for a grassroots environmental movement that is largely working class. This intersection of concerns that the mountain embodies has enormous potential to further dialogue between labour and environmental groups.

Currently, avenues to cultivate heritage tourism at the site are being discussed, such as developing ecologically low-impact hiking trails with educational markers that describe the history of the battle (as per Gonzalez 2007). Additionally, Kenneth King has long been a proponent of a museum or tourism centre near the mountain that discusses the history and labour struggles of the region. This is one of the long-term goals of our involvement, and we are attempting to lay the groundwork for a major investment such as a museum. We are also currently in the process of gathering and archiving key documents and artefacts regarding the miners' insurrection in 1921, with plans to curate them within the community. In addition, the data from the archaeological surveys as well as historical documents are being digitised and entered into a central database, with the intention of giving this to the WV State Historic Preservation Office to be stored for future scholars. These projects will serve to educate the public about Blair Mountain and its role in local history, and work to preserve its significance for future generations.

Future archaeological work

Archaeological work at Blair Mountain will continue with collaborative and collectivist methods. We are building upon the work of Ayers and King in exploring and documenting more sections of the battlefield. The ongoing archaeological research of the site is tied directly to the preservation of Blair Mountain, the betterment of the surrounding community and facilitating discussion of labour history. Future archaeological investigations promise to be exciting and rich with large areas of the battlefield yet to be examined. In addition, we are currently attempting to locate contextual tent colonies that housed striking miners in order to broaden the social dimension of our research. This will allow us to look at aspects of mining community life such as racial, ethnic and gender dynamics (Ludlow Collective 2001; Wood 2002).

Currently, we are surveying and locating the approaches and positions of the miners, which has had relatively little prior investigation. Archaeological investigations have just begun to shed light on the heavy fighting along Crooked Creek. From the survey conducted in 2006, the large quantity of bullets, short-range casings and evidence of close-quarter fighting behind the defensive line suggests this location was the site of a breakthrough (Ayers *et al.* 2006: 7). In addition, this location may have been only one of multiple instances of breakthroughs of the defensive lines due to similar evidence at other hotspots (Ayers *et al.* 2006:15–16). Current archaeological research is focusing on these locations in order to analyse the timeline and movements of the attackers. Our analysis utilises Geographic Information Systems software to model the topography and analyse viewsheds, line of sight, weaponry ranges and artefact patterning across the battlefield to more accurately understand troop movement.

Conclusion

Blair Mountain is a standing reminder of the long struggle for labour rights in West Virginia. Central Appalachia has for generations been a central battleground between owners and workers, even though the region has largely been decentred in both labour and American history. We intend this chapter to illustrate the fact that West Virginians have struggled for generations for the basic human rights to live and work in decent conditions. Especially important is the understanding that the conflicts of the early twentieth century are not detached from present struggles. While the issues and conditions may have changed, they are still instances in a steady stream of exploitation and resistance that continues today.

The issues discussed in this chapter are found not only in Appalachia. The deep structural problems we face are ones that many people globally are contending with – from indigenous peoples to inner city youth to factory workers in China. Activist research can and should be part of their struggle, serving to illuminate, connect and improve the lives of people living in systems of exploitation and domination. We hope this chapter demonstrates some ways in which collaborative efforts between academics, environmentalists, labour unions, social justice advocates and other community organisations can be used in the betterment of workers' lives today.

References

Anschuetz, K. F., Wilshusen, R.H. and Scheick, C. (2001) 'An archaeology of landscapes: perspectives and directions', *Journal of Archaeological Research*, 9(2): 157–211.

Associated Press (29 August 1921) 'Mingo Marchers Fight With Police; Five Miners Fall', *New York Times*: 1.

——(6 September 1921) 'Policing by the Army', *New York Times*: 13.

Ayers, H., Rothrock, Z. and King, K. (2006) *Archaeological Investigations of the Battle of Blair Mountain: May 13 to November 19, 2006*, on file (unpublished), West Virginia State Historic Preservation Office.

Badcock, A. and Johnston, R. (2009) 'Placemaking through protest: an archaeology of the Lees Cross and Endcliffe protest camp, Derbyshire, England', *Archaeologies*, 5(2): 306–22.

Bailey, R. (2001) *Matewan before the Massacre*, dissertation, Morgantown, WV: West Virginia University.

Ballard, C. (2002) 'The signature of terror, violence, memory, and landscape at Freeport', in B. David and M. Wilson (eds) *Inscribed Landscapes: Marking and Making Place*, Honolulu: University of Hawaii Press.

Blakey, M. and LaRoche, C. (1997) 'Seizing intellectual power: the dialogue at the New York African-American Burial Ground', *Historical Archaeology,* 31: 84–106.

Blizzard, W. C. (2004) *When Miners March*, Gay, WV: Appalachian Community Services.

Burns, S. S. (2007) *Bringing Down the Mountains*, Morgantown: West Virginia University Press.

Colwell-Chanthaphonh, C. and Ferguson, T. J. (2006) 'Memory pieces and footprints: multivocality and the meanings of ancient times and ancestral places among the Zuni and Hopi', *Current Anthropology,* 108: 148–62.

Corbin, D. A. (1981) *Life, Work, and Rebellion in the Coal Fields*, Chicago: University of Illinois Press.

Conkey, M. (2005) 'Dwelling at the margins, action at the intersection? Feminist and Indigenous Archaeologies', *Archaeologies* 1: 9–59.

Conkey, M. and Spector, J. (1984) 'Archaeology and the study of gender', *Advances in Archaeological Method and Theory,* 7: 1–29.

Duke, P., and Saitta, D. J. (1998) 'An emancipatory archaeology for the working class', *Assemblage* 4. Online journal. Available HTTP: <http://ads.ahds.ac.uk/catalogue/adsdata/assemblage/html/4/4duk_sai.html> (accessed 11 July 2009).

Durrenburger, P. (2006) 'On the invisibility of class in America', *Anthropology News* 47: 9–10.

Faulkner, N. (2000) 'Archaeology from below', *Public Archaeology,* 1(1): 21–33.

Fishback, P. V. (1995) 'An alternative view of violence in labor disputes in the early 1900s: the bituminous coal industry, 1890–1930', *Labor History*, 36(3): 426–56.

Foote, K. E. (2003) *Shadowed Ground: America's Landscapes of Violence and Tragedy*, 2nd edn, Austin: University of Texas Press.

Fowler, F. (1987) 'Uses of the past: archaeology in service of the state', *American Antiquity* 52 (2): 229–48.

Franklin M. (2001) 'A black feminist inspired archaeology?', *Journal of Social Archaeology,* 1: 108–25.

Giardina, D. (June 2005) 'The Battle of Blair Mountain. … revisited', *Appalachian Voices*. Online Journal. Available HTTP: <http://www.appvoices.org/index.php?/site/voice_stories/the_battle_of_blair_mountainrevisited/issues/29> (accessed 13 September 2009).

Gonzalez, S. A. (2007) 'Making pathways through traditions: an update on the Kashaya Pomo Interpretive Trail Project', *Society for California Archaeology Newsletter,* 41(1): 42–43.

Gramsci, A. (1971) *Selection from the Prison Notebooks of Antonio Gramsci*, Q. Hoare and G.N. Smith (eds), New York, NY: International Publishers.

Hamilakis, Y. (2005) 'Whose world and whose archaeology? The colonial present and the return of the political', *Archaeologies: Journal of the World Archaeological Congress* 1(2): 94–101.

Hamilakis, Y. and Duke, P. (2007) *Archaeology and Capitalism*, Walnut Creek, CA: Left Coast Press.

Harding, S. (2004) 'Introduction: standpoint theory as a site of political, philosophical, and scientific debate', in S. Harding (ed.) *The Feminist Standpoint Theory Reader*, New York, NY: Routledge.

Harris, H. (2005) 'Indigenous worldviews and ways of knowing as theoretical and methodological foundations for archaeological research', in C. Smith and H. M. Wobst (eds) *Indigenous Archaeologies: Decolonizing Theory and Practice*, New York, NY: Routledge.

House, S. and Howard, J. (2009) *Something's Rising: Appalachians fighting mountaintop removal*, Lexington, KY: The University Press of Kentucky.

Johnson, M. (2007) *Ideas of Landscape*, Malden, MA: Blackwell Publishing.

Little, B., and Shackel, P. (eds.) (2007) *Archaeology as a Tool of Civic Engagement*, Lanham, MD: AltaMira Press.

Ludlow Collective, The (2001) 'Archaeology of the Colorado Coal Field War 1913-1914', in V. Buchli and G. Lucas (eds.) *Archaeologies of the Contemporary Past*, New York, NY: Routledge: 94–107.

McGuire, R. H. (1992) *A Marxist Archaeology*, Orlando, Fla.: Academic Press.

——(2008) *Archaeology As Political Action*, Berkeley: University of California Press.

McGuire, R. H. and Reckner, P. (2003) 'Building a working-class archaeology: the Colorado Coal Field War Project', *Industrial Archaeology Review*, 25: 83–95.

McGuire, R. H. and Walker, M. (1999) 'Class confrontations in archaeology', *Historical Archaeology*, 33: 159–83.

Meador, M. (1991) 'The Redneck War of 1921: the Miner's March and the Battle of Blair Mountain', in K. Sullivan (ed.) (1991) *The Goldenseal Book of the West Virginia Mine Wars*, Charleston, WV: Quarrier Press.

Palmer, M. A., Bernhardt, E. S., Schlesinger, W. H. (2010) 'Mountaintop mining consequences', *Science* 327: 148–49.

Savage, L. (1990) *Thunder in the Mountains: The West Virginia Mine War 1920–21*, Pittsburgh, PA: University of Pittsburgh Press.

Shackel, P. A. (2001) *Myth, Memory, and the Making of the American Landscape*, Gainesville: University Press of Florida.

Shogan, R. (2004) *The Battle of Blair Mountain: The Story of America's Largest Labor Uprising*, Boulder, Colorado: Basic Books.

Smith, L. (2004) *Archaeological Theory and the Politics of Cultural Heritage*, London: Routledge.

——(2006) *Uses of Heritage*, London: Routledge.

——(2007) 'Empty gestures? Heritage and the politics of recognition', in H. Silverman and D. F. Ruggles (eds) *Cultural Heritage and Human Rights*, New York: Springer.

Steele, T. and Steele, W. (2009) 'United against MTR: red bandanas, dreadlocks, clean-cut, old folks and young', *Winds of Change*, newsletter of the Ohio Valley Environmental Coalition, October 2009, Huntington, WV.

Trigger, B. (2006) *A History of Archaeological Thought*, 2nd edn, Cambridge: Cambridge University Press.

United Mine Workers (May/June 2009) 'Don's World: Massey Energy's CEO defines a rogue coal company', *United Mine Workers Journal*, 120(3): 10–13.

Watkins, J. (2000) *Indigenous Archaeology: American Indian Values and Scientific Practice*, Walnut Creek, CA: Alta Mira Press.

Wheeler, H. N. (1976) 'Mountaineer Mine Wars: an analysis of the West Virginia Mine Wars of 1912–13 and 1920–21', *The Business History Review*, 50(1): 69–91.

Wilson, M. and David, B. (2002) 'Introduction', in B. David and M. Wilson (eds) *Inscribed Landscapes: Marking and Making Place*, Honolulu: University of Hawaii Press: 1–9.

Wobst, H. M., (2005) 'Power to the (indigenous) past and present! Or: The theory and method behind archaeological theory and method', in C. Smith and H. M. Wobst (eds) *Indigenous Archaeologies: Decolonizing Theory and Practice*, New York, NY: Routledge: 17–32.

Wood, M. C. (2002) 'Women's work and class conflict in a working-class coal mining community', in M. O'Donovan (ed.) *The Dynamics of Power*, Occasional Paper 30, Center for Archaeological Investigations, Carbondale: Southern Illinois University.

Zimmerman, L. J. (2005) 'First, be humble: working with indigenous peoples and other descendant communities', in C. Smith and H. M. Wobst (eds), *Indigenous Archaeologies: Decolonizing Theory and Practice*, London: Routledge.

Chapter 5

This is our island
Multiple class heritage or ethnic solidarities?

Richard Courtney

This chapter argues that the sociological importance of heritage is not to interpret the past, but to understand the way the past is used as a means to appropriate the present in order to call for social change and the implications of this practice on issues of multiplicity. The chapter will outline the sociological meaningfulness of heritage to the future of English Identity and separates this analysis from the conventional use of heritage as an object of historical study. The research in the borough of Thurrock, Essex, during the summer of 2006 was a community study that looked at the migration of Black British people from London, and the responses of the local majority white community. Thurrock was a traditionally 'white' urban area with a history in light manufacturing, quarrying and logistics. The borough had 19 wards at the time of study, and this chapter uses research data from two of the most socially and economically deprived wards, Ockendon and Tilbury. The research reveals the way in which social class, as a category of economic existence, was used as a cultural resource for respondents to legitimise their social memory. The legitimation that respondents desired was a strategy to attain heritage status in order to compete with claims for inclusion within the discourses of land and people made by newcomers to the locality. The chapter shows that heritage is central to an understanding of multi-culturalism, as it signals a domain of conflict over community and identity central to the definition of the nation-state. The research highlights that heritage is an aspiration for status by competing social and cultural groups; as such there is a conceptual separation of heritage from social memory. This highlights the processes of ethnic identification emergent amongst disenfranchised white working class groups and the political and sociological difficulties involved with reconciling this voice with wider political values of multi-culturalism.

Sociological and political considerations of heritage

The chapter identifies the central irony to emerge from a consideration of heritage within the context of British multiculturalism and English

Identity. The starting point of this irony emerges from the power of the authorized heritage discourse of the UK. The Authorized Heritage Discourse is identified by Smith (2006) as the official discourse on heritage that stands on high and bequeaths meaning and substance unto national identity. Heritage, in this sense, is a means by which authorised history anchors community identity to a meaning of place. The critical study of heritage has sought to challenge the solidity with which heritage discourse fuses the meaning of place with common identity to show the multiplicity of meaning and the power relations that obscure this from public view. It is in a context of heritage as a claim on history that heritage studies have attempted to explore unofficial and subaltern heritage as strategies of empowerment and autonomy from cultural domination. This direction of scholarly interest is one analogous to debates within the study of migration and ethnicity (Anthias 1998; Herbert 2008; Werbner 2005) and is paramount to the way in which English Identity can be theorised.

Heritage is widely recognised as being of central importance to the definition of ethnicity (Modood et al. 1997). This recognition has moved definitions of ethnicity away from explicitly racial criteria to substantiate the importance of cultural identity amongst recent migrant groups in Western societies. Whilst this shift from racial essence to historical movement and cultural heritage as an indicator of 'difference' should be welcomed, it presents a further problem when the concept of heritage is applied across all communities. The analysis of social class by reference to community heritage is a case in point as the analysis used in recent works is in itself an analysis of white ethnicity and not exclusively that of economic relations. In a world free from tyrannical and colonial history this would not present a problem; however, the heritage of class in Britain is entwined with colonial history and particularly discourses of whiteness (Bonnett 1996). The heritage of class and community is central to the pre-existing authorised discourse on heritage. Herein lies the central empirical problem; if heritage is sociologically meaningful to identity and community empowerment, how can we successfully negotiate a heritage of class when it is so emblazoned with the iconography of the heritage(s) that we are attempting to re-articulate for a multicultural future?

In order to overcome this conundrum a separation between concepts of heritage and social memory is required. Smith identifies a relationship between memory, identity and heritage that claims memory identifies heritage as 'a culturally directed personal and social act of making sense and understanding' (Smith 2006: 66). It is then suggested that via heritage one is subjectively bound to the national. This identifies the ultimately subjective aspects of heritage, in that its authority is drawn from its relativity to elites. However, there remains a conflation between memory and heritage as the two are represented as sharing the same function within social and political life. If social memory is defined, as Misztal argues, as intersubjective and shared between common people then at a theoretical level heritage and social memory are taut concepts (Misztal 2003). The problem rests with the fact that the difference between heritage and memory is that the former is not a separate aspect of national consciousness, but *is* national consciousness *sui generis*. The political and sociological relationship between heritage and memory is one of legitimation. The empirical questions ask *what* memory is legitimated as heritage and what are the political processes that allow the memories of some groups to be validated and not those of others. Consequently, social memory can be conceptualised along the same lines as Modood's conception of ethnicity as 'a community whose heritage [memory] offers important characteristics in common between its members and which makes them distinct from other communities' (Modood et al. 1997: 13). Heritage represents competing claims to institutionalise memory between specific social and cultural groups. As such, heritage provides legitimacy to reproduce social memory for future generations. The ultimate difference in the function of memory and heritage is that memory is about an historical consciousness of social groups and events, and heritage is about the right to take the meaning of those memories into future civic space; thus heritage is important for social and political change.

Social class is paramount in debates about social and political change in the UK as the concept of class fulfils a sociological and political function. Its sociological function determines levels of economic and social inequality and its political function highlights the undesirability and unjust nature of inequity. This is central to the understanding of heritage and social memory, because the ideological and emotional content of heritage is dependent upon the reflection of structural inequality in civil society. So for example, in a nation with a firm and stable stratified structure, heritage will consist of the memories most closely associated with the ruling classes. Conversely, a truly democratic society would represent heritage as a multitude of inter-related memories that provide a voice for the plethora of identities reflected in its civic sphere. In addition, there may be a form of universal heritage, which represents the nation's overarching respect for diversity. Each scenario is ultimately contingent upon the nature of social and political relations upon which it is founded. These relations are not just limited to ethnological ones, but also include economic relations as many of the boundaries to civic participation in the UK are founded upon issues of deprivation and disadvantage within the labour market (Sayer 2005).

If we define social class as an economic reality then social memories attached to class community are valid considerations when the heterogeneity of heritage is being understood. Social memory has become important within the field of class analysis simply because of its well-documented relationship to identity, and also the way in which it figures in class formation. The works of Skeggs (1997, 2004, 2005) and Savage (2000) argue that class should incorporate the subjective processes of class formation as local responses to post-industrialisation that have occurred over the past 25 years. Skeggs argues that sociology should provide a voice for social groups that are stigmatised and regulated by 'middle class' norms in the media, education and by entrepreneurial public policy (Skeggs 2005). Her argument is similar to those used by scholars interested in subaltern populations. This is because she argues that the post-industrial working classes in Britain lack a civic voice. She illustrates this by reference to 'reality television' that routinely commits symbolic violence upon the lifestyle and values of Britain's urban and impoverished citizens. Similarly, Dench *et al.* (2006) in their re-study of class and ethnicity in East London highlight the way multi-cultural public policy has rendered the working class voice as 'racist' and intolerable within a liberal society. The interest in class as community identity represents it in terms akin to an ethnicity, not as an economic reality. Consequently, their analysis 'forgets' that the concept of class was meant as a universal concept to be applied indiscriminately across communities otherwise labelled in cultural terms (Crompton 2001).

This is important for the discussion of heritage because what is being argued for is not the representation of the importance of class to British society, but the class of particular groups, namely the white working classes. The analytical importance of the political consideration of heritage presents a means to ask whether this is a just strategy, and whether sociology should see the position of white working class people as a subaltern population separate from other groups on the basis of whiteness and ethnicity. It is in this regard that class has become meaningful to white English Identity as an identity that fixes discourses of land and people in the public imagination. If, as it is argued, we consider heritage as a critical study of national and authoritative orthodoxy then the application of heritage to those identified as 'classed' citizens becomes ironic because these very people were effectively bound to the authorised discourse of heritage. To ascribe subaltern status to class identity and memory in this way is a 'red herring'. Many social scientists with an interest in class assume from the outset that those designated working class, are, due to a conceptual emphasis on ideology, subaltern to national identity (Meiksins Wood 1998). This is the case from within classic British community studies that discuss the importance of local economic relations and community as sociological domains 'hidden' from public view (Hill 1976). At a theoretical level, class has been viewed as divergent from the experience of the nation. However, the analysis of class in most studies is conducted within the shell of the British Nation (Giddens 1990, Urry 2000). Therefore it tells us more about the cultural existence of the majority population than the logic of economic relations and categories. An example is Bev Skeggs' work on dis-respectability amongst working class women (Skeggs 1997). Skeggs acknowledges that her analysis centres upon an experience of whiteness that is ultimately ethnically partial (Skeggs 2004). However, she neglects to theorise the implications of this partiality into notions of multiculturalism, in terms of relationships with issues of cultural marginality expressed by scholars researching the identity of groups classified primarily as ethnic (Anthias 2007; Werbner 2006). The relationship between white people and the nation is less distanced than it is for cultural minorities and it is argued to be primarily economic and not cultural (Bonnett 2000).

Bonnett (1998) has argued that working class people were included in the white 'race' during the construction of the National Health Service due to the state's recognition of their potential for social mobility; previously the ascripted nature of class along traditional hierarchies was considered to be something biological (Beck 1992). From the end of WWII the acceptance of class as a facet of national life changed from being one of ascription to one of mutability, regardless of the political differences over how to engender such mutability of status and dessert (Bauman 2001; Beck 2002). Continuous with this political development of the institutionalised recognition of class, was the aforementioned disaggregation of cultural minorities from the mainstream structures of citizenship (Solomos 2003). This ultimately led to the construction of a divide between the national population, again based upon ascription, but this time of 'heritage'. The expansion of state services in health, education and local population management fostered a sense of ownership in the local community (Dench et al. 2006). This is what is referred to as the 'golden days' of British community. Although many of these golden days did in fact include non-white citizens, they held white people as the focus of such glorified dessert (Back 1996). This was related to the fact that the solidarity fostered by the war effort, in the South East particularly, was incorporated into public space by both the Monarchy and the Parliamentary Labour Party. The Black and Minority Ethnic populations of the UK were perceived to have a peripheral attachment to white ethnocentricity due to the labour of war effort (Dench et al. 2006). The voice of the working class was thereafter part of national identity and a vocal participator in civil society. Ultimately, it was after 1979 that this voice waned and the identity of working class people was denigrated to a status of dis-respectability and became what was for a time known as the underclass, and to what is now colloquially referred to as 'chav culture' (Charlesworth 2000; Sayer 2005; Skeggs 2005). This denigration has precipitated the calls by sociologists to raise the civic voice of the working classes to emphasise not necessarily their immediate economic conditions, but to signal their formation as a post-industrial working class by reference to their social memory of denigration. This is ultimately about whiteness rather than class, because it doesn't account for the class mobilities and formation of other non-white groups and their occurrence within a national political environment. It is also geographically distinct from white communities within the English regions and neglects to represent the multiple experiences of class amongst the post-devolution administrative regions of the UK.

It is in the contexts of denigration and marginalisation that the 'English question' is raised because community renewal policies target local communities at the neighbourhood level within the English regions. So public policy bolsters a local identity that defaults to a sense of ordinary or folk sensibilities, regardless of whether this is in rural, urban, or suburban geographic contexts. The underlying communitarianism of New Labour public policy has been to inadvertently re-light English Identity, without ever muttering the word! This strategy has gone some way to allowing memory and identity to be imagined as quasi-autonomous at the local level. Public policy has provided the means to develop community identity, but has left the substance of such memory and identity for the market to decide. The market is of course England's population of white people; however, this market population is almost never explicitly referenced as a racialised group, but a socially excluded group. The discourses associated with social exclusion have been the means by which New Labour public policy has circumvented questions of 'race', whilst attempting to answer calls from disenfranchised white people about their social, cultural and economic futures. Localism, as a response to community renewal is a manifestation of a rising English Identity because it is a claim on heritage that is regionally located within England by people who view themselves as 'indigenous' and excluded from the civic multiculturalism of Britishness.

A well-referenced contradiction within New Labour multicultural and community renewal policy is the inconsistencies with which they have attempted to devise a 'liberal communitarianism' (Back et al. 2002; Shukra *et al.* 2004). The central idea is to foster a British civil society existent from a 'community of communities' (Parekh 2000). This creates a civic space occupied by multiple claims to particular forms of heritage, which within a truly abstract liberal environment is healthy and functional for social justice and democracy (Keane 1998). The idea of an emergent English Identity in such a context then appears to be anathema to the wider goals of multiculturalism; especially as such a national identity has conventionally been an expression of white exclusivity. The historian Rob Colls has characterised English Identity as a soft, emotionally and, geographically speaking, internal identity masked by the rational international appeal of Britishness. Colls claims that, in a sense, English Identity was colonised by British Identity as the former had more appeal on the colonial and imperial stage. It was the power accorded to Britishness via imperialism that made its appeal relevant to 'English' people: it was the identity that gave them power and a sense of continued purpose of global import (Colls 2002). In a social and economic domain of political disenfranchisement English Identity is a meaningful strategy for white people to reassert a former dominance via the legitimation of their social memory as a subaltern heritage to Britishness.

It has been argued thus far that heritage is an important sociological concept because it is a domain of cultural conflict with reference to its position as institutionalised social memory. The separation of memory and heritage shows the function of heritage to be future orientated as it defines the civic exclusion/inclusion for future generations. The sociological status of heritage is re-enforced by its futurity because it holds the power to consolidate identities and to precipitate future social and political change. The study of class is important because conceptually it presents sociology with a domain of exclusion that occupies a subaltern status to the orthodoxies of national heritage. This is a problem as the conceptualisation of class used in sociology is culturally distinct; in that whiteness is conflated with an economic reality subsumed by the nation-state. In regional contexts localism has emerged as a form of English Identity that makes claims for the heritage of white people. This presents a problem within considerations of multiculturalism because it attempts to articulate English Identity in relation to culturally defined marginal groups. As highlighted, the white working class communities despite denigration still retain an exclusive proximity to the state due to racial credentials. The following section illustrates this as an uneven strategy to legitimate the social memory of working class community as heritage, as the concept of class is considered to hold more just credence for white people than for cultural minorities.

The reassertion of class memory as heritage

The research was an ethnographic study that used qualitative interviews with 72 respondents from a variety of local businesses and local groups. The major empirical findings were that the more professionally successful people from London's Black-British population had begun an internal migratory journey similar to the 'white flight' which had led suburbanisation in South East Essex in the 1960s and 1970s. This meant that discursive control over the local area and its heritage was a major aspect of conflict between the new and established communities. It was in the context of this conflict over the meanings of land and identity that questions of English Identity emerged as a reassertion of claims to rights and centrality to discourses of heritage.

The study found there to be three major narratives on social memory that served to establish class as meaningful to heritage. These were the rural, industrial and civic narratives; the latter two narratives reflected the dominant economic histories of different wards within Thurrock. It was the social superstructure of these economic histories that respondents held lament for and wanted reasserted to create a better future. Taken together, the narratives provided evidence to suggest that the major cultural facet of English Identity was drawn from the symbolism of white labour from 1918 to the end of the 1960s.

The rural narrative

The rural narrative was found in wards that had some prior relationship to local agriculture. South Ockendon began the twentieth century as a small local farming community; however, after WWII many pre-fabricated houses were built to house workers from East London whose homes were destroyed as a result of war. Respondents' social memory was communal, convivial and highly personal. They referenced an intensely social area that was integrated by common institutions, such as local pubs, clubs, etc. However, their lament was not for a return to this era of budding suburbanisation, but for the imagery of England and ruralism that existed before. The rural narrative consisted of imagery of fields, farmers, toil and austerity, but above all else a desire to be self-sufficient – self-sufficiency was regarded as a virtuous outcome of the agricultural life. The following quote illustrates the narrative appeal of the rural.

> It used to be Orchards all around Ockendon, but now we've got Lakeside (a regional retail complex). Everything that's good about this place has gone, it's died of death this place has, it's killed our community ... You used to be able to get anything here, you never needed to go to Grays or Upminster, it was all here. We've got nothing now. This place has died of death. It was meant for farming, not flats and apartment for people that Tony Blair has chucked out of London. The new people that are coming in now, and I don't mean this in any bad way, but they are like fish out of water. This is a rural community, if you go outside Ockendon for a mile it's all fields, they don't know how to join into that ...
>
> (Brian, a local volunteer with the youth service)

Despite the fact that Ockendon had been surrounded by industrial manufacturing, and more ominously the M25 London Orbital for the past 40 years, was sequestered by Brian and most of the respondents from Ockendon. This sequestration of the reality that Ockendon was no longer a self-sufficient agricultural island signalled the power that a rural narrative had over claims to identity and local space. What the respondents desired most was to be able to define Ockendon with reference to its folk and rural past and to imagine that they themselves were the inheritors of such a legacy. Their resentment for newcomers was never explicitly racialised; few in Ockendon used racial stereotypes and labels for the mostly Black-British newcomers of African descent. Instead their cultural struggle existed over claims of ownership to the land based upon their assumption that they were the indigenous population and therefore had a natural right to own and define it. The rural narrative was their local social memory and it was used in triangulation with their perception of the present. Despite being a narrative that lamented a loss of autonomy and self-sufficiency, it also signified a former economic purpose central to the functioning of the nation, that being agriculture.

All of the respondents were critical of the current urban malaise in Ockendon. They characterised it as a place wrought by crime, vandalism and a loss of social and economic purpose. They were explicit in blaming the new community and asylum seekers for this plight. The rural narrative, however, structured their rationality to the problems of the present. The symbolic attraction of the rural narrative was that it reminded them of a time, not of when there were no 'foreigners', but a time when locals had the power to define and enjoy local spaces over and above 'others'. Their problems in the present were not directed at the new community first hand, they were directed at national government and British multiculturalism. They complained that as a local indigenous population they were ignored and instead the major voice which dictated the meaning of local land and people was an assumed sense of political correctness associated with Britishness. This perception signalled that the respondents felt that their social memory had been de-centred and removed from the heritage of the local area. It was here that they defined the local as English.

The industrial narrative

The industrial narrative drew many similarities to the previous narrative in that it expressed feelings of autonomy, self-sufficiency and economic purpose. The industrial narrative was used in Tilbury, a town that had a long-standing relationship to shipping and logistical distribution due to the docks. The difference however, was that the industrial narrative emerged from an immediate social memory of the decline of the docks. It used far less conventional symbols of English nostalgia than were seen in with the rural narrative, but still retained the same sociological function: to lament loss and to argue for change. Tilbury had developed from a locally envied sense of pride in its role in the industrial development of the nation. It was the loss of this central role in industrial development and the autonomy it allowed that respondents lamented when talking of the present. The following summed up this sentiment:

> Tilbury has had its own industrial revolution and that is the one thing that everyone has missed out. The industrial revolution was caused by the change in infrastructure and the modernisation of labour, containerisation, electrification of the railways, and Dartford Tunnel. That's what changed Tilbury people; because Tilbury was a main terminus for everything ... The MP wanted Tilbury to become the capital town of Thurrock. It was the biggest town in the world!
>
> (Tommy, a former local police officer)

An illuminating conclusion from the research in Tilbury was that local figureheads, councillors and local conservation groups were more aware of the requirement to be inclusive in their visions of local heritage. Many respondents from local conservation groups stressed the desirability of including the new community in their regeneration plans. This was interesting given that their regeneration plans were social, economic and cultural. They wanted to develop local areas of historical significance, not for their own purposes of self-identity, but for local prosperity for the entire Tilbury community. They were adamant that this would help foster a sense of social and cultural integration and would sideline the rise of the British National Party, who, given the extreme impoverishment of Tilbury, were politically highly significant. The BNP had come close second to Labour in both electoral wards since 2001. The response by local figureheads was not to decry the BNP as racist, but to highlight the sense of pride that Tilbury should have regarding the memory of its former social and economic glory. As opposed to being used as a 'call to arms' to generate cultural division, local groups signalled this pride in order to foster a local sharing of heritage, which regarded migration as integral to not just the area's development, but fundamental to its heritage due to the Commonwealth civic zeal generated by Tilbury Docks. Although politically distinct from Ockendon, respondents in Tilbury still defined their local heritage against a totalising national heritage represented by Britishness.

The civic narrative

The previous narratives referenced an economic reality of class and were materialist in the sense that they articulated the 'golden days' of local community as an existent superstructure founded upon economic reality. What was missing, and of course what is missing from many narratives of heritage and social memory, was class conflict. Instead class struggle was represented as a battle against non-local influence, namely Britishness. The civic narrative expressed in all cases the sense of communal identity fostered upon self-sufficient and purposeful economic activity at the local level. The following illustrates this social and economic relationship:

> This was a working class town, bustling with people everywhere. The toot was where everyone always went because that was the union you see. They used to have a lot of clubs, like for football or boxing. Clubs weren't just for going in and having a drink, they had other things too ... there was always sports stuff attached to the social clubs. We had everything we needed right here, in Tilbury.
> (Betty, elderly woman from Tilbury)

In Ockendon, many respondents spoke fondly of the jazz halls and dance clubs that were key sites of local social interaction. Boxing clubs and dance clubs were particularly cited as key institutions that governed the gendered development of local youngsters. The civic narrative expressed a sense of familiarity with the locality and its people. What was insightful in conversations about people's memories of community was that they referenced institutions rather than their neighbours or other identifiable persons. The power of civic institutions built on a solid economic geography was that they created definitive possibilities to know other locals. This was significant in conversation regarding local railway stations of which references to their former bustling glory were plentiful. These references registered the importance and centrality of the station as a means of logistical and leisurely transportation to and from the locality: they were sites that bounded local social order. This was due to the fact that all respondents interpreted the intentions and behaviours of others, regardless of social profile, by reference to their need to travel between the local and elsewhere. Respondents contrasted this stable past to their present orientation to the local railway stations. It was here that explicit racial demarcations were made, because the elderly respondents saw people they were unfamiliar with at the station. These were simply commuters from the new community who worked in London, but for the locals their presence perforated established boundaries between the local and non-local, which as a result were rendered as a 'known unknown'. Their presence caused a fear of crime in the elderly white respondents, because they saw the function of the railway station as different and alien from their familiarity with it in the past. An elderly woman made this statement in regard to her perception of young Black-British men at the railway station:

> Well I can remember it before there was never a bit of trouble, everyone was going to their work or to Leigh on holiday, or even onto the cruise terminal. It was bustling with different people, there was never a bit of trouble. Now, I'm not saying all of them, but a lot of them, start a lot of trouble don't they? You see it on the telly and then you start to worry and I don't go down there, I'd rather wait to get a bus …
>
> (Jean, East Tilbury)

The racialism in Jean's statement emerged from the fact that she no longer saw the railway station as a place where conduct was governed and this uncertainty became a risky situation for her as she applied media stereotypes to her reasoning. She made the connection to institutional past and identity explicit in her following remark: 'We used to have a lot of them when I was working at the hospital, but you knew who they were because you worked with them … ' The civic narrative that expressed the area's community and sociality was something embedded within familiar institutions founded upon the economic purpose and reality of the area. These had been swept away with the post-industrial economic tides of the 1980s and 1990s.

The civic narrative offered a means to justify why the institutions of the past were more socially functional than the lack of institutions experienced in the present. As social memories these narratives defined community identity with reference to the decline of these institutions and the power of localism to defend its social and cultural boundaries. In both the rural and industrial narratives, memory was used to reassert the 'glory' of the past to rectify the errant ways of the present in the hope of building a better economic future with stable local identities. The divergence was that in Tilbury the industrial memory was used to foster a more directed and integrative future with a consolidation of the memory as local heritage. In Ockendon the rural narrative held a more symbolic appeal and the lament of respondents was that this rural identity was not considered part of the civic heritage of the area; the relocation of the new community was seen to be symptomatic of neglect on behalf of national government. The heritage that residents wanted respect for was unavoidably ethnically exclusive to local whites and was aimed at elevating their status over newcomers. The following quote by Diane, a clerical worker from Grays, typified this resentment with reference to the establishment of the new community; it should be noted that her claims were proved by the research to be incredulous:

> I think it is the manner in which they have been brought into the area and it's the method whereby London are paying them 30K and that's now going to be increased to 50K to relocate in the sticks. So the locals take affront to that, they don't come in because they're working hard, they're not coming in for good jobs, they're coming here because London wants them out and they arrive in this area.
>
> (Diane, from Grays)

Conclusion

The research revealed that English Identity is a political manifestation of localism against a totalising national narrative of Britishness. In the locality of Thurrock, English Identity was contrasted against multiculturalism and acceptance of 'otherness' supposedly favoured by Britishness. There is a conceptual distinction to be drawn here between English Identity as a political voice and Englishness (Kumar 2003). In Thurrock, Englishness was the cultural facet of local people and their social memories drawn from local economic history. In all narratives economic history was referenced as central to the nation, and this bolstered the relevance and confidence of localism in the face of a denigrated present social, economic and political situation. It was the social memories attached to this former 'glory' that locals wanted restored in the face of challenges to the meanings of local space and identity by the non-white new community. These challenges represented the removal of their own social memory from the centre stage of national heritage and it was in this respect that they represented themselves as an indigenous subaltern.

Missing from the respondents' narratives of social memory was the means by which their own historical position shared an exclusive relationship to the power structures of colonial industrial capitalism. Multiculturalism in all its political, social and cultural forms is a partial reflection of a post-colonial acknowledgement of the heterogeneity of national heritage. In political and academic debates the respect for heterogeneity given by authorised versions of heritage is arguable in the sense that debate is about more respect for multiplicity not less (Shukra et al. 2004). The political advocacy of the ethnicised white English Identity found in Thurrock was an active argument for less diversity, but ironically used the language of asking for more on the basis of situating itself as a subaltern to Britishness. The subjective justification for English Identity as a political voice was due to its association with the memory of class and economics.

To conclude, heritage is an important sociological concept in that it can be used to assess the political legitimacy of the so-called silent majority voice in the public imagination. Regionally speaking, as the research suggests, this is most identifiable as a rising tide of English Identity. In the sociological literature this voice is being addressed as a phenomenon attached to post-industrial class formation (Savage 2001). In doing so the links between social class and ethnicity are obscured and class is rendered as a cultural resource, not an economic relation (Payne and Grew 2005). Consequently, many recent examples of class analysis and community study reduce class to the experience of whiteness, without providing an adequate theoretical rationale that is consistent with the wider democratic values held by social scientists. The research and focus of this area of study should ultimately be welcomed as a commitment to multiplicity of voice and interest in inequality, but it would do well to appreciate the memory of class held by the white community in terms of a struggle over claims to heritage. Ultimately, heritage provides an empirical means to judge the normativity inherent in the community relations understudy and establishes their position within the wider malaise of multicultural social relations that exist within the boundaries of the administrative region of England. In this way the social manifestation of heritage is an indicator of social and political change not yet achieved, but an aspiration of the substance of future civic space.

References

Anthias, F. (1998) 'Evaluating diaspora: beyond ethnicity?', *Sociology*, (32)3.
——(2007) 'Ethnic ties: social capital and the question of mobilisability', *The Sociological Review*, 155(4).
Back, L. (1996) *New Ethnicities and Urban Culture: Racism and Multi-Culture in Young Lives*, London: Routledge.
Back, L., Keith, M., Khan, A., Shukra, K. and Solomos, J. (2002) 'New Labour's white heart: politics, multi-culturalism and the return of assimilation', *Political Quarterly*, 73(4).
Bauman, Z. (2001) *Community: Seeking Safety in an Insecure World*, Cambridge: Polity Press.
Beck, U. (1992) *The Risk Society: Towards a New Modernity*, London: Sage.
——(2002) *Individualisation*, London: Sage.

Bonnett, A. (1998) 'How the British working class became white: the symbolic (re)formation of racialised capitalism', *Journal of Historical Sociology*, 11(3).
——(2000) *Anti-Racism*, London: Routledge.
Charlesworth, S. (2000) *A Phenomenology of Working Class Experience*, Cambridge: Cambridge University Press.
Colls, R. (2002) *The Identity of England*, Oxford: Oxford University Press.
Crompton, R. (2002) *Class and Stratification: An Introduction to Current Debates*, 2nd edn, Cambridge: Polity Press.
Dench, G., Gavron, K. and Young, M. (2006) *The New East End: Kinship, Race and Conflict*, London: Profile Books.
Giddens, A. (1990) *The Consequences of Modernity*, Cambridge: Polity Press.
Herbert, J. (2008) *Negotiating Ethnic Boundaries in the City: Migration, Gender, and Ethnicity in Britain*, Aldershot: Ashgate.
Hill, S. (1976) *The Dockers: Class and Tradition in London*, London: Heinemann.
Keane, J. (1998) *Democracy and Civil Society, Revised Edition*, London: University of Westminster Press.
Kumar, K. (2003) *The Making of English National Identity*, Cambridge: Cambridge University Press.
Misztal, B. (2003) *Theories of Social Remembering*, Buckingham: Open University Press.
Meiksins Wood, E. (1998) *The Retreat for Class: A True New Socialism*, London: Verso.
Modood, T., Berthoud, R., Lakey, J., Nazroo, J., Smith, P., Virdee, S. and Beishon, S. (1997) *Ethnic Minorities in Britain: Diversity and Disadvantage*, London: Policy Studies Institute.
Parekh, B. (2000) *The Future of Multi-Ethnic Britain: A Report of the Commission on the Future of Multi-Ethnic Britain*, London: Profile.
Savage, M. (2000) *Class Analysis and Social Transformation*, Buckingham: Open University Press.
Savage, M., Bagnall, G. and Longhurst, B. (2001) 'Ordinary, ambivalent and defensive: class identities in the north-west of England', *Sociology*, 35(4).
Sayer, A. (2005) 'Class, moral worth, and recognition', *Sociology*, 39(5).
Shukra, K., Back, L., Keith, M., Khan, A. and Solomos, J. (2004) 'Race, social cohesion and the changing politics of citizenship', *London Review of Education*, 2(3).
Skeggs, B. (1997) *Formations of Class and Gender: Becoming Respectable*, London: Sage.
——(2004), *Class, Self, Culture*, London: Routledge.
——(2005) 'The making of class and gender through visualising moral subject formation', *Sociology*, (39) 5.
Smith, L. (2006) *The Uses of Heritage*, London: Routledge.
Solomos, J. (2003) *Race and Racism in Britain*, 3rd edn, Basingstoke: Palgrave Macmillan.
Urry, J. (2000) Sociology Beyond Societies: Mobilities for the Twenty-First Century, London: Routledge.
Werbner, P. (2006) 'Vernacular cosmopolitanism', *Theory, Culture, and Society*, 23(2–3).

Part II

Recognising and Commemorating Communities

Chapter 6

Don't mourn organise[1]
Heritage, recognition and memory in Castleford, West Yorkshire

Laurajane Smith and Gary Campbell

Self-respect is a key issue in the study of heritage and class. As Andrew Sayer (2007: 94) notes, shame is a powerful emotion associated with class and is a response to the imagined or actual views of others. Class still matters, it defines the sorts of access people have to certain economic and material resources, and it 'affects how others value us and respond to us, which in turn affects our sense of self-worth' (Sayer 2005:1). This chapter, drawing on interviews conducted in the West Yorkshire, ex-coal-mining town of Castleford between 2003 and 2009, illustrates the ways in which 'heritage' has been used to assert self-worth and self-respect at both individual and community levels. In this context, heritage is used not only as a tool for collective remembering, but also in self-conscious and critical ways for negotiating and defining the social and moral values that underpin and define the cultural identity of a working class community.

In the face of de-industrialisation and the disastrous aftermath of the 1984–85 Miners' Strike, Castleford's identity as a mining town has been redefined. It is now a town commonly identified by what it has lost: it has become an 'ex-mining community'. In negotiating a new identity for Castleford, and in reasserting community self-respect and self-recognition, resident and community action groups have used and redefined 'heritage' in ways that question the legitimacy of dominant and authorised definitions of the term. In exploring the uses of heritage in Castleford, this chapter develops three aims. First, it outlines how ideas and discourses of 'heritage' are used in community debates and negotiations about what it meant to live in de-industrialised Castleford. Second, the chapter illustrates the linkages between these notions of 'heritage' and trade union legacies to argue that, after the defeat of the unions by the then conservative Prime Minister, Margaret Thatcher, in 1985, 'heritage' has taken on an 'organizing' role in the Castleford community. Finally, we discuss how the first two issues can illuminate attempts to theorise heritage as a cultural practice. In particular, we demonstrate how understandings of heritage in Castleford exist in opposition to the 'authorized heritage discourse' (AHD), and the implications of this for the development of a democratic sense of what heritage is, or can be.

Heritage and self-respect

If we take a casual glance at the World Heritage List, or the list of scheduled, listed or otherwise protected and conserved monuments, sites, buildings or other places of 'heritage' in most Western countries, we could be excused for taking away the image of a Western history full of triumph, glorious deeds and aesthetic wonders. It is true that 'places of pain and shame' (Foote 1997; Logan and Reeves 2009) or of dissonance (Tunbridge and Ashworth 1996) are included on these lists, but these are often simply gestured to, or seen as additions to the core pantheon of heritage marvels that make up such lists – and a certain assertion of Western 'self-respect'. The aggrandisement of national and international heritage lists has been well documented in the heritage literature (see for instance, Lowenthal 1985, 1998, 2006; Wright 1985; Hewison 1987; Cleere 2001; Meskell 2002; Labadi 2007 amongst others). Increasing national and international interest in heritage since the 1960s can be tracked by the growing numbers of international treaties, as well as national laws and policies developed since this time, that aim to preserve and conserve material culture and, recently, intangible heritage. Some commentators have argued that such a concern has tended to be a symptom of cultural decline or angst (Hewison 1984), and that it simply maps out Western societies' insecurities and nostalgic yearnings for grander, 'better' times in the face of environmental and economic uncertainty (Wright 1985, 1991; Hewison 1987; Walsh 1992; Lowenthal 1985, 1998, 2006; McCrone *et al.* 1995; Brett 1996). Heritage, it is argued, refocuses history via nostalgic yearnings (Hewison 2009). This is indeed *one* of the things that heritage can do (Smith 2006). The point here, however, is that the activities we engage in around concerns for 'heritage' *do* things beyond the often simple and stated aims of conservation. What is defined as heritage, how it is managed, conserved and interpreted has a cultural and social consequence.

The difficulty with much of the writing on heritage is the assumption that heritage, as a thing, monument, site or place, has inherent meaning and that this meaning is somehow uncritically tied to the material symbolism of national or other community identity. Thus, 'heritage' becomes the focus of critique concerning social and cultural conservatism, rather than the social values, hierarchies and practices that privilege and champion certain forms of 'heritage' and history. However, 'heritage' is, as one of us has argued before, not the site, place or monument listed on some national or international 'list', rather heritage can more usefully be defined as a cultural process in which cultural and social meanings are negotiated, made, re-made and/or rehearsed (Smith 2006). Heritage is a discourse, by which we mean it offers a framework for thinking about and acting on social 'problems' associated with the past. As a discourse heritage becomes 'a practice not just of representing the world, but of signifying the world, constituting and constructing the world in meaning' (Fairclough 1992: 64, see also Fairclough 2001). Thus, heritage discourses work to make the past meaningful and actively negotiate the meaning of the past for the present. National and international heritage lists have often championed triumphal elite versions of history and, in an international context, Eurocentric versions (Byrne 1991; Cleere 2001), because they are constructed within the Western Authorized Heritage Discourse (AHD). The AHD owes much to nineteenth-century European architectural conservation and archaeological debates about the inherent aesthetic worth of 'heritage' sites and to understandings of history predicated on the historical experiences of the social and economic elites (Smith 2006: 29–34). The AHD is not the only discourse of heritage, but it is the dominant one, and underpins professional practice within Western heritage management today and within intergovernmental institutions such as UNESCO (Smith 2006; Waterton 2010). The AHD constructs heritage as inherently valuable, subject to the stewardship of expertise (primarily architects, archaeologists and historians), and as inextricably tied to 'identity' and national identity in particular; moreover, it is also constructed as aesthetically and historically 'good' (see Smith 2006; Smith and Waterton 2009: 27–30, 2011).

The ways in which heritage lists are often constituted has tended to tell the story not simply of nostalgic yearnings for 'better' times, but rather a version of history and the past that privileges certain historical experiences or perceptions. Thus, as Raphael Samuel (1994) argues, what the heritage-baiters, such as Hewison and Wright, misunderstand is that heritage can, and sometimes does, have meaning beyond attempts by elites to represent their heritage as nationally legitimate and significant. However, this misunderstanding itself has consequences, as it has tended to dismiss heritage practices altogether as uncritical nostalgic yearning. Heritage projects taken up in de-industrialised contexts, for instance, are often dismissed as attempts to sanctify and sanitise a dismal and difficult history. For instance, Hewison (1987: 95) has argued that 'the heritage solution' has been increasingly applied to ease the emotional and economic losses of de-industrialisation. This argument is reinforced by the tendency of dominant and traditional heritage practices and the associated tourist industry to sidestep class histories that acknowledge trauma and loss (Barthel 1996: 69, 125; Brower 1999; Debary 2004). However, interviews of visitors to museums that aim to remember and commemorate working class history has revealed that visitors to such places engage in quite mindful and critical memory work during their visits. Indeed, they were generally found to be using visits to develop or reinforce critical social commentary about both the past and present, suggesting that something more complex is occurring with this heritage than most critics allow (see Smith 2006: 195f). Although there has been more critical interest in class heritage of late (see not only chapters in this book, but also Irving and Taksa 2002; Oliver and Reeves 2003; Pickering and Tyrrell 2004; Stephenson and Wray 2005; Carnegie 2006; Richardson 2008;

Taksa 2009; Wedgwood 2009; Strangleman 2010 among others) there has nonetheless been a tendency for working class heritage to be ignored or obscured by the AHD or for it to be dismissed as representing nostalgic sanitisation that glosses over class inequality and historical trauma (Strangleman 1999: 741).

What becomes lost in this process is the role heritage plays not just in identity construction, but also in the construction of the emotional energies of self-respect and recognition. Heritage is a cultural process not just about the construction and negotiation of abstract identities, but is also about negotiating the values and cultural meanings that underpin those identities, as much as it is about negotiating the *feelings* and emotions that also underpin identity. That such feelings become entangled with nationalism and patriotism at national levels does not negate the importance that heritage, and the discourses that frame it, play in negotiating and regulating emotional meaning. The AHD, however, tends to privilege 'feel good' qualities about heritage, so much so that dissonance and the contested nature of history becomes something which the AHD cannot adequately address (see Smith 2010). Thus, the emotional aspects of the cultural processes that engage with heritage become hidden or obscured. Nonetheless, heritage is a discourse or cultural tool that is used to help us to not only remember and forget, but also to negotiate the social values, meanings and emotional landscapes that define and express group and individual identity.

The ways in which the AHD and other discourses of heritage negotiate identity does not only define the way heritage lists are constructed, it has wider political consequences as well. The political and social significance of heritage can be understood in the context of the growing recognition of 'identity politics', or more usefully the 'politics of recognition' (Fraser 1995; 2000). Recognition of difference has become, during the last decades of the twentieth century, an identifiable arena of political conflict (Kymlicka and Norman 2000; Lovell 2007). Claims for the recognition of difference and identity have become a recognised platform from which to engage in struggles for social justice, and parity in negotiations over the distribution of resources of power (such as finance, welfare, housing and education, etc.). This growth has occurred simultaneously with increasing post-war national and international institutional interest in heritage. This is not to suggest a direct correlation between heritage and the politics of recognition, but it highlights two issues. First, it underscores the intensity often identified in heritage conflicts over whether to preserve or not certain heritage places, or how such places should be valued and interpreted, by placing these conflicts within a wider understanding of the political consequences that identity claims can have (see Smith and Waterton 2009 for fuller discussion). Second, the desire and need by States and their heritage agencies to control and regulate identity claims acquire a certain urgency in the context of increasing demands for the political recognition of cultural and identity claims. In this latter context, however, the AHD can only acquire further authority and utility through its ability to help states and their policy makers to regulate and govern competing claims to identity based on appeals to heritage and the past (see Smith 2007). For Nancy Fraser (2000, 2001) the 'politics of recognition', acknowledges that different community groups, with different histories, needs and aspirations may make claims for recognition in both symbolic and material forms. Further, these claims will have material consequences for equity and justice as they become involved in negotiations over access to and redistribution of resources. Andrew Sayer (2005, 2007), however, warns that a shift in focus from the politics of redistribution to recognition has tended to ignore class politics. He notes that the politics of class does not fall neatly into the politics of recognition as framed by Fraser, as the 'poor are not clamouring for poverty to be legitimized and valued' (2005: 52). While he notes that class struggles are primarily about the distribution of resources, they also involve a different recognition from that often highlighted in identity politics, and argues that recognition in the case of working class communities and individuals is about respect for their 'moral worth as a person, rather than as a person of a particular identity' (2007: 96). The moral concerns and sense of injustice that underpin class struggles should not be devalued or ignored, and as Sayer notes, a strong sense of self-recognition and self-respect are vital standpoints from which to assert the morality and justice of working class political and economic aspirations.

So what does all this mean for heritage in Castleford? The framework we are developing here asserts that heritage is a cultural process engaged in mediating the meaning of the past, which has implications for contemporary expressions of identity, memory and emotion. This process is often, but not always, framed by the AHD, although other discourses of heritage may exist outside or in opposition to the AHD. Moreover, heritage, with its close association with 'identity', has a consequence for political struggles based on recognition, and in the case of class conflict, recognition may start with self-recognition of moral worth. Thus, it becomes useful to ask, what were the issues of self-recognition and moral worth that were at stake in Castleford, and how did heritage work to help negotiate those issues?

Castleford – a background

To understand what was at stake it is important to outline what was both lost and gained in Castleford during de-industrialisation. Founded in AD 71 by the Romans, Castleford grew as an industrial centre during the eighteenth century, and the underlying deposits of coal, sand and clay, together with the existence of two navigable rivers, saw the early development of coal mining, glass making and pottery manufacturing (Wilders 1995, 2003). Confectionery manufacturing, flour milling and tailoring also developed, with the confectionary factories targeting the employment of the wives and daughters of mineworkers, while women were also employed in the pottery industry and worked in decorating and glazing (Wilders 2003). A chemical works, which opened in 1915, was also a significant employer within the town (Wilders 1995: 72). Surface mining for coal occurred from the 1500s; however, it was in the nineteenth century that coal mining came to dominate the town with the opening of Whitwood, Wheldale, Glasshoughton and Fryston Collieries (Wilders 1995).

During the early 1960s the potteries closed, followed by the glassworks in 1983 and the chemical works in 2005, together with a general reduction of staff in other industries. The 1984–85 Miners' Strike resulted in the loss of 3000 jobs in Castleford as most of the Castleford and nearby mines closed shortly after the strike, with other pits closing during the 1990s and the last closing in the wider Castleford-Wakefield region in 2002 (see Bailey and Popple, this volume, for history of the Strike). Not only did the closures of the mines have a major economic impact, they also had an immeasurable consequence for community pride and self-esteem. The extent of the emotional impact of the Strike, and de-industrialisation more generally, have been documented for the Durham region by Stephenson and Wray (2005:177), who identify what they termed the long term 'emotional degeneration' that occurred in mining communities following the loss of the industry.

With the loss of industry also came a remodelling of the Castleford urban landscape with the demolition of not only industrial buildings and pithead winding gears, but also much of the high-density housing associated with British nineteenth- and early twentieth-century industrial towns. Replaced by modern lower density housing estates, it is probably safe to say no one in Castleford laments the loss of the previous housing stock, however, the impact of the changes to the urban streetscapes adds to the sense of change in Castleford. Many who we interviewed lamented the loss of the ability that previous terraced housing had provided in facilitating community interaction (CAS02, 05, 09, 10, 50, 51 among others).[2] Adding to a sense of loss of community identity is also the fact that many of the workers in Castleford now commute to Leeds, Wakefield or other regional centres, an issue also frequently reiterated in interviews.

It is important not to underestimate the impact that the loss of industries, together with the aftermath of the 1984–85 miners' strike has had on community cohesion and pride. The strong social and cultural ties that bind industrial communities are well documented (see Richards 1997; Crang 2001; Hutton 2005 for coal; and also Bruno 1999; Linkon and Russo 2002; Nadel-Klein 2003; Stenning 2005; Strangleman 2010 for other industries). These ties have not only been threatened by mass job losses and unemployment, but were also explicitly attacked during the 1984–85 miners' strike. Under the leadership of Margaret Thatcher, the then Conservative

Government targeted the social and cultural foundations that underpinned the identity of mining communities, as part of their strategy to break the National Union of Mineworkers (NUM) and ultimately undermine the power of the British Union Movement. The impact of this strike not only on mining communities and the NUM, but also on the power of British Trade Unions has been well documented (Bailey and Popple this volume; Richards 1997; Milne 2004; Hutton 2005; Williams 2009). One of Thatcher's enduring legacies, defining the mine-workers and their communities as 'the enemy within', was to leave a raft of un-repealed legislation that has severely weakened the unions and has seen trade union membership drop from its peak of just under 60% nationally in 1979 (Disney *et al*. 1998) to 25.8% of all workers in 2006 (ONS 2007). The sense of distress in Castleford following the Strike, and de-industrialisation more generally, remains strong:

> After the strike, it were bloody, people were dead on their feet just about. Places were shutting down, there were shops shutting down, people with no money. Basically you are talking about depression for a quite a few years after the strike ... Emotional and economic depression both of them.
> (CAS44, 2009)

The strike itself was a 'year of, oh, psychological trauma, it really really was, as I said it probably took me about twelve years to actually admit that' (CAS47, 2009). De-industrialised communities, facing all the social problems that they have, and in this case the added insult of the Conservative Party's attack on mining communities and the NUM, have faced events that were literally traumatic. There is a wider literature on dissonance and 'dark' heritage, which stresses how profoundly negative events are dealt with in social memory and we think that these insights are relevant to Castleford (see in particular Tunbridge and Ashworth 1996; Logan and Revees 2009). Though no-one we spoke to saw themselves as helpless victims, the level of individual and collective distress is palpable, as is the feeling that after over 20 years both individuals and the community are using processes of social memory, and heritage-making to deal with the emotional cost of what they have lost. As one community member had noted it had taken her 20 years for the shock of that period to recede and to remember that 'Castleford, as a community, mattered' (CAS19 2004).

Not mourning, organising

Between 2003 and 2009, the authors conducted semi-structured interviews with over 60 people involved with the Castleford Heritage Trust,[3] other community activists involved with other local community groups, local politicians, councillors, artists, ex-miners, ex-pottery workers; former and current confectionery workers and other interested residents of Castleford. In many of these interviews we asked the question 'who represents Castleford?'. This question often generated an interesting discussion, with various people noting it used to be the unions, the Labour Party at local government level and local councillors. The emphasis was, however, always on 'used to be'. A particular issue with almost everyone was the amalgamation of Castleford's local government with the Wakefield Metropolitan District Council. This amalgamation was seen to have resulted in Castleford being under-represented and marginalised at regional government level. Moreover, local councillors were no longer seen as representing local issues, as one woman noted:

> the people who represented the Labour Party [locally] when I was young probably worked down the pit with me granddad. The first mayor of Castleford had been a boyfriend of me grandma's at one time. These [were] people who lived *in* the community, they don't do that now, they come from somewhere else.
> (CAS33, 2008, interviewee's emphasis)

However, many noted more general trends, stating that the power of the unions had eroded considerably and that the Labour Party no longer represented working communities:

> The reason its changed is because the situation has changed from heavy industry to service industries and the Labour Party changing as well knowing that if its going to get in government then its got to appeal to a larger spectrum of population, you know, rather than pleasing trade unions whose membership have dropped down now.
> (CAS42, 2008)

Many of the men we interviewed, who had been actively involved in the Labour Party at a local or regional level, noted that not only had membership fallen, but also that debate at branch meetings had lost its depth and urgency:

> *Interviewer (clarifying): Historically there used to be more activity at the local branch level?*
> Yes. And at constituency level, not a lot going off. Also at district level. There's nothing – there's nobody challenging everything. Now I'm a Labour Party man. There's nobody organized against what Tony Blair's [the then Labour Prime Minister] done. If it were Margaret Thatcher who were slipping all these arrogant policies through we'd be marching behind the banners in millions down at London, but it just doesn't happen anymore.
> (CAS14, 2004)

Many people who we interviewed stressed the degree of political debate that occurred at community and workplace level (CAS05, 15, 19, 41, 42, 48, 51, 53). As another noted, the degree of political debate in the community had been lost, and this was explained as resulting from:

> Lack of trade unions, I would say that one of the reasons why we are in that position because we don't have the trade union movement that we used to have. As I say I used to go to branch meetings as a young man and I used to hear the debate, but there is none of that now. I used to listen to the debates and take part in the debates, and that debate continued in the pub and it continued in the pit so we had a general discussion going all the time on politics, on the industry and what was happening. So there was a general feeling of being part of the business of politics and trade unions. We had a trades council in Castleford, a very strong trades council but none of that now.
> (CAS35, 2008)

As in many working class communities, the link between industry, union activity and municipal representation in Castleford was very strong, as this man illustrates:

> I think it has changed [representation] because when you look back 30 years ago the mines were still strong, the unions were a lot stronger, Labour Party membership was a lot bigger. So you had a very unionized and strong labour base, or activist base, and you know, supposing you look back at the municipal history of Castleford it was definitely very strongly based through that industrialised unionised environment and that was great, and that really summed up the town in a lot of ways.
> (CAS48, 2008)

The culture of the Labour Party was also seen to have changed, first because you 'can't talk' union:

> we lived in an industry we worked in an industry, it were part of our life, and that's why the trade unions played a big role and it's a shame that you can't have a union now, you can't talk about unions now, why the heck not?
> (CAS51, 2009)

Second, because what were identified as service industries were seen as dominating party concerns, as CAS14 states in response to the question 'does the Labour Party represent working people now?':

> I'd throw that back at you and say 'is there any working people left or are they all in the service industries'? There's no roughty-toughty man sort of stuff, you know, nowt like that.

Castleford as a mining town and as a town known also for the local rugby league team, the Castleford Tigers, presents a masculine image. Although many of the industries in the town, such as the potteries, confectionary manufacturing and tailoring, were dominated by female employees, the masculinity of the town's image is important. Although often not explicitly discussed by residents, the gendered image of the town is in flux. Not only challenged by the 'end of work' and changing work patterns, but by the changing prominence of women. As one man noted about life before the Strike: 'I think women were sort of in the background, I think, up to a point' (CAS39, 2009). However, for women the miners' strike resulted in increasing the numbers of women becoming involved in unions and wider politics, as one elderly woman and daughter of a mining family noted:

> The women became very strong during the miner's strike! They had to go out and do something because their husbands were sat at home moaning about being on strike. And women organised food parcels, places where they go and children be fed, it was the women who organized that. The women became involved in the unions, the women formed self-help groups and learnt to do things that they hadn't had a chance to do, one lady took herself to classes and learnt to write poetry and another one learnt how to make sandals and shoes, she could make her own shoes! Wouldn't have done that before the strike. The women did come together doing during the strike.
>
> (CAS33, 2008)

The highly successful Castleford Community Learning Centre,[4] an organisation involved in running a range of courses for local residents, including re-training and skills development and which works in partnership with local universities, 'was born out of the Miners Strike by a group of women who had been part of the women's support groups during that year's struggle' (CAS47, 2009). To what extent, however, women's roles changed due to their involvement in union activism is unclear, as Shaw and Mundy (2005) report; changes in gender relations in some mining communities perhaps owe more to changes in the labour market and the loss of jobs following pit closures than to experiences during the Strike. Whatever the cause, however, gender relations in Castleford are undergoing change.

The organisations that had previously represented the town and its working class community were seen by many to have failed, weakened or turned elsewhere. The change in the gendered image of the town, and gender relations generally, in many ways reinforced the sense in which the Labour Party and the trade unions no longer adequately represented a community that many of the older residents remembered. Prior to the Strike it was largely and traditionally men that were involved in trade union and Labour Party activities; however, with the growth of service industries and the loss of mining, Castleford's previous sense of masculine self-respect and self-recognition could no longer be called upon. Many of the changes, it needs to be noted, were not seen as bad. No one for instance wanted to go back to the working conditions that miners worked under, no one lamented the changing position of women, no one wanted to go back to the polluted and over-crowded housing conditions, but what emerges from the interview data is a strong sense that people were looking for ways to navigate those changes:

> there has been an eroding away of that culture, you know, and now we have got a town that is, you know, more outward looking in the sense that, you know, the communities that were there based around those industries are just not there any more. Although a lot of the families still live in these communities and have got an identity with that, and the roots are still there, but there's a lot, you know, a lot more people now coming in and out of the town who rent properties. And you know that's not a bad thing, um, its just the way society has changed and, ah, you know, I think Castleford's trying to adapt to that.
> (CAS48, 2008)

It was to 'heritage' that sectors of the community, particularly older residents, turned to help navigate the cultural, industrial and social changes experienced in Castleford. However, the trade union legacy has been significant in the way the concept of heritage has been mobilised, as we will see below.

The Castleford Heritage Trust (CHT) organised by both men and women, and, led by community activists, such as the current chair Alison Drake, originally came together as a residents' action group to restore a clock to the then disused market hall in the main street of Castleford (Drake 2008). Meeting someone 'under the clock' had an important resonance for Castleford residents, and the successful campaign to have a clock restored to the hall galvanised both the group and the wider community. Indeed early community meetings about heritage issues regularly attract over 300 people while public meetings called by local councils about economic renewal often struggled to get 30 attendees (CAS19, 2004). What is interesting about the clock was that it was not the original but a new one that had been designed by a local artisan. The point here is that what was important to what was to become the CHT, was not a sense of 'authenticity' of fabric that normally drives professional heritage experts, but rather recreating a sense of place to facilitate community remembering and interaction. Heritage here was not about an 'authentic' clock, but rather the sense of place and communal practice having a clock on the market hall symbolised and recreated.

From the clock, the CHT moved to a campaign to uncover and interpret the remains of a Roman bathhouse and to develop plans for a community forum that would consist of a local museum, gallery space, meeting place and other community amenities. Although still campaigning for this project, a gallery and meeting place have been developed (see Drake 2008 for details). The community has also engaged in repatriation debates with museums outside of Castleford for the return of Roman artefacts excavated and removed from the town by archaeologists:

> Most of the historical remains, for some reason were taken away by Leeds or Wakefield, and are stored there. In fact most of them are not even open to viewing, so what we do need in Castleford is a large centre where all these things can be brought together to show Castleford's heritage and history so that the children of Castleford have something to be really proud of instead of looking upon Castleford, as some people do, as an old mining town.
>
> (CAS09, 2004)

The concern for Roman remains, while very real, works to attract the attention of external heritage agencies that have tended to dismiss the town as having no heritage of value. The AHD does not recognise the validity of Castleford's industrial heritage, an issue reinforced by the fact that much of the material heritage of this period has been torn down (see Smith 2006; Drake 2008 for fuller discussion). The Roman heritage is also used unconsciously by local residents, as one of us has argued elsewhere (Smith 2006: 255), to legitimise a local sense that Castleford's industrial and recent heritage matters. In the interviews when asked 'what is Castleford's heritage', many respond by noting 'it is Roman', but then immediately jump to deeper discussions of industrial and other more recent histories and events. The Roman heritage is validated by the AHD, and is often used to flag or signify that the next thing talked about, that is industrial life and experiences, is heritage too. The naming of Roman history is not a passive use of the AHD, as documented previously (Smith 2006:259). Roman and other pre-industrial periods of the town have been redrawn, literally, on to banners designed and styled after union and pit banners. The iconography used renders this heritage as part of the heritage of Castleford within cultural terms that draw on union and industrial legacies.

The CHT organises an annual heritage festival during July. At this festival a range of activities takes place including, pottery painting and glazing, rag rug making, dancing, singing, exhibitions that include mining history and local natural heritage, and poetry, art and craft displays are also mounted. Local schools actively participate in the festival, with some teachers organising their teaching around festival activities (Drake 2008). The pit banners hold pride of place in these festivals, either carried during the parade that is a feature of the festival, or hung to decorate the old market hall. The festival is characterised as:

It's a community thing. I think anything that draws community together is a good thing. It makes people aware of their surroundings and what's happening in the town. It celebrates things.
(CAS10, 2004)

This viewpoint was reinforced by the majority of the 107 people surveyed through structured interviews undertaken on the streets of Castleford in and around the festivals of 2004 and 2005:

Opportunity for different groups in Castleford to get involved in one annual project. Gives children something to remember when they get older. Memory jogger for older people. ... Because it gives them a sense of community. Without a sense of community you get antisocial behaviour and crime. It creates and jogs memory. It's something to look forward to as an annual event. Best thing about it is that it is coming from the community and not forced on them – it gives them a sense of pride.
(CF7, 2004, male, 40–60, laboratory technician)

Because it builds a sense of community and goodwill between people.
(CF65 2004, male, 30–40, unemployed)

To keep up the community spirit. It was divided during the miners' strike – some families still don't speak. But a thing like this brings people together and gets young people involved in the community and they get to learn about their traditions.
(CF54, 2004, female, 40–60, funeral director)

So Castleford can maintain its identity. Castleford has a lot going for it and it's important to get that message out there.
(CF67, 2004, male, 40–60, bank auditor)

The heritage festival and other activities organised by the CHT were seen by the residents surveyed above as events that showed and generated pride in Castleford (see Smith 2006:261f) and that: 'That community does matter. Community spirit does matter. That change can be happy as well as hard' (CF65, 2004, male, 30–40, unemployed). Self-respect and self-recognition are key issues here. The audience of the CHT heritage festivals and other heritage activities is very much a local one – the community is speaking to itself, redefining and asserting its moral worth. One of the key issues for many in both the street interviews and more formal interviews was not only regenerating community pride, but also reinforcing community values. One of the changes that was very much lamented in Castleford was a sense that community friendliness was being eroded. Almost everyone we spoke to pointed out that the real heritage of Castleford lay in the friendly and supportive community and that 'everybody helped everybody else' (CAS33, 2008).

In addition to concerns over changing community values, some of those interviewed also noted that the reduction of both apprenticeship training and trade union participation had had an impact on community values. Not only did apprenticeships and trade union participation provide work skill training they also, some reported, socialised young men, as indeed did the social networks of the mining communities themselves (see Strangleman 2001, 2005). The following account from CAS35 (2008) maps the lines of influence that underpinned community values in the town:

> the good trade union leaders they had defended the industry and defended the men who worked in the industry very strongly and made Castleford stronger because of the dependency of the mining industry, and therefore the industry was strong and the trade union movement was strong and the unity in the town, unity in the area, was very pronounced. If you hurt him you hurt me ... and that [value] used to [be] reflected when we go out dancing and socializing. People they used to have their differences, but nothing we have today, nobody stabbing one another, nobody, all right they used to fight after a drink, Friday, Saturday night, but the next day they would be drinking together they'd be working together within the week. So I think the trade union movement developed a great deal of strength in the area and some of the trade union leaders were also the political leaders like [name given] and so together it built Castleford and made Castleford strong both in the educational scene, the social areas and rugby, a lot of the lads who played rugby worked at the pits and because of the fact that the trade unions were part of the structure of the culture to develop, to progress, to support, they would defend the rights of these rugby players to work in the pits although their jobs weren't the same jobs as some of the other people [who] worked on the coal face, but they used to get the training and were supported by the industry, I think that was because of the trade union movement.

The CHT and the festival and other events it organises are about creating a sense of place and self-respect, and they also, as one person identified in the street interviews said, 'creates and jogs memories', and are about 'producing heritage and creating something now' (CF17 2004). This sense of agency is vital. The festival and exhibitions that the CHT mount are very much interactive, nobody comes to gaze dispassionately at art works or exhibitions, but rather they come and are encouraged to engage and experience. Exhibitions on mining, for instance, require children to crawl through dark tunnels while ex-miners hide and squirt them with water to simulate the dark, hot and wet conditions of the mines, pottery exhibitions encourage you to don an apron and try your hand at decorating and so forth. Not only are memories being jogged for older residents, but they are also being created for younger people as they are engaged in acts of collective remembering of not only past events but the community values that they generated. The way heritage is used in Castleford is similar to that reported in mining communities in County Durham, as Stephenson and Wray (2005) argue, where the re-invigorated Durham Miner's Gala is an example of what they refer to as 'emotional regeneration'. Participation in the Gala they note 'represents a restatement of allegiance to the community, to the union, and to a unique culture' (2005:184). As in Castleford, heritage here is not about sentimentality, but is also concerned with acknowledging the brutalities of mining (see also Wray this volume).

Not only has the CHT represented Castleford to itself, but also to wider audiences. Castleford has been one of the centres targeted by government policies of regeneration. One of these projects, filmed by the commercial television station, Channel 4, saw the building of new infrastructure in the town that centred on an elegant footbridge completed in 2008 across the River Aire, making access between two areas of the town much easier while also creating a space to encounter and meet other residents. The CHT was, and continues to be, active in asserting its views to regional and national governments about the nature and impact of regeneration agendas in Castleford. In some ways the CHT, and discourses of heritage within the town more generally, are playing a role in 'emotional regeneration', but also an 'organising' role. This organisation revolves around asserting self-respect and pride, defining and redefining community values, attempts to socialise or teach younger residents those values and representing community interests and issues to government policy bodies. As one retired unionist and Labour Party activist noted, community groups tend to represent Castleford today:

> People goes to these things [community groups] and they start talking to each other and it grows, this is like what happens, you get a bud and it grows into a big flower, and it seeds, and it spreads about, and this is what the heritage of Castleford is to me, its people not just talking to people, its getting on with it and working with each other, and the heritage of Cas[5] is what has gone off, but it's the future as well, we have got to work and get a future as well, we can't just lapse on what it used to be, let's get a new one.
>
> (CAS50, 2009)

Not only is it community groups that are representing the town, but it is also 'heritage'. Heritage in terms of not only 'what has gone off' (that is, what happened in the past), but it is also people 'getting on' with each other. What heritage is also doing is negotiating a future for Castleford as well. Heritage as a cultural process becomes not about 'saving' 'what has gone off' as Castleford 'can't lapse on what it used to be', but rather it is about acknowledging or recognising the past and using that as a starting point for negotiating its new future. The CHT and community discourses of heritage are, in the absence of strong union and political representation, working to not only represent working class Castleford, but to negotiate new identities and the sense of geographical, social and political 'place' (Hayden 1997). We are not suggesting that the filling of the vacuum left by the unions is a 'good' thing, simply that it has happened, but also that the way heritage is being utilised has a legacy in the union movement. In the following extract, CAS50 talks about a sense of inheritance:

> Well everyone joined unions then. You have got to have union backing, in that day and age, and I say it to this day, you have got to have a big lump of people behind you [CAS51 makes agreeing noises]. The union is the men, the working men, the union is that to me. And if you don't fight for your rights, and this is what it all goes by, you got to turn around and fight for your rights. That's the way I was brought up. I used to sit with me granddad, we were only on about this before you [interviewer] come, how I used to spend a lot of time with old men. When I got to work plus when you went into pubs in them days it was, it was not all discos and this, that and the other, I used to go in quiet back rooms where old guys used to sit and you used to hear all the tales. You used to sit in front of a big roaring fire, give them a couple of pints, you tapped them up with pints, they, you [becoming excited], they leaked and I mean leaked, they told you everything. This is where I get my union bits from is what these guys have had to put up with in past and what I had to like carry on. This is the way I always thought about it, I always had to carry on from what these guys started …
>
> (CAS50, 2009)

What is being said here, the idea of collective power, of learning values through talking with elders and noting the importance of acknowledging what was put up with and what was achieved and carrying on those values to maintain or improve conditions, maps on to what is being done with heritage in contemporary Castleford. The discourses and practices of heritage are used to redefine community and re-knit and strengthen community ties and to transmit certain social and cultural values. They also acknowledge a sense of inheritance that revolves around working for improvements, and by definition, change. The important point to stress here is that heritage in Castleford is not about nostalgic yearning for days gone by, but acknowledging those days – recognising them and understanding their moral worth and using that recognition as a point from which to 'carry on' and to get a new and improved future.

Conclusions

Heritage in Castleford sits outside of and, in many ways, in opposition to the AHD; the AHD and its traditional understanding of heritage simply offers no way of understanding what is defined as heritage in Castleford. In some ways, when residents talk about heritage as being 'people', 'community values', or 'industrial work experiences', heritage in Castleford could be classified as 'intangible heritage' as defined by UNESCO. However, that definition also misses the point. Heritage for the residents of Castleford is not so much about conserving 'things' or 'intangible traditions' from the past, but rather it is an active process of *making*, negotiating and transmitting memories and social values for and in terms of present needs and aspirations. It is about generating pride and self-respect in the face of historical trauma and economic and political change. Ultimately, it is about self-recognition.

Importantly this self-recognition does not rest on, nor is it a prelude to, nostalgic attempts to 'save' or 'conserve' the past, but rather underwrites and focuses community gaze on both the present and the future. Heritage, here, does in fact what the critics Hewison (1987, 2009) and Wright (1985) warn against, it refocuses history, although not in the sense that traditional heritage lists do in providing institutional recognition of elite historical experiences, but in terms of a critical refocusing that recognises the moral worth of working class experiences. This process is not something in and of itself to warn and rail against, as some commentators tend to do, but rather to understand as a focus of analysis and critical debate.

Castleford illustrates that heritage is indeed an active process of making and re-creating both historical and contemporary social meaning and values. It is a process or a performance that utilises the past, certain material objects, places or intangible traditions, around which individuals, communities and nations decide not only what is to be remembered and what forgotten, but also how those memories are used to understand and negotiate the present. In short, heritage is actually not all about the past nor conserving things untouched and unchanged, rather it is ultimately about negotiating historical and cultural *change*. The implications of this are that heritage, potentially, can provide a forum or focus for democratic debate and negotiation about cultural, social and political change.

Critical and self-conscious engagement with heritage does not necessarily lead to cultural and social stasis, but whatever the outcome of heritage negotiations, it is important to note that heritage practices will intersect with the politics of recognition. In whatever ways heritage is used to define identity it will have implications for struggles over how communities and other interests are or are not recognised. Recognition has been identified as a new form of political conflict (Fraser 1995, 2000), a form in which heritage becomes a recognisable resource of power as identity becomes a plank in such struggles. Identifying this interplay and the consequences heritage thus has will only advance our abilities to critically and consciously use heritage as a tool for negotiating cultural values and meanings. It may be, as Sayer (2007) warns, that in terms of working class communities self-recognition is more important than broader 'recognition' as framed by Fraser and others. However, as Castleford, in the face of de-industrialisation, loss of union power and seemingly increasing Labour Party disinterest in its traditional grass roots, engages with new forms of community and political representation, heritage has been taken up to provide the resources for self-recognition from which to mount new ways of 'doing' politics and securing social and economic justice.

Acknowledgements

This study was funded by a British Academy grant (SG-46739). The authors would like to thank all those who allowed us to interview them for this study and the members of the Castleford Heritage Trust who facilitated this study and welcomed us to Castleford.

Notes

1 The words 'don't mourn organise' are reputed to have been written by the Swedish-American activist and singer Joe Hill just prior to his execution in 1915 for murder. He is popularly believed to have been 'framed' for this murder.
2 Interviews are referenced anonymously by the abbreviation 'Cas' followed by a field number and the year date of the interview.
3 The Castleford Heritage Trust, originally the Castleford Heritage Group, maintain a drop-in centre and gallery in Sager Street, Castleford, and have been agitating for heritage issues in Castleford since 1999. They maintain a website at: http://www.castlefordheritagetrust.org.uk/
4 For more information about the Castleford Community Learning Centre see http://cclc.co.uk/about.html
5 'Cas' is the diminutive and affectionate term for Castleford.

References

Barthel, D. (1996) *Historic Preservation: Collective Memory and Historical Identity*, New Jersey: Rutgers University Press.
Brett, D. (1996) *The Construction of Heritage*, Cork: Cork University Press.
Brower, B. C. (1999) 'The Preserving Machine: The "New" museum and working through trauma – *the Musée Memorial pour la Paix of Caen*', *History and Memory*, 11 (1): 77–103.
Bruno, R. (1999) *Steelworker Alley: How Class Works in Youngstown*, Ithaca: Cornell University Press.
Byrne, D. (1991) 'Western hegemony in archaeological heritage management', *History and Anthropology*, 5:269–76.
Carnegie, E. (2006) ' "It wasn't all bad": representations of working class cultures within social history museums and their impacts on audiences', *Museum and Society*, 4 (2): 69–83.
Cleere, H. (2001) 'The uneasy bedfellows: universality and cultural heritage', in R. Layton, P. G. Stone and J. Thomas (eds) *Destruction and Conservation of Cultural Property*, London: Routledge.

Crang, M. (2001) *Cultural Geography*, London: Routledge.
Debary, O. (2004) 'Deindustrialisation and museumification: From exhibited memory to forgotten history', *Annals of the American Academy of Political and Social Science*, 595 (1): 122–33.
Disney, R., Gosling, A., Machin, S. and McCrae, J. (1998) *The Dynamics of Union membership in Britain: A Study Using the Family and Working Lives Survey*, Department of Trade and Industry. Online. Available HTTP: <http://www.berr.gov.uk/files/file11634.pdf> (accessed 16 October 2010).
Drake, A. (2008) 'The use of a community heritage in pursuit of social inclusion: A case study of Castleford, West Yorkshire'. Unpublished MA dissertation, University of York, UK.
Fairclough, N. (1992) *Discourse and Social Change*, Polity Press, Cambridge.
——(2001) 'The discourse of New Labour: Critical Discourse Analysis', in M. Wetherell, S. Taylor and S. J. Yates (eds) *Discourse as Data: A Guide for Analysis*, London: Sage.
Foote, K. E. (1997) *Shadowed Ground: America's Landscapes of Violence and Tragedy*, Austin: University of Texas Press.
Fraser, N. (1995) 'From redistribution to recognition? Dilemmas of justice in a "post-socialist" age', *New Left Review* 212:68–93.
——(2000) 'Rethinking recognition', *New Left Review*, 3 (May/June), 107–20.
——(2001) 'Recognition without ethics?' *Theory, Culture and Society*, 18 (2–3), 21–42.
Hayden, D. (1997) *The Power of Place*, Cambridge, Mass.: The MIT Press.
Hewison, R. (1981) *In Anger: British Culture and the Cold War, 1945–60'*, New York: Oxford University Press.
——(1987) *The Heritage Industry: Britain in a Climate of Decline*, London: Methuen.
——(2009) 'The heritage sector and social class: past events and present performance', unpublished conference paper, Missing Out Conference, English Heritage, London, March.
Hutton, G. (2005) *Coal not Dole: Memories of the 1984/85 Miners' Strike*, Catrine: Stenlake Publishing.
Irving T. and Taksa L. (2002) *Places, Protests and Memorabilia, the Labour Heritage Register of New South Wales*, Industrial Relations Research Centre, University of New South Wales.
Kymlicka, W. and Norman, W. (2000) 'Citizenship in culturally diverse societies: Issues, contexts, concepts', in W. Kymlicka and W. Norman (eds) *Citizenship in Diverse Societies*, Oxford University Press.
Labadi, S. (2007) 'Representations of the nation and cultural diversity in discourses on World Heritage', *Journal of Social Archaeology*, 7(2): 147–70.
Linkon, S. L. and Russo, J. (2002) *Steeltown U.S.A.: Work and memory in Youngstown*, Lawrence: University of Press of Kansas.
Logan, W. and Reeves, K. (2009) *Places of Pain and Shame: Dealing with 'Difficult' Heritage*, London: Routledge.
Lowenthal, D. (1985) *The Past is a Foreign Country*, Cambridge: Cambridge University Press.
——(1998) *The heritage crusade and the spoils of history*, 2nd edn. Cambridge: Cambridge University Press.
——(2006) 'Stewarding the future', *Norwegian Journal of Geography*, 60 (1): 15–23.
Lovell, T. (ed.) (2007) *(Mis)recognition, Social Inequality and Social Justice Nancy Fraser and Pierre Bourdieu*, London: Routledge.
McCrone, D., Morris, A. and Kiely, R. (1995) *Scotland – The Brand: The Making of Scottish Heritage*, Edinburgh: Edinburgh University Press.
Meskell, L. (2002) 'The intersections of identity and politics in archaeology', *Annual Review of Anthropology*, 31: 279–301.
Milne, S. (2004) *The Enemy Within: Thatcher's Secret War Against the Miners*, London: Verso.

Nadel-Klein, J. (2003) *Fishing for Heritage: Modernity and Loss Along the Scottish Coast*, Oxford: Berg.

Oliver, B. and Reeves, A. (2003) 'Crossing disciplinary boundaries: Labour history and museum studies', *Labour History*. Online. Available HTTP: <http:www.historycooperative.org/journals/lab/85/oliver.html> (accessed 1 August 2005).

ONS (Office for National Statistics) (2007) *Union Membership: Union Density Down Slightly in 2006*. Online. Available HTTP: <http://www.statistics.gov.uk/CCI/nugget.asp?ID=4&Pos=&ColRank=1&Rank=74> (accessed 16 October 2010).

Pickering, P. A. and Tyrrell, A. (eds) (2004) *Contested Sites: Commemoration, Memorial and Popular Politics in Nineteenth-Century Britain*, London: Ashgate.

Richards, A. J. (1997) *Miners on Strike: Class Solidarity and Division in Britain*, London: Berg.

Robertson, I. J. M. (2008) 'Heritage from below: Class, social protest and resistance', in B. Graham and P. Howard (eds) *Heritage and Identity*, Aldershot: Ashgate.

Samuel, R. (1994) *Theatres of Memory. Volume 1: Past and Present in Contemporary Culture*, London: Verso.

Sayer, A. (2005) *The Moral Significance of Class*, Cambridge: Cambridge University Press.

——(2007) 'Class, moral worth and recognition', in T. Lovell (ed.) *(Mis)recognition, Social Inequality and Social Justice Nancy Fraser and Pierre Bourdieu,* London: Routledge.

Shaw, M. and Mundy, M. (2005) 'Complexities of class and gender relations: recollections of women active in the 1984–85 miners' strike', *Capital and Class*, 87(1): 151–76.

Stenning, A. (2005) 'Re-placing work: economic transformations and the shape of a community in post-socialist Poland', *Work, Employment and Society,* 19(2): 235–59.

Stephenson, C. and Wray, D. (2005) 'Emotional regeneration through community action in post-industrial mining communities: The New Herrington Minder's Banner Partnership', *Capital and Class,* 87(1): 175–99.

Strangleman, T. (1999) 'The nostalgia of organisations and the organisation of nostalgia: Past and present in the contemporary railway industry', *Sociology,* 33 (4): 725–46.

——(2001) 'Network, place and identities in post-industrial mining communities', *International Journal of Urban and Regional Research*, 25(2): 253–67.

——(2005) 'Class memory: Autobiography and the art of forgetting', in J. Russo and S. L. Linkon (eds) *New Working-class Studies,* Ithaca: Cornell University Press.

——(2010) 'Food, drink and the cultures of work: consumption in the life and death of an English factory', *Food, Culture and Society: An International Journal of Multidisciplinary Research,* 13(2): 257–78.

Smith, L. (2006) *Uses of Heritage*, London: Routledge.

——(2007) 'Empty Gestures? Heritage and the Politics of Recognition', in H. Silberman and D.R. Fairchild (eds) *Cultural Heritage and Human Rights*, New York: Springer.

——(2010) ' "Man's inhumanity to man" and other platitudes of avoidance and misrecognition: an analysis of visitor responses to exhibitions marking the 1807 bicentenary', *Museum and Society*, 8(3): 193–214.

Smith, L. and Waterton, E. (2009) *Heritage, Communities and Archaeology*, London: Duckworth.

——(2011, in press) 'Constrained by common sense: the Authorized Heritage Discourse in contemporary debates', in J. Carman, R. Skeats and C. McDavid (eds) *The Oxford Handbook of Public Archaeology*. Oxford University Press.

Taksa, L. (2009) 'Labor history and public history in Australia: Allies or uneasy bedfellows', *International Labor and Working class History,* 76: 82–104.

Tunbridge, J.E. and Ashworth, G. (1996) *Dissonant Heritage: The Management of the Past as a Resource in Conflict*, Chichester: Wiley.

Walsh, K. (1992) *The Representation of the Past: Museums and Heritage in the Post-Modern World*, London: Routledge.

Waterton, E. (2010) *Politics, Policy and the Discourses of Heritage in Britain*, Basingstoke: Palgrave Macmillan.

Wedgwood, T. (2009) 'History in Two Dimensions or Three? Working Class Responses to History', *International Journal of Heritage Studies,* 15(4): 277–97.

Wilders, D. G. (1995) *History of Castleford*, Castleford: Briton Press.

——(2003) *Hartleys: Brick by Brick, Pot by Pot*, Castleford: Castleford Press.

Williams, G. (2009) *Shafted! The Media, the Miners' Strike and the Aftermath*, London: Campaign for Press and Broadcasting Freedom.

Wright, P. (1985) *On Living in an Old Country*, London: Verso.

——(1991) *A Journey Through Ruins – The Last Days of London*, Hutchinson Radius.

Chapter 7

Images, icons and artefacts
Maintaining an industrial culture in
a post-industrial environment

David Wray

> The reality of community lies in its members perceptions of the vitality of its culture. People construct community symbolically, making it a resource and a repository of meaning, and a referent of their identity.
>
> (Cohen 1985:118)

Following the failure of the 1984–85 British miners' strike, and subsequent closure of the remaining mines in Co. Durham (in the North East of England), the mining communities of what was once the largest coalfield in the world were left without the industry that had created and defined them. As well as producing the coal that fuelled British industry for centuries, those mines also produced a clearly defined and socially embedded industrial culture, a culture created within the intersections of community, occupation and trade union; and it is one that has survived beyond the industry itself into the now post-industrial reality of the twenty-first century. While formal representations of that industry, and the heritage it left behind, can still be seen in museums across the region, particularly at the Beamish Open Air Museum, the artefacts, exhibitions and displays are primarily representations of how others interpret the residual fabric of that industry and culture.

For one group of community-based activists in Co. Durham, the New Herrington Miners Banner Partnership, (hereafter the Partnership) this type of historical and cultural representation is neither owned nor presented by miners, and is therefore divorced from what they see as their own cultural identity. In an attempt to present *their* understandings of *their* cultural heritage, they have embarked upon a series of projects that culminated in the creation of their own museum, located within their own community, and made freely available to all. Within the museum, physical and representational artefacts portray their understandings of the reality within which mining life in Co. Durham was grounded. Images of mines; of miners; and of mining hang alongside iconic trade union banners; banners that proudly state within their imagery the class identities and allegiances of those that carried them. All of these are surrounded by artefacts, both industrial and social, that collectively articulate an industry and a culture. The museum, located in a large space provided for them in the community by the YMCA, has been self-funded by the Partnership, and is their attempt to define themselves within the context of their own history, and to provide a resource available to their community, particularly the local schools.

I will critically locate the efforts and aspirations of the Partnership within the contexts of their community, and in doing so will define the term 'community' as an amalgam of place; occupation; class; and culture; and not simply a geographically specific area of living space. The data on which the chapter is based comes from focus group discussions, individual interviews, observation of Partnership meetings, and general discussions with Partnership members, as well as participant observation of school and community group presentations.

Culture and class in mining communities

When we use the term 'community', care must be taken, as it is a complex and contestable concept. In a criticism of some academic approaches to the term (including his own), McCulloch (2002) identifies the need for definitional clarity arguing against the indiscriminate use of the term, and warns that 'community' often appears to be treated as 'a quality relationship rather than being a type of social structure which can take a number of distinct forms' (2002: 15). In other words, to fully understand the complexities of any community, we must first understand the social, economic and political forces that were contingent on its formation. In terms of the mining communities of Co. Durham, no definition can be made without an understanding of the relationship between the communities and the industry that brought them into existence. It should also be noted that mining communities cannot be seen simply as homogeneous social organisations related to a specific industry, as each has its own unique identity (Williamson 1982; Beynon and Austrin 1994; Gilbert 1995). Nevertheless, just as human beings, mining communities are of the same genus, and are clearly recognisable through a common genetic code.

Found spatially organised across the coal measures, mining communities were initially what Williamson (1982: 62) describes as 'constructed communities'; little more than work camps constructed to house the workers and their families, who were brought in to meet the needs of the mine. As they developed, the social relations within both the community and the mine shaped and moulded the community into a 'rich mosaic of subjective meanings which people attach to the place itself, and to the social relationships of which they are a part' (Williamson 1982: 6).

The social relationships in mining communities are therefore unique, standing their inhabitants apart from the general population in terms of a cultural identity forged by the nature of the industry. Studies of mining communities, and there have been too many to recount here, all identify a culture that is unique and intrinsically different from other forms of social organisation (see for instance, Dennis *et al.* 1976; Douglas 1974; Warwick and Littlejohn 1992). Perhaps Bulmer, in his attempt to define a stereotypical mining community, best captures the forces and influences that shape them:

> Physical isolation, economic predominance of mining, dangerous work, social insularity arising from occupational homogeneity and isolation, communal leisure activities, rigid division of labour between the sexes, economic and political conflict between mine owner and miner, and the communal character of social relationships.
>
> (Bulmer 1976: 76)

Social interactions obviously existed within the community but, in mining communities, they also existed within the mine itself. The significance of this is that miners, living in isolated occupational communities, by necessity interacted with the same people in all aspects of their lives, both socially and professionally. They worked together, played together and lived together, to the point that some of the more isolated communities could be described as closed communities. Salaman (1975: 231) describes the social relationships in mining communities as 'preferential associations' where friendships inside and outside the mines enhanced social solidarity and occupational identity.

The social relations of labour in the mine were set and controlled by the miners themselves, as tasks and responsibilities were organised around autonomous work groups, subject to no external authority other than the general requirements of hours of work; discipline and health and safety legislation. This form of work organisation created social relations of labour within the mine that were then transferred to the wider community. The leadership of these work groups, informally selected from within the workforce, had an authority that extended well beyond the confines of the mine (Trist and Bamforth 1951; Herbst 1962; Allsop and Wray 2002). These men, because of their occupational leadership, became individuals with significant influence within their respective communities.

These unique social relations of labour also impacted upon the development and organisation of the trade union. The occupational leaders underground, because of their status within the workforce, became the nucleus of resistance to the mine owners, and they built and shaped the Durham Miners Association (DMA), a constituent part of the National Union of Mineworkers (NUM). The DMA was conceived within the mining communities of Co. Durham, maturing and developing alongside those communities to the extent that each is reflected in the other, and neither can be fully understood individually (Williamson 1982; Beynon and Austrin 1994; Stephenson and Wray 2009). Williamson best captures this relationship when he states that 'Trade unionism for miners was not something removed from their daily experiences and organized by strangers: it was a major part of that experience' (1982: 96).

Each mine/community had its own 'Lodge', the term used within the DMA to describe the organisation of the union at a colliery level, that was, at the same time, in and of the community. The extent of this symbiotic relationship impacted on all aspects of life, creating strong occupational and cultural identities. Mining communities have been described as an amalgam of family, community, Chapel and Co-operative store (Ackers 1996), with the union at the heart of all (Beynon and Austrin 1994). There in times of need, either industrial or social, the DMA always provided a constant and pervasive presence. These social and industrial relations, developed over succeeding generations, created traditions, attitudes and beliefs that together created an institution that both serviced, and in many ways controlled, those communities (Douglas 1974; Allsop and Wray 2002).

In developing the social and industrial forces that shaped the individuals living and working in mining communities, we must also consider class. Williamson, in offering us what is perhaps the most insightful view of class in mining communities, argues that class is a social relationship rather than a category in that class is something which is experienced, something that brings a 'consciousness of belonging ... to the street, the village and the pit' (1982: 7). Linking class to biography, he argues that class cannot be separated from the 'self', as class is a set of socially sanctioned criteria for 'recognizing inferiority and superiority' (1982: 8) which shape the individuals' feelings of self-worth. The consequences for those identified as inferior he describes as 'the subtle injuries of class' (1982: 10), and in response to this that he calls the 'injuries of inferiority' (1982: 9), he argues that miners built their own standards by which individuals should be judged, standards that no outsider could influence. These he describes as 'a reputation in work, in the home and in their dealings with neighbours' (1982: 8).

Dennis *et al.* (1976: 33) also identify concrete, rather than abstract standards miners used to classify themselves: 'in the pride of being a worker, and in solidarity to other workers'. This statement is a correct assumption, but one that could have been more clearly defined, in that miners primarily classify themselves in the pride of being a miner and in solidarity with other miners.[1] This self-classification has been recognised elsewhere as the creation of social (rather than class) consciousness that created a situation where those outside the community were seen as different from those within (Lockwood 1975; Salaman 1975; Richards 1996). The work of miners takes place out of sight of the rest of society; they belong to a hidden world known and understood only by themselves, and the geographical isolation of their communities reinforced this difference. Here we are talking about identity rather than class, and if miners saw themselves as different from outsiders, there is ample evidence that they themselves have historically been seen as different by outsiders looking in. When, during the miners' strike of 1984–85,

Margaret Thatcher described the miners as the 'enemy within' she was simply reiterating the long established impression of 'otherness', a view common within the literature on miners and mining communities (Reese 1985; Gilbert 1995; Ackers 1996). This otherness was perhaps best summed up in 1840 in a letter by a mine manager who described his workforce as 'this peculiar race of pitmen' whose 'numbers can only be kept up through breading' (Beynon and Austrin 1994: 27). This otherness was maintained, if not strengthened, by the harsh realities of life and work in the coalfields, and was undoubtedly strengthened by the experiences of those communities during the year long strike of 1984–85, and by the consequences of defeat.

The last word on the subject of identity should be left to Williamson:

> Through their unions and co-operative societies they built their own institutions. Through family and kinship they built defensive walls against chance and circumstance, constructing a way of life that was theirs.
> (Williamson 1982: 6)

Industrial closure and the inevitable redundancy, both human and spatial, have broken down those walls, threatening all the old certainties underpinning mining communities. The response, led by small groups of activists in many of the mining communities of Co. Durham, has seen an upsurge of interest in all aspects of mining heritage, allied to a determination that this unique culture will not pass into history unrecognised. The extent of this determination is exemplified by the work of the New Herrington Miners Banner Partnership.

Images, icons and artefacts

In order to fully understand the aims and ambitions of the individuals involved in the Partnership, it is important to understand the social and cultural imperatives that brought the group into existence. It is here that we first encounter iconography and imagery, and the importance of these cannot be overstated. Annually, on the second Saturday in July the DMA holds the Durham Miners Gala, a huge event that continues to draw crowds of over 70,000 people to Durham city, despite the fact that the last mine in Co. Durham closed in 1993. At the Gala, each mining community carries a huge Banner, the physical representation of the community and Lodge, through the streets of the city to the area where the Gala is held. For a more comprehensive understanding of the importance of these Banners to the communities they represent and the imagery carried on them, see Emery (1998) and Wray (2009).

Each Lodge Banner identifies the mine and community it represents and, through the imagery on both the front and back, can be seen the history, the hopes and the aspirations of all the generations who have followed it into the Gala since 1872. That this annual event continues 18 years after the coalfield ceased to exist is visible and graphic evidence of its importance as the last remaining link to the complex matrix of influences that defined the lives of all who were connected to the industry: occupation, class, community and trade union.

These Banners have always had an important iconic place in the cultural and occupational identity of the communities they represent, and since the bitter year-long strike of 1984–85 (a strike to protect jobs and communities), that importance has increased significantly. During that year, and particularly at the end of the dispute when miners marched back to work carrying them in an act of defiance to the State, those Banners took the form of battle standards. I have previously discussed the cultural importance of the Banners, and argue that they may be more important today than they were when the mines were open, in that they possess the collective memories of the now post-industrial communities they represent (Wray 2009).

For the Partnership, the importance of their Banner can be seen through the more recent history of their community. The mine that brought New Herrington into existence closed on the last day of 1985, one of a group of mines in Co. Durham in the first tranche identified for closure following the defeat of the 1984–85 strike. In common with most post-industrial mining communities, the new reality for New Herrington was a slow decline into long-term unemployment, social decay and all the concomitant problems associated with poverty (Coalfield Taskforce 1998; Stephenson and Wray 2005, Waddington 2004; Waddington *et al.* 2001). The following year the community decided, despite the closure of their mine, to carry the Lodge Banner into the Gala, more as an act of defiance to the closure than a simple adherence to tradition. However, when the Banner was unfurled in preparation it was damaged by the wind to the point where it could never be carried again. The relationship between Banner and community was graphically highlighted when one of those present stated that: 'We knew that the banner would never go back into Durham again, and we realized then that the village had died' (Pat: Partnership Treasurer). This may seem to be a dramatic, even melodramatic, statement but it is clearly indicative of the iconic nature of these Banners for the communities they represent. In their study of New Herrington, Stephenson and Wray (2005: 180) conclude that the Banner was the 'representational heart of the community' and, for the people who went on to form the partnership, its loss represented the end of their emotional attachment to 'place'; to occupation; to culture; and to tradition. All had now passed into history.

Having gone through what can only be described as period of mourning, the Partnership was formed in 1999, around a nucleus of local activists including the last Lodge Official at the mine. The goal of the Partnership was to re-establish the old collective identity lost following the closure of the mine, around which a new sense of community could coalesce.

Setting themselves a five-year plan their first goal was to raise the funds to purchase a replica Banner,[2] a goal achieved within two years, with the new Banner carried into the Gala of 2001. While the possession of a Banner able to be carried into the Gala was important, it was also recognised by the members of the Partnership that with the end of the industry, the reasons for carrying it had changed. For them the Banner was now a physical representation of a unique way of life that had been destroyed. It was carried now in a celebration of, and commitment to, the maintenance of a social order and occupational identity that underpinned all that they were. It was no less than a defiant and iconic emblem upon which their lives and the life of their community were represented. As one partnership member put it:

> What is important for people to understand is that the Banner is representative of a way of life that goes back centuries, rather than a battle standard from a 20 year old industrial dispute. Part of what we do is about letting Thatcher and her like know we are still here. They closed the pits and took the jobs, but every time we take that Banner out, we are saying to them we're still here, and we are still fighting for our communities.
>
> (Bob: Partnership committee member)

These efforts undertaken by the Partnership have led the way to more widespread attempts to maintain a tradition and a cultural identity in communities across the Co. Durham coalfield, with replica Banners now being commissioned for communities whose mines closed generations ago. Each year increasing numbers of Banners are carried at the Gala to the extent that at the 2009 Gala, more than 70 were carried through the streets of Durham, more than had been carried in any year since the 1960s, when the Durham coalfield had been the largest in the UK (see Figure 7.1). The police estimate that more than 100,000 people had also attended the Gala that day. The importance of these Banners to the community groups that have organised around them cannot be overstated. As I have argued elsewhere (Wray 2009), it is as if the Banners have gone through some kind of anthropomorphic process assuming an individual identity that possesses all the collective memories of the community it represents.

Within three more years, the Partnership had raised the funds to create a memorial garden on the former site of New Herrington colliery. Designed to commemorate the lives of all those who had worked at the mine, as well as all those miners from around the world who had lost their lives underground, this garden was opened in July 2004. The garden stands directly above one of the shafts of the colliery, and consists of a memorial stone flanked by the old pulley wheels that served that shaft, surrounded by black slate to represent the coal seams (Figure 7.2). A Miners Memorial Service is

Figure 7.1 The Durham Gala, 2009. Photo David Wray.

Figure 7.2 The memorial garden on the former site of New Herrington colliery. Photo David Wray.

now held annually, and in a speech at the inaugural Memorial Service a member of the Partnership described the garden as being:

> ... here to mark our passing, mining is not here anymore and before this Memorial Garden there was no evidence of the mine left above ground. We cannot forget why this place is here.
> (Pat: Partnership Treasurer)

In 2004, to mark the 20th Anniversary of the beginning of the 1984–85 strike, the Partnership, in a joint venture with a local University, raised the funding to commission a photographic exhibition depicting the changes to mining communities, and their inhabitants, in the 20 years since that strike. The imperative behind this project was primarily educational, and the Partnership developed plans to use the exhibition as a learning resource that could be taken to schools and community groups, an initiative welcomed by all of the local schools in the area. While the exhibition was to be the centrepiece of the learning material, the members of the Partnership began to accumulate artefacts associated with the mining industry and mining communities, artefacts that they describe as memorabilia. Beginning with their own memorabilia, accumulated over many years working in the industry and living in the community, the Partnership developed a small resource that, along with the Banner, was taken on visits to community groups and schools in and around New Herrington.

Just as New Herrington had led the way in the acquisition of new Banners to take into the Gala, so they have been an example for other groups, who have also visited schools. As a result of these activities there has been an upsurge in interest in all types of artefacts associated with mining. In New Herrington, local people responded to the educational programme by offering the Partnership items of their own. So much has been accumulated that storage space was required, and a local Church offered a room in the Church community centre and provided a large van to assist in the transportation of the displays.

These artefacts range from: the tools used in mining; books on how to mine and about mining; photographs of mines, mining and miners, as well as mining communities; items that reflect life in a mining household; and a myriad artefacts, both large and small, that are too many to list here. All were catalogued, repaired if necessary and prepared for exhibition. In order to do this further funding was required to provide display boards and tables, as well as the equipment to show moving and still images, all successfully raised by the Partnership. All presentations were undertaken by the Partnership, with the members of the group developing presentational skills as they progressed.

The emergence of groups providing oral and physical presentations in schools around the area coincided with an initiative launched by the Beamish

Open Air Museum aimed at providing a service that would be available to schools throughout the region. The aim was to provide ex-miners with the training and support needed to undertake such visits, who would then go to their own local schools to introduce mining to the pupils, and to answer any questions. These visits would be accompanied by a representative of the Museum, and followed up by funded visits to the comprehensive mining exhibits at the Museum itself. To initiate the programme, individuals from the communities were invited to the Museum, and Museum staff visited all the groups already involved in school visits.

When contacted, the Partnership were initially interested, and a delegation visited the mining exhibitions at the Museum, while Museum staff also examined the artefacts gathered by the Partnership. It became apparent to the members of the Partnership that some of what was presented and said during these exchanges was either inaccurate or demonstrated only partial understandings of the artefacts and the Partnership exhibits. This resulted in some concerns over the motivations of people who were perceived as outsiders, coming in to their community and trying to involve themselves in well-established programmes. There were also peripheral concerns that all of the funding for the project was to go to the Museum, with nothing allocated to the contributing community groups. After much discussion, the Partnership decided that they were better custodians of mining heritage and culture, and they would attempt to create their own museum. This discussion also coincided with the realization that it would be more efficient to bring school and community groups to them. Following a search for accommodation that would not be financially prohibitive, the Partnership were offered a large space at the community's YMCA, with the only cost the insurance needed to cover the exhibits.

Using the full space available, the Partnership were able to exhibit their whole collection of artefacts and memorabilia, with the new Banner and the damaged one it replaced, as the centrepiece of the exhibition. The exhibit itself is organised along thematic strands: the mine; the community; the home; miners; and with a special alcove given over to the photographic exhibition mentioned above. Formally opened by the General Secretary of the DMA, and the focus of a great deal of media interest, the museum is open three days per week from 4pm until 7pm for the general public, and will open during the day on request from schools and community groups. No charge is made, but donations are accepted. Since opening, the rate of donated and loaned artefacts has increased dramatically to the point that the Partnership has difficulty exhibiting it all. The museum also exhibits Banners from other groups, who have difficulty storing them when not in use.

While the activities and endeavours of the Partnership outlined above are, by any standards, significant achievements, to understand them properly we need to do so in the context of the motives of the individuals concerned.

116   Images, icons and artefacts

These are best summed up in the following statement by the Treasurer of the Partnership:

> We want a proper history written, a people's history; the truth. We have to keep it alive ourselves because no one else will tell the kids what our lives were about and how those lives have changed. We are talking about educating the kids, so that they will know what it was like to live in a mining community. The miners are a class in themselves, different from the rest of the working class. This is what we are trying tell our children, to give them some pride in who they are.

Conclusion

When we come to discuss the activities of the Partnership; their aims and ambitions, and particularly the creation of the museum and their attitudes to the historians from the Beamish Open Air Museum, we have to return to the issues of 'class' and 'otherness'. The statement from the Treasurer above clearly identifies both of these issues. They are concerned to ensure that *their* understanding of *their* history is correctly represented to the general public, and more importantly to the children of their own community, and they do not trust outsiders to do that. As Williamson (1982) points out in an earlier discussion above, miners established their own standards by which they should be judged, standards that no outsider could influence, and the Partnership take this further in that no outsider should attempt to represent those standards to their children, nor to the wider world. Such representations can, and should, only be made by miners themselves.

These insular attitudes may seem a little eccentric, even extreme, but they must be seen within the context of the history of their community since the 1984–85 strike. During that strike, when mining communities were exposed to the full weight of the State's power, miners and their families were portrayed as the enemy within. Always seen as different, they were now isolated from the general working class by that struggle, and because of the bitterness of the defeat, those involved were politicised to the point that this difference was now something to be celebrated.

With the loss of the mines, the inhabitants of mining communities were stripped of more than their jobs and livelihoods. They were stripped of their occupational identity, their identity as miners. The reality of unemployment is such that individuals are not unemployed miners, or any other occupation, they are simply unemployed. In such communities as these where occupational identity is so fundamental, that loss was also a threat to culture and tradition. Faced with being stripped of a culture and traditions created and defined by occupation, many in these communities have attempted to keep those traditions and that culture alive. Evidence of this can be seen in the efforts within post-industrial mining communities across Co. Durham in maintaining the annual Gala, and through an increased attachment to a now redundant occupational identity. At the forefront of these efforts have been the Partnership, determined that these traditions and this culture will not be lost with their passing.

In doing so they are attempting to maintain the memory of a way of life, however harsh, that provided them with stability, security and a certainty of 'self'. The importance of memory in these attempts to maintain a way of life has been recognised elsewhere. Writing about the now post-industrial community of Youngstown, in the USA, Linkon and Russo (2002: 249) conclude that: 'The recovery of a positive memory of itself is the first important step toward reconstructing a sense of place, belonging and ownership.' It is that sense of ownership that the Partnership has over their own past that refuses to allow professional historians to tell their story. They fully intend to do that for themselves.

The 'subtle injuries to class' suffered by these individuals have nothing in common with those caused by feelings of inferiority outlined by Williamson (1982) above. These individuals do not see themselves as inferior to anyone. They see themselves as guardians of a collective memory of occupation, trade union and community that they are determined to pass on to a generation that, in these social excluded communities, will never be able to achieve for themselves.

Notes

1 The author of this article worked as a miner for 24 years in the Co Durham coalfield.
2 A typical 8 ft by 6 ft Banner costs in the region of £7,000.

References

Ackers, P. (1996) 'Life after death: mining history without a coal industry', *Historical Studies in Industrial Relations*, March, 159–70.
Allsop, D. and Wray, D. (2002) 'The rise and fall of autonomous group working in the British coal mining industry', *Employment Studies Paper 41*: University of Hertfordshire Business School.
Beynon, H. and Austrin, T. (1994) *Masters and Servants*, London: Rivers Oram Press.
Bulmer, M. (1975) *Working Class Images of Society*, London: Routledge and Kegan Paul.
Coalfields Taskforce (1998) *Making a Difference: a new start for England's coalfield communities*, London: DETR.
Cohen, A. P. (1985) *The Symbolic Construction of Community*, Milton Keynes: Open University Press.
Dennis, N., Henriques, F. and Slaughter, C. (1976) *Coal is our Life: An analysis of a Yorkshire mining community*, Milton Keynes: Open University Press.
Douglas, D. (1974) 'Pit Life in Co. Durham', *History Workshop Pamphlet*, Oxford: Ruskin College.
Emery, N. (1998) *The Banners of the Durham Coalfield*, Sutton Publishing: Phoenix Mill.

Gilbert, D. 'Imagined Communities and Mining Communities', *Labour History Review*, Autumn 1995, 60(2): 47–55.

Herbst, P. G. (1962) *Autonomous Group Functioning*, London: Tavistock Publications.

Linkon, S. L. and Russo, J. (2002) *Steel Town USA: Work and Memory in Youngstown*, Lawrence: University of Kansas.

Lockwood, D. (1975) 'Sources of Variation in Working-Class Images of Society', in M. Bulmer (ed.) *Working Class Images of Society*, London: Routledge and Kegan Paul.

Mayo, M. (1997) 'Partnerships for regeneration and community development: some opportunities, challenges and constraints', *Critical Social Policy*, 17: 3–36.

McCulloch, A. (2000) 'Evaluations of a community regeneration project: case studies of a Cruddas Park development trust Newcastle upon Tyne', *Journal of Social Policy*, 29(3): 397–420.

Rees, G. (1985) 'Regional restructuring, class change and political action: preliminary comments on the 1984/5 miners strike in South Wales', *Environment and Planning D: Society and Space*, 4: 369–406.

Richards, A. J. (1996) *Miners on Strike*, Oxford: Berg.

Salaman, G. 'Occupations, community, and consciousness', in M. Bulmer (ed.) (1975) *Working Class Images of Society*, London: Routledge and Kegan Paul.

Stephenson, C. and Wray, D. (2005) 'Cultural regeneration in post-industrial mining communities: the New Herrington Miners Banner Partnership', *Capital and Class*, 87: 175–99.

Stephenson C. and Wray D. 'Now that the work is done: community Unionism in a post-industrial context', in J. McBride and I. Greenwood (eds) (2009) *Community Unionism: A comparative analysis of concepts and contexts,* Houndmills: Palgrave Macmillan.

Trist, E. L. and Bamforth, K.W. (1951) 'Some sociological and psychological consequences of the Longwall method of coal getting', *Human Relations*, 4.

Waddington, D., Critcher, C., Dicks, B. and Parry, D. (2001) *Out of the Ashes?: The social impact of industrial contraction and regeneration on Britain's mining communities*, Norwich: The Stationery Office.

Waddington D. (2004) *Developing Coalfield Communities: Breathing New Life into Worksop Vale*, International Specialised Book Service.

Warrick, D. and Littlejohn, G. (1992) *Coal, Capital and Culture: A sociological analysis of mining communities in West Yorkshire*, London: Routledge and Kegan Paul.

Williamson, Bill (1982) *Class, Culture and Community: A biographical study of social change in mining*, London: Routledge.

Wray, D. (2009) 'The Place of Imagery in the Transmission of Culture: The Banners of the Durham Coalfield', *International Labor and Working-Class History*, 76(1): 147–63.

Chapter 8

A working town empowered
Retelling textile history at Cooleemee, North Carolina

Tamasin Wedgwood

> I came to realise the inadequacy of our understanding not so much of the objective conditions of class but of its subjective experience. ...
>
> I find ... that the items I have been given and the stories I hear don't fit the labor history I teach or that most people know
>
> (Faue 2002)

Piedmont North Carolina is a still largely rural region dotted with numerous textile mills and associated mill villages. Today few mills are operational, and during the 1980s–90s, many mill villages were abandoned or demolished. Today, increasing numbers of mill villages are experiencing rebirth as both living communities and newly valued historic assets. Beginning in 1989, Cooleemee, North Carolina, was in the vanguard of this movement. The town rallied behind preservation projects and history teaching, reinvigorating community and reinventing identity. This mill town's dedication to history work formed a case study for original research (Wedgwood 2007) into how museums might rebuild community esteem after widespread industrial job losses. Cooleemee's significance lies in the way this effort is entirely community-led.

Since there was no textile story, or at least no worker-oriented textile story being told in museums or taught in schools, Cooleemeeans found themselves performing research and archaeology; teaching school history lessons; and writing articles for distribution to other textile towns. Learning that this was 'their story' to tell, filled townspeople with a new confidence in themselves and their future. They also discovered that first-hand experience could fill gaps in academic understanding, for while academic history forms tidy chapters lodged under defining headings life-experience is more complex.

The role of history in local and personal identity involves such subjective influences as memory, song and story. These tell us how people see themselves. They describe history experienced 'on the ground' rather than what Dicks described as the simplified, homogeneous 'view of our town from the hill' (1999: 352). 'Hilltop' observers gain objectivity with distance, but some complex information is unique to the 'view from the valley'. Faue (2002) found that having 'reached the limits' of theoretical understandings of class, academics need insight into 'subjective dimensions' that only working people themselves are equipped to explain. Taksa (2002) identified four of these dimensions. These are 'the private underpinnings of working class life' in family and community; the 'contingent nature of opportunities'; the 'malleability' and complexity of class identity, and the way workers use their labour heritage to 'engage with the past and draw meaning from it'. A fifth subjective dimension is motivation, for 'Oral sources tell us not just what people did, but what they wanted to do, what they believed they were doing and what they now think they did' (attributed to Portelli, quoted in Stille 2001).

As Faue observed: 'Because labor historians have so often assumed that the workers are already at the factory gate ... we don't often consider how they got there' (2002: 13). Such assumptions motivated research at Cooleemee where there was a 'huge piece missing' concerning the migration of rural people into millwork. Without understanding this, Cooleemeeans felt their story was incomplete, 'Our only other alternative ... the notion that simply crossing into a mill town and taking a mill job removed all consciousness of the past and of who they were' (Rumley, J. 2001: 2–3).

For the Carolinas, the period immediately after the American Civil War saw the rapid rise of sharecropping, a high birth rate and, with the advent of the railways, a move from a subsistence to a cash economy. Small farmers who had previously been self-sufficient moved towards dependence on a single cash crop – tobacco or cotton. Unfortunately, while merchants and manufacturers benefited, 'the results for farmers were not so clear' (Tullos 1989: 139). In fact, the result for many was a mass migration into factory work. Plummeting cotton prices and the control of tobacco by monopolies forced many off the land at a time when capital was accumulating in the hands of a small merchant class. These merchants were poised for investment in industry in a region devastated by war, yet blessed with cheap land, plenteous waterpower and increasingly large numbers of impoverished wage-seekers. Lured by waged work in a cash-dry economy, 150–200,000 Piedmont North Carolinians moved from farm to mill village between 1885 and 1905 (see Rumley, J. 2001: 63, 68). Although mill designs were borrowed from the Northern industry, this was an investment by Southern entrepreneurs in a Southern industry. Prime investors were the Duke family who built three fortunes after the Civil War: first in tobacco; then hydro-electric power and finally textile production.

In tandem with ideas of business and 'progress', came a genuine belief that industrialisation could result in moral and social improvements. The building of the mill at Cooleemee by Duke subsidiary, Erwin Mills, was described by the manager thus:

> That section of the state was a wild one – without schools and without religious influence ... I personally, had the village built, and it was

through me that the company has spent thousands of dollars in the promotion of education, moral uplift, and religion.

(W.A. Erwin, quoted in Rumley, J. 2001: 71)

Carolina architects modelled mill housing on rural designs on large plots[1] with additional commons and community hog lots. Enabling families to continue smallholding would attract and retain the 'right sort' of worker. Village amenities were designed to encourage that worker to become increasingly 'civilized' and educated, while retaining a sort of rural simplicity. The Piedmont's availability of 'Scotch-Irish' and German farmers was almost as attractive to entrepreneurs as were its natural watercourses. During the 1920s, 'when tenancy engulfed nearly 50% of Carolina farmers, and when thousands of families had already fled the land ... Duke power dangled these displaced and desperate folk before prospective manufacturers' (Tullos 1989: 170):

Greater than any resource of the Piedmont Carolinas is the character of its men and women ... 99% native born, Americans of old pioneer stock ... keen, teachable, and ambitious to work and get ahead. ... Small town life is an underlying cause of the stable, productive industrial conditions you find here. There are no slums, no breeding places of unrest. It makes for a wholesome point of view.

(Duke advertising reproduced in Tullos 1989: 170)

Mill-town residents, as much as would-be investors, believed the copy. For many sharecroppers the mill village was as utopian as Duke's advertising implied. Having struggled hand-to-mouth, these people were paid in cash, had subsidised housing, their children could attend school, refuse was collected, there were shops, social clubs, entertainments; ultimately even electric light and indoor plumbing.[2] At the same time, attempts at paternalistic control were not as successful as it might appear. Workers were perfectly capable of using the aspects of 'paternalism' that they liked, and scorning others – for example accepting the free medical care, but refusing to attend childcare classes and shunning social workers (see Hall *et al.* 1987: 138–39). While Cooleemee was a planned model community, there grew up on the outskirts, 'North Cooleemee' – home of bootleg taverns, non-conformist sects and African-Americans, who although excluded from millwork, serviced mill employees and performed manual labour in the mill yards. Wingerd suggests Erwin Mills could have clamped down on disreputable North Cooleemee, but:

turned a blind eye ... probably regarding the settlement as a relatively harmless safety-valve for worker discontent ... of equal importance was North Cooleemee's symbolic function in workers' lives. Whether or not individuals chose to participate in the unsanctioned activities it harbored, its very existence asserted their right to direct their lives as they pleased.

(Wingerd 1996: 886)

Visitors to Cooleemee today hear about Dora Cope. Aged fifteen around 1903, Dora was one of the first females trained in weaving, and when her promised skilled post did not materialise, her extended family walked out. Dora remembered Cooleemee's supervisor grumbling 'You Copes always get the cream of the jobs', and her brother's retort: 'We always do the cream of the work.' Dora explained family honour could not countenance the Company's broken promise and claimed Company agents in subsequent years repeatedly asked the family to return. Records confirm that by 1910, the Copes were back in Cooleemee, and Dora was a weaver (Rumley, J. 2001: 113–14). Stories like these shed new light on industrial relations and worker self-image.

Unfortunately, this idyllic heyday was to be short-lived. Between 1925 and the mid-1930s, increasing 'scientific management', combined with the Depression, plunged Carolina's textile industry into strikes and picket-line violence that would taint the industry with a sense of bitterness and betrayal that never entirely dissipated. Daughters of D.W. League, who lost his job because he refused to make weavers into 'slaves', remembered: 'It bothered him a great deal … this change that had come about. People were not given the consideration that they had been before' (Shirley Whitmire, in Tullos 1989: 190). Newspaper reports on the untimely death of League's politically active son described 'a "cotton mill boy" who sincerely and seriously thought of himself as a rising Moses to lead his people out of the wilderness' (Tullos 1989: 192).

A strike at Loray Mill, Gastonia, North Carolina, in 1929 became iconic in the public and academic imagination after sensational news that strikers accused of murdering Gastonia's Police Chief had escaped to the Soviet Union.[3] Meanwhile, the shooting at Gastonia of Ella Mae Wiggins, textile worker and songwriter, created a labour martyr. The twenty-nine-year-old mother of nine was shot on her way to a Union meeting, run off the road by a gang hired by the Mill (see Hall *et al.* 1987: 214–27). Her killers were never brought to justice, and her fate re-entered the public imagination in 1955 when this 'Ballad of Ella Mae Wiggins' appeared:

> … She never had had much schooling,
> Because she went to the mills so young,
> But the songs came like cool spring water
> To Ella Mae's mountain tongue. …
> . … The Company killed Ella's children,
> And they feared the power of her song,

So they shot Ella Mae on Gastonia's streets
And they never have paid for their wrong.
Gastonia's unions are growing,
The workers are stronger each day,
And the voice that sounds clearest among them all
Is the singing of young Ella Mae.[4]

Wiggins' own 'Mill Mother's Lament' entered the musical memory locally and nationally, recorded by Pete Seeger in 1956.

Although rural mills like Cooleemee often avoided the violence that scarred larger textile towns, sensational headlines and unsolved murders cast long shadows. Exploitation and violence became the dominant images of millwork in the collective psyche and the academic perception. Images of 'white slavery' tended to erase those images of idyllic model communities, superior modern conveniences and the exemplary thrifty workforce that had held the public imagination in earlier times.

The bitterness of the 1930s generation was repeated in the bitterness of the last textile generation who saw mills closing and jobs going overseas. By the 1990s, Carolina textile workers were tired of being 'victims'. It was time to remember that before the bloodshed of the 1920s and 1930s, and before the lay-offs and closures of the 1960s–90s, there had been something better – something of which a whole region had once been proud. Mill villagers began to think about how they wanted to be defined – was it as 'poor', 'oppressed', 'obsolete', or as hard workers, proud citizens; descendants of pioneers? And who should do the defining? Was that for academics to decide, or could people choose to define themselves?

The catalysts for change at Cooleemee were self-taught historians Jim and Lynn Rumley. From their example grew extensive practical preservation, and serious lay research. Raised on ideas of class conflict, active in left-wing causes since the 1960s, seeing a 1938 film of Cooleemee shook their assumptions about working class experience. Providing the impetus to question 'official' history, and interview Cooleemeeans, this 'bootleg' copy of an H. Lee Waters film[5] held images of well-fed, well-dressed, relaxed and cheerful workers in an industry that according to accepted history, was bitter, 'exploitative' and emerging from a national depression. It contrasted sharply with iconic images of child labour in Carolinian mills captured by Lewis Hind 30 years earlier. Seeing the surprises held within this film initiated over 20 years of painstaking study. The results, Lynn Rumley avers, compel the revision of academic interpretations of Southern textile history.

Watching this film today as a European, 1930s Cooleemeeans seem more prosperous than comparable Britons of that era. Certainly, these images compare favourably with 1930s photographs of Carolinian sharecroppers. Cooleemee's children of 1938 appear at least as well clothed as Cooleemee's children of 2008, and with an extensive, well-equipped playground including ping-pong tables, youth club and swimming pool, they were vastly better provided with recreational facilities. One elderly Cooleemeean's lament in interview that compared to his depression-era childhood, Cooleemee's 1990s children 'didn't have a thing in the world' suddenly made sense (CLM15, 2007).[6]

In 1969, three generations of millwork in single-industry Cooleemee ended. From then until 1990, decline, decay and depopulation set in. The aging population worried about increasing drug-use among the young, whom they felt had been short-changed, even 'disinherited' by progress. Asked how they had felt at this period, Cooleemeeans explained: 'Well, the mill was all we had', and 'it was as if the town had lost everything' (CLM12, 2007; CLM08, 2007).

Moving to Cooleemee in 1986, the Rumleys experienced the last decade of this physical, social and emotional decline. Like many residents of their adopted community, both had left school at fifteen. A hosiery knitter, Jim was a union organiser in the Carolinas, Georgia and Alabama during the 1960s–70s. A local leader of the National Caucus of Labor Committees, he was fired and blacklisted for union activity. During the same period, Lynn's similarly egalitarian social fervour led her into Civil Rights activism (see Michel 2004), and thus to the South, and ultimately into partnership with Jim. As political radicalism mellowed into conviction that people need a sense of historic identity the Rumleys entered a new phase. Enlisting town support behind the teaching of local history in school, they began an infectious process of volunteerism and civic engagement. From a town of just 800 mostly blue-collar workers, 21 attended the initial public meeting to found the Cooleemee Historical Association (CHA). Representatives of Cooleemee's African-American minority attended, as did the 'type of people who don't attend meetings' (Rumley, L. 2007c). CHA immediately developed a social mission, since all attendees shared concerns about housing, crime, drugs and lack of opportunities for youth. Today CHA has over 700 member households.

When CHA proposed a Textile Heritage Festival, offers of help, photographs and artefacts poured in. The resultant temporary 'museum' attracted queues throughout Heritage Day. Queues so long, that some locals actually 'broke in' after closing to see the displays (Rumley, L. 2007c; Wedgwood 2009). Coupled with an influx of over 4,000 visitors, many of them former residents, this left no doubt that Cooleemeeans needed a museum. Interviewees remembered the excitement that seized them, ensuring that before the second annual Festival they had opened Cooleemee Textile Heritage Center as a permanent museum. Townspeople have since opened a Mill House Family Museum, and have plans for several others – including Bootleggers' and Trades Union museums. Interviewees believed CHA galvanised existing civic groups, and inspired the formation of new ones, so that Cooleemee now 'gets-together' regularly in 'positive social gatherings of people of all ages and types ... I think this will continue and be an ongoing impetus ...

binding people together in all sorts of projects ... through bad times as well as celebrations' (CLM05, 2007).

Through CHA's schools program, 'Discovering our Heritage', children learn local history, beginning by researching their own families: 'if a child learns to appreciate ... their ancestors, it opens a window for them onto history ... an anchor, or point of reference' (Rumley L. 2007b). Progressing in successive Grades into town geography and economics, history is an expanding story. Children visit the museum to hear 'elders' recount their childhoods and are encouraged to ask grandparents to tell them about the past. Textile Heritage Week begins in the cemetery, with elders sitting holding enlarged photographs of their younger selves, while children gather to listen.[7] Storytelling teaches Cooleemee's children their origins, and how they can lay claim to the future: 'it's teaching them to volunteer; to be good citizens ... it makes them feel they've come a long way' (CLM12, 2007). Sandra Ferrell, Mill House Museum committee member, explained, 'The idea that a family can be rich in ways other than money is a concept that a lot of children don't have today ... Teaching those values is this museum's unique mission. I think it can have a big impact on our community' (*Cooleemee History Loom* 2006: 3).

Discovering that children were interested in their memories, collections and opinions surprised Cooleemee's elderly, and gave them hope that 'Cooleemee will carry on – the children will carry it on' (CLM12, 2007). Children discovered 'that this is their town ... they are the guardians of it for the future' and 'ordinary people have a real hand in history' (Rumley 2007a, 2007b). CHA, the schools programming, museums and the History/Archaeology Summer Camps held at 'Riverpark' are all places 'where lots of people with different talents can be utilized' (CLM08, 2007) – for example Riverpark's outdoor classrooms are visited by local hunters and fisherman. Through sharing their knowledge and memories with children, Cooleemee's adults develop a sense of pride:

> Cooleemee people are proud of being cotton mill people and believe it was a status worth praise and recognition (as opposed to the degrading 'linthead' stereotype). But their real pride comes from describing and passing on what they consider the community's main traditions ... values of family, neighborhood, work ethic, individual identity.
> (Rumley, L. 2009a)

From this success, CHA widened community renewal to the regional level through a Textile Heritage Initiative (THI) proposing the South-wide teaching of textile history. Through their newsletter, *The Mill Whistle*, publicity sent a clear message about from whose ranks THI expected fellow-preservationists to come: 'Remember the old mill whistle? ... the first blast was to wake you up ... The whistle blew again to summon millhands to work' (THI 2005: 3). CHA now has links with 150 mill-villages across the South East. Textile Heritage Week is now celebrated in North and South Carolina, Georgia and Alabama.

Lynn Rumley asked me to review *Saving Legacy Stories*, a self-help manual on oral history collecting co-written with folklorist Sarah Bryan. My research on small community museums' role in rebuilding community esteem (2007) was entitled: 'Your history matters'; Rumley and Bryan's manual ends: 'You are a part of history, and your efforts will make history.' As an academic 'view from the hill', mine discussed an issue; as the heart-felt living experience of townspeople themselves, theirs was more 'political' and empowering. The Cooleemee manual is remarkable for being written for other lay historians and communities. From the invitation of its opening sentence: 'Look at this photo', it approaches readers as equal partners in preservation: 'Consider this an informal guide. Take what you can from it' (Rumley and Bryan 2007: 6). Since working class efforts to preserve and record history are underrepresented in the literature, Cooleemeeans operated by trial and error. In distilling their experience into a useable tool, they hope to spare other communities the same struggle. Inspiring examples are given of lay groups achieving community revival through preservation. Encouraging towns and individuals to tell their own stories, the manual leaves readers with the confidence that we can all be oral history collectors.

The authors blend their practical advice with philosophical observations about the nature of history, including useful insights into how local histories can shed light on national events, and challenge accepted 'truths'. They explain that academics too are 'constructing a narrative', and encourage communities to take ownership of their story. Lay people are encouraged to educate themselves through research, but at the same time are reminded: 'Never fail to acknowledge your expertise, gained from your own firsthand witness ... Be confident that you too, are an expert' (2007: 50). Above all, Rumley and Bryan make history personal: 'If you're depending on the professionals to do this for you, we guarantee you will be saddened by your deference. If this legacy is to remain, it is up to you ... The questions you ask of your own history will shape the answers it will reveal' (2007: 6).

The guarantee of 'sadness' if communities rely on 'professionals' originates in bitterness over some of the encounters CHA has had with academics, and with the North Carolina Humanities Council. When authoring their own histories, communities sometimes meet rejection or condescension. A friend recounted his similar dismay at witnessing preservationists talking a local expert down – an insult aggravated because it occurred at an 'Open Day' presented as an opportunity for information exchange: '"Anorak" referred to "the authoritative book" ... The local man said quietly: "I know. I wrote that book." Still "Anorak" did not hear ... just kept right on talking. ... These guys wanted to tell, not listen' (GCW01, 2009). Taksa (2003) has vividly described the disservice to history when memories are collected, yet not used to inform exhibits that remain at odds with working people's experience.[8] As Portelli has written, to tell accurately 'requires the presence of someone who will listen' (2003: 15).

At Cooleemee, Jim Rumley listened carefully. He distilled local memories and extensive research into a book described by Fink, Professor of History at the University of Illinois, as an 'iconoclastic' interpretation that 'tilts at the windmills of academic wisdom' 'rather than a sentimental heirloom a serious attempt to authorize a ... version of the region's past' (2006). Ultimately, Fink was very negative about Rumley's research and conclusions, writing: 'The chasm in the worlds of historical studies between academic and local or "amateurish" publication is evident in the lack of any journal review of Rumley's work' (2006). However, this dismissive comment seems unfair. How does a self-educated ex-trades unionist from an unknown small town obtain academic 'peer' review – even without the negative connotations (in America) of his Marxist-Leninist past? Paul Escott, Reynolds Professor of History at Wake Forest, reviewed Rumley's book favourably (Escott, 2009). Additionally, the Rumleys believe Fink's published criticism of their work, rather than stimulating the discussion they hoped for, hardened the academic community against taking them seriously. They insist their research is rigorous:

> We have sought proofs and background. We have devoured what has been written by historians, sociologists, folklorists, novelists, essayists ... What they offer in books about us often argues with what we have discovered, and what we discover argues back, and then we argue with ourselves.
> (Rumley and Bryan 2007: 9–10).

Escott (2009) believes Jim's work to be based on impressive research, with 'intelligent and sophisticated analysis'. He found discussions of history amongst Cooleemeeans were at a level 'found in few graduate-school seminars' (Escott, 1992). While local history may be a microcosm of national events, it is equally likely to diverge from national and dominant historical narratives. Jim Rumley, blacklisted trades unionist, was raised by a stepfather with a bitter view of the textile industry, informed by personal experience of Depression, strikes and picket line violence. If a history of exploitation was to be found, one might reasonably expect Rumley to find it. Instead, he describes a negotiated balance of class power. Professor Gary Freeze described Rumley's contribution to this new perspective:

> Rumley has tapped into Rousseauian philosophy to describe a 'social contract' ... between owner and operative ... This was not a particularly paternalistic relationship ... nor was it the more explicitly exploitative mill society ... others have portrayed ... In this way, Rumley departs

from a scholarship that waits like a bridesmaid for the class-conflict approach to labor history work.

(Quoted in Rumley, J. 2001: ix)

Rumley does not gloss over the bitter class conflict of the 1920–30s. Of 1934's general textile strike he writes: 'unless this ... becomes the target of more local research, its full ... meaning will never be recorded. ... Whether one's ancestors were rebels, foes or neutrals in this revolt, it is a chapter no one can afford to skip' (Rumley, J. 2009: 12). However, Cooleemee's workers neither joined the 1934 strike, nor unionised until much later than either the national or regional pattern. 'Scientific management' and 'stretch-out' had not been introduced at Coolemee, and assurances that management would 'stick by' Cooleemeeans were understood to mean they never would be. It was the company 'breaking its word' (introducing time-management studies in 1937) that provoked unionisation. Prior to this, Cooleemeeans reported excellent industrial relations, including remarkable freedom to pursue agriculture, hunting and fishing on Company land. Some hands retained family smallholdings, rotating between mill and farm on a seasonal basis. This pattern of tending 'livestock ... and gardens as well as power looms', holds true across the South, although 'Cooleemee was exceptional in the scope of Erwin Mills' vast landholdings ... the degree to which the company made them available for workers' use', and the degree to which this allowed workers 'a sense of self-sufficiency and independence' (Wingerd 1996: 879–80).

During slack times, Cooleemee's mill warehoused fabrics to keep hands working, and 'distributed work', ensuring each family had some income. Through this benevolent expediency, management 'retained its trained workforce intact and loyal, ready for better times', while Cooleemee's workers were insulated from the Depression (Rumley L. 2009a,b). This relative advantage was verified by interview evidence – at Glencoe, North Carolina, the museum director (GLC01, 2007) described growing up as a farmer's daughter envying mill-village lifestyles. A West Virginian visitor to Glencoe concurred: 'At least they were paid in cash! Do you know how they paid us in the coal camps?' (GLC06, 2007). Hall *et al.* (1987) found that although interviewees might have negative memories of millwork, life in the mill village was universally remembered positively.

Experience is always relative and subjective: although Portelli (1991: 202–15) found shocking abuses in Kentucky mining camps, he found miners themselves considered their lifestyles good – compared to other camps or previous experience. Comparing American workers to Frederick Douglass, who believed his master 'kind' because he could compare him only to other slaveholders, Portelli identifies other uniquely American factors in workers' perceptions of their lot. American workers 'take it for granted that their country's standards can only be the best', and without an accepted politics of class-conflict, 'do not primarily think of themselves as an exploited class ... there is something personally demeaning – rather than collectively legitimizing – in appearing to have been exploited' (1991: 202; 213). For these reasons, American workers prefer to see history as a story of rugged independence, the overcoming of hardships and the making of individual choices.

The Rumleys allow that exploitation and poverty represent part of the 'truth' – but only part. By indicating that Cooleemee's history does not follow patterns described in academic texts, they do not declare accepted views invalid, merely that reality was more complex. At minimum, Cooleemee demonstrates that exceptions exist to generalised 'truths', but when Cooleemee reached out to other textile communities, similar patterns emerged. Across the South, the long-accepted image of a degraded, subjugated white workforce is being questioned. Even in the now notorious West Virginian coal camps, miners operated smallholdings, and took game from Company land. These country lifestyles supplemented miners' diets, provided enjoyment and made miners 'less willing to take the risks ... of forming a union, demanding recognition, and securing a contract' (Montrie 2007: 1–11, 28). This is the same complex and paradoxical pattern described at Cooleemee: providing commons both reinforced workers' dependence on the company, and gave them 'a realm of independence' (Montrie 2007: 9).

Portelli identified other paradoxes: increased productivity could be seen as exploitation, yet was often a source of pride for workers (1991: 138–42). Works sports teams or works bands concretised workplace 'team spirit'. While Hall *et al.* (1987: 137) suggest this heightened loyalty to the village and the boss, cut down on the time workers could spend 'loafing', and through having teams, rules and set times of play 'trained' workers for the regulated workplace, Portelli found playing for the Company team was perceived as 'over-time', and could be used by workers as a bargaining chip (1991: 151). By emphasising that they chose restrictive working conditions in exchange for some other benefit, workers are empowered. In 1934, Cooleemeeans *chose* not to strike in exchange for a promise that management would 'stick-by' them – a promise they *chose* to believe in, sugared by management providing a new baseball field (Rumley, J. 2001: 327–29). Perceiving historical experience as a series of choices workers made means workers were neither 'passive' nor subjugated. They directed their history, and could have made it take another route (Portelli 1991:113–14). Acknowledging both the complexity of historical 'truths', and their potential to empower, Watson (2007) suggests communities consciously present selective histories for self-assertion, and are fully aware of the complexities, contradictions and partial truths.

Cooleemee's oral history project met 'instant recognition that we could not record every ... story'; accepting that the process was selective, Cooleemeeans 'offered ... a community consensus as to who were the priority people'

(Rumley and Bryan 2007: 15). People have always chosen in which light to present themselves; which things to perpetuate, which to let be forgotten. The result at Cooleemee is a depiction of the town as 'one big family' – an image that, as Fink indicates, ignores African-Americans who lived outside this 'family'. Yet even Fink, a strong critic, observes the intelligent deliberation (rather than naive nostalgia) behind this: 'the heritage emphasis determinedly deflects the focus from class to culture, and from labour politics to identity politics' (2006). Cooleemee's memory is selective, but townspeople focused on the memories they felt most important to preserve. They continue to gather new stories that will eventually tell their community's collective experience. In Taksa's (2002) estimation, rather than being biased, 'the more recent work on community ... has produced a more nuanced understanding of working class experiences'.

Memories of the KKK in Cooleemee became contentious when some oral testimonies recalled Klansmen merely disciplining drunks and wife-beaters (Fink 2006). It is known that the Klan presented itself as a 'moral' organisation that would 'clean-up' a town, and deliver charity to the poor – so long as they were white Protestant poor (see Hesse 2001: 69). To our modern sensibilities, this is sinister. To a poor white protestant in the 1930s Cooleemee it might feel different. White Coleemeeans reported what they remembered, and this is at least honest. Jim's book suggests white and African-American Cooleemeeans united in outwitting Klan attempts to clamp down on North Cooleemee during prohibition (2001: 188–92). The unsettling evidence of that 1938 film shows African-American Cooleemeeans looking prosperous and elegantly dressed, and young African-American boys showing off to white children who watch with delighted applause. On the one hand this is the face of segregation, on the other, there seems genuine interaction and good humour between the two groups. Clearly black life experience in Cooleemee is as complex and stereotype defying as white, and needs further investigation. African-American testimonies from the region confirm that even for them, mill-villages provided a certain insulation from social ills: Cone Mills of Greensboro built a separate village for black operatives, who were thus: 'sort of isolated. ... We didn't know about the cruel things ... of segregation and Jim Crow in this community because we were not exposed to it until we went outside of it' (Franklin Richmond, quoted in Patterson 2009). An African-American interviewee who lived through segregation and integration, never remembered feeling afraid in Cooleemee, and attributed this lack of racial tension to white and black being on approximately the same economic level (CLM20, 2009).

The role of the Klan in Cooleemeean memory is disconcerting, yet we cannot simply reject memories that represent perspectives we prefer not to contemplate. Furthermore, white Southerners today may have learned to abhor racism; yet know that their own grandparents perhaps were Klan members – how does one reconcile that? Absolutely it is right to denounce the Klan. However, in order to overcome racism, society needs to understand the social, historical and experiential factors from which that racism formed. The voice of white Southerners is part of understanding that process of class, race and exclusion. We might disagree with white memories of the Klan at Cooleemee, yet should remember Portelli's comment on inaccurate community memories: 'if oral sources had given us "accurate" ... reconstructions of the death of Luigi Trastulli, we would know much less about it' (Portelli 1991: 26).

African-American history in Southern towns meets two significant difficulties: the preferred bias and just simple experience of the dominant white culture, and a lack of artefacts and documents giving the black point of view. However, Jim Rumley's book documents African-American history such as worker unrest at the proposed employment of a black weaver, or a 1934 African-American Cooleemeean demanding to know why the minimum wage did not apply to Cooleemee's black mill-hands (2001: 323, 345–47). Lynn Rumley is adamant:

> CHA members would NEVER have gone along with leaving out [African Americans] of Cooleemee. ... Given the photos and information that we have had the opportunity to receive, [we] not only acknowledge black Cooleemeeans' 'existence' but ensure their contributions ... are recognized. There were two cultural communities here, living side-by-side ... but not equal. When Genelle Watkins came to see the new Mill House Museum ... I asked her whether it portrayed lifestyles black families lived. She answered with a pretty absolute, 'yes'. She was proud to have her daughter see it.
>
> (Rumley 2008)

Today CLM20 is actively promoting the commemoration of black history at Cooleemee and her photographs of the segregated Rosenwald School are being scanned for the museum collection. In interview she was adamant that she has experienced no sense of racism or exclusion in CHA projects, and that when she looks around at other preservation projects across the region she thinks proudly: 'We started that!' (CLM20, 2009).

Conclusions

Cooleemee faces the difficult task of coming together to renew, redefine and celebrate a town that was once segregated. In selecting those aspects that unite a town in newfound 'community', locals are pursuing a social and psychological agenda. However, African-Americans and whites interviewed shared the same agenda: to accentuate the positive and move on, and to choose people from Cooleemee's past who might 'be an inspiration for a young person' (CLM20, 2009).

A survey by Rosenzweig and Thelen (1998) documented this use of the past to inspire. They also discovered that of the lowest US income group ($0–$14,999/annum), a large majority watched history programmes, 48 per cent visited historical sites, 40 per cent read history, and 21 per cent participated in 'groups devoted to studying, preserving, or presenting history' (1998: 242–46). Added to the high level of historical interest amongst lower income groups is the hugely democratising influence of the Internet. Communities and individuals today can build their own websites, post articles, and circulate their views to a worldwide audience. History is no longer the preserve of the intellectual, and many more 'versions' are being authorised. What matters, Nadel-Klein finds, is not whose version is 'true' but what each version tells us about the worldview and social position of the teller (2003: 109). High (2007: 14) notes that 'memory should not be seen as a "problem" ... to be "overcome", but rather as a unique resource'. As Portelli states: 'Historical work using oral sources is unfinished ... historical work excluding oral sources ... is incomplete' (1991: 55).

Rumley and Bryan make an analogy between history and a quilt. Each story is a scrap in the quilt. The view of the quilt, like the 'view from the hill', varies with the viewer: the pattern seen by the visiting collector differing from that seen by locals who recognise the fabrics, own the quilt, and can wrap it around themselves for comfort and remembrance. There is always selection, always voices yet to be heard, but rather than a problem, this is a limitless opportunity: patterns repeat, echo, clash and shift in an ever-widening spectrum of knowledge, memory, opinion and interpretation. 'Truth' is a continuum, rather than a specific entity – found not in any single scrap of the quilt, but in the resonances created between them. The title of CHA's *History Loom*, reminds us history is constructed here, not merely recorded.

In 1997, Governor James B. Hunt recognised the Rumleys for 'outstanding service to the State of North Carolina'. The North Carolina Society of Historians named Jim 'Historian of the Year' in 2002, and gave CHA awards for the *Loom*, for a documentary video and for 'outstanding involvement of elementary school-age children in learning and preserving history'. In 2004, CHA appeared in *National Geographic News* (Drye 2004), and received the Albert Ray Newsome Award for 'general excellence' from the Federation of North Carolina Historical Societies. Lynn Rumley ponders: ' ... think what this would have been like if we had had an infusion of money and professional advice ... coupled with the outstanding dedication of this community' (2007d).

The enormous pool of lay knowledge discovered by Rosenzweig and Thelen provoked them to issue this challenge: 'Why not increase collaboration between professional historians and popular history makers? ... bring together Civil War reenactors and Civil War historians? ... make use of the World Wide Web ... to create virtual meeting grounds for professionals and non-professionals?' (1998: 183–84). The reason for this meeting of minds is clear: each lacks skills or knowledge the other can provide. A free exchange will create a system of constant checks, balances and adjustments between accepted history and community memory, thus avoiding the greatest errors of both. Learning to listen rather than merely tell will enrich historical understanding.

Notes

1 In Cooleemee plots average 70'x150', see Rumley 2001: 72–73.
2 In Cooleemee free electric light was installed in worker housing in 1927; indoor plumbing in 1932 (Rumley, L. 2009b).
3 See Rumley, J. and Rumley, L. 2009:58.
4 'The Ballad of Ella Mae Wiggins' by Malvina Reynolds, copyright 1955 Schroder Music Company, renewed 1983.
5 Edited versions of four of H. Lee Waters' films of Cooleemee are now released on DVD (2007).
6 Interviewees are referenced anonymously by the abbreviation CLM (Cooleemee), GLC (Glencoe), or GCW (Glyn Ceiriog) followed by a field number and the year date of the interview.
7 'Learning from the Elders', Davie County Record, 4 October 2007; 'Keeping their Heritage Alive', *Salisbury Post*, 4 October 2007.
8 According to testimonies at Eveleigh Railway Workshops, most workers did not live in the 'typical' house displayed. They did not remember the rosy 'hearth and home' of the exhibit's title – one described his boarding house as 'a brothel', another as 'my little Black Hole of Calcutta' (Taksa 2003).

References

Cooleemee Historical Association (1992 video, 2007 DVD) *Good Times in Old Cooleemee – 1938–1942*, films by H. Lee Waters, Copyright CHA.
——(2006) *Cooleemee History Loom*, 63:3.
Dicks, A. (1999) 'The view of our town from the hill: communities on display as local heritage', *International Journal of Cultural Studies*, 2(3): 349–69.
Drye, W. (2004) 'In U.S. South, textile mills gone but not forgotten', *National Geographic News*, 19 October 2004.
Escott, P. (1992) 'Letter to funding agencies re "The History is People" proposal of the Cooleemee Historical Association', 29 January 1992, Cooleemee, North Carolina, Cooleemee Historical Association Archives.
——(2009) emails to author (10–11 November, 2009).
Faue, E. (2002) 'SYMPOSIUM: Retooling the Class Factory: United States labor history after Marx, Montgomery, and Postmodernism', *Labor History*, May 2002, 82.
Fink, L. (2006) 'When community comes home to roost: the Southern milltown as lost cause', *Journal of Social History*, Fall 2006.
Hall, J. D., Leloudis, J., Korstad, R., Murphy, M., Jones, L., and Daly, C. (1987) *Like a Family the Making of a Southern Cotton Mill World*, Chapel Hill and London: University of North Carolina Press.
Hesse, K. (2001) *Witness*, New York: Scholastic.

High, S. and Lewis, D. (2007) *Corporate Wasteland The Landscape and Memory of Deindustrialization*, Ithaca and London: Cornell University Press.

Michel, G. (2004) *Struggle for a Better South: The Student Organizing Committeee, 1964–1969*, New York: Palgrave Macmillan.

Montrie, C. (2007) 'Continuity in the Midst of Change: Work and Environment for West Virginia Mountaineers', *West Virginia History,* New Series, Spring 2007, 1(1): 1–22.

Nadel-Klein, J. (2003) *Fishing for Heritage, Modernity and Loss along the Scottish Coast*, Oxford: Berg.

Patterson, D. W. (2009) 'Cone Mills villages', *Greensboro News and Record*, 3 May 2009, Online. Available HTTP: <http://www.newsrecord.com/content/2009/05/03/article/cone_mills_villages_stir_fond_memories/>.

Portelli, A. (1991) *The Death of Luigi Trastulli and other stories: Form and Meaning in Oral History*, Albany: State University Press of New York.

Rosenzweig, R. and Thelen, D. (1998) *The Presence of the Past Popular Uses of History in American Life*, New York: Columbia University Press.

Rumley, J. (2001) *Cooleemee, The Life and Times of a Mill Town*, Cooleemee: Cooleemee Historical Association.

——(2009) 'The rising', *Bobbin and Shuttle,* 6 (2009): 12–15, 57.

Rumley, J. and Rumley, L. (2009) 'Loray', *Bobbin and Shuttle,* 6 (2009): 56–58.

Rumley, L. (2007) Interview by author, Textile Heritage Center, Cooleemee, North Carolina (21 April 2007).

——(2007a) 'Back from Cooleemee re-Research on community identity/ regeneration'. E-mail, (8 March 2007).

——(2007b) 'Answering your questions'. E-mail (27 March 2007).

——(2007c) 'Community embracing museum, museum embracing community'. E-mail (13 April 2007).

——(2007d) 'Back from Lynn re-your research paper'. E-mail (4 May 2007).

——(2008) 'The difficulties of interpreting an African American historical culture experience from the outside'. E-mail (22 March 2008).

——(2009a) 'Community pride'. E-mail (14 January 2009).

——(2009b) 'How the South's cotton mill people survived the Great Depression', *Bobbin and Shuttle,* 6 (2009): 6–7, 60–61.

Rumley, L. and Bryan, S. (2007) *Saving Legacy Stories of the Vanishing World of Southern Cotton Mill People*, Cooleemee: Cooleemee Historical Association.

Stille, A. (2001) 'Prospecting for truth amid the distortions of oral history', IDEAS March 10, 2001. Online. Available HTTP: <http://www.racematters.org/distortionoforalhistory.htm> (accessed 28 June 2009).

Taksa, L. (2002) 'Retooling the class factory, response 3: family, childhood and identities: working class history from a personalised perspective', *Labor History*, May 2002, 82: 127–34.

——(2003) 'Machines and Ghosts : politics, industrial heritage and the history of working life at the Eveleigh workshops', *Labor History,* 85 (November 2003).

Textile Heritage Initiative (2005) *The Mill Whistle*, August 2005, 1(1).

Tullos, A. (1989) *Habits of Industry White Culture and the Transformation of the Carolina Piedmont*, Chapel Hill and London: University of North Carolina Press.

Watson, S. (2007) 'History museums, community identities and a sense of place: Rewriting histories' in S. Knell, S. MacLeod, and S. Watson (eds) (2007) Museum Revolutions, London: Routledge.

Wedgwood T. (2007) 'Your history matters: museums building community identity after industrial decline', unpublished M.A. dissertation, University of Leicester.
——(2009) 'History in two dimensions or three? Working class responses to history', *International Journal of Heritage Studies,* July 2009, 15(4): 277–97.
Wingerd, M. (1996) 'Rethinking paternalism: power and parochialism in a Southern mill village', *The Journal of American History,* December 1996, 82(3): 872–902.

Chapter 9

The silencing of Blackball working class heritage, New Zealand

Paul Maunder

> This article is an act of storytelling. As Walter Benjamin required, the story-teller is a moral figure.
>
> (Benjamin 1978)

In New Zealand, the 1990s were the zenith (or nadir), of the practice of neo-liberal ideology. As a country, in a strange act of masochism, we imposed upon ourselves the extreme form of the market-based economy much in favour with the World Bank and the IMF. Using a blitzgreig approach, the Labour government of 1984 had, according to Jane Kesley:

> ... lifted exchange controls, deregulated the financial markets and floated the dollar. Price stability was made the Reserve Bank's sole objective. Foreign investment rules were relaxed, and state assets (notably telecommunications, forests and the Post Office Savings Bank) were sold to foreign companies. Domestic subsidies were withdrawn and domestic markets deregulated. Tariffs were reduced, and other trade protections removed. Internationally the Labour government pursued a vigorous free trade position.
>
> (Kesley 1999: 9–11)

When a National Party came to power in 1990, unions were in turn attacked, benefits were cut, more central and local government assets sold offshore, and public and social services contracted out. These changes were embodied in law through the Commerce Act (1986), the Investment Act (1986), the State-Owned Enterprises Act (1986), the State Sector Act (1988), the Public Finance Act (1989), the Reserve Bank Act (1989), the Employment Contracts Act (1991) and the Fiscal Responsibility Act (1994).

As an essential part of this revolution, an Employment Contracts Act (1991) was introduced to clear the labour market of the hindrances represented by traditional unionism. Accordingly, unions found themselves facing a drastic loss of membership and an extremely difficult organising landscape. Their statutory right to represent workers was removed, so that any agent could do so, and rights of access to workplaces were severely curtailed. Consequently, collective bargaining became difficult and as unions struggled to survive, a culture of competitive unionism arose. Many of the celebratory aspects of working class culture disappeared, including May Day events.

By the end of the 1990s, one of the few places in which May Day was celebrated was the small village of Blackball, on the West Coast of the South Island. Founded as a coal-mining community in the late nineteenth century, the village had a proud union tradition and, until the mine closed in 1964, the union ran the town, employed a doctor, organised the bus timetable and operated a picture theatre from the miners' hall. When I moved there in 2002, it was no longer a union town, but the pub had inherited two banners from the 1930s, sewn by wives of the miners during a particularly bitter dispute. The proprietor had pinned these on one wall of the bar. 'Solidarity Forever', read one; 'United We Stand, Divided We Fall', read the other.

They were a fragile inheritance I suppose, and gave the hotel an unusual ambience. The proprietor, as part of an annual calendar of events designed to entice outsiders to this remote location, had from the mid-1990s, held a May Day celebration each year. At first it was a simple soap-box event, but as unionists and cultural workers were attracted because of the vacuum elsewhere, singing and theatre were added, plus a symbolic march through town. A pilgrimage began to take place annually, with unionists, MPs and activists coming from far afield.

There was a historical logic behind this. In 1908, when it was a town centred on the coal mine, a famous strike took place in Blackball. Activists schooled in socialism and Industrial Workers of the World syndicalist ideas, had arrived to work in the mine after being blacklisted in other places (including Australia and the US). Peter Clayworth writes:

> The Wobblies were formed with the intention of carrying on the class struggle through the creation of one big industrial union of workers. The final goal was the destruction of capitalism and the abolition of the wage system. This was seen as leading to the creation of a co-operative commonwealth, where all production was for the benefit of all workers and the union would provide the basis for the organisation of society. The general consensus was that this would ultimately be achieved through the weapon of the general strike, rather than through violent revolution ...
>
> (Clayworth 2008: 6–7)

The activists, Pat Hickey, Bob Semple and Paddy Webb, seized on local anger over a very short lunch break (known as cribtime) of 15 minutes, as well as frustration at an arbitration regime set up by the state, which consistently favoured the employer.

After establishing a local branch of the Socialist Party, they organised wildcat strike action over the crib time issue and the union withdrew from the arbitration system. An aggressive management response saw the issue escalate and become the object of national media attention. As a result of speaking tours by the key activists, the miners received financial and moral support from workers throughout New Zealand, and after three months the company caved in. This victory led to the formation of the first National Federation of Miners and then to the first Federation of Labour (the Red Feds). The subsequent five years saw a period of socialist/syndicalist activism in New Zealand never since repeated in its intensity, including a strike in the gold mining town of Waihi which saw a worker killed by police, and a waterfront strike quelled by special constables. The movement was eventually disrupted both by vicious employer and state response and the beginning of WW1.

From this point, a parliamentary party wing of the movement was formed, leading two decades later, to the victory of the Labour Party in the 1935 elections, helped of course by the Depression crisis. This government, which held power for the following 14 years, established the infrastructure of social democracy in New Zealand, including free universal health care and education, and a welfare system for the unemployed and the elderly.

It was then, fitting, in the dark times of the 1990s, that Blackball should become something of a shrine. At the 2001 celebration, as the neo-liberal cloud began to lift, I passed on the suggestion made to me by a colleague, that a Museum of Working Class History should be established in the village. There was a positive response and a Trust was formed, which included two MPs, senior union activists and local people. I was elected Chairperson and, shortly after, moved to Blackball.

None of us were museum professionals, but I had spent the latter part of my career in community arts, a field which had included an art in working life arm. I knew therefore, that representing working class stories and values required different expressive forms from those favoured by middle class culture. I was also versed in community cultural development philosophy and saw this project taking place within that paradigm.

A perusal of funding guides revealed the initial need for a feasibility study. We decided this required a scoping of the contents of the proposed museum, the building which would be required, costs associated with both building and contents, a business plan, the support that might exist for the project, and a look at similar institutions overseas. We raised sufficient funds to do the above, including the purchase of some land, the preparing of a set of drawings for the building, and the sketching of exhibition concepts. Most of the work, apart from the architect, was done by volunteers, or by 'friends', for a small payment.

We had realised from the outset that the museum would need to tell a story, or a series of linked stories:

i   the creating of a proletariat in New Zealand;
ii the 1908, IWW, 'Wobbly' phase, including the strike and subsequent events;
iii the Communist inspiration during the 1920s;
iv the adopting of a Fabian-style parliamentary solution, leading to the 1935 victory.

As well, there should be a changing, current exhibition, and the exhibitions should include the Maori story and the women's story. Aware that museum 'experts' would be unlikely to have a background knowledge of these matters, we contacted art in working life sculptor, Phill Rooke, to design the stories in partnership with labour historians. And as we began to attend museum gatherings, we were pleased to find that current museum culture favours storytelling over 'displays of dead and dusty objects', to quote from notes taken at one of these seminars. As well, we were keen to preserve the shrine aspect of Blackball and to build on the notion of pilgrimage. To counter the problem of isolation, exhibitions would be available on CD Rom, and a website with downloadable items would be essential. As well, the temporary exhibition could travel to main centres. At an all up cost of $1.3 million, we felt the project was feasible, and inexpensive.

But, as soon as we began applying for funding, issues arose, in a curiously enigmatic manner. For with neo-liberal ideology and its TINA (There Is No Alternative) viewpoint, political issues are reduced to the level of subtext, and history as praxis disappears. I therefore make the following interpretations as a reading of this subtext.

The first reading involves the concept of heritage, which has become a part of the creative industries, that joining of the cultural to market-based economic forces. Heritage becomes then a vehicle for providing increasingly sophisticated consumer opportunities, especially for tourists. Along with art works, heritage can be used to 'brand' a region or a country. Corporate partners see their involvement as a marketing exercise, so that their brand is associated with a particular heritage. Of course, this, in turn, begins to create its own praxis. For Baz Kershaw (1992: 174), the English writer on cultural matters, it produces 'a decontextualised culture, a culture without roots'. For Hewison (1995: 135), it 'conspires to create a shallow screen that intervenes between our present life and our history. We are offered a contemporary creation, more costume drama and re-enactment, rather than critical discourse.' And as Kershaw (1999: 39) writes, 'the process of commodification begins even before anything is bought'.

However, when it comes to the working class, there are no castles to be decorated by mannequins or people in fine costumes. Nor are there beautiful objects. For the working class sell their labour. That is the essence. Even the machines they worked, or the factories or mines in which they worked, did not belong to them. So, in terms of inheritance, all we gain from our working class forebears are ideas and events, which resulted from the selling of their labour. On the cultural front there are banners, songs, some literature based on these events and ideas. But as an inheritance, it is not object-based.

In numerous ways then, our story did not fit the heritage norm. For a start, it was a story inspired by socialist ideals. It could never be an easily digestible consumer opportunity. It was about a culture within a socialist context and it was about roots. It was also a story about production rather than about consumption.

The second issue, we began to realise, was posed by postmodernism, which as a cultural paradigm, shines with two different lights. One is technical: all the stories have been told and all the genre created, so that we simply play with the retelling. We could perhaps live with that, despite its feeling of decadence. The other is the embracing of diversity, and this presents a bigger problem. While I would argue that class is part of diversity, the working class is seen by postmodernists as inextricably tangled with the discredited Marxist meta-narrative, so that it has been dismissed from the *politics of identity* spectrum. Even more extremely,

> Notions of the common good are frequently viewed, paradoxically, as potentially coercive. Anything that smacks of collectivism ... is treated with suspicion, so that sometimes even the slightest hint of 'community' becomes a disease of the imagination, a nostalgic hankering after a shared sense of the human that never actually existed.
> (White 1991: 125)

Not a conducive cultural climate for the singing of Solidarity Forever or for unionism per se, despite moves within the union movement to encompass a growing gender and ethnic diversity in the membership. The story we wished to tell was then, unfashionable, despite its crucial importance in the making of the nation.

But it is necessary to ask, unfashionable for whom? How did we know this? Was it ever stated? Of course not. There are no funding guides which state that working class projects are excluded. But one senses it. Hints are dropped. Conversations are reported at a later date. One becomes aware of networks of 'the important'. The government was pushing a Creative Industries paradigm, which saw art and heritage as having an important role to play in the creating of a post-industrial economy, and in branding the country. The Lord of the Rings multi-national film project, based in New Zealand, was flavour of the month. We were faced with Gramsci's hegemony, that web of consciousness which pervades and which is created daily.

But there were faces. We began to deal with advisors, generally of Generation X age and they raised compliance issues:

(1) The feasibility study hadn't been carried out by one of the experts on writing feasibility studies.

— But, we replied, we needed to decide on shape and form, how could an outside expert do that?
— Sorry, those are the rules. You'll need to do it again.
— We've used up the money.
— How unfortunate.

(2) How could we prove ourselves sustainable? In our view, a community development approach develops the community to the point (hopefully) of sustainability. It is also an approach which emphasises process as much as product, with often the process revealing the product.

— Sorry, figures are required, market-based research carried out, what entry fee will people be prepared to pay, what is the demand from the school market?

Another well paid expert was required, to produce a document which would in turn determine the product and place it firmly within a consumer paradigm.

But we picked up another agenda to these dialogues, an unspoken politics. A colleague from an organisation which monitors the excesses of the free market (trade agreements, overseas investments and the like) said, 'You're probably on their Black List.'

— Black list?
— Yes, they've got one. Organisations that don't get funded for political reasons. We found out about it.

The other realisation, as the advisors began to suggest names of people who we might like to work with in order to become compliant, was the existence of a croneyism within the sector; of advisors giving work to their colleagues, of advisors and consultants easily changing roles, so that state funds are generally not going out into the communities, but rather, circulating, like a lot of aid money, within a state/corporate circle.

Another potential funder began to insist on 'co-location', which involved siting the museum within the local 'heritage theme park', an institution which is obedient to the demands of the heritage industry. And then a local mining company which trucks coal through Blackball, proposed a partnership whereby they would provide infrastructural funding annually. For a moment we thought we had the system beat, before the Belgian partner in the company decided they had no wish to promote the political content of the proposal. At least, and at last, the political censorship was out in the open.

We were ready to give up at that point, but the centenary of the strike was such a successful celebration that we decided we at least had to build a memorial/shrine. This we are now doing, with a Phill Rooke sculpture from the original concept fronting a cheap industrial shelter system which will have some information panels, a small shop and resource centre. A portion of the money required arrived when a supporter insisted that a Power Corporation that wanted to put a road through his land in order to build a dam must make a substantial donation to the project.

As a final irony, when we applied to the local Council to waive the building consent fee, the politics once more came out in the open, with some Councillors refusing to put ratepayers' money into something that espoused 'communism'. The national press had a field day about 'reds under the bed', leading to some embarrassment, the vote being retaken and the motion approved. As the mayor then memorably said, 'Some people mightn't like it, but this is part of our history.'

I am left with the realisation of how important it is to continue to articulate the story of the contribution that working people made, and continue to make, to the system of social democracy, and to identify the forces which somewhat stupidly, and almost unwittingly, wish to silence this story. For without this story to ground us, the political system we have, for all its faults, is under threat.

A further realisation comes from current theorising of the place of community under neo-liberalism (Defilippis, Fisher and Shragge 2006). As an ideology, neo-liberalism attacks community structures, but at the same time gives these structures a formal role to play in the new order. For as the state withdraws from direct provision of services, community groups are required to fill the vacuum: in health, education, housing and in culture. Most often, this role is filled under a neo-communitarian philosophy uncritical of the wider forces operating, with community romantically envisaged as providing a social glue to cure the ills besetting increasingly fragmented societies. As well, community groupings often provide services far more cheaply than the state, with poorer wages and conditions.

But if community groups, including a local working class, can hold the state to account, remain critically aware of the forces of global capital, ground capital within the local setting, and establish truly democratic relations at the local level, then this is a promising basis for struggle.

References

Benjamin, W. (1978) *Reflections*, New York: Schocken Books.
Clayworth, P. (2008) 'Pat Hickey, the making of a homegrown revolutionary', talk delivered at Blackball Cribtime Strike Centenary Celebrations, 23 March 2008. Available online. HTTP: <http://www.blackballmuseum,org.nz>.
Defilippis, J., Fisher, R. and Shragge, E. (2006) 'Neither romance nor regulation: re-evaluating community', *International Journal of Urban and Regional Research*, September 2006, 30 (3): 673–89, Oxford: Blackwell Publishing Ltd.

Derby, Mark (2008) '"Where the light of their glory leads": the international context of the Blackball strike', adapted from a talk given to the seminar to mark the centenary of the 1908 strike, Blackball, 23 March 2008.

Hewison, R. (1995) *Culture and Consensus: England, art and politics since 1940*, London: Methuen.

Kelsey, J. (1999) *Reclaiming The Future*, Wellington: Bridget Williams Books.

Kershaw, B. (1992) *The Politics of Performance: Radical theatre as cultural intervention*, London and New York: Routledge.

——(1999) *The Radical in Performance: between Brecht and Baudrillard*, New York: Routledge.

White, Stephen K. (1991) *Political Theory and Postmodernism*, Cambridge and New York: Cambridge University Press.

Part III

Working Class Self-Representation and Intangible Heritage

Chapter 10

Working class autobiography as cultural heritage

Tim Strangleman

In a period of just under four years in the 1960s, the *New Left Review* published a series of accounts of work by non-academics in the pages of its journal. These were later published as *Work* and *Work 2* and were edited and given a foreword by Ronald Fraser (1968, 1969). The accounts ranged from blue to white collar employees, male and female, in a variety of occupations and professions. What was valuable then, and now, is the way these autobiographical pieces tell us something profound about the everyday experience of 'ordinary' people given a platform to think, reflect and write about their working lives. We will return to the '*Work*' collections later, but for the time being it is important to put that publication in context and try and make some broader points about working class history and heritage. It is important to see autobiography produced by working class people, often in the context of work and the workplace, as a vital part of cultural heritage, one that is often undervalued, ignored or in some cases vilified. The chapter begins by exploring debates about autobiography and its value to historians and sociologists and draws on discussions from the related field of oral history. In turn, it examines the range of working class autobiography available to us, examples ranging from those of professional writers published by major publishing houses through to short pamphlets produced by local history groups. Finally, the chapter draws on a number of examples from published autobiographies to explore in greater depth the kinds of rich access this genre gives us to a wider and deeper appreciation of working class heritage and the hidden meanings and processes of class.

Autobiography

Autobiography has been seen as a controversial source for social scientists and humanities scholars, however over the last two or more decades it has gained a measure of acceptance amongst the mainstream. Arguably this has occurred as part of a wider shift in academic fashions associated with post-structuralism and the cultural turn, but has its roots in an older tradition of feminism and the radical 'history from below' movement which emerged alongside the New Left during the 1950s and 1960s. In essence the acceptance of autobiographical reflection as legitimate material for understanding the social world reflects the recognition of the need for a plurality of view points as well as a wider questioning of the foundations of 'hard fact' found in official documentation and archives. As part of the process of gaining acceptance in the field, scholars using autobiography as part of their research have engaged in a fascinating and protracted series of reflexive debates about the validity of their material (see Plummer 2001; Stanley 1992). In many ways debates about autobiography parallel those taking place in the field of oral history, indeed these debates and the fields themselves creatively bleed in to one another (see Perks and Thomson 1998, Portelli 1998, 2001; Thompson 1978). At the heart of the question is a concern about issues of validity and generalisability. There is a fear that experience is too vulnerable to partiality, selectivity and straightforward falsification. In the field of oral history, these charges have been met straight on. For many the style of the narrative told is as important as the content of what is being said. Here Italian oral historian Alessando Portelli explains why this is the case:

> The oral sources used in this essay are not always fully reliable in point of fact. Rather than being a weakness, this is however, their strength: errors, invention and myths lead us through and beyond facts to their meanings.
>
> (Portelli 2001: 2)

This is quite a step for many academics to take. What is being highlighted here is that there is a whole level of meaning that needs to be attended to if sociologists are to fully understand work, or any set of social relations. In their collection *The Myths We Live By*, social historians Raphael Samuel and Paul Thompson talk about the importance of taking myth seriously and that 'what is forgotten may be as important as what is remembered' (Samuel and Thompson 1990: 7).

In the context of autobiographical studies, there are similar concerns which beg questions not only of material but also the methods and epistemologies deployed. Plummer, in his discussion of Liz Stanley's work, offers two models for conceptualising autobiography; a strongly realist approach she likens to a microscope 'the more information about the subject you collect, the closer to "the truth" – the "whole truth" – you get' (Stanley 1992: 158 cited in Plummer 2001: 87). Stanley's second and preferred way of thinking about the autobiography is that of a kaleidoscope, where 'Each time you look you see something rather different, composed mainly of the same elements but in new configuration' (Stanley 1992: 158 cited in Plummer 2001: 88). As with oral history, it is the shift in meaning and perspective that is recognszed as valuable, rather than a naive attempt to pin down and collate 'absolute truth'. What both oral histories and autobiography have in common then is a shared reflexivity on the part of the producer and those who choose to use them in understanding the social world.

This issue of the unreliability of memory and experience is echoed in Martin Jay's (2005) thought-provoking book on experience. Discussing the ideas of American pragmatist philosopher John Dewey Jay notes:

> According to Dewey, the classical denigration of experience prevailed until the seventeenth century and was based on contempt for the imperfections of mere opinion, as opposed to the certainties of science. ... [Plato] disliked it not because it was 'subjective,' a charge later leveled by modern defenders of a putatively 'objective' science, but because it dealt with matters of chance and contingency.
>
> (Jay 2005: 13)

In his book *Songs of Experience,* Jay charts the changing fortunes of 'experience', for some it gives the actor status and legitimacy, while for others it is dangerously subjective and emotional. We turn now to an explicit consideration of working class autobiography.

Working class autobiography

When one considers autobiography the natural tendency is to think of it as the realm of elites and the famous, and not those from more humble backgrounds. While contemporary publishing houses and the bookstores that stock their product may reinforce this view with the seemingly endless supply of 'celebrity' memoir, the truth is somewhat different. In reality, there has been a long tradition of autobiographical writing by working class people. John Burnett's (1994) *Useful Toil* is an edited collection of such writing from 1820 to 1920. In his introduction Burnett notes that Matthews identified ' ... some 6,500 published British autobiographies and over 2,000 diaries covering the sixteenth to the twentieth centuries' (Burnett 1994: xi). It is important to recognise the range of this type of material, and as part of this process develop an awareness that the status of the publication may not be a reliable indicator of quality or usefulness. Perhaps the most obvious and that which enjoys the highest profile of working class autobiography has traditionally been from labour leaders and politicians, whose careers elevate them to the position where writing an autobiography is seen as the norm. Examples here would be such as trade unions leaders, one of the oldest being Joseph Arch (1898/1986) the pioneer agricultural organiser, other later examples include London docker Jack Dash (1987) and labour politicians such as Durham Miners leader and MP John Wilson (1910/1980).

While these types of autobiography fit in, however uncomfortably, to the more usual elite patterns of publishing there are other examples that are somewhat different. Two examples in particular are Reg Theriault's *How to tell when you are tired*, and Ben Hamper's *Rivethead*. The reason these are bracketed together here is that they represent, in slightly different ways, accomplished writers who reflect on the meaning of work from within a working class paradigm. Theriault's book is an excursus on the joys and pain of blue-collar work and includes accounts of fruit picking, tramping as well as working as a longshoreman on the San Franciscan waterfront. *How to tell when you are tired* is more than a simple recollection of a life as blue-collar worker, but offers a proto-sociological reflection on both work as well as working class culture. Hamper's (1991) book *Rivethead*, subtitled 'tales from the assembly line', is equally richly reflective on these themes but more narrowly focused on automotive assembly line work. Hamper is a very skilful writer who eventually became a journalist in his own right. *Rivethead* is in turn a tragic and humorous account of working on and off the line. Like Theriault, Hamper explores the Janus-face nature of work, its ability to fulfil and to alienate in equal measure. Here Hamper gives one of the best illustrations of the monotony of work:

> However, my ascension into this new sense of dominance didn't rid me of the age-old plight that came to haunt every screw jockey: what the fuck do you do to kill the clock? There were ways of handling nimwit supervisors or banana sticker rednecks and lopsided rails. But the clock was a whole different mammal altogether. It sucked on you as you awaited the next job. It ridiculed you each time you'd take a peek. The more irritated you became, the slower it moved. The slower it moved, the more you thought. Thinking was very slow death at times. Desperation led me to all the usual dreary tactics used to fight back the clock. Boring excursions like racing to the water fountain and back, chain-smoking, feeding Cheetos to mice, skeet shooting Milk Duds with rubber bands, punting washers into the rafters high above the train depot, spitting contests. Any method was viable just as long as it was able to evaporate one more stubborn minute.
>
> (Hamper 1991: 94–95)

Hamper and Theriault then represent an important but arguably quite rare form of working class reflection on life and labour. More numerous and illustrative of the general genre are the mass of books published by workers who more simply reflect on their lives. It is impossible to list all of these, and this article, of necessity has to be brief, so it can only mention a few and these could include stonemason Seamus Murphy's (1997) *Stone Mad*, which in particular focuses on the author's seven-year period of apprenticeship, or Sussex labourer Peter Richards' (2001) *Thirty-three years in the trenches*.

Some industries enjoy more autobiographies than others. One of the most interesting sources of examples of working class autobiography is from the railway industry where the sheer amount of material is astonishing (see Strangleman 2002; 2004; 2005). The reasons for the volume of books from the railway industry is quite simple, the market. There has been for a long time now a huge appetite for anything written about railways and as part of that a significant body of autobiographical material has emerged by railway workers, both blue and white collar. What is interesting is the way this market has meant that the most high profile grades of workers engaged in the most visible and exciting work, whilst dominant, do not monopolise the genre. Over recent decades increasing numbers of signal workers, train staff and others have published their accounts of life on the rails and this is not simply a British phenomena. There are other industries and sectors where there is a growing number of publications; these include other transport occupations, the navy and the military. Again, much of this publication has at its root the readership for it. There is a strong tendency towards white male authors in autobiography and it would be interesting to speculate why this is. Finally, there is a new phenomenon in working class autobiography, the work-themed or -based blog that are often then turned into books (see for example Reynolds 2006). What links all these examples is the fact that working class autobiography is predicated on work and working life. Work is what allows or legitimates an author's decision to write their story.

Working class autobiography as cultural heritage

In what sense then can we make an argument for autobiography written by working class people as in any way representing cultural heritage? Here it is worth looking closely at some of these accounts of working life and reflecting on what they might tell us and represent. In doing this I want to examine in detail sections from a number of autobiographies and select various themes, the first of which is the initial experience of work. The event of starting work usually makes a big impression on workers, and one that sticks in the memory in a way that subsequent events may not. Here is the account of toolmaker Jack Pomlet, published in the *New Left Review* collection mentioned above and is worth quoting at length:

> I was instructed to report to the foreman of a small workshop which produced components out of which electrical instruments were constructed. My future place of work lay on the far side of the plant, in that part which dated back to the firm's origins in the late nineteenth century. To reach it I had to pass through sights as alien to my past boyhood experiences as the moon's landscape will appear to the first men to tread it. On every piece of open ground lay mental shapes; some mere bars and sheets straight from the steelworks; others gigantic welded constructs covered in a deep brown rust. Besides these objects in the

open spaces of the plant were small huts reminiscent of building site 'cabins'. Then I entered the great main workshops. Each chamber, or 'aisle' as they were called, was about one hundred and fifty feet across and anything between five hundred and seven hundred yards long. Several of these great Vulcan halls lay parallel to each other. Within them the huge steam turbines which drove the equally massive electrical generators were built. Overhead rolled the girdered cranes capable of carrying weights of more than two hundred tons. As I made my bewildered way through this strange place one passed over my head. At once I understood the instinct which makes small creatures freeze as the birds of prey encircles overhead. My startled attitude to the crane's passage amused the men at work upon the turbine shells. One glance revealed my newness and a series of catcalls followed my passage down the 'aisle'. Mostly the shouts were good-natured advice to get out of the plant while I had the youth to do so. Such advice never even penetrated my outer consciousness, for how could anybody abhor this great masculine domain with its endless overtones of power and violence? During my short journey through that place of steel and power my memories of school and all it stood for were largely erased. It must have been an experience similar to that of young country boys recruited from the old English shires, and then thrust into the trenches of the Somme.

(Pomlet, in Fraser 1969: 22–23)

It is obvious that this is a stunning piece of writing about work. What makes it especially valuable is the way it captures the duel nature of work, the shock and awe coupled with attraction to the majesty of work and workplace. Pomlet's quote displays the profound sense of desire and excitement about work. It speaks to the sense of being different from, but aspiring to be like, the established workers in the plant and in that space a transformation is occurring wherein the boy becomes a man through the work performed or the anticipation of it. We can see here identity in its raw form being created or at least aspired to if not achieved instantaneously. Crucially, we see the power of this form of reflection as opposed to say oral history. For while the oral historian may prompt and prod their subject the written form of memoir allows the author to reformulate, to reflect and to question their memories. It is precisely the ability to revise their experience in the context of later events and knowledge that gives these studies their power and reach. Put differently it would be difficult, if not impossible, to imagine that same fifteen-year-old being able to fully appreciate the combination of experiences and social forces playing on him at the time.

We can gain access to this same quality of experience from the autobiography of a railway worker, Ron Bradshaw who describes here his feelings about his entry into the adult world of work:

> At fifteen and a half years of age, I was quickly to learn the meaning of maturity and manhood, for here I was a lone teenager thrown into a world of adult working men, without a single person of my own age group for companionship or consolation.
>
> (Bradshaw 1993: 25)

Bradshaw describes in great and moving detail the difficulty of adjusting to this new way of life, the sense of strangeness in relating to an adult worker, in negotiating a new sense of self. He also articulates beautifully the process of socialisation in his discussion of his growing relationship with the older man who was training him as a junior signal worker:

> By the eighth day that hitherto impenetrable barrier had been conquered and Ted Cox's face broke down into a satisfied smile. With a pat on the back he announced 'You'll make it lad. Now we'll show you how to write. Your script is appalling.' ... Up to then, I had secretly feared him; now I felt a conversion to almost hero worship.
>
> (Bradshaw 1993: 21)

The point to make here is that it would be difficult to imagine the fifteen-year-old Ted Cox being able to make these observations, nor the much older self being able to articulate it in a straightforward oral history, it is the very process of reflection, thinking and writing which produces the depth of the account and hence its value.

Working class autobiography then opens up a vision of the affectual realm of working life and a study of examples from the genre throws up numerous illustrations of this. Thinking about Stanley's image of the kaleidoscope we can read any autobiography in lots of ways. There follow two different extracts here from *The Heat*, a collection of autobiographical writing, part of a collection based on a writing project for steel workers, which illustrates this (Baca 2001). Jennifer Jones describes her first shift at a steel mill:

> Now the low rumble is a loud roar. My heart is beating so loud I am sure everyone can hear it. ... My legs are trembling and I'm really afraid but I have to go on. I climb the steps, reach the top of the opening, and my eyes stretch open wide. How do I begin to describe what I am seeing? How can I describe things I have never seen before?
>
> (Jones 2001: 28)

Jones' story portrays the fear of a new worker as well as that of a female in a male dominated industry. Her desire to control her emotions is a mixture of wanting to be seen as able to cope as a woman, and not wanting to seem gauche, as was the case with Pomlet. Jones' gender gives her the status of outsider in a dual sense. In the same collection, steel worker Gary Markley reflects on the leader of his crew, in the process making almost ethnographic observations in terms of character:

> I find out later that Papa Dunn is the emotional glue that holds this band of misfits together. He's six feet tall and thin as a rail. For a man in his sixties, though, he has the thickest head of silver hair I have ever seen. His eyes and cheeks show the wrinkles of time, but overall, he seems healthy and smart as a whip. He leads quietly by example. Only when things are about to explode does he speak with an angry voice. This always ends any uprising because – and I'm not sure why – no one wants to disappoint Papa.
>
> (Markley 2001:105)

Markley's short piece of autobiographical writing is just a bare fifteen pages in length but illustrates the emotional ties that bind workers together, how workers become embedded in their work and the lives of others. His piece emphasises the way autobiography makes explicit what is often known, felt and taken for granted. The piece shows the affective contract made between workmates, based largely in this example on the charismatic leadership of one respected foreman. Another example from the US can be seen in Marian Swerdlow's *Underground Woman,* which is an account of her experiences as a New York City train conductor and is a good illustration of the subtleness of working class work culture. In the book she balances her affection for subway work with reflections on its less attractive aspects: 'I loved it. I felt immersed in the legends of the railroad. To me it was a railroad, and the railroad was a romance' (Swerdlow 1998: 20).

This romance is leavened by frank discussions of sexism and awkwardness, and in doing so produces a richer, more complex picture of work and the way new and established workers have to negotiate the foibles of others. What is produced, or captured in the telling of a working life, are the numerous and discrete ways in which individual identity is formed within collective work cultures.

Some autobiographical writing is obviously more reflective on what it is to work. One of the more philosophical engagements with this question can be seen in Jock Keenan's (1968) chapter in the initial *Work* collection. Here he portrays his feelings about being without work:

> Most men can learn to live with most forms of adversity. But what scarcely any man can bear with any degree of equanimity is to be undermined in his natural pride; to be stripped of his native dignity; to be left naked and defenceless, beaten and broken, a fit object for little more than charity. That is when the cold winds blow.
>
> (Keenan 1968: 272)

In a later passage, he mulls over the contradictions of being on the dole:

> Frankly, I hate work. Of course I could also say with equal truth that I love work; that is it is a supremely interesting activity; that is it is often fascinating; that I wish I didn't have to do it; that I wish I had a job at which I could earn a decent wage. That makes six subjective statements about work and all of them are true for me.
>
> (Keenan 1968: 273)

One of the most interesting aspects of working class autobiography is when a worker reflects on the ending of work, the either voluntarily or involuntarily loss of employment. There are numerous examples of this from the railway industry where rationalisation, closure and redundancy were commonplace from the 1950s onward. In Adrian Vaughan's (1981) *Signalman's Twilight* we get an illustration of the affective attachment to work in his retelling of an incident after his beloved signal box was closed and in the process of being demolished:

> The great goods shed – Brunel's goods shed – was being demolished by a gang of contractor's men wielding sledgehammers and to my admittedly unhappy gaze they had the appearance of particularly loutish pirates. One of them called to me: 'Hey! If you're looking round – go up into the signal box – the whole place is polished up as if it would never close – they were some daft beggars those signalmen'. I said nothing but crossed the tracks, entered the door and climbed to the operating floor. The room was cold, damp and strangely silent, a coating of dullness was on the bell domes and their tappers seemed to reach out to be worked. Faint spots of rust were beginning to grow on the silver-handled levers.
>
> (Vaughan 1981:354)

There are many observations one could make about the form and content of this passage and indeed Vaughan's whole autobiography. What is clear is that this is someone who clearly loved their work, the people he worked with and the idea of being a railwayman. There is also a strong streak of morality running through the account in that Vaughan sees himself as part of a privileged group that had known real fulfilling and meaningful work. In saying nothing to the demolition crew he maintains a dignified silence around railway lore, custom and practice. Those outside the railway fail to pick up on the meaning of taking pride in the job, even, or especially to the last in terms of polishing the signal levers. Vaughan does not have to say to the contractors, nor to his readers by that stage in the book, that to be a 'proper railwayman' was to take pride in doing a job well. To not maintain standards would be to let themselves down as well as others. Vaughan's book is an implicit account of the way workers are embedded in their work, the way their character is formed by their interaction with material culture as well as with one another. In this sense then Vaughan captures, in retrospect at least, something powerful about occupational identity and culture.

There was a rash of autobiographies from workers who had left railway service during the 1960s as part of the major industrial restructuring going on in that decade. These have produced a wide range of firsthand accounts of workers rationalising their action in leaving a job they often loved. Take for example signalman Harold Gasson who left railway service for the then Morris Motors:

> Bill Prior [another signalman] ... asked me if I was aware of the opportunities only a few miles away at the Morris Motors car factory. It seemed from his information that his son-in-law had joined the security staff there working the same hours as we were doing but for five pounds a week more, plus a pension and pay, when off sick ... I wrote to the factory for an interview and a couple of weeks later I was called to attend, and found everything that I had been told was true. I left that interview to discuss things with my wife, and although she knew that the railway was my life, that extra money and the conditions that went with it, were an opportunity not to be missed.
>
> (Gasson 1981: 117)

The passage talks to the tensions in work and the choices people have to make about their lives and the lives of others. It reflects issues of identity, security, basic economics as well as attachment and affect for ones' work.

Discussion

So in what sense can we think of the autobiography of working class people as 'heritage', and what are the implications of this? It has clearly been the argument thus far that this kind of autobiography *does* count as a form of heritage. Any form of autobiographical writing tells us something about the person as well as the age in which they live. This can be thought of most directly in terms of the descriptive accounts of places, events and people. Where autobiographies are especially powerful is in the ability they give later readers to appreciate the ideas and emotions of actors involved in a particular historical period. They allow us access, in the context of the work autobiography, to the affective attachment to work, to the ways in which people are embedded and become embedded in their work and the way in which this is a tremendously *social* process occurring over time. Autobiography sheds light on what T. H. Marshall (1992) termed 'industrial citizenship', the sense of presence and ownership in work of working people, the ability to have a say in what was done and done to them and the way confidence in the economic realm legitimates activity on a wider political stage. In a slightly different setting, US labour historian Jefferson Cowie[1] recently talked of 'cultural enfranchisement of working people' in a discussion of the characters in John Steinbeck's *The Grapes of Wrath*. These two ideas help us to think about the way autobiography can be seen as heritage in a fairly direct sense. This is the idea that to fully understand the workplace and the role of workers we need to understand the way work is inhabited and transformed by those undertaking it. This is in contrast to accounts that view workers as passive dupes undertaking work as a drudge in order to fund their lives *outside* work. Working class autobiography is heritage in that it records, and is attentive to the social processes of being and becoming, of agency being formed and exercised.

There are clearly contrasts with other modes of heritage and difficulties in how we understand and draw on this type of material. The last 20 or more years has marked a recognition that heritage and what counts as history has to be expanded beyond what Raphael Samuel (1994) once described as 'drum and trumpet history', the privileging of elite forms of material culture and knowledge. The recognition of the importance of 'history from below' has been a gradual process of discovery since the early post-war period, and is now beyond an article of faith of those on the left. Arguably, the main problem with autobiography is that of subjectivity and the concern over the reliability of experience. Memory and the memoirs that are produced by it are notoriously selective both in terms of what they include as well as what they exclude. As we saw earlier those who study autobiography have rejected simplistic accounts of the genre as offering a straightforward truth about the world, rather autobiography gives us a series of cuts, or glimpses, into a particular world. To draw on Stanley's work we must think of the autobiography in kaleidoscopic rather than microscopic terms. Writing in the introduction to his collection of observations on the industrial revolution, *Pandaemonium*, Humphrey Jennings (1985) describes his project as trying to present what he calls an 'imaginative history' of the period and goes on to write:

> I do not claim that they represent the truth – they are too varied, even contradictory, for that. But they represent human experience. They are the record of mental events. Events of the heart. They are facts (the historian's kind of facts) which have been passed through the feelings and the mind of an individual and have forced him to write. And what he wrote is a picture – a coloured picture of them. His personality has coloured them and selected and altered and pruned and enlarged and minimised and exaggerated. Admitted. But he himself is part, was part of the period, even part of the event itself – he was an actor, a spectator in it.
>
> (Jennings 1985: xxxv)

Like Stanley's kaleidoscopic vision of autobiography, Jennings' imaginative history offers a vision of captured experience, of reflection and to what is so often intangible and unremarked and unrecorded.

All work autobiography offers something of value to us in its rereading. Taken as a whole the range of working class autobiography in existence is immense and yet is undervalued. Its study allows us to understand changes in attitudes to work, its value and meaning, its organisation and social relations. This is true of any era, but it is worth considering the changing nature of work over the last three decades or so. During this period whole industries, communities and ways of life have been irrevocably changed beyond recognition. While a pithead wheel, a piece of industrially inspired art or even a heritage centre may mark the site, little remains of former industrial development. While material remains and their preservation are crucial in terms of heritage, we should not neglect the role and value of working class testimony to bygone ways of being and sociality, and as such working class autobiography deserves to be recognised as heritage in its own right.

As has been argued here, working class autobiography has been increasingly recognised as valuable and important. It can be found in national chain bookstores as well as in local heritage centres, and has been published by multinational publishing houses as well as in the form of local history group pamphlets with limited circulation. These memoirs can be read in many ways and for wildly different purposes – be they academic or by local writing groups. Their existence offers a powerful counter to the trivialising effects of celebrity culture by validating the importance of everyday life and in the process legitimising others to tell their own stories.

Note

1 See http://reading.cornnell.edu/panel_discussion.cfm.

References

Arch, J. (1986) *From Ploughtail to Parliament: An Autobiography*, London: Cresset.
Baca, J. S. (ed.) (2001) *The Heat: Steelworker Lives and Legends*, West Mena: Cedar Hill.
Bradshaw, R. (1993) *Railway Lines and Levers*, Paddock Wood: Unicorn Books.
Burnett, J. (ed.) (1994) *Useful Toil: Autobiographies of Working People from the 1820s to the 1920s*, London: Routledge.
Dash, J. (1987) *Good Morning Brothers!*, London: London Borough of Tower Hamlets/Wapping Standing Neighbourhood Committee.
Fraser, R (ed.) (1968) *Work: Twenty Personal Accounts*, London: Pelican.
——(1969) *Work 2: Twenty Personal Accounts*, London: Pelican.
Gasson, H. (1981) *Signalling Days: Final Reminiscences of a Great Western Railwayman*, Oxford: Oxford Publishing Company.
Hamper, B. (1991) *Rivethead: tales from the assembly line*, New York: Warner Books.
Jay, M. (2005) *Songs of Experience: Modern American and European variations on a universal theme*, Berkeley: University of California.

Jennings, H. (1985) *Pandaemonium: The coming of the machine as seen by contemporary observers*, London: Picador.

Jones, J. (2001) 'Day one', in J. S. Baca (ed.) *The Heat: Steelworker Lives and Legends*, West Mena: Cedar Hill.

Keenan, J. (1968) 'On the dole', in R. Fraser (ed.) *Work: Twenty Personal Accounts*, London: Pelican.

Markley, G. (2001) 'Long live "D" crew', in J. S. Baca (ed.) *The Heat: Steelworker Lives and Legends*, West Mena: Cedar Hill.

Marshall, T. H. (1992) *Citizenship and Social Class*, London: Pluto.

Murphy, S. (1997) *Stone Mad*, Belfast: The Blackstaff Press.

Plummer, K. (2001) *Documents of life 2: An invitation to a critical humanism*, London: Sage.

Pomlet, J. (1969) 'The Toolmaker', in R. Fraser (ed.) *Work 2: Twenty Personal Accounts*, London: Pelican.

Portelli, A. (1998) 'What makes oral history different', in R. Perks and A. Thomson (eds.) *The Oral History Reader*, London: Routledge.

——(2001) *The Death of Luigi Trastulli and Other Stories: Form and Meaning in Oral History*, Albany: SUNY Press.

Reynolds, T. (2006) *Blood, Sweat and Tea: Real-Life Adventures in an Inner-City Ambulance*, London: The Friday Project.

Richards, P. (2001) *Thirty-Three Years in the Trenches: Memoirs of a Sussex Working Man*, Oxford: White Cockade.

Samuel, R. (1994) *Theatres of Memory: Past and Present in Contemporary Culture*, London: Verso.

Samuel, R. and Thompson, P. (1990) *The Myths We Live By*, London: Routledge.

Stanley, L. (1992) *The Auto/Biographical I; Theory and Practice of Feminist Auto/Biography*, Manchester: Manchester University Press.

Strangleman, T. (2002) 'Constructing the past: Railway history from below or a study in nostalgia?', *Journal of Transport History*, 23(2): 147–58.

——(2004) *Work Identity at the End of the Line?: Privatisation and Culture Change in the UK Rail Industry*, Basingstoke: Palgrave.

——(2005) 'Class memory: working-class autobiography and the art of forgetting', in J. Russo and S. Linkon (eds.) *New Working-Class Studies*, Ithaca: Cornell University Press.

Swerdlow, M. (1998) *Underground Woman: My four years as a New York City subway conductor*, Philadelphia: Temple University Press.

Theriault, R. (1995) *How to tell when you're tired: A brief examination of work*, New York: Norton.

Thompson, P. (1978) *Voice of the Past: Oral History*, Oxford: Oxford University Press.

Vaughan, A. (1981) *Signalman's Morning/Signalman's Twilight*, London: Pan.

Wilson, J. (1910; reprinted 1980) *Memories of a Labour Leader*, Firle: Caliban Books.

Chapter 11

You say 'po' boy', I say poor boy
New Orleans culinary and labour history sandwiched together

Michael Mizell-Nelson

The decision to order either a poor boy sandwich or a po-boy sandwich in New Orleans transmits a surprising amount of cultural baggage. Most New Orleanians are accustomed to saying po-boy and seeing the French bread sandwich name written in its contracted form on signs and menus. When someone such as local food guru Tom Fitzmorris insists upon saying poor boy, the original term, he invites ridicule for being an elitist.

In a heated exchange during a panel discussion at the 2007 Po-Boy Preservation Festival, food writer Tom Fitzmorris faced off against poor boy expert and cartoonist Bunny Matthews. The latter favours 'po-boy', and the two men represent two sides of a generational shift:

FITZMORRIS: I have a gut-level aversion to something that started in New Orleans somewhere in the 1970s. It seems to me that something could not possibly be authentic New Orleans unless it were seedy, a little sleazy, a little funky—which strikes me as funny because we have historically been thought of as a cultured city.
   ... whoever uses the term po' when you mean to use the word poor when you talk about anything else [besides the sandwich]?
MATTHEWS: *Everybody in New Orleans does.* That's an absurd thing to say! You don't tell your kids you're going to get a *poor* boy sandwich.
FITZMORRIS: *Yes I do!*
MATTHEWS: Oh, you're full of shit, boy. Nobody says that.
FITZMORRIS: See? This is a perfect example. Here I am trying to make a cogent comment on this, and I'm being accused of being full of bullshit.

Following a few more minutes of argument, Fitzmorris concluded that 'this is the most ridiculous controversy imaginable' (*Poor Boy Sandwich History Panel Discussion* 2007).[1] As depicted in a recent book by food writer Sara Roahen (2008: 99–118), Fitzmorris' argument seems to end with the idea that the original restauranteurs called it a poor boy and spelled it that way on their menus, so Fitzmorris is going to abide by their wishes. He appears to be a stodgy traditionalist unwilling to account for shifts in language. It might seem that one could not find a less significant debate, even in culinary history. After all, who in the United States orders a submarine sandwich instead of a sub?[2]

Nevertheless, the po-boy/poor boy debate is more than simply an entertaining sidelight about quirky New Orleanians. The argument symbolises the general disappearance of a vibrant working class history from New Orleans' consciousness as older residents have died off. Fitzmorris is historically correct, and he is not the only one who insists upon the non-contracted form.

Descendants of the baker and restaurant owners who invented the sandwich and older New Orleanians use only the poor boy term. Dwindling numbers of people whose memories stretch far enough back understand the term's significance. 'Poor boy' memorialises the 1,100 street railway workers whose union was broken during a 1929 strike. Oral history interviews I conducted with many who had first-hand knowledge of the strike and the sandwich name reveal that none of these older New Orleanians ever broke from the standard poor boy nomenclature.[3]

My examination of poor boy sandwich origins began as research for a video documentary on New Orleans streetcar history I was producing in the mid-1990s. Delving into sandwich history, I had expected to trace the several different origin stories and, I hoped, substantiate some link to the streetcar strike featured in my documentary. Despite my doubts, archival and oral history evidence revealed that working class New Orleanians had maintained a consistent story that conformed with established facts. The name and remarkable size of the French bread sandwich had sprung directly from the strike. Brothers and former streetcar conductors Bennie and Clovis Martin turned lunch stand operators in the French Market had supported the strikers in 1929 by providing free meals for their former union brothers. Those meals eventually turned into large sandwiches made from especially long loaves of French bread created to fill this need.[4]

Following the video documentary's release, reporters often sought my interpretation of poor boy history. Knowing that archived news articles featured the strike origin story, I considered the factual version of its history to be readily available, so I did not plan to publish on the topic. A couple of younger journalists began to refer to the strike story as the most prominent creation myth among several and used qualifiers such as 'alleged' and 'legend' when writing about the poor boy's labour history origins.

Community versus culinary history

Popular interest and confrontations with bad poor boy history finally moved me to write a scholarly article on the sandwich's history. Even as food writing and culinary history have burgeoned in the last several years, the authors too often end their research after having located one old newspaper article or reference work. Seldom do food writers look beyond a previously published source. The adventurous ones might rely on interviews, but then they usually stop short of seeking any primary sources or other methods for verifying information conveyed through oral history. While culinary history is fascinating, it's all just a bunch of legends, they tend to claim; therefore, one should never expect to ferret out the actual origins. *Select a story that sounds right and stick with it* tends to characterise too much published food history.

This scenario confronted me more than a decade after I had engaged in my earlier research. When one of the journalists I shared my findings with opted to refute the information for no apparent reason, I decided I needed to write about New Orleans food history. In responding to freelance writer Pableaux Johnson's initial phone call, I explained how, despite my original doubts, I had found that the most popular story about the sandwich's origins was accurate. As I do with all journalists, I offered to provide copies of my source material, including a letter from the Martin Brothers pledging to feed the strikers free meals. I never heard from Johnson again, but several months later I received a list of excellent questions from a fact checker at the national magazine publishing his piece. I was amazed at how specifically focused her questions were, so I thought that finally I would be able to refer other journalists to a detailed, well-researched synopsis.

The published article portrayed the strike story as 'apocryphal' (Johnson 2005) and argued that the sandwich had been named in the 1800s – long before the 1929 streetcar strike. New Orleans' alternative weekly newspaper praised the article for disproving some myths (Price 2005).[5] Ironically, the journalist had sold the article to a national publication by claiming to set the record straight about the history of the sandwich.

Considering that I had missed some essential evidence that Johnson had uncovered, I set out to write my account by contacting the author and asking about his research material. He had consulted one source, John Mariani's *Encyclopedia of American Food and Drink* (1999). After first relating the Martin Brothers' strike account, Mariani added, 'Another story says the term is related to the French for a gratuity, *pourboire*. Nonetheless, the term 'poor boy' for a sandwich goes back to 1875' (p. 246).

I then exchanged emails with Mariani, who told me that he had found the citation in the *Random House Unabridged Dictionary* (1999), which reports the term first being used between 1875 and 1880. This is where the correcting of an 'apocryphal' legend dead-ends. Much more detailed treatments are found in the *Oxford English Dictionary* (1989) and the *Dictionary of American Regional English* (1985), and both cite 1931 as the first published use. As of yet, no menus, restaurant signage or other evidence has been found to support the term poor boy being used to describe French bread sandwiches before the strike.[6] The historical method had lost out to one book with 'Encyclopedia' in its title and one dictionary reference.[7]

A sense of pride in my own work certainly motivated my decision to write down a history ignored by scholars and given short shrift by foodies; however, I also recollected the voices of many deceased New Orleanians who had related the poor boy sandwich origins when I had videotaped interviews during the mid-1990s. The term 'apocryphal' resonated as I thought of one such voice, the former New Orleans Fire Department Superintendent Bill McCrossen, who responded with, 'You could get a sandwich anywhere, but you could only get a poor boy at Martin Brothers' (1995).

Every voice I recorded spoke with a working class dialect. Most were quite distinct while a few reflected a smoother, lilting quality. Interestingly, the voices of those who write about the sandwich, including my own, tend to reflect no such inborn connection to the New Orleans culture we profess to comprehend. The voices of the living grandchildren of the families who developed the sandwich are just as adamant in defending the use of poor boy; these descendants, whom we celebrate during the Po-Boy Festival as the 'founding families of the Poor Boy', are three and four generations removed from the originators, yet their voices also sound with authentic New Orleans dialects. Attempts to negate their family and community history incensed some of the descendants. They transmit an oral history that my research confirmed and enhanced using documentary evidence as well as interviews.

Pursuing sandwich history may seem laughable to traditional history scholars and many others. A graduate student responded to news of my work with comic disbelief. Nevertheless, food history is often so elusive and generally poorly researched that when essential elements about origins can be understood, one should attempt to tell the story as fully as possible. However, a scholarly article alone would not amend the record because most academics continue to have little impact upon the general public. A 1950 linguist's scholarly account of the poor boy sandwich origins floats around the Internet with scarcely any attention paid to it (Cohen 1950: 67–69).[8] The best way to reconnect the public to its own history would be via a much more substantial and lively medium.

Public history and the poor boy

I engaged in my first poor boy public history experience during a 2004 event welcoming the return of streetcar service to the city's main thoroughfare, Canal Street, and marking the 75th anniversary of the poor boy streetcar strike. A farmer's market sponsored a poor boy tasting to accompany the history. The poor boy shop owner near the market site had reopened a famous restaurant known as the Parkway Bakery because long ago it had baked its own loaves. He decorated his restaurant with nostalgic icons of local history as well as sandwich artefacts; therefore, he had developed a reputation as an authoritative source on the sandwich's history.

This poor boy shop owner is a great restaurateur, and nobody quarrels with his expertise in the kitchen. While few historians would consider themselves prepared to step into a commercial kitchen and begin serving food, this restaurant owner feels no such qualms. Like me, he, too, drew upon oral history to back up his stories. However, he had no inclination to examine the stories he had been told.

The owner of the Parkway Bakery had told the farmer's market staff an old story about the first poor boy sandwiches having been made with fried potatoes. The market folk loved the legend and produced signs and press materials proclaiming that everyone could taste the original poor boy served to the strikers. The media and others remarked upon how they had never known that the first poor boy had been the French-fried one, and they assumed that my research had revealed this information. A few wanted to know exactly how I had discovered that it was the first one. While answering their questions in advance of the main presentation, I debated whether to discuss this aspect at all before making brief comments and distributing a short handout describing the history of the sandwich. I know that most public historians have encountered those moments when one treads the line between correcting a well-loved story and appearing to be an anal-retentive killjoy.

This French-fry tale appeals to many because it melds poverty with one of its hallmark foods: potatoes. Few hearing this story in a twenty-first century city infamous for its impoverished residents would consider how insulting such an action would have been in the context of 1929. Early twentieth-century New Orleans was still a union labour stronghold, so to offer former union brothers a meal of fried potatoes instead of a more substantial sandwich with meat would have been disrespectful. The restaurateurs promised a 'free meal' to the strikers.

Beggars in this period probably received either plain stale bread or perhaps sections of loaves moistened with roast beef gravy, termed 'debris' in New Orleans; the more telling examples of poverty were over-ripe banana French bread sandwiches, often served with mayonnaise. Since New Orleans served as one of the most important entry points for the banana into the US diet, rotten and over-ripe bananas were often available either inexpensively or free. This story, even more interesting than the fried potato one, is scarcely known; children growing up in the slums near the docks, however, were well aware of this meal.

I decided to point out that the potato origin story was just one of the many colourful tales connected to the sandwich history, and I had already prepared a brief historical account on a handout that included my contact information for anyone interested in helping me to preserve similar stories about the poor boy. Following the market presentation, I told the restaurant owner in private that I had a colourfully illustrated newspaper photo essay from 1949 with an interview of the originator of the sandwich ('Poor Boy

Gets Rich' c. 1949). Clovis Martin explained that the French-fry poor boy was a post-World War II innovation owing to teenagers not having enough money for a regular sandwich. I let the restaurateur know that I could provide him with a copy of the clipping for display in his restaurant, but this artefact did not appeal to his sense of history.[9]

In 2007, the restaurant owner told a *New Yorker* journalist the same fried potato po-boy story. I learned this when the writer remarked to me how interesting the French fry sandwich story was. He had blogged about this story days earlier, so even though we were supposed to discuss race relations on the streetcars, he asked me to clarify the sandwich origins so he could correct the earlier article (Baum 2007a, 2007b).

Po-Boy Preservation Festival

As part of their participation in the National Trust for Historic Preservation's Main Street programme, Oak Street Association leaders sought a festival to bring people to the street. Veneration of the poor boy is part of a larger post-Katrina movement that treasures New Orleans cultural history, so the association settled upon the poor boy as a quintessential local food around which to develop a festival, although few of the merchants were connected to the sandwich trade.[10] Serendipitously, I was completing a scholarly essay for a New Orleans culinary history collection when a group of merchants from the Carrollton neighbourhood's business district approached me in 2007 about their developing a po-boy festival. After recent experiences with inaccurate culinary history in print, I was happy to work on the inaugural event.

The Po-Boy Fest provides an artificial celebration of uncommonly good food originally meant for common folk. 'S.O.S'. – Save Our Sandwich – is a catchphrase adopted by the festival organisers in marketing the festival. The concept of preserving the sandwich against the onslaught of Subway, Quiznos, and other fast-food chain restaurants succeeded from the outset. What many expected to be a small-scale neighbourhood festival brought more than 10,000 people onto three blocks of Oak Street during the first year. The poor boy and the sandwich shops and groceries that had long purveyed the sandwich symbolised small family businesses and local culture, just as Oak Street epitomises one of the city's hardscrabble, not completely gentrified commercial districts. Family-owned sandwich shops, and the family-owned bakeries that supplied them with bread, had already declined in number after suffering decades of competition from fast food franchises selling inexpensive hamburger and fried chicken.[11]

Po-boy: racial epithet, down-home southernism, or both?

No debate over po-boy versus poor boy occurred in deciding the festival name, since the organisers were unfamiliar with the term's history. So many decades had elapsed since the sandwich name had shortened, that most New Orleanians discern no racial overtones to the po-boy term. However, a recent arrival in the community, food writer Sara Roahen (2008: 104), reports that she initially felt like a white rapper and had to overcome an aversion to the term when ordering the sandwich.

The term 'po' has emerged in other mainstream contexts, serving most notably as the name for a regional franchise of restaurants named Po' Folks. Headquartered in the panhandle of Florida, all but one of its ten locations are in Florida and Alabama. The corporation's website depicts the Po' in its name as symbolic of its down-home, 'folksy' nature; nevertheless, this quaint expression does not seem to resonate beyond the restaurant's Deep South customer base.

Well before its culinary application, the term had circulated in wide enough use among Blues musicians early in the twentieth century that a white folklorist included two songs with 'Po' Boy' in their titles in a 1911 scholarly article (Odum: 270).[12] Langston Hughes' poem 'Po' Boy Blues' demonstrates that African-American intellectuals were well aware of the term during the Harlem Renaissance. The term 'poor boy' was commonly used during the early twentieth century to denote schools and orphanages for children, e.g., 'The instruction in said school shall be free for poor boys.' Both terms existed well before the 1929 streetcar strike, but neither one was tied to a sandwich name beforehand. However, the terms were likely racialised in conversational use from the outset. White impoverished children probably enjoyed the dignity of being labelled 'poor', while black kids, and some of the whites, may have been 'po'.

The term po-boy in the years before the strike likely may have referred to beggars seeking leftover bits of food in the French Market. Almost all legends of the sandwich name attribute its origins to the city's largest and oldest public market, and a couple of the stories centre upon the dismissive term 'boy' as used to describe African American men.[13] Some of the most offensive accounts, recorded during the Great Depression, describe poor African-American youth begging in the French Market. They were described as moving from stall to stall with loaves of stale bread, acquiring limp lettuce from one vendor and over-ripe tomatoes from another, and then scraps of meat from another. One version published in 1937 (Cora and Brown: 187) accepts the Martin Brothers origin and then states that '[t]he story goes that Martin couldn't resist little negro boys who eyed his snacks wistfully and finally came out with, 'Mistah, could you-all spa'h a sandwich fo' a po' boy'.' This tale turns upon both the racially derisive meaning of boy and the surprising generosity of one of the Martins who responds by filling a full loaf of bread with fried oysters, ham and cheese, and other meat. It ends by suggesting that 'in retelling the Martin story, all New Orleans puts a great deal of pathos and feeling into pronouncing "po" boy', so the sandwich is better known that way than as a 'poor boy'. Despite this account, interviews reveal that many white and black New Orleanians assiduously avoided the contracted form.

You say 'po' boy', I say poor boy   167

One local culinary researcher refuses to use 'po-boy' because she believes that it originated 'to mock black dialect' (Detweiler). Given the sandwich's origins in the mixed-race working class French Quarter neighbourhood, however, the term more likely mocked white as well as black speech. Nevertheless, cognizance of a shared dialect seems to have disappeared simultaneously with the movement of white residents from the downtown neighbourhoods and blacks from the French Quarter during the mid-twentieth century. The term carried at least two meanings. As 'poor boy', it spoke to the tragedy of union men who faced off against the city utility only to be reduced to the level of beggars relying upon handouts. Applying the term to men who had once been considered to be among the aristocrats of labour provided an ironic twist. As 'po-boy', it could conjure up a scene that racists might depict as comical, the sight and sound of black men or boys begging for food or ordering a sandwich. Few twenty-first century New Orleans diners associate the sandwich with racist origins; time also has eroded the sense of what used to be common knowledge: the sandwich's connection to a violent labour strike. For most, the sandwich name represents just one of the city's many culinary hallmarks.[14]

Careful use of 'poor boy' rather than 'po-boy' may be somewhat analogous to use of the terms 'woman' and 'lady' in the Jim Crow South. Either a black or white female could be identified as a woman; however, only white women could be called 'ladies'. The strikers memorialised by the sandwich were all white.[15] Steadfast use of the term poor boy may have indicated that there would be no mistaking these white strikers for the familiar beggars. Adherence to poor boy on most white-owned restaurant menus might represent a distancing from poorly educated white as well as black neighbourhood residents.

Photographs shared by descendants of the Martin family prove to be telling.[16] The earliest surviving photograph of Martin Brothers Coffee Stand and Restaurant depicts a takeaway French Market stall located in the French Quarter when it was an integrated slum housing poor African- and Italian-American families. The Martins served black and white workers from the nearby, biracially unionised docks. The commercial photographer's print features white owners and employees formally posed, but the image includes an African-American customer seated at one of the counters. The restaurant's move to a much larger location on a main thoroughfare following the strike represented success. The larger restaurant also included a black service window. The move from the waterfront to true public space reveals that the black 'po-boys' now endured window service.

Rise of the po-boy in post-civil rights New Orleans

Despite early conversational use of the contracted form, 'poor boy' rather than 'po-boy' predominated on menus and sandwich shop signage more than four decades after the strike. The 1970 edition of *The New Orleans*

Underground Gourmet included reviews of several poor boy and 'working man' restaurants (Collin 1970). Po-boy does not appear anywhere in the book.[17] The transition to po-boy in print represents several changes. Increased use of the colloquial term symbolises the familiar radical transformations experienced throughout the US during the late 1960s and early 1970s, refracted through the lens of New Orleans. Tom Fitzmorris hinted at the transition when he argued in the Po-Boy Festival debate that in the last few decades, culture associated with New Orleans needed to be 'dirty, or funky'.

Yats and po-boys

The colloquial version of the sandwich name rose to prominence amid a great cultural shift reflected in a slew of jokes made at the expense of white working class residents termed 'yats'. The relatively recent label stemmed from a popular greeting often heard among white and black working class New Orleanians: 'Where Y'at'. The alternative media led the way – cartoon renderings of the working class as caricatures appeared in the city's major underground weekly newspaper, *Figaro,* and other publications.[18]

This generation did not 'discover' the working class, obviously. The 1930s Louisiana Federal Writer's Project, for example, had produced a good number of observations about working class New Orleans in the *New Orleans City Guide, Gumbo Ya-Ya* and other publications. One of the most prominent voices belonged to one of the combatants in the Po-Boy Fest debate. Bunny Matthews' cartoons featured a New Orleans element long extant but rarely commented upon in print. Matthews' New Orleans variation of Stan Mack's 'Real Life Funnies' strip in the *Village Voice,* based on conversations heard in New York City, also used verbatim conversations. Matthews' series title was rendered in dialect, 'f Sure'. In the 1970s, cultural commentators such as Matthews steeped their work in grotesque caricatures of working class life, attempting to replicate and celebrate in text and illustrations the visceral sensations of New Orleans' neighbourhood culture. Such awareness became a hallmark of the New Orleans counterculture. One of the most prominent organic food stores in New Orleans featured as its slogan on shopping carts and print material, 'Eat Mo' Bettah'.[19]

The broadcast and print media help to date the increasing appropriation of the city's working class localisms as it moved beyond the alternative culture. Before the mid-1970s, television programming featured professional broadcast voices and advertising jingles that hardly distinguished New Orleans from any other city. One exception was newspaper sports reporter Hap Glaudi, who had migrated from sports print journalism to television with his New Orleans dialect intact. Glaudi also was noted for his neighbourly behaviour on camera in an era when news was delivered in a straightforward manner. A beloved weatherman, Nash Roberts, featured a softer version of a New Orleans dialect. Both were employed long term at the same station,

WWL, and their presence played an important role in establishing their employer as the city's leading local news station. Other television anchors and reporters continued to adhere to the industry practice of speaking in standard English.

By the late 1970s, even local television advertising reflected a cultural shift started among the city's youth. One of the most prominent ad campaigns during this period was created for a regional convenience store chain. Time-Saver television commercials featured two actresses portraying workers making a mass-produced version of poor boy sandwiches. Two actors performed as caricatures of New Orleans working class women who assembled po-boy sandwiches with a lot of 'my-nez' (i.e., mayonnaise rendered in dialect). Their speech underscored the convenience store's message that these refrigerated sandwiches were just as good as traditional po-boys – despite the fact that they were mass-produced, wrapped in plastic and stored in coolers. In no way could this have replaced a sandwich famed for its fresh French bread and crisp outer crust. These ersatz 'yats' were meant to help replace excellent local cuisine with convenience. Unlike some of the more colourful late night commercials that made comic use of more authentic working class business owners as media personalities, these ads featured actors and they aired during prime viewing hours.

The fact that it was no longer acceptable to denigrate African-Americans in mainstream publications and general conversation probably factored into the elevation of what had once been routine denigration of white working class New Orleanians into comic caricatures. Slumming, once a more informal practice among intellectuals and upper middle class New Orleanians, had now been foregrounded. The delayed release of *A Confederacy of Dunces* also highlights this change. Written during the 1960s, John Kennedy Toole's novel preserves an intellectual's satirical interpretation of black and white working class dialect and the working class nature of the city's dominant culture. Published in 1980 and awarded the Pulitzer Prize for fiction the following year, Toole's book is celebrated by many New Orleanians for 'getting the New Orleans dialect right'. The book reached the public at a time when many New Orleanians had already developed an appreciation for the city's spoken English. Four years later, the yat dialect also attracted two video documentary producers whose 1984 *Yeh You Rite* helped establish their reputations as national documentarians. Their low budget New Orleans program helped them to garner funding for a documentary series on regional dialects.[20]

While the former examples may have reflected an intellectual interest in the city's street culture, the majority of thought given over to yats was intended to ridicule. Much of the humour regarding yats was generated by the working class themselves. However, most was generated by people who viewed themselves as being outside the culture. For two decades, the daily newspaper allowed one staff writer to publish feature articles based on rendering interviews with New Orleans natives in dialect and depicting them in ways more characteristic of minstrel characters than human beings. The headline for one of reporter Bill Grady's articles conveys the spirit of this exercise: 'Yat Carries "Hood Close to the Hawt"'. Front-page caricatures in the newspaper reflected a region-wide practice of telling jokes about working class men and women – typically in dialect.[21] The wide adoption of the 'po-boy' term – and the seeming loss of its racial and classist origins – symbolises this rapid cultural transformation. Mocking working class speech and culture is so widespread that terms such as 'po-boy' are typically viewed as having no negative associations.

Historical method in public history environs

On the day of the festival, the history venue is the least popular area as people fill the streets to eat the sandwich, drink beer and dance to music rather than study the food or learn from those who have. However, the online history posted to the festival's permanent website has already begun to sway people from other versions of poor boy history.[22]

The Po-Boy Fest has not ossified the historical process, however. Many details about the origins remain to be learned. An audience member sought me out during the history panel discussions at the November 2008 festival with information about yet another origin story. He presented information about *his* family's former French Market restaurant and their claims to having created the first poor boy sandwiches. I had heard several mentions of this story before, but never enough to pursue it beforehand. The Battistella family operated a restaurant in the French Market in the early twentieth century, and this family member argues that the Martins became famous for serving large sandwiches created in the Battistella restaurant. What might have seemed antagonistic has developed into a sharing of resources and information: the Battistella family's story was featured as part of the third annual festival's panel discussions on lost poor boy restaurants.

Much remains to be clarified about the sandwich origin stories. The French Market birthed a number of New Orleans culinary traditions, including the Muffuletta olive salad sandwich and *café au lait* stands. Fortunately, the festival provides opportunities for community members to engage in the process of establishing their own history. Expanding the developing scholarly history of the sandwich is exactly the sort of exchange that a festival allows. Scholarship enriched by the public's memory, which often survives only as family stories and photographs, is the ultimate benefit of public history presented via old and new media.

Rather than having to answer basic questions from travel writers and other journalists confused by the various stories, I can now refer them to the Po-Boy Fest history section. Food journalists often find the web-based history before approaching me. Online debate over sandwich history developed even before the first festival had taken place. The value of posting vetted information on the Internet is plainly apparent, and the festival's online component has inspired various creative responses to and challenges to local history.

The advent of the festival and its web history exhibit triggered an online discussion (Price and Uzee 2007) among a group of local food journalists days before the street component:

> Here is what I don't get. The streetcar strike was actually in 1929, right? Here is the *po-boy history* [the underlined words are linked to <http://www.poboyfest.com/history>] from the recent festival written by a local historian. I agree that dropping the final consonant is a common feature of local dialect. But does it seem odd that in 1929 the Martin Brothers would coin the term 'poor boy' and by 1931 it had become so common and widely spoken that the written form had evolved to 'po-boy' (or po boi)? I'm no linguist, but that strikes me as unlikely. It makes me question the 1929 origin of the term.
>
> (Price 2007)

No mention of a rapid transition to po-boy in written form is made in the online history. Later in the thread, the same journalist writes:

> My bullshit detector goes off every time I read that the Martin Brothers invented the sandwich and the name. I think part of the problem is that much food history is written by food writers, many of whom are trained neither as journalists nor scholars. Without the background in journalism or scholarship, they're not skeptical enough of their sources. Also, writers tend to like a good story, when they should really distrust every good story.[23]

This food writer is stuck in 'bullshit detector' mode and unwilling to consider evidence that supports the working class version of its own history. The festival's online and pamphlet history states emphatically that 'your grandparents were right' because the folk version turned out to be the accurate one. The terms had existed well before the strike; they had not yet been connected to the sandwich. This exchange exemplifies how much simpler it is to argue plausibility or implausibility. Nevertheless, incremental progress is being made: late in 2009 another food writer (McNulty 2009) chose the phrase 'purported origins' instead of 'apocryphal'[24] when describing the strike story.

The dilemma of this newer generation of food writers suggests that the popular sense of history as a canonised timeline of dates and information continues to affect people's perspective. The complexity of history is lost, and people look either for the definitive narrative or an account they can define as correct – or incorrect because, in this case, it sounds like too good a story.

These particular food writers, all of whom are relatively young and none of whom grew up in New Orleans, exhibit quite a lot of scepticism. However, in dismissing the working class story altogether, they miss the ironic application of the term 'poor boy'. The Martins did not name the sandwich. They seemed to have picked up upon a new use for an old term and capitalised on their own generosity. If food writers insist on engaging in history, they should spend more time researching and less time on the artifice of writing. A food review can be finessed, but history demands substantial evidence and not just opinion.[25]

The most sensible explanation I have unearthed about the naming process is part of the baker's family history. John Gendusa remembers a newspaper clipping from the time of the strike that may have recorded a key moment in the sandwich naming process. Because it was posted on a wall in the bakery, he read this article many times through the years. Essentially, someone made a dark joke about the formerly unionised 'aristocrats of labour' seeming to be like 'poor boys' begging for food. A reporter repeated the quip in a news article, and the strikers began to use the term to describe themselves. That the media would play a role in capturing a phrase that the strikers and their supporters used ironically makes sense, but it is only a clue. Maybe one day I can locate this article. For now, the genesis of the sandwich name, like the origins of life on Earth, will remain mysterious, in part.

My involvement with the Po-Boy Fest provided an opportunity to reach new audiences by capitalising on the post-Katrina nostalgia for all things connected to New Orleans culture. As a result, people are delving into poor boy history and even challenging what we now know. An online cooking and food history website has taken elements from the festival website and made them part of its own extensive web exhibit.[26] In another example, a young man built upon the festival's sandwich focus and posted a video tour of an abandoned bread bakery in a part of the city that once held many family-run French bread bakeries and poor boy shops (Robeson 2009). A few older residents still refer to this area as the 'po-boy belt' because of the proliferation of bakeries and poor boy shops that developed in the 7th and 8th Ward downtown neighbourhoods. The first of two video clips began with a synopsis of our festival website's sandwich history as the title card before the camera navigated the abandoned rooms, brick ovens and other parts of what the videographer thought was the bakery that 80 years earlier had originated the extra-long French bread loaf tailored for serving poor boy sandwiches.[27]

The minimalist video artistry was created by the owner of the defunct building, which had, until Katrina, been the site of the Angelo Gendusa Bakery – not the John Gendusa Bakery. However, his video touched upon yet another element in the story of working class New Orleans. This contributor focused upon what many would consider to be an arcane topic. His indirect, creative response may be interpreted as a product of the new media revolution, which seems to have encouraged more assertive responses to historic as well as other topics. This video artist did not feel inclined to notify the festival organisers about his work. I stumbled upon it after viewing a more traditional video response to the festival posted by another attendee.

His interesting piece conveys the sense of cultural loss the city has suffered over many decades. It is especially noteworthy because few in the city even remark upon the loss of the neighbourhood bakery tradition. The proliferation of fast food restaurants beginning in the 1960s and 1970s and the ongoing intrusion of franchise submarine sandwich shops that started in the 1990s continue to damage the city's culture. The neighbourhood groceries and sandwich shops that had served most poor boys for years declined rapidly following World War II. Likewise, the neighbourhood bakeries that had provided the crucial ingredient of 'poor boy loaves' have become even scarcer.

If the sandwiches and sandwich shops are endangered, the small bakeries in the city are nearly extinct. New Orleans once boasted more than 150 family-run bread bakeries; a handful remain. Post-Katrina, the French bread trade is now dominated by one large-scale bakery. Meanwhile, the third and fourth generations of the John Gendusa Bakery struggle to regain their market share following flooding devastation and a delayed reopening.[28]

Scholarly methods alone were insufficient to convey the story via the old media. Assembling an online version of poor boy history featuring interviews with descendants of those who developed the sandwich has proved to be more convincing than academic credentials. Archival images, family photographs, streaming video excerpted from my documentary, and some of the crucial documents available via the same website have proved to be most effective. I had long ago uncovered the letter through which the Martin Brothers pledged to feed their former union brothers free of charge, and I had provided photocopies to individual culinary historians and journalists.

However, when presented in its naturally aged sepia tones as a downloadable jpeg, the letter connects much more viscerally with the public.[29] The president of Leidenheimer Baking Company has framed a copy of the letter and hung it among his collection of family business history. Its online presence also has made it much easier to convey how the sandwich is connected to the city's labour and working class history and is not just part of a hazy past of feeding poor people. More than any other element, this letter seems to have silenced many of the sceptics. A foodie or a culinary historian never would have unearthed it. An interest in labour history led me to discover the letter during my research into the streetcar union's archival records, territory far removed from foodway resources. The *Magna Cart*a of poor boy history, the Martin Brothers letter, aids in verifying a crucial part of the story.

Preservation is part of the festival's mission, and it appears to be making progress towards that end. A well-regarded young chef sold sandwiches during the first festival and was moved to develop a gourmet poor boy shop rather than return to a *haute cuisine* kitchen.[30] One of my favourite moments stemming from the re-emergence of the poor boy origin story resulted from distributing the festival's history pamphlet through various sandwich shops. Big Shirley's, a family-run restaurant, now boasts window signage stating, 'We serve Poor Boy, not Po-Boy sandwiches.' The African-American owner later told me that the pamphlet history awakened memories of the way her grandparents had ordered the sandwich. The pamphlet moved her to make the change.

I personally do not care whether the sandwich is ordered as po-boy or as poor boy – as long as the customer knows the history. The pathway reconnecting New Orleanians to their rich labour and working class heritage runs through their neighbourhood sandwich shop.

Notes

1 Videotape, Poor Boy Sandwich History Panel Discussion, History Venue, 2007 Po-Boy Preservation Festival, 18 November 2007, Bunny Matthews (Artist & Culinary Historian); Tom Fitzmorris (WWL-AM Food Show & Culinary Historian); Vance Vaucresson (Vaucresson's Sausage Company); Moderator: Michael Mizell-Nelson (University of New Orleans), author's personal collection.
2 Sarah Roahen, *Gumbo Tales: Finding My Place at the New Orleans Table*, W.W. Norton & Company, 2008, 99–118.
3 Each videotaped interview I conducted in the early and mid-1990s regarding the 1929 strike included questions regarding the poor boy sandwich origins. The video documentary, Streetcar Stories, was produced in cooperation with New Orleans PBS affiliate WYES-TV. It first aired in 1995.
4 For my brief account of the sandwich name origins, please see the Po-boy Preservation Festival history webpage: <http://www.poboyfest.com/history>. A fuller account, including citations, is available in my essay 'French Bread', in *New Orleans Cuisine: Fourteen Signature Dishes and Their Stories*, Susan Tucker, editor, University of Mississippi Press, 2009. An online version of the essay can be found in the Louisiana Endowment for the Humanities' quarterly publication. See 'Our Daily Bread', in *Louisiana Cultural Vistas*, Summer 2009: 54–65.
5 See Johnson's article in *Saveur Magazine*, February 2005, and cited in Todd A. Price, 'Food News', [New Orleans] *Gambit Weekly*, 22 February 2005. <www.bestofneworleans.com>, Price noted, 'In Saveur's February issue, local writer Pableaux Johnson profiles the oyster po-boy and dispels some myths about its origins.'
6 John Mariani. Email to author, 12 July 2007, and *Encyclopedia of American Food and Drink*, New York: Lebhar-Friedman, 1999. The citation was in the 2nd edition of the *Random House Dictionary* (1999). Only recently available to researchers, an online, searchable database, America's Historical Newspaper Database, allows searches of New Orleans newspapers. As of 2010, the database allows access to articles through the 1930s. No article or advertisement mentions poor boy sandwiches before 1931.
7 The magazine editors also chose wrong on the correct spelling for Po-Boy. They had asked for my opinion on how to punctuate the term. I had noted that po' boy was grammatically correct, but most New Orleanians and even the daily newspaper used a hyphen instead. The New Yorkers ignored my advice on that question, too.

8 In a follow-up article published later the same year, Cohen discovered that Louisiana oil field workers had adopted the sandwich name to describe various aspects of their work. See Cohen, H. (1950). ' "Poor Boy" as an Old Field Term', *American Speech*, 25 (3) pp. 233–34.
9 Unearthing this clipping owes to my working with the descendants of the baker responsible for creating the poor boy loaf. The clipping had hung for decades in the John Gendusa Bakery. Sharing their family history and photographs with me had helped to preserve a crucial part of local culinary history. When these materials were lost to Hurricane Katrina's floodwaters, I was able to give them duplicates made from my copies.
10 More information about the National Trust for Historic Preservation's Main Street program can be found here: <http://www.preservationnation.org/main-street/>. The twenty-first century attempts to establish a festival for the sandwich were preceded by one in the early 1980s. Po-boy historian Bunny Matthews staged a festival that featured about eight food vendors, but did not attract many attendees.
11 Decades earlier, Bunny Matthews researched a perceptive assessment of the role the fast food industry played in endangering the poor boy shop. See Matthews, B. (1981) 'The making of a po-boy', (New Orleans) *Times-Picayune Dixie Magazine*, 29 November. It remains the most detailed newspaper article regarding the sandwich origins. Matthews also noted the rapid demise of the sandwich shops and corner groceries that once provided New Orleanians with the majority of their fast food eaten away from home.
12 'Po' Boy A Long Way from Home' and 'Po' Boy 'Way From Home', quoted in Howard W. Odum, 'Folk-Song and Folk-Poetry as Found in the Secular Songs of the Southern Negroes', *The Journal of American Folklore*, 24: 93 Jul. – Sep., 1911, 255–94.
13 Another journalist's account worth consulting was written in 1970 for the New Orleans Archdioceses' *Clarion Herald* newspaper. Mel Leavitt interviewed the surviving Martin brother, Bennie. See vertical files, 'Po-Boy Sandwiches', Louisiana Collection, New Orleans Public Library.
14 For use of the term poor boy in music and work contexts, see Hennig Cohen, ' "Poor Boy" as an old Field Term', *American Speech*, vol. 25, no. 3, Oct. 1950: 233–34. All references cited in the article date from after the use of the term for the sandwich in New Orleans and are sited in the Gulf South.
15 More complicated than labour history in most southern cities, the New Orleans union actually had admitted black members from 1918–26. See fn 14 for a citation about the period in which the traditional AFL local included about one-third black membership.
16 A New Orleans chef who grew up in Mid-City in the 1950s and 1960s theorises that white restaurant owners may have resisted changing their menus from poor to po- in part to retain some distinction from their black neighbours amid the changes created by the civil rights movement. This may partly explain why Tom Fitzmorris found the Martin Brothers' menu unchanged in the mid-1970s. Many more natives may deny such arguments any validity.
17 Five years later, Collin continues this usage in a newspaper feature, 'The Golden Poor Boy Awards', New Orleans States-Item, 20 December 1975, Lagniappe, 10.
18 In the 1950s and 1960s, the term 'pit' was used to distinguish young working class white males from middle class and wealthier white males, who were often described as 'socs', an abbreviated reference to their higher social status.
19 Matthews' earlier cartoons were extremely popular during the 1970s. His cartoon strip, 'f'Sure!' first appeared in the weekly *Figaro* in 1976. Compilations sold well in a few books, all of which are now out of print. Matthews, B. (1978) *F'Sure!: Actual Dialogue Heard on the Streets of New Orleans*, New Orleans: Neeteof Press. Two later books centred upon two fictional characters who owned a neighbourhood restaurant and bar in the Ninth Ward of the city: (1983) *Vic and Nat'ly*, New Orleans: Jumawid Press, and (1985) *Vic & Nat'ly*, Volume II. New Orleans: Rosina V. Casselli Press. Vic and Natl'y have become his most popular and longest-lived characters. In 2009, Vic and Natl'y appeared on the Po-Boy Fest poster.

20 Andrew Kolker and Louis Alvarez created the Center for New American Media in the late 1970s. Their early documentary works produced as members of the New Orleans Video Access Center interpreted Louisiana political and cultural history. These programmes catapulted them to national prominence on PBS and helped to relocate their production facilities to Manhattan. See their website for more information about their work as well as a transcript of Yeh You Rite!: http://www.cnam.com/flash/index.html

21 From the 1980s up to 2006, Times Picayune staff writer Bill Grady seemingly enjoyed carte blanche from his editors to render in dialect much of the interviews he conducted with New Orleans working class residents. Not surprisingly, this treatment was largely used for white New Orleanians and not used as often in interviews with black citizens. See 'Hollywood Can't Copy This Cabbie; Yat Carries "Hood Close to the Hawt"', *Times-Picayune*, 27 September 1998, B1.

22 The Po-Boy Festival history website: <http://www.poboyfest.com/history>.

23 eGForums, Gullet Society for Culinary Arts & Letters, online bulletin boards, Todd A. Price, <http://forums.egullet.org/index.php?showtopic=109880>. Here the author concedes that he is no linguist while refuting the work of a linguist who supports the Martin Brothers poor boy name argument. eG Forums > Regional Cuisine > United States > Louisiana > Louisiana Dining 'Po-boys gone by What's gone, gone, gone'. 7–14 November 2007.

24 The phrase is: 'its purported origins as a portable meal for striking New Orleans streetcar workers'. See Ian McNulty, 'Saving an Appetite', *Gambit Weekly*, August 2009, Annual Student Guide, 3.

25 This also means that food writers will have to become more closely connected to serious study of the topic. It is not in any journalist's job description to research any topic over long periods of time, so they need to better acquaint themselves with those who do. Years before local food writers dug into history, archivist and historian Susan Tucker had started to lead the careful study of New Orleans culinary history. Unfortunately, her voice is too often backgrounded. New Orleans food writers must begin to consult her considerable research before writing. Much of Tucker's work remains housed in archival collections. Nevertheless, her efforts are quite visible among food historians. As leader of the New Orleans Culinary History Group, Tucker has overseen the development of a research bibliography and a collection of research files for New Orleans food history. See Tucker, editor, *New Orleans Cuisine: Fourteen Signature Dishes and Their Histories*, University Press of Mississippi, 2009.

26 See What's Cooking in America: <http://whatscookingamerica.net/History/Hoagie-SubmarinePoBoy.htm>.

27 The video was formerly posted to Youtube, <http://www.youtube.com/watch?v=Pm9yZBHGk9Q>, but the owner removed it. I have a copy of the video in my possession.

28 The footage depicts the former site of the recently closed Angelo Gendusa Bakery on North Rampart Street (which was famous for its bullet-proof, glass-enclosed, bread delivery system during its last years of operation). The John Gendusa Bakery, located a few blocks away, birthed the poor boy sandwich loaf. A family argument back in the 1920s split the Gendusa Brothers Bakery. Both had flourished for decades until Katrina caused Angelo Gendusa to close permanently.

29 The letter is available via: <http://www.poboyfest.com/files/images/MartinBrothersletter.jpg>.

30 Mahony's Po-Boy Shop features classic sandwiches and fine ingredients, as well as some innovative additions.

References

Baum, D. (2007a) 'Those poor boys', *The New Yorker* 11 April. Online. Available HTTP: <http://www.newyorker.com/online/blogs/neworleansjournal/2007/04/those_poor_boys.html>.

——(2007b) 'The black star', *The New Yorker*, 19 April. Online. Available HTTP: <http://www.newyorker.com/online/blogs/neworleansjournal/2007/04/the_black_star.html>.

Cohen, H. (1950) 'The history of "Poor Boy," the New Orleans bargain sandwich', *American Speech*, 25: 67–69.

Collin, R. H. (1970) *The New Orleans Underground Gourmet*, New York: Simon and Schuster.

Cora, R. and Brown, B. (1937) *10,000 Snacks: A cookbook of delicious canapes, relishes, hors d'oeuvres, sandwiches, and appetizers for all occasions*, Garden City, New York: Halcyon House.

Detweiler, M. (n.d.) 'New Orleans bread'. [note] Research Binder. Culinary Research Group. Newcomb Archives, Newcomb Center for Research on Women, Tulane University.

Johnson, P. (2005) *Saveur*, 81.

——(2007) 'Re: Poor Boy Sandwich', E-mail (12 July 2007).

Mariani, J. (1999) *The Encyclopedia of American Food and Drink*, New York: Lebhar-Friedman Books.

——(2007) 'Re: Poor Boy Sandwich', E-mail (12 July 2007).

McCrossen, B. (1995) [Interview—video recording] New Orleans Fire Museum with M. Mizell-Nelson. June 3.

McNulty, I. (2009) 'Saving an Appetite', *Gambit Weekly*, Annual Student Guide, August: 3.

Mizell-Nelson, M. (2009) 'French Bread', in S. Tucker (ed.) *New Orleans Cuisine: Fourteen Signature Dishes and Their Stories*, Jackson: University Press of Mississippi.

Odum, H. W. (1911) 'Folk-song and folk-poetry as found in the secular songs of the Southern Negroes', *The Journal of American Folklore*, 24: 255–94.

New Orleans Item (c. 1949) 'Poor boy gets rich', news clipping, Gendusa family collection.

Poor Boy Sandwich History Panel Discussion (2007) video recording, Po-Boy Preservation Festival History Venue, New Orleans. 17 November 2007. Author's personal collection.

Price, T. A. (2005) 'Food News', *Gambit Weekly*, 22 February. Online. Available HTTP: <http://bestofneworleans.com/gyrobase/Content?oid=oid%3A33990> (accessed 21 July 2009).

Price, T. A. and [Uzee], C. (2007) eGForums, Gullet Society for Culinary Arts & Letters. Online posting. Available HTTP: <http://forums.egullet.org/index.php?showtopic=109880> (14–21 November 2007).

Roahen, S. (2008) *Gumbo Tales: Finding My Place at the New Orleans Table*, New York: W.W. Norton & Company.

Robeson, Anthony. (2009) 'Bakery', video recording, vacant Angelo Gendusa Bakery, May, collection of the author.

Chapter 12

Swedish working class literature and the class politics of heritage

Magnus Nilsson

The main argument in this chapter is that the emergence of group-specific literary heritages constitutes a major challenge to the notion of national heritage, but that the promotion of working class literature as heritage also challenges the standard conceptualisation of the politics of heritage as identity or recognition politics. This argument is first presented in theoretical terms, and thereafter illustrated by an analysis of the politics of the promotion of Swedish working class literature as heritage.

The main reason for choosing Swedish working class literature as an example is the fact that this literature has gained a very strong position in the national Swedish literature during the twentieth century. Thus it represents one of the most successful working class challenges to a national heritage. Furthermore, the nature of this challenge has changed over time, which makes it illustrative of several aspects of the class politics of heritage.

Literature as heritage

Despite it seldom receiving much attention within heritage studies, literature – understood both as a body of artistic or aesthetic texts, and as an academic discipline – has for centuries been one of the most important institutions for the promotion of intangible heritage.[1] Above all, it has played a central role in the creation of national heritages. This has been pointed out by, among others, Simon Gaunt (2003: 91), who argues that 'the task of claiming and shaping a national literature as the nation's cultural heritage' has been a 'crucial element in the construction of modern European national identities since the nineteenth century'. As can be illustrated with Andrew Milner's analysis of the emergence of English literature as an academic subject, this task was to a large extent carried out by literary scholars, primarily through their efforts to establish national literary canons. According to Milner (1996: 8–9), F.R Leavis – whom Milner calls 'perhaps the single most important figure in the twentieth century history of the discipline' – argued that the national literary canon had a peculiar significance to the wider national culture, defined as 'a social culture and an art of living', in that it embodied the latter's true values. Thus, the canon of English literature 'justified itself as the best of the national (and imperial) culture'.

I would like to argue that literature's role as heritage can be conceptualised in two ways. According to one view, literature's heritage-aspect lies in its content – in what Stephanos Stephanides (2003: 49), following Walter Benjamin, has called the 'factual "information"' communicated by textual artifacts. In this view, literature is seen as a *source of information* about an intangible cultural heritage which is believed to exist also outside, and independent of, the literary work, as when Leavis argues that the national literary canon embodies the true values of the national culture. The second view is that literary works can be heritage in their capacity of what Gaunt (2003: 91) calls 'textual monuments'. According to this view the heritage-aspect of literature lies not in its content, but *in itself*, in its status as a collection of 'great works'.[2]

The distinction between these two views is analytical, and in practice they often overlap. This is the case in what Robert Eaglestone (2000: 62–63) calls the 'traditionalist's argument' for reading one of the most obvious examples of a writer who has become an integral part of a national heritage, namely Shakespeare.[3] According to this argument, Shakespeare should be read because the 'aesthetic worth' of his plays cannot be rivalled, and because he is 'the best teacher of values'. The reference to unrivalled aesthetic worth indicates that Shakespeare is seen as a monument, whereas the insistence that he is a 'teacher of values' shows that his works are viewed as sources of information about a text-external intangible cultural heritage.

The distinction between these views brings to the fore two different aspects of the function of literary heritage. The first of these is heritage's role in the formation of collective identities, and the second is its role in the production of collective beliefs. When a literary monument is claimed as heritage, those claiming it are – by the very act of claiming it as *their* heritage – conferring their collective identity. And at the same time they are also attributing status to this identity by connecting it to a work considered to be 'great'. Literature whose heritage-aspect lies in its content can also be used to confer and attribute status to identities. As David Lowenthal (1996: 128) puts it, heritage 'passes on exclusive myths of origin and continuance, endowing a select group with prestige and common purpose'. At the same time, however, literary content may also be connected to *beliefs*, rather than to identities. For, as has been pointed out by Tunbridge and Ashworth (1996: 27), heritage 'cannot avoid' containing 'messages' which 'stem from the conscious choices […] made on the basis of sets of […] values […] of those exercising these choices'. Thus the claiming of literature as heritage can also be understood as a manifestation of collective beliefs.[4]

The emergence of group-specific literary heritages

During the second half of the twentieth century, academic literary studies in the advanced capitalist countries to some extent withdrew from explicit involvement in the construction of national literary heritages. One reason for (or, perhaps, consequence of?) this was, as Herbert Grabes (2003: 240) has argued, the development of new theoretical paradigms – such as New Criticism, structuralism and deconstruction – which 'bracketed the links between literary texts, their authors, and the cultural and historical conditions under which they were written'.

But despite these changes in academic literary studies, literature was, of course, still used for nationalistic purposes. Not only did the already existing nation states continue to rely on their literary heritages for the conferring and re-producing of national identities and nationalistic beliefs, the emerging post-colonial nations, as well as nations who underwent revolutionary change, also put great emphasis on the creation of national literary heritages in order to construct imagined political communities.[5]

Nations are, however, far from the only actors using literary heritage to forge collective identities. As has been pointed out by Wolfgang Behschnitt and Thomas Mohnike (2006: 203–4), the emergence of such literary phenomena as working class literature, women's literature and immigrant literature shows that various subordinate social groups have begun to use literature to constitute themselves as imagined communities. In this process, the creation of *group-specific literary heritages* has played an important role.[6] The ethnic revival among the Tornedalian minority in northern Sweden in recent years, for example, has not only led to an increased production of literature in meänkieli (Tornedalian Finnish), aiming to construct a Tornedalian identity, but also to the creation of a Tornedalian literary heritage which is used to manifest the Torndalians' 'singularity' as an ethnic group, and to 'demand its right to exist in the face of a majority society' (Gröndahl, Hellberg and Ojanen 2002: 166).

The emergence of group-specific literary heritages constitutes a critical response to the obscuring of 'sub-national cultural and social experiences' (Smith 2006: 30) produced by the promotion of national heritages. To some extent, this has triggered a counter reaction. Above all the promotion of immigrant and minority literary heritages has provoked nationalistic reactions from governments who, in the face of increasing cultural diversity, try to use literature to promote national identification. One example of this is the recent attempt by the Danish government to create an official 'cultural canon' – which includes literature, architecture, design, film, etc. – aiming to start 'a debate … about our cultural heritage and what it means to be Danish' (Bjärstorp 2007: 3).[7]

Parallel to this, however, the construction of post-colonial, gendered, ethnic, etc. literary heritages has received a high degree of support from scholars within such fields as post-colonial literature, women's literature and immigrant and minority literature. Thus literature – understood both as a body of literary works and as an academic discipline – continues to be one of the most important institutions for the promotion of heritage.

Challenging the idea of heritage

At the same time, however, the emergence within nation states of group-specific literary heritages constitutes a challenge to what Stuart Hall (1999: 7) in his seminal article 'Whose Heritage?' calls the 'idea of Heritage'.

Hall (1999: 5) proposes that 'The Heritage' (by which he means the *national* heritage) be viewed as 'a discursive practice', as 'one of the ways in which the nation slowly constructs for itself a sort of collective social memory', by 'selectively binding ... chosen high points and memorable achievements into an unfolding "national story"'.[8] That this practice is selective means that at the same time as it 'highlights and foregrounds', it also 'foreshortens, silences, disavows, forgets and elides' (Hall 1999: 5). Thus, heritage, as Hall (1999: 6) puts it, is 'always inflected by the power and authority of those who have colonised the past, whose versions of history matter'.[9] The emergence of group-specific literary heritages can be seen as a return of some of the things repressed in what Hall (1999: 6) calls 'the Heritage's version of the dominant national narrative'. Thereby, it contributes to 'a major transformation in our relation to the activity of constructing a "Heritage"' (Hall 1999: 7). This transformation is described by Hall (1999: 7–8) as 'a number of conceptual shifts' which, taken together, mark 'an unsettling and subversion of the foundational ground on which the process of heritage-construction has until very recently proceeded', including

> a radical awareness by the marginalised of the symbolic power involved in the activity of representation; a growing sense of the centrality of culture and its relation to *identity*; the rise amongst the excluded of a 'politics of recognition' along the older politics of equality; a growing reflexivity about the constructed and thus contestable nature of the authority which some people acquire to 'write the culture' of others; a decline in the acceptance of the traditional authorities in authenticating the interpretative and analytic frameworks which classify, place, compare and evaluate culture; and the concomitant rise in the demand to re-appropriate control over the 'writing of one's own story' as part of cultural liberation ....

According to Hall, these shifts can give rise to different political projects. One is that of re-defining heritage in 'a more profoundly inclusive manner', by demanding 'that the majority, mainstream versions of the Heritage should revise their own self-conceptions and rewrite the margins into the centre, the outside into the inside' (Hall 1999: 10). Another project is that of demanding the 'preservation and presentation of "other cultures"' (Hall 1999: 12). In the field of literature, these two projects often correspond to what John Guillory (1993: 3), in his analysis of different kinds of demands for revision of the literary canon, calls the 'integrationist' and 'separatist' strategies. When groups hitherto made invisible in the national heritage demand that their literature be included in the 'mainstream versions of the Heritage', they are demanding integration, whereas demands for 'preservation and presentation' of group-specific literary heritages usually take the form of separatist struggles for cultural autonomy.

The identity politics and class politics of heritage

That the understanding of heritage is often connected to its role in the construction of identities is almost a truism. As Laurajane Smith (2007: 164) puts it, 'the dominant discourse of heritage naturalizes the assumption that heritage is inextricably linked to identity' (see also Smith 2006: 30). An important consequence of this focus on heritage's identity-conferring status is that the politics of the construction and promotion of group-specific heritages is often understood as a form of *recognition* or *identity politics* – as a politics which, in Nancy Fraser's (1997: 11) words, views 'cultural recognition' as 'the remedy for injustice and the goal of political struggle'. This has been underlined by, among others, Lindsay Weiss (2010), who points out that the concept of heritage has 'a tendency to be deployed according to a very familiar set of expectations having to do with identity rights or rights to recognition generally'.

A good example of how the politics of heritage is conceptualised as a politics of recognition or identity can be found in Marta Anico's and Elsa Peralta's (2009: 2) argument that heritage is 'an influential device … in the identity politics led by multiple groups', and that 'heritage is a social and cultural arena where disputes concerning the affirmation of identities take place'.

According to Anico and Peralta (2009: 2), one consequence of heritage's ties to the politics of identity or recognition is that 'conflict emerges as a prominent aspect of contemporary heritage'. This claim is, however, rather weak. For, as Tunbridge and Ashworth (1996: 30–31) have shown, 'a society composed of different social groups is fully capable of encompassing a number of different but exclusive heritages without these leading to conflict'. The main ways in which this may occur are, according to Tunbridge and Ashworth, 'mutual indifference, tolerant acceptance as of necessity, or a mutuality of esteem leading to mutual association and participation'.

The fundamental reason that it is possible for different groups to assert different heritage-based identities without this resulting in antagonisms is, however, that identities express difference rather than conflict (Michaels 2004). But when heritage is used to express beliefs, it is hard to avoid antagonism. For, as Walter Benn Michaels (2004: 38) has pointed out, 'the relevant thing about beliefs' is 'that they are true or false'. Therefore, heritages expressing beliefs foment, in Lowenthal's (1996: 227) words, 'conflicts between rival claimants, rival visions of past and present, and rival views of truth and error'. And from this follows, as Michaels (2004: 46) puts it in a statement where the words 'culture' and 'values' can easily be substituted with 'heritage' and 'beliefs', that 'if we think of cultures as shared values, it becomes impossible to commit ourselves in principle to respecting other cultures'. 'Why should we', Michaels asks, 'respect values that are different from ours, which is to say, values that (insofar as they are different) we must find mistaken and that we may even find repugnant?'

The conceptualisation of the politics of group-specific heritages as identity or recognition politics obviously risks making invisible the challenges arising from the fact that these heritages may also be used to express collective beliefs. But the politics of beliefs is not the only aspect of the politics of heritage that risks being obscured or misconstrued by the focus on identity or recognition politics characteristic of contemporary heritage studies. The same can be said about the class politics of heritage.

From a Marxist perspective, class is not an identity, but a social relation of production. This is put well by Barbara Foley (2002: 28). 'Although membership in the working class may give rise to various modes of identity', she writes, 'the working class is defined as class through the process of exploitation – that is, the unequal exchange of wages for labor-power that results in the production of surplus value'. This means that class politics is based on a different logic from recognition or identity politics. What identities want is, as Michaels (2006: 297) puts it, 'respect'. They do not want their 'difference' to be 'understood as and treated as inferiority'. The working class, on the other hand, doesn't need respect. And the most obvious argument for this is the one put forward by Michaels (2004: 132), namely that 'the capitalist steals the worker's labor, not his identity'. Thus, recognition or identity politics not only fails to address the fundamental class injustice – i.e. exploitation – but may also be *counterproductive* in the struggle against this injustice. The reason for this is that since classes *are* social relations of production, the working class is *constituted* by exploitation. Therefore, the aim of the working class is – as Fraser (1997: 17), following Marx, puts it – 'to abolish itself as class'. And this means that the 'last thing it needs is recognition of its difference'. On the contrary, 'the only way to remedy the injustice (of exploitation) is to put the proletariat out of business as a group' (Fraser 1997: 18).

Swedish working class literature as heritage

Working class literature is a central, but highly heterogeneous current in modern Swedish literature.[10] Its starting point was the political literature – mainly poetry, songs and short prose – created within the Labour movement in the late nineteenth century. During the early twentieth century, working class writers began reaching out to audiences outside the labour movement, primarily with realistic prose fiction describing working class life. In the 1930s working class literature had its breakthrough in the national literary sphere with the emergence of a new generation of writers, who became successful mostly with autobiographical novels about their childhood and youth, but also with modernist poetry. These writers then played a central role in Swedish literature during several decades, as indicated not just by the fact that their works became very popular among both critics and readers, but also by the facts that three of them – Harry Martinson, Eyvind Johnson and Artur Lundkvist – became members of the Swedish Academy, and two of them – Martinson and Johnson – were awarded the Nobel Prize in literature. After World War II, several new generations of Swedish working class writers have emerged, and after a relative decline during the 1980s and early 1990s, working class literature has once again become a central current in Swedish literature, mainly in the form of more or less autobiographical novels such as Susanna Alakoski's *Svinalängorna* [The Swine Houses] (2006), Åsa Linderborg's *Mig äger ingen* [Owned by No One] (2007) and Kristian Lundberg's *Yarden* [The Yard] (2009).

The important role played by working class writers in modern Swedish literature has led to the integration of working class literature into the national literary heritage. This was stressed by Karl Ragnar Gierow of the Swedish Academy in his presentation speech when Johnson and Martinson were awarded the Nobel Prize in 1974. According to Gierow (2010), Johnson and Martinson are 'representative of the many proletarian writers or working class poets who, on a wide front, broke into our literature [...] to enrich it with their fortunes'. Gierow's comment about working class writers enriching 'our literature' signals that he views them as literary monuments. At the same time, however, he also describes the breakthrough for working class literature as an important 'influx of experience', which indicates that he also sees it as a source of information about hitherto neglected aspects of the national heritage (Gierow 2010).

Alongside the understanding of working class literature as a literature that has (or should) become integrated into the national heritage, there have also been tendencies to view it as a separate, class-specific heritage. This was, for example, the view held within the Swedish labour movement during the decades around the year 1900, when a relatively autonomous counter public sphere ('Öffentlichkeit'), including an 'institution of literature', was created (Mral 1985: 14–15).

Within this institution, attempts were made to construct a working class literary heritage defined in absolute opposition to the bourgeois literary heritage. Initially, these attempts were often focused on creating what Guillory (1993: 9) calls 'a non-canonical canon', consisting of works 'actively excluded' from the national canon by the bourgeoisie. One example of this can be found in an article from 1886 by the social democratic politician and journalist Axel Danielsson (1972: 31), where it is argued that August Strindberg has been driven into exile by the bourgeoisie because he is a mouthpiece for 'the era of the proletariat'. Danielsson thus claims Strindberg as a writer connected to the working class, and hence as a part of its literary heritage.[11] At the same time, other writers were declared to be fundamentally alien, or even antagonistic, to the working class and to the labour movement. Perhaps the best example of this is the attack by the leader of the Social Democratic Party – Hjalmar Branting – on the poet Viktor Rydberg in four articles published in the party newspaper *Social-Demokraten* in December 1891 and January 1892. The bottom line in Branting's argument is that Rydberg – who was very popular among workers because of his radical views on religious and social issues – was a fundamentally liberal thinker and writer who had no place in the working class literary heritage (Nilsson 2009: 73).

Danielsson makes no comments about the content of Strindberg's work. The argument that he is a mouthpiece for the proletariat is based entirely on the fact that he has been driven into exile by a bourgeoisie which is blind to his genius. Thus Danielsson claims Strindberg as part of the working class literary heritage in his capacity as a literary monument. Branting, on the other hand, excludes Rydberg from the working class literary heritage on the basis of the liberal beliefs expressed in his works.

Danielsson's and Branting's attempts to create an autonomous, group-specific working class literary heritage are focused on claiming and rejecting bourgeois writers. Parallel to this, however, a literary heritage consisting of literature written by working class writers emerged within the labour movement. Among the most important writers belonging to this category were the poets Karl Johan Gabrielsson (who used the pen name 'Karolus'), Johan Berndt Johansson ('Bertila'), Atterdag Wermelin and Leon Larsson.

Few efforts have been made to integrate this literature into the national literary heritage, and since the disintegration of the working class counter public sphere during the first decades of the twentieth century, it is virtually unknown to most Swedes (Nilsson 2006: 48). In some circles, however, attempts have been made to re-claim it as an autonomous working class literary heritage. One example of this is the argument put forward by the labour politician, journalist and poet Axel Uhlén in his book *Arbetardiktningens pionjärperiod 1885–1909* [The Pioneer Period of Working class Literature 1885–1909], that even if the early working class writers do not 'belong to the literary history' they are nevertheless part of 'the cultural history of the labor movement' (Uhlén 1978: 7).

The political function of the working class literature written within the labour movement during the late nineteenth and early twentieth century was to create 'a feeling of solidarity and willingness to fight among the workers' as well as promoting 'certain political dogmas and beliefs' (Nilsson 2006: 39). Or, in other words: to make workers class-conscious. The class consciousness that the labour movement tried to create consisted in the insight that workers had common political and economic interests which were antagonistic to those of the ruling classes. Thus it rested on a set of beliefs about the social reality. And therefore it is hardly surprising that the heritage-value of working class literature was seen to lie mainly in its content, and that its aesthetic worth – as has been pointed out by Brigitte Mral (1985: 15) – was considered secondary to its political (propagandistic) functions. It is also not surprising that the labour movement chose the separatist strategy when promoting a working class literary heritage. For the fact that this heritage expressed beliefs contradictory to those held by the bourgeoisie made the integration of working class literature into the national literary heritage virtually impossible.

During the first decades of the twentieth century, the Swedish labour movement rapidly gained political influence, and eventually the Social Democratic Party became the dominating force in Swedish politics.[12] One result of this transformation of the labour movement from an oppositional movement to a ruling party was the dismantling of the working class counter public sphere, and the abandonment of its separatist cultural politics.[13] And as a consequence of this development, the labour movement ceased to promote a group-specific working class literary heritage. Instead, leading representatives for the labour movement tried to deconstruct the dichotomy between working class and bourgeois literature that had been established a couple of decades earlier. A good example of this is the attempt made in 1950 by the former minister of finance Ernst Wigforss to rehabilitate Viktor Rydberg. Wigforss argues that Rydberg's critique of industrialism was an important source of inspiration for many leading social democrats, and thereby tries to undo the opposition between socialism and liberalism which was the leitmotif in Branting's critique, as well as in later attacks on Rydberg from other labour movement representatives such as Bengt Lidforss and Zeth Höglund (Nilsson 2009: 83–85). Another expression of the same development was the relative indifference (or even hostility) from parts of the labour movement towards the working class writers who became successful in the national literary sphere during the 1930s (Nilsson 2006: 135; Linderborg 2001: 323). This indifference did, however, soon give way to a more benevolent attitude towards the new working class literature, which was celebrated as a symbol for the democratisation of Swedish society brought about by the labour movement, and thus viewed as an important addition to the national literary heritage. That this view soon became accepted also outside the labour movement can be illustrated with a quotation from Gierow (2010):

> Eyvind Johnson's education – that is, the education provided by society at that time – ended when he was thirteen and was imparted to him at a little village school north of the Arctic Circle. The future awaiting the

young Harry Martinson opened up to him when, at the age of six, as a so-called child of the parish, he was sold by auction to the lowest bidder – that is, to the person who took charge of the forsaken boy for the smallest payment out of parochial funds. The fact that, with such a start in life, both of them have their places on this platform today, is the visible testimony to a transformation of society, which, step by step, is still going on all over the world. With us it came unusually early; it is perhaps our country's biggest blessing, perhaps, also, its most remarkable achievement during the last thousand years.

To some extent, working class literature still has this function. This can be illustrated with a short description of how it is presented at one of the finest working class heritage museums in Sweden, namely Statarmuséet [The 'statare' museum] in Torup.

The 'statare' were a class of farm labourers, who were paid in kind, and contracted for a year at the time. This type of employment existed until 1945 and its abolishment was seen as a symbol of the modernisation of Sweden, and of the inclusion of the last sector of Swedish society (the countryside) in the welfare state. Several leading working class writers came from the statare class, and three of them – Moa Martinson, Ivar Lo-Johansson and Jan Fridegård – are sometimes referred to as 'the statare school', mainly because they all published autobiographical novels about their childhood in statare families in 1933. In 2008, the 75th anniversary of the publication of these novels was commemorated with a special exhibition at Statarmus. One of the central ideas behind this exhibition is captured in the following formulation, which can be found on the museum's web page: 'Today we know that the books became effective documents about parts of our history' (Statarmuséet 2009). The novels about the statare are here presented as sources of information about a part of the national history or heritage. And this seems to be in accordance with the writers' own understandings of their work. On the museum's web page, Jan Fridegård is quoted, saying that he is grateful that he was given the chance to act as a 'mouthpiece for many who lead hard lives and die quietly – without the possibility of speaking for themselves' (Statarmuséet 2009). Fridegård thus views his literary work as a kind of heritage management – as a way of making sure that significant information about a group of people with limited possibilities of 'speaking for themselves' is preserved, and passed on to coming generations.

The Swedish labour movement's abandoning of the separatist strategy for constructing and promoting working class literature as a working class heritage may be seen as a move away from class politics. For the integration of working class literature into the national literary heritage seems to follow the logic of identity or recognition politics. What this integration made possible was the creation of a national identity based on a narrative in which the working class was included. Thereby this literature was recognised as a source of information about important aspects of the national history. And this, in turn, meant that the experiences of the working class were acknowledged as being equally important as the experiences expressed in the canonised aristocratic and bourgeois literature. Hence, the working class gained cultural recognition. And the same thing was achieved when working class writers and their works were recognised as literary monuments, since this was an acknowledgement that workers were capable of producing 'great works'.

That the integrationist strategy follows the logic of identity politics, rather than the logic of class politics, doesn't, however, mean that the construction and promotion of working class literature as part of the national heritage didn't serve the interests of the working class. For, even if exploitation may be the fundamental class injustice suffered by the working class, it is certainly not the only one. In addition to being exploited workers have historically also been subjected to the cultural injustice of misrecognition.[14] The integration of working class literature into the national heritage did indeed serve as a remedy for this injustice. Furthermore, as has been underlined by Smith (2006: 50–51; 2007: 160), recognition or identity politics may very well have vital importance in wider struggles for equity. It is also obvious that identities formed around the concept of class can be of fundamental importance for class politics (Nilsson 2008: 37), and that, as long as the fundamental distinction between class politics and the politics of recognition or identity is upheld, the latter kind of politics need not obscure or displace the struggle against the class injustice of exploitation (Nilsson 2008: 43).

Nevertheless, there does exist a contradiction between the integrationist and separatist strategies of promoting working class literature as a means for class politics. The construction and promotion of working class literature as part of the national heritage is made possible by the understanding of class as an identity and, consequently, of class politics as identity or recognition politics. And the logic of this politics is fundamentally incompatible with that of a class politics aiming at the abolition of exploitation.

Conclusion

The main argument in this chapter is that the politics of the construction and promotion of Swedish working class literature as heritage cannot be satisfactorily conceptualised within the discourse of identity politics. And since this discourse has become more or less hegemonic within heritage studies, this argument should be seen as a call for a re-theorising of the class politics of heritage in general. Thus, the construction and promotion of working class literature as a group-specific heritage not only challenges the 'idea of Heritage' underpinning national heritages, it also challenges the dominant 'idea of heritage politics' within heritage studies.

Notes

1 I agree with Laurajane Simith's argument that heritage is ultimately and inherently intangible (Smith 2006: 3, 56; Smith 2007: 164), and that whereas material heritage objects may certainly be useful for making heritage 'tangible', they are not 'in and of themselves "heritage"' (Smith 2006: 2). This is especially true for literature, which – because of the reproducibility of literary texts and the consequential absence of a concrete, material work-object – lacks much of the tangible quality of heritage phenomena such as buildings, landscapes or, even, other artistic works such as paintings or sculptures.
2 In reality it is of course the other way around. Literature never describes anything existing outside itself – the intangible cultural heritage which it is believed to bear witness about is always constructed in the text. And the monumentality of literary works is always a product of external factors, of what John Guillory (1993: ix) calls 'the context of their institutional presentation'.
3 Shakespeare's status as part of the British (or English?) heritage can be illustrated with the fact that he is the only compulsory author on the National Curriculum and the only author named by the Qualifications and Curriculum Authority in their guidelines. One can also mention the several heritage sites dedicated to him and his work, such as his birthplace in Stratford-upon-Avon, the reconstructed Globe Theatre in London and Kronborg Castle near Helsingør in Denmark (also known as Elsinore Castle).
4 This 'dual quality' of heritage – its function as both a 'myth-making display-case' and as an 'identity-conferring arena' – has been highlighted by Bella Dicks (2000: 70).
5 For a discussion of the relationship between literature and post-colonial nationalism, see Innes (1996).
6 This development can be seen as an example of the 'vernacular aspiration' underlying the contemporary 'heritage phenomenon' (Dicks 2000: 37).
7 Bjärstorp quotes a statement made by the Danish minister of culture, Brian Mikkelsen, in 'What Does It Mean to Be Danish', Copenhagen post Online, 9 December 2004.
8 A similar, but more elaborate, view of heritage is put forward by Smith (2006: 17) in her analysis of the 'dominant heritage discourse', whose origins are said to be 'linked to the development of nineteenth century nationalism and liberal modernity'.
9 See also Smith (2006: 80–82).
10 The Swedish term for 'working class literature' is 'arbetarlitteratur', which literally translates into 'worker literature'.
11 That Strindberg indeed did become part of the working class literary heritage is indicated by the respect paid to him towards the end of his life: 'In January 1912 a torchlight procession, headed by members of the Stockholm Worker's Commune, celebrated the sixty-third birthday of August Strindberg. Red flags were carried and revolutionary anthems were sung' (Williams 1996:49). And in the official social-democratic writing of history, Strindberg is presented as 'the workers' own bard' (Linderborg 2001: 322.)
12 The first social democratic government was elected in 1920, and the social democrats held government uninterrupted from 1932 to 1976.
13 This politics had already been challenged within the labour movement in the 1880s, and during the early twentieth century it rapidly became marginalised (Linderborg 2001).
14 For an analysis of how members of the working class are subjected to misrecognition – in the form of status subordination – see Skeggs (1997).

References

Anico, M. and Peralta, E. (2009) 'Introduction', in M. Anico and E. Peralta (eds) *Heritage and Identity: Engagement and Demission in the Contemporary World*, London: Routledge.

Behschnitt, W. and Mohnike, T. (2006) 'Bildung und Alteritätskonstitution in der jüngsten schwedischen Migrantenliteratur', in C. Barz and W. Behschnitt (eds) *Bildung und anderes: Alterität in Bildungsdiskursen in den skandinavischen Literaturen*, Würzburg: Ergon.

Bjärstorp, S. (2007) 'Cultural canons, cultured citizens: a reconsideration of the Nordic canon debates', paper presented at the 14th Nordic Migration Researchers' Conference at the University of Bergen, Norway, November 2007.

Danielsson, A. (1972) 'Tre artiklar om August Strindberg', in M. Bergom Larsson (ed.) *Svensk socialistisk litteraturkritik*, Hedemora: Gidlunds.

Dicks, B. (2000) *Heritage, Place and Community*, Cardiff: University of Wales Press.

Eaglestone, R. (2000) *Doing English: a Guide for Literature Students*, London: Routledge.

Foley, B. (2002) 'Ten propositions on the role played by Marxism in working class studies', *Rethinking Marxism*, 14(3): 28–31.

Fraser, N. (1997) *Justice Interruptus: Critical Reflections on the 'Postsocialist' Condition*, New York: Routledge.

Gaunt, S. (2003) 'The *Chanson de Roland* and the invention of France', in R. Shannan Peckham (ed.), *Rethinking Heritage: Culture and Politics in Europe*, London: I. B. Tauris.

Gierow, K. R. (2010) 'Presentation Speech'. Online. Available HTTP: <http://nobelprize.org/nobel_prizes/literature/laureates/1974/press.html> (accessed 22 February 2010).

Grabes, H. (2003) 'Cultivating a common literary heritage: British histories of English literature since World War II', *Modern Language Quarterly*, 64: 239–54.

Guillory, J. (1993) *Cultural Capital: The Problem of Literary Canon Formation*, Chicago: The University of Chicago Press.

Gröndahl, S., Hellberg, M. and Ojanen, M. (2002) 'Den tornedalska litteraturen', in S. Gröndahl (ed.), *Litteraturens gränsland: Invandrar-och minoritetslitteratur i nordiskt perspektiv*, Uppsala: Centrum för multietnisk forskning.

Hall, S. (1999) 'Whose heritage? Un-settling "The Heritage", re-imagining the post-nation', *Third Text*, 13(49): 3–13.

Innes, C. L. (1996) '"Forging the conscience of their race": nationalist writers', in *New National and Post-Colonial Literature: An Introduction*, B. King (ed.), Oxford: Clarendon Press.

Linderborg, Å. (2001) *Socialdemokraterna skriver historia: Historieskrivning som ideologisk maktresurs 1892–2000*, Stockholm: Atlas.

Lowenthal, D. (1996) *Possessed by the Past: The Heritage Crusade and the Spoils of History*, New York: Free Press.

Michaels, W. B. (2004) *The Shape of the Signifier: From 1967 to the End of History*, Princeton: Princeton University Press.

——(2006) 'Plots against America: neoliberalism and antiracism', *American Literary History*, 18: 288–302.

Milner, A. (1996) *Literature, Culture and Society*, London: UCL Press.

Mral, B. (1985) *Frühe schwedische Arbeiterdichtung: Poetische Beiträge in sozialdemokratischen Zeitungen 1882–1900*, Uppsala: Uppsala University.

Nilsson, M. (2006) *Arbetarlitteratur*, Lund: Studentlitteratur.

——(2008) 'Rethinking redistribution and recognition: class, identity, and the conditions for radical politics in the "postsocialist" age', *New Proposals*, 2(1): 31–44.

——(2009) 'Radikalen och offentligheterna', in B. Sjöberg and B. Svensson (eds), *Kulturhjälten: Viktor Rydbergs humanism*, Stockholm: Atlantis.

Skeggs, B. (1997) *Formations of Class and Gender: Becoming Respectable*, London: Sage.

Smith, L. (2006) *Uses of Heritage*, London and New York: Routledge.

——(2007) 'Empty Gestures? Heritage and the Politics of Recognition', in H. Silverman and D. F. Ruggles (eds), *Cultural Heritage and Human Rights*, New York: Springer.
Statarmuséet (2009) Online Posting. Available HTTP: <http://www.statarmuseet.com/Arets_utstallning.html> (accessed 21 July 2009).
Stephanides, S. (2003) 'The translation of heritage: multiculturalism in the "new" Europe', in *Rethinking Heritage: Culture and Politics in Europe*, R. Shannan Peckham (ed.), London: I. B. Tauris.
Tunbridge, J. E. and Ashworth, G. J. (1996) *Dissonant Heritage: The Management of the Past as a Resource in Conflict*, Chichester: Wiley.
Uhlén, A. (1978) *Arbetardiktningens pionjärperiod 1885–1909*, Stockholm: Ordfront.
Weiss, L. (2010) 'Heritage-making and political identity', *Journal of Social Archeology*, 7(3): 413–31.
Williams, R. (1996) *The Politics of Modernism: Against the New Conformists*, London: Verso.

Chapter 13

Singing for socialism

Kate Bowan and Paul A. Pickering

In 1963, Race Mathews edited a book of 'Socialist Songs' for the Fabian Society of Victoria. In his introduction, Mathews, a future Labor member of both the Australian Federal Parliament and the Victorian Legislative Assembly and a Cabinet Minister for nearly a decade in the reformist Cain government in Victoria, lamented the loss of a tradition of singing for socialism. 'The student socialist movements of the thirties and forties had a singing tradition', he wrote, 'those who belonged to them may forget the politics, but they do not forget the songs. During the early fifties this tradition was lost … ' 'Somewhere along the line', he continued, ' a generation of young socialists moved on without teaching its songs to its successors, and a chain stretching back to the first formation of the Labor Clubs was broken' (Mathews 1963: 1).[1] Mathews' volume was what we would nowadays call an act of historical reconstruction but the chain he sought to repair was linked to a more distant past.

For the student of commemoration and tangible heritage this humble volume opens up a number of potential lines of enquiry. Here we will discuss three. First, we will consider socialist songbooks as cultural artefacts, as *lieux de mémoire* to borrow Pierre Nora's well-known phrase. For Nora a site of memory is a significant entity 'which by dint of human will or the work of time has become a symbolic element of the memorial heritage of any community' (Nora 1996: xvii). Second, we will open the covers of the books to examine the song lyrics, both for the way in which they were used to commemorate historical events, or were themselves links in Mathews' chain: songs of the past. Third, and most importantly, we will explore the role of music in socialist heritage and commemoration. If socialist songsters were *lieux de mémoire* they were also *sons de mémoire*. Our study draws upon a large corpus of songbooks traversing the anglophone world, but looks in particular at Britain's colonies of settlement, and by so doing highlights the transnationalism of the genre. From this cacophonous congeries we examine two iconic labour anthems that captured the hearts and minds of at least two generations of socialists and, taken together, provide points for comparison with regard to questions of heritage and commemoration.

The songbook, a secular counterpart to the hymnal, has a long history in anglophone culture. Closely related to the street ballad, songbooks had been in circulation since at least the English Civil War.[2] Arm in arm with Mathews and Quintus Fabius Maximus marched generations of chroniclers and warblers. For radicals the political songbook reached its heyday at the end of the nineteenth century and into the early decades of the twentieth. The Chartists, the first nation-wide movement of working people animated by a fierce sense of independence and abrasive class-consciousness, had earlier produced a number of songbooks.[3] The form was enthusiastically embraced by subsequent labour, radical and socialist movements. Their songsters were widely circulated. Writing in 1913, Howard Evans claimed egregiously to be the originator of the genre, and noted that the first edition of his *Labourer's Songbook* sold 120,000 copies (Evans 1913: 42). *Labour's Songbook*, produced by the Independent Labour Party (ILP) went through three editions in 1926, 1926 and 1931; likewise James Leatham's *Songs for Socialists* had gone through three editions by 1890, two in one year.[4] Formal sales figures only tell half of the story. As with most of the literature of radicalism a single copy could undoubtedly serve a community (Allen and Ashton 2005). When pressed into the service of electioneering, song sheets were mass-produced in quantities that are impressive even to the modern eye: during the Liberal campaign of 1906, for example, an estimated 1,000,000 were printed (Trentmann 2008: 101).

The form lent itself to this type of mass circulation. Printed collections of songbooks came in many shapes and sizes: from bound works of reference intended for pride of place on the shelves in working class homes to more ephemeral pocket-sized chapbooks, and single song sheets, in the tradition of the street ballad, unlikely to last more than a few public outings. For example, the *Socialist Sunday School Songbook*, published in 1912 by the flourishing Socialist Sunday School organisation in England, was accompanied by single sheets printed on heavier card; the *Liberal Song Book*, compiled by the Women's Liberation Federation, offered word sheets at 2 shillings per hundred; the *Women + Suffrage Campaign Song Book*, published across the Atlantic in 1892, advertised single sheets for 5 cents, 50 cents per dozen and $2.00 for 50.[5]

The best-known socialist songbook was *Chants of Labour*, edited by Edward Carpenter. Characterised by the incorrigibly obstreperous George Orwell as a 'fruit-juice drinker, nudist, sandal wearer and sex maniac' and even less generously as a 'pious sodomite' (Orwell 1937: 206; Rowbotham 2008: 442), Carpenter advocated a cocktail of socialism, eastern mysticism, homosexual rights, communitarianism and health reform (including sandal wearing). In *Chants of Labour* he penned what quickly and enduringly became a paean of socialist faith, 'England Arise!'

> Forth, then, ye heroes, patriots, and lovers!
> Comrades of danger, poverty, and scorn!

> Mighty in faith of Freedom your great Mother!
> Giants refreshed in Joy's new-rising morn!
> Come and swell the song,
> Silent now so long:
> England is risen! – and the day is here
>
> (Carpenter 1888: 19)

This anthem was almost ubiquitous in collections of left-wing political songs for several generations; *Chants of Labour* defined a socialist musical canon in at least seven editions between 1888 and 1922 (Waters 1990: 107).

Songbooks performed several roles in radical politics. As Michael Saunders (2009: 22) has recently argued, Chartist poetry played a central role in sustaining the movement. While poetry was often performed it was also a form of private entertainment; singing, on the other hand, was quintessentially a communal activity that entertained, inspired, mobilised and proselytised. As the editors of the *Left Song Book*, published in the shadow of the coming Second World War, wrote: 'Music has been one of the banners at the head of every great progressive movement.' 'For music', they continued, 'has the faculty of binding together in a single emotion all those who are united by a common interest and a common purpose' (Bush and Swingler 1938). Singing was seen by many as a weapon in political struggle. According to the editors of Australian Student Labor Federation's *Rebel Songs*, published in 1947, for example, 'Lilliburlero', a song of the 1688 English Revolution, was 'said to have "sung a deluded prince out of three kingdoms"' (Waters; Murray-Smith 1947: 11); the cover of Mathews' Fabian volume carried a well-used quotation from Anatole France: 'La Marseillaise and the Carmagnole have overthrown the armies of Kings and Emperors.' The editor of an anti-slavery songster waxed even more lyrical claiming that music was the 'handmaid of Liberty, attending her steps, celebrating her triumphs, or sharing her defeats' (*Free Soil Minstrel* 1848: preface).

Most importantly for the present purpose, songbooks were explicit acts of commemoration: self-conscious links to the past, material place holders in a political continuum. Without exception, socialist and radical songbooks presented a mix of traditional and original compositions. The lyrics of these songs were commemorative in at least three discrete senses. First, there are songs that commemorated contemporaneous events. An example that was republished in numerous collections is the death march composed in 1887 by William Morris for the funeral of Alfred Linnell, a man killed on 'Bloody Sunday' when police broke up a peaceful protest rally in Trafalgar Square. J. Bruce Glasier, a veteran of the Social Democratic Federation, prominent leader of the ILP and an inveterate compiler of songbooks, argued that 'only on rare occasions' did 'contemporary political agitation or public excitement … evoke topical verse of notable merit' (Glasier 1919: ix). The reason is easy to understand. Morris' song, undoubtedly one of the 'rare' exceptions for Glasier, as well as the numerous others that did not meet his aesthetic standards, shared an important feature with the venerable ballad tradition: almost instantaneous communication. Again, Morris' death march is a case in point. Newspaper reports of the funeral show that the song had been performed before the ink on the paper had dried.[6] Radical audiences had grown up expecting balladeers to report the news. Charles Thatcher, the most prominent antipodean ballad singer, for example, attended the election hustings one day and sang of it the next (*Daily Southern Cross* 1862: 6 November).

Second, these books invariably contained songs that served to commemorate past events. By reaching back across time to recruit the heroes of struggles gone into the ranks of a universal political tradition they could be pressed into the service of the present. Almost invariably these ethereal appeals were couched in abstract terms. Published in London in 1887, *Socialist Songs*, for example, included Morris' 'All for the Cause':

> Hear a word, a word in season, for the day is drawing nigh
> When the Cause shall call upon us, some to live, and
> some to die!
> He that dies lonely, many a one hath gone before,
> He that lives shall bear no burden heavier than the life they bore
> (*Socialist Songs* 1887: 3)

The *Clarion Song Book*, published in 1906, included Clara Thomson's 'Borne Adown the Distant Ages' which expressed a similar sentiment to the musing of the Communist poet-laureate:

> Borne adown the distant ages,
> Comes the echo of a song,
> Voice of heroes and of sages,
> How it swells and rolls along!
> Tones of those who never faltered,
> Accents of the good and wise,
> Those who never blenched or faltered,
> Never stooped to play with lies.
> Now, adown the ages ringing,
> Comes their song of hope and cheer,
> As the voice of angels bringing
> Hope to those who labour here
> (*Socialist Songs* 1896; Pearce 1906: 56)

Unlike the toasts that were invariably interspersed with singing and dancing at radical and socialist festivities, songs rarely honoured the feats of individuals. Morris' first foray into political song, 'Wake, London Lads!', written in

1878 for a protest rally against the prospect of Britain's involvement in an 'unjust war' in support of the Turks, drew upon the English Civil War as its didactic premise and singled out Oliver Cromwell for special praise (Salmon 2001: 31–32). This is understandable given the mid-nineteenth century enthusiasm for The Protector; it is, nevertheless, one of the exceptions to prove the rule among socialist and radical songs (Pickering 2003: 230–31). The individual most commonly celebrated in later radical and socialist songbooks, especially in the US and Australia, was Joe Hill, himself a well-known composer of radical songs. Born in Sweden, Hill migrated to the United States in 1902 where he became a leading figure in the Industrial Workers of the World (known as the Wobblies), an organisation committed to revolutionary struggle via militant trade unionism. Hill gained international notoriety in 1915 when he was executed for the murder of a policeman. Hill's legion of supporters at home and abroad was convinced that he had been framed and his execution took place in a storm of protest that echoed down the years (Smith 1969).

Hill's legacy was not only ensured by the executioner's bullet or by his defiant last words – 'don't mourn, organise', but also by song. Homilies to Hill found their way into countless songbooks and his memory inspired two famous songs – 'I dreamed I saw Joe Hill Last Night' and 'Joe Hill' – that have been performed by the likes of Paul Robeson, Pete Seeger, Bruce Springsteen and England's radical minstrel, Billy Bragg. Bragg's interest is a reminder that Hill's flame also burned outside the United States, a fact that is further evident in numerous radical songbooks.[7] Race Mathews found a place for one in his collection; his attempt to directly link past and present mirrors the defiant words themselves:

> I dreamt I saw Joe Hill last night,
> Alive as you and me –
> But Joe, said I, You're ten years dead –
> I never died, said he.
> The cartel bosses killed you Joe,
> They shot you, Joe, said I –
> Takes more than guns to kill a man,
> Said Joe, I didn't die.
> Joe Hill ain't dead, he says to me,
> Joe Hill ain't never died,
> Where working men are out on strike,
> Joe Hill is at their side
>
> (Mathews 1963: 24)

Hill's legacy was also a corpus of didactic songs that, but for the circumstances of his death, might otherwise have struggled to find their way into the socialist canon. Hill's music in particular attracted harsh criticism for its banality even from his acolytes, although this did not stop his songs being widely circulated.

Of equal importance to songs that looked to the past for inspiration were the numerous songs that commemorated past events. Mathews' collection, for example, included 'The Ballad of 1891 Shearers' Strike', a song penned in 1917 by Helen Palmer, herself a political activist, which chronicled the fierce industrial dispute over pay and conditions as well as closed-shop union power:

> When through the west like thunder rang out the union's call,
> The sheds'll be shore union or they won't be shore at all!
>
> (Mathews 1963: 51–52)

The Shearers' Union was defeated but not before bringing central Queensland to the brink of civil war and earning themselves a place in the pantheon of labour (Svensen 1989). Australia's greatest poet, Henry Lawson, was inspired to write the famous lines that envisaged blood staining the wattle. By flying the Eureka Flag[8] the union leaders had appealed directly to the past, a heritage that was reflected in Palmer's lyrics:

> The flag of blue above them, they spoke Eureka's name.

By publishing the song Race Mathews was linking arms with Helen Palmer who, in turn, had stretched out her hand in a year of revolution to those shearers who, in turn, had embraced the leaders of Australia's 'own little revolt' in 1854.

At the time the strike had also spawned one of Australia's most famous election ballads: 'The Ballot is the Thing' by William Kidston. An iron moulder by trade, moderate socialist, democrat, trade unionist and future Premier of Queensland, Kidston set his ballad to the 'Wearing of the Green', an Irish revolutionary song of the 1790s. Mathews effectively completed the circle by including this song in his collection (Mathews 1963: 35; Murphy 2003).

Another example from Mathews' collection that shows how commemorative songs not only crossed the boundaries of nation and language but also accumulated meaning over time is 'La Carmagnole'. The version Mathews selected for his fellow Fabians was a conflation of the 1871 version – a lament for the Paris Commune – with the version dedicated to the Russian Revolution of 1917:

> Vive la Commune de Paris
> Vive la Commune de Paris
> Ses mitrailieuses [sic] et son [sic] fusils (Their machine guns and their guns)
> Ses mitrailieuses et son fusils
>
> (Mathews 1963: 19)[9]

The song was composed, however, much earlier in August 1792. It derived its name from the short jacket that distinguished the militant *sans culottes*, but its lyrics had more to do with their attitudes than their appearance:

> Antoinette avait résolu (Antoinette had decided)
> De nous faire tomber sur le cul; (To drop us on our arses)
> Mais le coup a manqué (But the plan was foiled)
> Elle a le nez cassé. (And she fell on her face)

In 1792 the *sans culottes* reputedly sang 'La Carmagnole' as they stormed the Tuileries, the king's palace, and they sang it later that year as they went into battle at Jemappes against the invading Austrians bent on suppressing the revolution. Not surprisingly, 'La Carmagnole' became a central component of revolutionary consciousness (Lefebvre 1962: 261; Soboul 1980: 228). As we have seen the song's meaning was mutable, absorbing successive accounts of revolution in 1830, 1848 and 1871 (as well as in the period 1880–1917 and beyond).[10] As Alexander McKinley has written, 'With every revolutionary convulsion, the *sans-culotte* folk song was there' (McKinley 2008: 143).[11]

Writing in 1895 Glasier, was of the view that the best songs of socialism were yet to be written but, having said that, his collections included many songs of the past (Glasier 1895: preface). This was true of the genre *per se*. Even Robert Blatchford, who vehemently advocated a new socialist aestheticism that would generate songs written by socialists for socialists, included renowned songs from the past in his *Clarion Songbook*, published in 1906. The appropriation of the past via songs unchanged from their original context was, in some ways, the simplest form of heritage management. The overwhelming majority of songs in Mathews' collection, for example, fall into this category: from 'The Internationale' to Blake's 'Jerusalem'; from 'Bandiera Rossa' to 'The Wearing of the Green'.

One of the most widely used of the songs of the past was 'The Vicar of Bray', an unlikely satirical ditty written during the eighteenth century. The song appears in Mathews' collection (and many besides) under the rubric 'traditional songs' without any other justification for its inclusion. Its appeal to earnest radicals with unshakeable convictions is not immediately obvious, unless it is seen as an account of an anti-hero characterised by political opportunism and compromise. The lyrics tell the story of a wily Vicar who clung tenaciously onto his post for half a century during the religious upheavals that occurred between the reigns of Charles II and George I by using whichever liturgy – Catholic or Protestant – was favoured by the incumbent. Yet popular it was. Open house at Frederick Engels', for example, involved the consumption of large amounts of champagne, pilsner, claret and May wine and raucous renditions of the 'Vicar of Bray', reputedly the host's favourite song. Engels certainly liked the song sufficiently to translate it into German and publish it in *Sozialdemokrat* in 1862 (*Rebel Songs*

1953: 28–29; Hunt 2009). What his compatriots made of the quirky tale is not recorded.

Other common inclusions from the more recent past are easier to understand. 'The Truth is Growing' appeared in many collections with the attribution 'from the "Chartist Chaunt" by Thomas Cooper'.[12] Cooper was one of the most prominent Chartist leaders who superintended the publication of a Chartist hymn book in Leicester. In later years Cooper was equally well known for his poetry as he was for his politics, although the two avocations were hard to extricate: he completed his most famous lines – 'The Purgatory of Suicides' – in his prison cell in 1845 (Cooper [1871] 1971).

Given that the 'Chaunt' was also one of Cooper's 'Prison Rhymes', written while he languished at Her Majesty's pleasure, it sounded a remarkably optimistic note:

> Truth is growing – hearts are glowing
> With the flame of liberty:
> Light is breaking – Thrones are quaking –
> Hark! – the trumpet of the Free!
>
> (Cooper 1877: 283)

Although changing the title removed the direct reference to Chartism, the attribution in the songbooks invariably mentioned Cooper and the original title. For later radicals and socialists there was much to admire about Cooper. A man who began his working life as a humble shoemaker's apprentice, Cooper typified the politics of the 1830s and 1840s, including the rough edges that led him to fight for a better world with his fists as well as his ideas. Here was a man who embodied the Chartist mantra, 'No Surrender'. At the same time, Cooper was a model working class autodidact; despite little formal schooling, he taught himself Latin and Greek, history and practical science and composed his verse while hammering at his last. In later life, he lived as a lecturer discoursing on an extraordinary range of subjects.

Better known to socialists and radicals of later generations was Ebenezer Elliott, a radical mechanic in Sheffield, the heart of the Yorkshire steel industry. The publication of his *Corn Law Rhymes* in 1831 earned him sobriquets such as the 'Corn Law Rhymer' and the 'Yorkshire Burns' as well as international renown for his poetry and his politics (Watkins 1850). Even the irredeemably acerbic Thomas Carlyle praised Elliott for his ability to 'handle both pen and hammer' (although he typically qualified this with the observation that Elliott's poetry had 'the tang of the Circulating Libraries' to it) (Carlyle 1832: 351). The *Rhymes* were a stringent criticism of the catastrophic effects of the Corn Laws – a tariff designed to keep the price of grain high so as to buttress the incomes of the landed aristocracy – on the lives of the working poor. The *Rhymes* were used by reformers across a wide spectrum including the middle class liberals who converted the Anti-Corn

Law League into a machine of political warfare (Pickering and Tyrrell 2000). It was one of his later poems, however, that attracted the attention of those who compiled songbooks. Published in 1848, 'The People's Anthem' was sung to 'The Commonwealth' composed by Josiah Booth in 1888, just in time for Carpenter's *Chants of Labour*. To the modern eye (ear) it is a pedestrian warble; for his contemporaries and for generations since it was a staple of the public commemoration of their struggle and prominent in their published collections of songs. Part of this appeal must have been due to its author. Elliott epitomised the radical labouring man at a time when, to borrow E.P. Thompson's famous conception, class happened among Britain's working poor. Here was a man among the first to stand alone against privilege not as a gentleman radical or a middle-class reformer but as one of the people. Carlyle found Elliott to be 'sturdy, defiant, almost menacing', characteristics that later in the decade he feared would result in 'brickbats, cheap pikes, and ... sputterings of conflagration' (Carlyle 1832: 344: Carlyle 1840: 1). Where better for Elliott to feature than in the pages of compendiums intended for the people by the people.[13]

Historians have lingered over the poetry generated in pursuit of radical reform either of the political system, the relationship of capital and labour or both, but it is also worth remembering the fact that Elliott's poetry was set to music. Song, or more precisely the act of communal singing, was a central part of socialism. Socialist song takes its place at the end of a longstanding politico-musical tradition – one that Anne Janowitz has identified as a 'counter-cultural' tradition of 'interventionist song' (Janowitz 1998: 195–96) – that can be traced back beyond Chartism to the Jacobites. While the songbook as an artefact may constitute tangible heritage, by opening the covers again and considering the tunes to which the poetry was sung we enter the realm of the intangible. This was a tradition of sung performance, of active heritage, a process, to borrow the words of Laurajane Smith, 'of engagement, an act of communication and an act of making meaning in and for the present' (2006: 1). Performed words *and* music was heritage through doing. This musical heritage is worth lingering over.

If we turn to the tunes supporting the texts already mentioned, a wide range of musical traditions is brought into view. As noted, Elliott's anthem 'God save the people' was most often sung to the hymn 'Commonwealth'; Cooper's 'Truth is growing' to the 'Anvil Chorus' from Verdi's opera *Il Trovatore*. Engels' beloved ballad, the 'Vicar of Bray', was printed as broadside ballad both in its own right and as an air to new texts, and 'La Carmagnole' and 'Austria', the tune accompanying Clara Thomson's 'Borne Down the Distant Ages' were two of several European songs that found their way into the radical song repertoire (chief among them was 'La Marseillaise'), reflecting not only the influx of European political exiles into Britain but also the international reach of British radical sympathies.[14] This small sample reflects the various and diverse strands of musical heritage that coalesced to form what one commentator has described as 'a usable past' (Eyerman 1998: 29).

The musical activities of the later socialists and radicals had much in common with previous practices and older traditions. There is an enduring link between the hymnody of the nonconformist churches and radical politics such as the one forged between the Chartists and nonconformists. The most prominent manifestation of this was the Labour Church movement formed in 1891. The *Labour Church Hymn Book* and its companion, the *Labour Church Tune Book*, published in 1892, is a direct heir of the *National Chartist Hymn Book* and *Democratic Hymns and Songs*, a link expressed in the reuse of songs by Elliott, Cooper and the mystical Chartist, Gerald Massey. Writing in the late 1920s, Joseph Clayton remembered the singing of Socialist songs and Labour hymns as 'a great feature of the meetings of the Labour Church', noting that it both revived an old custom of the Chartists and encouraged nonconformists of the Free Churches to associate themselves with the Labour movement. Although the Labour Church was, in Clayton's words, 'by no means professedly Christian', it nonetheless held Sunday meetings that again performed a dual purpose of creating an atmosphere of a place of worship and reinvoking 'similar festivities in Nonconformist circles' (Clayton 1926: 95).

Freethought also produced its own particular genre of ethical and progressive hymnbooks sharing many of the authors found in the socialist songbooks, including Morris, Shelley, John G. Whittier, Robert Lowell, W.J. Fox and Charles Mackay as well as more extreme figures such as the renowned anarchist, Louise S. Gugenberger (Bevington) and drew upon the same musical traditions.[15] From the late eighteenth century onward to late Victorian socialism, institutions such as the South Place Chapel not only produced these hymnbooks, but also provided the venue for countless musical performances by radical dissenters. Many of the tunes popular on the streets in the late nineteenth century, such as 'Hearts of Oak', 'Scot wha hae', 'and 'Men of Harlech', which had served the Chartists and later the Liberals so well, were also pressed into service by the socialists. Italian opera, a staple of working class music-making, particularly in the brass band movement, also found its way into the socialist repertoire, as did the melodies of Gilbert and Sullivan.

Socialism then, like previous radical movements, drew on a large body of popular music with which to sing its songs. In an 1889 review of the Carpenters' *Chants of Labour*, Oscar Wilde applauded this very eclecticism, praising socialism for not allowing 'herself to be trammelled by any hard and fast creed, or to be stereotyped into an iron formula'. He noted their openness to 'many and multiform natures' and welcomed their decisions to not only educate the people in political science but also in a wide range of music 'entirely free from any narrow bias or formal prejudice' so that 'Mendelssohn was followed by the "Marseillaise", and "Lillibulero," a chorus from "Norma", "John Brown" and an air from Beethoven's Ninth Symphony are all delightful to them' (Wilde 1889).[16]

Although socialists drew on their literary heritage in a relatively straightforward way to create what H.S. Salt called 'a tradition of sympathy' (Salt [1893]: xv)[17] that suited their ideological needs, their relationship to musical heritage was more complex, involving questions of musical literacy and popular memory. Socialists had less control over musical choices that were subject to exterior pressures other than ideology. It was one thing to read a new text from a song sheet, it was another to read musical notation. Tapping into collective memory – remembering the tune from its title on the page – was a basic requirement for popular singing. Songbooks with musical scores were the exception rather than the rule and only a very few newly composed songs achieved mass appeal for this reason. Shared memory was a primary concern: utility played a critical role in decisions about music.

Some socialists were very concerned by the tension between, on the one hand, ideological and aesthetic value and on the other pragmatic demands. Blatchford, Glasier, Georgia Pearce and, to a lesser extent, Carpenter, had concerns about the use of unsuitable tunes (Waters 1990: 116–18). In their utopian desire to create a new culture for a new age they rejected contemporary popular culture as irredeemably tainted by commercialism. In his *Socialism in Song*, Glasier left many ideologically uplifting poems without a tune, fearing that they would be ruined if associated with 'airs of the past, many of which are instinct with feeling or reminiscences of an anti-Socialist character'. Going one step further, he also omitted 'suitable' songs because it was impossible to wrest them from the melodies to which they had 'long been wedded' (Glasier 1895). Finding their musical heritage difficult to control Pearce and Blatchford almost exclusively used new music composed specifically for their *Clarion Song Book*. Only five pre-existing popular tunes survived, whose provenances were stripped down to their national origins so as erase any connection to popular culture. Amusingly, Salt's classic 'Hark! The Battle Cry' is no longer sung to the 'Men of Harlech' but to a 'Welsh air arranged'; Burn's immensely popular 'A man's a man for a' that' becomes merely a 'Scotch air'; the Civil War song which so successfully accompanied Morris' 'March of the Workers', 'John Brown's Body', becomes an 'American air' and the English drinking song 'Down among the dead men' supporting Morris' 'Come, comrades, come', is identified simply as an 'Old air', even 'God Save the Queen' becomes a non-specific 'National Anthem' to preserve the purity of 'Hail Sacred Comradeship'.

Pearce and Blatchford were clearly amongst a small minority who did not share Wilde's catholic taste nor his sense of humour which appreciated the 'amusing transpositions' that often occurred.[18] Wilde took particular enjoyment when 'Up, ye people' ('a very revolutionary song by Mr. John Gregory, bootmaker') was set to 'Rule Britannia' with the refrain beginning:

> Up ye People! Or down into your graves!
> Cowards ever will be slaves!
>
> (Wilde 1889)

It was exactly these amusing instances of Thompsonian counter-theatre that worried the more staid Socialists. They were most concerned for instance about the use of 'The British Grenadiers' for the German anarchist exile, Johann Most's 'Hymn of the Proletariat' (Waters 1990: 116).[19] However, the satirical use of this song can be found both in the earlier street ballad tradition and in numerous mainstream political songbooks.[20] It is clear, moreover, that these 'inappropriate' tunes were not always hastily added but were in the mind of the author when the new words were penned. This was often evident in the title or the text. The connection to the past was embedded rather than 'wedded'.

Writing in 1916 Edward Carpenter looked back on the compilation of *Chants of Labour* as a 'thing which might have been much better done by some one else', but he could find no one else to do it. 'And it was a queer experience', he recalled, 'collecting these songs of hope and enthusiasm, and composing such answering tunes and harmonies as I could ... ' (Carpenter 1916: 136). The production of *Chants of Labour* was an intimate affair, drawing upon many close friends for new music as well as re-casting and adapting 'the accompaniments and arrangements of old and standard airs' (Carpenter 1888: vi). The songbook was soon considered 'one of the best of the many Socialist song books' and came to function as a kind of a source book for subsequent collections (Clayton 1926: 17). As noted, Carpenter's own original contribution 'England arise, the long, long night is over', quickly gained a 'great vogue'. By 1897 at Leeds' May Day on Woodhouse Moor, 'twenty-thousand voices called for England to arise ... ' (Rowbotham 2008: 249).

Unlike the effete sandal-wearing Carpenter, Jim Connell was 'an enormous man, who invariably affected a flowing cloak, and a gigantic, wide-brimmed hat of picturesque appearance' (Clynes 1937: 87). In 1889, Connell, an Irish Land Leaguer, union agitator and secretary of the Workingmen's Legal Aid Society, boarded a train at Charing Cross Station in a high state of excitement after hearing a lecture by fellow Socialist, Herbert Burrows (Clynes 1937: 87). Burrows, a 'facile talker and emotional orator' (Stenning 1970: 32), so inspired Connell that in the fifteen minutes it took to reach his destination of New Cross Station he had finished the first two stanzas and chorus and mapped out the rest of what was to become one of the most powerful anthems of the international labour movement, 'The Red Flag'. It appeared in the SDF newspaper, *Justice*, on the Thursday before Christmas and by the following Sunday it was being sung in Liverpool and Glasgow (Connell 1889).

Both Carpenter and Connell attended a Birmingham ILP Conference in 1898. It was fitting that they were both there as, for one commentator, it marked a musical rite of passage:

> [Carpenter's] hymn 'England, arise!' was the marching song to which our Forlorn Hopes tramped to meet victory or defeat. But, by the time of

the 1898 Conference, another song was replacing it; one which has since been heard all over the world. I refer, of course to 'The Red Flag'
(Clynes 1937: 86)

This sense of succession from Carpenter to Connell is seen again in the celebrations of the socialist and labour successes following the 1906 and 1924 General Elections. In 1906 '"England arise, the long, long night is over", was chanted all over the country with fervour ... ' (Clayton 1926: 130). Whereas in 1924, following the election of the first Labour government, the 'whole assembly rose in chorus, and raised the roof of the mighty building, as together they sang the most fervent of all socialist anthems ever, "The Red Flag"' (Granville 3 October 2002).

The celebratory and overtly nationalist 'England Arise' is one of many radical responses to the questions raised in Shelley's 'Song to the Men of England', itself a staple of socialist song books, and foreshadowed Blatchford's enormously popular and yearningly nostalgic *Merrie England* (1894). It is one of only a few songs with original music that gained enormous popularity. Hubert Parry's setting of Blake's 'Jerusalem' would be a later example. Carpenter, however, not only wrote the words but also the hymn-like music. Music had preoccupied him from an early age. A largely self-taught pianist, Carpenter's determined efforts at the keyboard late at night and natural talent brought him to, as he described it, 'the far borderland of Beethoven's Sonatas'. This urge to play was accompanied by one to create: 'Indeed, it is curious', he remembered later in life, 'but I took to composing, or attempting to compose music, before I ever thought of composing or attempting to compose poetry' (Carpenter 1916: 23–24).

Connell's detailed account of the Red Flag's gestation revealed that it came into being as an act of many commemorations (Connell 1920: 5). Connell's fifteen minutes on the train from Charing Cross took place during the London Dockers' Strike which he considered to be 'the biggest thing of its kind that occurred up to that date'; he was also inspired 'by the Paris Commune, the heroism of the Russian Nihilists, the firmness and self-sacrifice of the Irish Land Leaguers, the devotion unto death of the Chicago Anarchists, and of other similar events' (Mann [1923] 1967: 68). Unlike Carpenter, Connell was no composer but had a popular tune firmly in mind when he wrote the poem. 'There is only one air which suits the words of "The Red Flag",' he declared, 'and that is the one which I hummed as I wrote it. I mean "The White Cockade".' Unfortunately, Connell's musical intent fell victim to the vagaries of the oral tradition. Subsequent alterations to 'The White Cockade' had rendered it, in his estimation, 'nearly a jig' and therefore unsuitable to his words; perhaps in response to these changes, fellow socialist Adolphe Smith Headingley replaced the tune in the mid-1890s with 'Maryland' (Mann [1923] 1967: 68–69; Connell 1920: 5). In this Connell was also profoundly disappointed and bitterly denounced the change. 'Headingley might as well have set the song to "The Dead March" in Saul', he fumed, '"Maryland" acquired that name during the American War of Secession'. If this was not bad enough, he continued, 'It is really an old German Roman Catholic hymn ... composed ... to remind people of their sins.' We know it as 'Tannenbaum'.

The story of 'The Red Flag' is well rehearsed; for our purposes, it epitomises the struggle between ideological sympathy and singability. A key problem for the outraged Connell was the disjuncture between the meaning of the words and music. 'Maryland' did not even reinforce the radical message of his poem through irony. Very different ideological heritage is embedded in each of the tunes. Connell's intention to sing the poem to the Jacobite song, 'The White Cockade', connected him to a long tradition of dissent, and Robert Burns, who wrote a version of the song, joined Shelley and Byron as a special hero of British radicalism. 'Maryland', however, was problematic in terms of radical heritage and became the subject of some dispute, not only because the tune's origins as 'church music' clashed with Connell's own atheism, but because of its place in Civil War history. Popular songs from the American Civil War had appeared as airs well before the rise of socialism, in broadside ballads and Liberal songbooks. William Morris' very popular 'March of the Workers', for example, was set to 'John Brown's Body' and 'Marching through Georgia' and 'Tramp, tramp, tramp' were standard tunes in the popular repertoire. 'Maryland, my Maryland', however was not such a straightforward appropriation. It was written in 1861 by the Southerner, James Ryder Randall, and was adopted as an anthem of the Confederacy and much later as the state song of Maryland. During the Civil War, several different versions of the words were published and, like the border state itself, the song was fiercely contested. In recent years Randall's lyrics have attracted criticism for their allegedly racist overtones. Ironically, Connell was unconcerned by the words; his objection was to the tune.

In his opinion the substitution did not even correct the problem of singability, 'Every time the song is sung to "Maryland" the words are murdered', he despaired (Connell 1920: 5). A few, such as George Bernard Shaw, agreed with Connell's damning assessment, decrying the song somewhat maliciously (and mysteriously) as 'the funeral march of a fried eel' (Churchill 1937: 53). Others, notably a proud Scotsman, Keir Hardie, made concerted efforts to remain true to Connell's wishes, taking the trouble while touring South Africa to give some Cape Town socialists 'a few lessons on how to sing the song ... to the more harmonious tune of "The White Cockade"' (Wyk 1998: 123). 'Maryland' was generally considered to be an easier tune to sing and over time it became 'The Red Flag'.

Music travels vast distances with ease as does its ability to commemorate. It is both moveable heritage and an efficient conveyor of heritage. Tunes and songbooks flowed out to the colonies of settlement in the minds and suitcases of the socialist immigrants and touring activists who moved around the

British world, from Melbourne, Johannesburg and Dunedin to Broken Hill, Wellington and Cape Town. The Dominions experienced the wholesale transplant of socialist musical culture – bands, choirs and orchestras – as well as the allied modes of performance and traditions of understanding. Music's power to disrupt, to question, to unify, to uplift was brought into play in public meetings, lectures, on street corners and at open air rallies as an integral part of radical political agitation.

The plethora of Australasian songbooks that appeared during the first two decades of the twentieth century generally replicated the British socialist canon. In the main, the songs of the late nineteenth-century socialist generation dominated, although important earlier figures such as Shelley, Lowell, Cooper and Elliot continued to appear. Like their British counterparts, these songbooks also displayed idiosyncratic features in response to their particular time and place. For instance Tom Mann's 'As Men We Must Fight' appears only in Australasian songbooks, presumably written during his years in New Zealand and Australia. In similar ways songbooks from the industrial north of England differed in their selections, both poetic and musical, to those produced in London reflecting different personalities and capabilities. Carpenter's reach extended well into the southern hemisphere. As most songbooks were produced without music, *Chants of Labour* (as well as the *Labour Church Tune Book*) became a reference book in Australasia as it did in Britain. It was so influential and available that it was sufficient to include an abbreviation and tune number at the top of a song.[21] Many Australian songbooks made explicit their debt to Carpenter by paying homage to him on the front cover with his own inscription from *Chants of Labour*, 'And they sang a new song'.

The 43rd song of *Chants of Labour*, 'The Fatherhood of God, and the Brotherhood of Man' provides a fascinating example of transnational movement in the other direction. Carpenter attributes the words of this poem to the *Otago Witness*. How Carpenter acquired the 31 May 1873 issue of this newspaper is unknown, but it is a telling instance of the way that printed material easily negotiated the vast distances of the British world. As the song became a regular feature in socialist collections, it lost its original attribution. By the time it appeared in Wellington's *Songs of Revolt* a decade later its tune was simply given as 'No. 43' from *Chants of Labour*. Ironically the song had come full circle without knowing it.[22]

'England Arise' was an example of the socialist ideal of creating a new art for a new age. Composing new words and new music was a practice taken up by socialists in both Australia and New Zealand. In Melbourne, an anarchist, J.A. Andrews, contributed 'Sons of the South' to the *Labour Song Book*; whereas 'Our Country' and 'A Marching Song' penned by his friends, Bernard O'Dowd and Marie E.J. Pitt, appeared in the *Socialist Songs* series. Party treasurer and amateur composer, Frank Vernon, contributed new music to O'Dowd's and Pitt's poems as well as to old standards including Cooper's

'Truth is Growing' and D.J. Nicoll's 'The Coming of the Light'. Across the Tasman Sea, the Scottish immigrant and secretary of the New Zealand Socialist party, Robert Hogg, mined his own poetic heritage (he traced his lineage back to the Ettrick Shepherd) to produce 'Demos is our King' and 'Workers of the World Unite' (the latter made its way into Australian collections), and J.B. Hulbert included his own setting of the 'The Red Flag' in his *Socialist Songs* in 1906.

Despite the enormous popularity of 'England Arise', its constraining nationalist agenda required textual adjustment to be relevant in other parts of the world. The solution was easy: the problematic 'England' was simply replaced, and it emerged as either 'Toilers Arise' or 'Labour Arise'. The Red Flag suffered no such impediment and became internationally popular without changing a word. Mann remembered it as 'the most popular song of its kind in Victoria'. It was sung at all their meetings. 'The Red Flag' was a powerful symbolic reminder to socialists like Mann of their movement's goals to wipe out all racial hatreds, get rid of national frontiers and to treat 'all men as brothers but in deed and in truth' (Mann [1923] 1967: 165–66). A South African socialist remembered the song attaining a similar significance for South African unionists early last century (Wyk 1998: 188–19, 123). It was sung by Taffy Long, Herbert Hull and David Lewis as they walked to the gallows, sentenced to death for murder during the 1922 Rand Miners' Strike in Johannesburg. A witness remembered the execution scene vividly: 'the prison seemed to be like a church with not a sound to be heard. The great audience became silent as the three started on the path to death singing:

> Then raise the scarlet standard high!
> Within its shade we'll live or die.
> Tho' cowards flinch and traitors sneer
> We'll keep the red flag flying here.
>
> (Verwey 1995)

Their funeral, attended by over 10,000 people, commenced and concluded with the singing of the same words.

Invariably, 'The Red Flag' opens or closes the songbooks in the same way as it opened and closed meetings amongst socialists of all stripes. The selection of songbooks under consideration here also reveals the stubborn persistence of 'The White Cockade'. In a few books only the Jacobite tune is given, while in others the singers are given a choice.[23] By the time it became a staple of the IWW repertoire 'Maryland' had taken hold, although it was not until 1953 in an Australian student songbook that the title 'Tannenbaum' appeared (*Rebel Songs: Song Book of the Australian Student Labour Federation* 1953).

Unlike 'England Arise', 'The Red Flag' assumed an equivalent position of importance in the American socialist tradition as the one it held in the

British. It was one of only a handful of British songs to do so, alongside H.S. Salt's 'Hark! The Battle-Cry is Ringing' and Edith Nesbit's 'Hope of the Ages'. The increasing presence of Wobbly songs after the First World War and the appearance of separate IWW songbooks in Australia reflect Australian socialism's openness, at least for a period, to Wobbly extremism and opened up another source of musical heritage from which to draw.[24]

Australasian songbooks from the 1950s and 1960s were explicitly historical and commemorative, consciously constructing a direct lineage to their past. In many cases an account of the song's history appeared under the title. An Australian student songbook published in 1947 reminded the singers of the 'Red Flag' that Australian workers contributed £30,000 to the strike fund, whereas a decade later *Kiwi Youth Sings* noted the use of the song in the 1890 Maritime Strike in New Zealand. Two inverse tendencies are present in the inter-generational transfer of this song tradition. Some iconic tunes such as 'Wearing of the Green', 'Scots wha hae', 'Men of Harlech' and the 'Vicar of Bray', long used to set other political texts, now appear in their own right with their original meaning laid bare. Others, such as the 'Red Flag', become the tune for more topical lyrics. In Race Mathews' edition it not only appears in its own right but also as a tune for 'The Shirker's Flag' and in *Freedom Songs*, a collection produced by the Eureka Youth League, it has the more sombre duty of supporting 'November 19 (1915)', a commemoration of the 'murder' of Joe Hill. Becoming part of an ongoing commemorative process Connell's song joined the 'usable past'. On the one hand his prediction that his song would live on was realised (Connell 1920: 5); on the other, he would have been bitterly disappointed to learn that not only had 'The White Cockade' been ruined, but the reviled tune, 'Maryland'-cum-'Tannenbaum', had in fact *become* 'The Red Flag'; a powerful reminder that heritage is always at the whim of the present.

For the student of heritage and commemoration an examination of singing for socialism through tangible and intangible heritage throws up a range of important issues. The first conclusion that can be drawn is historiographical. In contrast to the orthodox view of late Victorian socialist politics as fissiparous and irredeemably fractured, exploring socialist culture through the medium of the songbook reveals a common heritage. For all that they refused to march in step with each other, socialists often marched arm in arm with heroes of the past: the likes of Cooper, Elliott, Joe Hill and even the Vicar of Bray. Second, the pages of their songbooks suggest that commemoration was a process. By reaching into the past to draw on shared history, knowledge and understandings, radicals and socialists enlisted it into the service of the present. They performed their songs in the now.

Third, taken together the expansive collection of songbooks considered here are a reminder of the ready circulation of cultural forms, as well as ideas and individuals, around the globe. Those who struggled at the edge of the

British world had access to a rich repertoire augmented by the burgeoning tradition of radical songs across the Atlantic. At the same time it is clear that the radical and socialist song tradition in the Great Republic owed much to the toil of comrades in Britain. When sung to 'Austria', Morris' 'All for the Cause' sounded much the same in Chicago as it did in London, Sydney, or on the Veldt. At first glance the specificity of the title might have condemned Edward Carpenter's 'England Arise' to the narrow confines of Blake's 'green and pleasant land'. It nevertheless resounded around the Anglophone world – sometimes modified – but usually as a rousing incongruity. Carpenter's seminal composition pointed the way to a new aesthetic ideal that, at one and the same time, liberated socialists from the weight of the past and engaged them in the act of creating it.

The process of simultaneously using, making and performing heritage was enhanced every time a new set of lyrics was written, new melody composed, an old tune enlisted or discarded. This nexus between past and present is an aspect of using heritage that has attracted scant sustained attention. Venerable words spoke of past champions and heroic deeds, but even when the words were new the tunes provided continuity and reveal a longer if often complex teleology. This is evident on almost every page of the songbooks examined here. They are both *lieux de mémoire* and *sons de mémoire*.

Our case studies then show that heritage is mutable, crossing the boundaries of time, language and nation. Songbooks were the most important receptacle of this practice. No one exemplified the difficulties of negotiating and managing heritage more than Jim Connell when he penned 'The Red Flag'. As we have seen, his desire to support his message with a Jacobite song was thwarted by forces he could not control. The struggle continued long after he died. In 1945, the newly elected Labour government marched into the House of Commons singing Connell's anthem. Fifty-two years later at the conclusion of the Labour Party's Annual Conference in 2007, cards with the words of the 'The Red Flag' were handed out to delegates. As Simon Hoggart quipped, 'Some of us can remember a time when you would no more have needed the song's lyrics than you would have to teach Happy Birthday at a children's party.' 'There was a brief period during the Blair years when it was banned altogether', he continued, 'but once it had been safely defused, it returned – sung yesterday by a willowy soprano, so it sounded less like a call to the barricades than Proms in the Park' (Hoggart 2007).

Has it been defused? Perhaps Connell will have the last laugh. At about the same time as Tony Blair banished the 'The Red Flag' from its place in Labour ritual, Billy Bragg was recording it on compact disc. Not only has Bragg refused to let the song fade away, he honours Connell's original intention by restoring the 'White Cockade' (Bragg 1990). By joining Connell in singing for socialism, Bragg, like many before him, joined a chorus that has echoed across the years to the field of Culloden. The booklet accompanying Bragg's recording includes the lyrics to the 'The Red Flag' and a number of other radical and protest songs he has recorded; it is a socialist songbook for today.

Acknowledgements

We would like to thank the librarians at Hocken Library, University of Otago, Working Class Museum Library, Salford and the Socialist Party of Great Britain for helping us to access sources in their collections.

Notes

1 All songbooks referred to in this chapter are listed in chronological order in an appendix and not in the bibliography. For Mathews see *Biographical Register of the Victorian Parliament, 1900–84* (Melbourne 1985: 151).
2 See William Cartwright, *A Cavalier Song* (London, 1647); *The Fourth (and last) Collection of Poems, Satyrs, Songs, &c. Containing, I. A panegyrick on O. Cromwell, and his victories:* By E. Waller, Esquire (London 1689). See also: *The Cavalier Songs and Ballads of England from 1642 to 1684*, edited by Charles Mackay (London: G. Bohn, 1863); J. Bruce Glasier, *Socialism in Song*, (Manchester: National Labour Press 1919), p. xi.
3 See William Hick, *Chartist Songs and Other Pieces* (Leeds 1840); Patrick Brewster, *Chartist Songs and Socialist Sermons* (Glasgow n.d.); P. Brown, *Reform Songs and Squibs* (Edinburgh 1839); Thomas Cooper (ed.) *Shakespearean Chartist Hymn Book* (Leicester, 2nd edition 1843); Ernest Jones, *Chartist Songs and Festive Pieces* (London 1846).
4 Independent Labour Party Archive, Box 7, Working Class Movement Library, Salford; *Songs for Socialists*, Third and Enlarged Edition (Aberdeen 1890).
5 Ivy Tribe Collection, National Museum of Labour History, Manchester, Box 9: Various hymn books; Women's Liberation Federation, *Words of the Liberal Song Book*, n.d; Ada M. Bittenbender, *Women + Suffrage Campaign Song Book* (Lincoln, 1892, Huntington Library, San Marino).
6 See *Pall Mall Gazette* (1887: 7 December); *Daily News* (1887: 8 December). Morris, one of the best-known socialist aesthetes of his day, was a poet of prodigious talent and his Death March travelled across the Atlantic: it was used on May Day 1892 at the anniversary service of the execution of the Haymarket 'martyrs' in Chicago.
7 See *Proletarian Song Book*, (School Edition, First edition Glasgow 1918: 20–21, 29–30, 43, 45, 50–51); *I.W.W. Songs To Fan the Flames of Discontent* (nineteenth edition by 1923); *Rebel Songs* (Melbourne: 1953).
8 The Eureka Flag, or Southern Cross, was flown by miners protesting over a tax on the Victorian goldfields in 1854. The rebels swore an oath of independence under the flag during what is now known as the Eureka rebellion which has become an iconic event in Australian history.
9 The song was often sung with the chorus of *Ça Ira*.
10 See 'The Worker's Carmagnole', in Samuel Friedman, *Rebel Song Book* (New York, Rand School Press, 1935), 29.
11 McKinley shows how the sung was subsequently taken up by French anarchists and was used until the First World War at least.
12 See inter alia: *Labour Church Hymn Book*, London, 1892; *Songs for Socialists, Compiled by The Fabian Society* (London 1912), p. 47; Socialist Party of Australia, *Socialist Songs* (Melbourne, n.d.), song 13; The I.L.P. *Song Book*, 'The Worker' Socialist Newspaper Society, Huddersfield, [c.1925], pp. 2–3; *Labour Song Book*, [Melbourne, n.d], pp. 25–26.

13 See Carpenter *Chants of Labour*, p. vi: 'They are for the use of the people, and they are mainly the product of the people'.
14 The tune ' Austria' was taken from Josef Haydn's anthem, 'Gott erhalte Franz den Kaiser', written for Emperor Francis II. Later in 1797, Haydn himself used the melody in the second movement of his String Quartet op. 76 no. 3, which was given the nickname 'Emperor'. In 1841, the revolutionary republican poet, August Hoffmann von Fallersleben, used the tune to set his then inflammatory poem, 'Das Lied der Deutschen', which was, in 1922, to become the German national anthem, better known as 'Deutschland über alles'. It was not only the socialists that found the embedded radical heritage of this melody attractive; on 19 July 1908 it was sung to a 'A Liberal Programme' at the Great Demonstration held by the Wirral Liberal Association (Bodleian Library Broadside Ballads 2010).
15 See for example *Victorian Band of Hope Union Hymn Book* (Melbourne: Edwin Wilson 1860); *The Secularist's Manual of Songs and Ceremonies* (London: Austin and Co. [1871]); *Secular Songs and Gems of Thought* (Canterbury NZ: Canterbury Freethought Association 1892); *Hymns of Progress* (London: Progressive Association 1883); *Ethical Hymns* (London: Swann Sonnenschein 1899); *Hymns of Modern Thought* (London: Hampstead Ethical Institute 1900); *The Fellowship Hymn Book* (London: W.A. Hammond 1908).
16 The prevalence of art music in Carpenter's collection is unusual, as it is in the *Clarion Song Book*. In general the presence of classical music was restricted to Italian opera and extracts from Gilbert and Sullivan.
17 Salt's preface to *Songs of Freedom* provides a clear explanation and justification for this literary tradition. Its pillars included Romantic poets such as Shelley, Byron and Blake, Chartist and earlier radical poets, notably Robert Burns, and the American romantics, Lowell and Whittier, and preeminently Walt Whitman, all of whom in Salt's eyes struck a chord with socialist ideology. Music, however, plays no role at all in Salt's 'songs'.
18 The aesthetic concerns and goals of these few individuals are not reflected in the contents of the majority of the songbooks.
19 Waters relates how H.W. Hobart, the cultural writer for the SDF, in particular could not reconcile the 'ideological conflict' inherent in the combination of Most's poem and the 'The British Grenadiers'.
20 See for example the 1892 Home Rule ballad, 'Ulsters Defiance: A Ballad of the North' (Bodleian Library Broadside Ballads 2010), and Mr J. and Miss F. Payne's *Toilers and Moilers Patriotic Free Trade Songs* of 1904 in which two of three songs, 'Freedom of England' and 'A Cry to the Nation on behalf of willing workers' are both set to 'The British Grenadiers', the remaining 'Free Trade Fight' to 'Tramp, Tramp, Tramp'.
21 See for example *Socialist Songs* (London 1896); *I.L.P. Song Book* (Manchester 1896); *Songs of Revolt* (Wellington, NZ 1909); *Labour Song Book* (Melbourne 192?).
22 This example of transnational flow from periphery to centre is not isolated; earlier in 1892, the Manchester song book, *Songs for Co-Operators with Music*, issued by the educational committee of the Co-operative Union in Manchester, included a song, 'Maker of Earth and Sea: An Australian National Anthem' by J. Brunton Stephens to music by Giordani. It also is a rare collection that acknowledges the *Otago Witness* for the 'Fatherhood of God', thereby showing its indebtedness to Carpenter.
23 In two surviving songbooks from Dunedin, both from 1908, 'The White Cockade' is given as the only tune as it is in Melbourne's *Labour Song Book* and the Sydney Socialist Democratic League's *Songs of Socialism* over ten years later. Both options are given in the 1907 and 1909 editions of *Socialist Songs* in Melbourne and Wellington's socialists are also given a choice in *Songs of Revolt* as are the Americans in 1935 in Friedman and Bachman's *Rebel Song Book*.
24 An internationally popular Wobbly song 'Bump me into Parliament' was actually written by a Melbourne Wobbly – 'Casey of the One Big Union League, Melbourne'.

References

A.C. (31 May 1873) 'Fatherhood and Brotherhood, *Otago Witness*.
Allen, J. and Ashton, O. (2005) *Papers for the People*, London: Merlin.
Bodleian Library Broadsheet Ballads. 'Ulster's Defiance: A Ballad of the North'. Available HTTP: <http://bodley24.bodley.ox.ac.uk/cgi-bin/acwwweng/ballads/image.pl?ref=Johnson+Ballads+1342A&id=21072.jpg&seq=1&size=1> (accessed 7 September 2010).
Bodleian Library Broadside Ballads. 'A Liberal Programme'. Available HTTP: http://bodley24.bodley.ox.ac.uk/cgi-bin/acwwweng/ballads/image.pl?ref=Johnson+Ballads+1389&id=21125.gif&seq=1&size=0 (accessed 7 September 2010).
Bragg, B. (1990) *The Internationale*, Liberation Records.
Carlyle, T. (1831) 'Corn Law Rhymes', *Edinburgh Review*, July: 338–61.
——(1840) *Chartism*, London: James Fraser.
Carpenter, E. (1916) *My Days and Dreams being Autobiographical Notes*, London: Allen and Unwin.
Churchill, W. (1937) *Great Contemporaries*, London: T. Butterworth.
Clayton, J. (1926) *The Rise and Decline of Socialism in Great Britain 1884–1924*, London: Faber and Gwyer.
Clynes, J. R. (1937) *Memoirs 1869–1924*, vol. 1, London: Hutchinson and Co.
Connell, J. (21 December 1889) 'A Christmas Carol: The Red Flag', *Justice*.
——(6 May 1920) 'How I wrote the "Red Flag"', *The Call*: 5.
Cooper, T. ([1872] 1971) *The Life of Thomas Cooper by Himself*, Leicester: Leicester University Press.
——(1877) *Poetical Works of Thomas Cooper*, London: Hodder and Stoughton.
Dawson, S. (n.d.) 'Carpenter's Music', in Dawson, *The Edward Carpenter Archive*. Available HTTP: <http://www.edwardcarpenter.net/ecmusic.htm> (accessed 18 August 2010).
Evans, H. (1913) *Radical Fights of Forty Years*, London; Manchester: Daily News and Leader.
Eyerman R. and Jamison, A. (1998) *Music and Social Movements: Mobilizing Traditions in the Twentieth Century*, Cambridge: Cambridge University Press.
Frith, S. (1996) *Performing Rites: On the Value of Popular Music*, Cambridge: Harvard University Press.
Granville, D. (3 November 2002) 'The song for all socialists', *The Irish Democrat*. Available HTTP <http://www.irishdemocrat.co.uk/features/red-flag/> (accessed 25 August 2010).
Hall, D. (2001) *'A Pleasant Change From Politics': Music and the British Labour Movement Between the Wars*, Cheltenham, New Clarion Press.
Hoggart, S. (2007) 'Red Flag rises above a dodgy future', *Guardian*, 28 September.
Hunt, T. 'Eat, drink and be a communist', *Spectator*, 15 April 2009.
Janowitz, A. (1998) *Lyric and Labour in the Romantic Tradition*, Cambridge: Cambridge University Press.
Lefebvre, G. (1962) *The French Revolution*, London: Routledge.
Mackay, Charles (ed.) (1863) *The cavalier songs and ballads of England from 1642 to 1684*, London: G. Bohn.
McKinley, A. (2008) *Illegitimate Children of the Enlightenment: Anarchists and the French Revolution, 1880–1914*, New York: Peter Lang.
Mann, T. ([1923] 1967) *Tom Mann's Memoirs*, London: MacGibbon and Kee.
Murphy, D. *et al.* (eds) (2003) *The Premiers of Queensland*, St. Lucia: University of Queensland Press.
Nora, P. (1996) *Realms of Memory. Rethinking the French Past*, vol. 1, New York: Columbia University Press.

Orwell, G. (1937) *The Road to Wigan Pier*, London: V. Gollancz.
Pickering, P. A. (2003) 'The Hearts of the Millions: Chartism and Popular Monarchism in the 1840s', *History*, 88/2/290: 227–48.
Pickering, P. A. and Tyrrell, A. (2000) *The People's Bread*, Leicester: Leicester University Press.
Rowbotham, S. (2008) *Edward Carpenter: A Life of Liberty and Love*, London: Verso.
Salmon, N. (2001) 'The Communist Poet-Laureate: William Morris's Chants for Socialists', *Journal of William Morris Studies*, 14/3: 31–40. Available HTTP: http://www.morrissociety.org/JWMS/W01.14.3.SalmonSocialists.pdf (accessed 6 June 2010).
Salt, H.S. (1893) *Songs of Freedom*, London: Walter Scott Publishing Co.
Saunders, M. (2009) *The Poetry of Chartism*, Cambridge: Cambridge University Press.
Smith, G. M. (1969) *Joe Hill*, Salt Lake City: University of Utah Press.
Smith, L. (2006) *Uses of Heritage*, London; New York: Routledge.
Soboul, A. ([1968]; 1980) *The Sans-Culottes*, Princeton: Princeton University Press.
Stenning, H. J. (1970) '1906 and all that', *Journal of William Morris Studies*, 2/4: 31–33. Available HTTP: <http://www.morrissociety.org/JWMS/SU70.2.4.Stenning.pdf> (accessed 25 August 2010).
Svensen, S. *The Shearers' War*, Queensland University Press: St. Lucia.
Trentmann, F. (2008) *Free Trade Nation: Commerce, Consumption, and Civil Society in Modern Britain*, Oxford: Oxford University Press.
Ivy Tribe Collection, National Museum of Labour History, Manchester, Box 9: Various hymn books.
Verwey, E. J. (ed.) (1995) 'Samuel Alfred (Taffy) Long 1891–1922', in *New Dictionary of South African Biography*, vol. 1, Pretoria: HSRC. Available HTTP: <http://sahistory.org.za/pages/people/bios/long-sa.htm> (accessed 6 January 2010).
Waters, C. (1990) *British Socialists and the Politics of Popular Culture 1884–1914*, Stanford: Stanford University Press.
Waters E. and Murray-Smith, S. (1947) *Rebel Songs*, [Melbourne?] Australian Student Labor Federation.
Watkins, J. *Life, Poetry and Letters of Ebenezer Elliott, the Corn-Law Rhymer*, London?: n.p.
[Wilde, O.] (15 February 1889) 'Poetical Socialists', *Pall Mall Gazette*.
Wyk, J. (1998) ' "Volcano Needing Constant Watching": South African White Labour and Socialist Culture 1900–924', *Journal of Literary Studies*, 14/1: 116–35.

Selected songbooks in chronological order

Reform Songs and Squibs. (1839) By P. Brown. Edinburgh.
Shakespearean Chartist Hymn Book. ([1839] 2nd edition 1843) Edited by Thomas Cooper 1839 Leicester.
Chartist Songs and Other Pieces. (1840) By William Hick. Leeds.
Chartist Songs and Socialist Sermons. (n.d.) By Patrick Brewster. Glasgow.
Chartist Songs and Festive Pieces. (1846) By Ernest Jones. London.
The Free Soil Minstrel. (1848) New York, Martyn and Ely.
Victorian Band of Hope Union Hymn Book. (1860) Compiled under the direction of The Union Melbourne: Edwin Wilson.
Reform Songs. [1867] London: Farrah.
The Secularist's Manual of Songs and Ceremonies. [1871] Edited by Austin Holyoake and Charles Watts. London: Austin.

Hymns of Progress. (1883) London: The Progressive Association.
Songs for Liberal Electors. (1886) London: Manchester.
Radical Rhymes no. 1. (1887) By W.C. Bennett. London: Hart.
Socialist Songs. [1887] Aberdeen: M'Kay.
Socialist Songs. [1887] London n.p.
Chants of Labour: A Song Book of the People with Music. (1888) Edited by Edward Carpenter. London: Swan Sonnenschein.
Socialist Songs (1889) Aberdeen: Committee of the Aberdeen Branch, Socialist League.
A Songbook for Socialists. [1890] London: William Reeves.
Secular Songs and Gems of Thought. (1892) Canterbury [N.Z.]: Canterbury Freethought Association.
Songs for Co-Operators with music. (1892) Manchester: Co-operative Union.
Words of the Liberal Song Book. (n.d.) London: Women's Liberation Federation.
Women + Suffrage Campaign Song Book. (1892) Edited by Ada M. Bittenbender. Lincoln: Tribune.
The Labour Church Hymn and Tune Book. (1893) Edited by E. and J. Trevor. London; Manchester: Labour Prophet Publishing Offices.
Socialist Songs. (1894) Edited by John Bruce Glasier. Glasgow: Labour Literature Society.
I.L.P. Song Book. (1896) Compiled by Harry Henshall. Manchester.
Socialist Songs. (1896) London n.p.
S.D.F. Song Book. (1898) London: Twentieth Century Press.
Songs issued by the Liberal and Radical Union. [18 – ?] London.
Liberal Election Songs. [18 – ?] London; Manchester.
Liberal Election Songs. [18 – ?] [version with music] London; Manchester.
Liberal Song Sheet. (n.d.) s.l.
Hymns of Modern Thought. (1900) London: Hampstead Ethical Institute.
Socialist Songs with Music. Edited by Charles H. Kerr. (1902) Chicago: Charles H. Kerr and Co. Cooperative.
Labour Songs. (1902) Wellington: Wellington Branch of the New Zealand Socialist Party.
Toilers and Moilers Patriotic Free Trade Songs. (1904) By Mr J. and Miss F. Payne. Aldershot, UK s.l: n.p.
Socialist Songs with Music. (1906) Edited by J.B. Hulbert. Wellington: J.B. Hulbert.
Clarion Song Book. (1906) Edited by Georgia Pearce. London: Clarion Press.
Socialist Songs with Music. [1906–23] Melbourne: Fraser and Jenkinson.
Socialist Songs. (1907) Melbourne: The Socialist Party.
Fellowship Hymn Book. (1908) London: W.A. Hammond.
Socialist Songs. [1908] Dunedin [N.Z.]: Fergusson and Mitchell.
Socialist Songs. [1908] Dunedin [N.Z.]: New Zealand Socialist Party.
Songs of Revolt no. 1. (1909) Wellington: New Zealand Socialist Party.
Socialist Songs. [1909–12] Melbourne: The Socialist Party (Affiliated with the Socialist Federation of Australasia).
I.W.W. Songs and Poems: To Fan the Flames of Discontent, 5th ed. [19 – ?] Adelaide: I.W.W.
Songs for Socialists. Compiled by the Fabian Society. (1912) London: The Fabian Society.
Socialist Song Book. [1917] Sydney: Social Democratic League.
Proletarian Song Book. (1918) Glasgow n.p.
Songs of Socialism. [1918?] Sydney: Social Democratic League.
Demonstration on the Domain: Songs of Freedom. [1919–39?] Sydney: I.W.W.
Barrier Socialist Songster. [191-?] Issued by the Barrier Social-Democratic Club, Broken Hill. Broken Hill [NSW]: The Club.
I.W.W. Songs. [191-?] Sydney: I.W.W. Publishing Bureau.

The Socialist Labor Party Book of Socialist Songs. (1927) Sydney: The Party.
Socialist Songs, 10th edn, enlarged. [192-?] Melbourne: The Socialist Party (Affiliated with the Socialist Federation of Australasia).
Songs to Fan the Flames of Discontent. [192-?] Sydney: I.W.W.
The Communist Song Book. [192-?] London: The Workers' Socialist Federation.
Labour Song Book. [192?] Melbourne: Tocsin Print.
Labour's Song Book. [1931] London: I.L.P. Publication Department.
Rebel Song Book: Eighty-Seven Socialist and Labor Songs for Voice and Piano. (1935) Edited by Samuel H. Friedman and Dorothy Bachman. New York: Rand School Press.
The Left Song Book. (1938) Edited by Alan Bush and Randall Swingler. London: V. Gollancz.
Rebel Songs. (1947) Edited by Edgar Waters and S. Murray-Smith. [Melbourne?] Australian Student Labor Federation.
Kiwi Youth Sings. (1951) Wellington: The New Zealand Student Labour Federation and The New Zealand Progressive Youth League.
Rebel Songs. (1953) [Sydney?]: Australian Student Labour Federation.
The Songs of Joe Hill. (1960) Edited by Barrie Stavis and Frank Harmon. New York: Oak Publications.
Socialist Songs. (1963) Edited by Race Mathews. Melbourne: Victorian Fabian Society.
Freedom Songs. [196-?] Melbourne: Eureka Youth League.

Chapter 14

'Faces in the Street'
The Australian poetic working class heritage

Sarah Attfield

> Working-class literature is not only a grouping of novels, poems, plays, autobiographies, *et cetera* ... it is also a name we can give to a literary/social/critical practice that is informed by a consciousness of the social and historical importance of class antagonisms.
>
> (Syson 1993: 87)

> It is in literature, above all, that we observe in a peculiarly complex coherent, intensive and immediate fashion the workings of ideology in the textures of lived experience of class-societies.
>
> (Eagleton 2006: 101)

Australia has a rich history of working class poetry that includes poetry of lament and protest from eighteenth-century transported convicts, nineteenth- and early twentieth-century poems of colonial settlement in the bush and developing city slums, 1940s and 1950s poetry with socialist leanings and links to the Communist Party of Australia; union songs, 1970s and early 1980s worker and performance poetry, Aboriginal poetry dealing with hardship and discrimination and contemporary poets from working class backgrounds who continue to explore working class experience.

According to Silverman and Ruggles, heritage can be tangible and intangible and is important for creating a sense of 'personal and community identity' (2007: 3). Heritage in this sense is not neutral and is entwined with notions of power and control (Silverman and Ruggles 2007). What is interesting is who and how certain types of heritage gain credence over others and how exclusions occur. Trouillot (1995) emphasises the importance of history outside official, academic sources – history instead that is produced and learned through popular culture and unofficial narratives. He describes writers as 'field labourers' in the production of history (1995: 25), and suggests that it is necessary to access histories that are written in the 'home, in poetry and childhood games' (1995: 71). For Trouillot (1995), the past and present are implicated in each other and poetry from the past can thus help us to understand the poetry of today and provides continuity for a shared culture.

The work of past and present poets demonstrates some of the ways in which working class Australians have expressed themselves. Their poetry is diverse, energetic, playful and committed. The poetry reveals a strong sense of working class culture and stands as a record of working class cultural heritage. Their voices should be heard and acknowledged but, because working class writing is mostly 'rooted outside the academy' (Coles and Zandy 2007: xix) their work has been marginalised – many Australian working class poets have struggled to gain recognition within the literary mainstream and their work has been 'hidden or forgotten ... or actively suppressed as political propaganda' (Coles and Zandy 2007: xix). They have also fought against stereotypes as they have challenged the views within their communities that poetry is elitist or too difficult and the views from outside that have suggested that working class poetry is a literary inferior, unsophisticated and too grim. Poetry that engages with the variety of working class experience is an important method of highlighting class issues in Australia – working class writing can reveal how class has operated as a 'shaping force' (Coles and Zandy 2007: xx) and provides an alternative narrative; one which presents the 'perspective and circumstances of the least powerful' (Coles and Zandy 2007: xx). Working class writing also shows that artistic and cultural production has never been the exclusive domain of the elite and offers a way of inclusion for working class heritage – bringing past and present working class voices and stories to the fore and contributing to a shared understanding of working class history and culture.

History of Australian working class poetry

According to historians Jordan and Pierce (1990), in eighteenth- and nineteenth-century Australia, poetry was not necessarily thought of as an elitist pastime and the poetry pages of newspapers such as the *Bulletin* were often used to comment on politics, life in the settlements and the various social issues of the day and provided 'a means of expression' (Jordan and Pierce 1990: 12). This poetry was generally accessible – catering for readers from a variety of backgrounds (Inglis Moore 1971). Despite the majority of colonial Australians living in the growing cities, there was a general sense of romanticism for the bush as expressed by poets such as A.B. 'Banjo' Patterson; however, some poets such as Henry Lawson and Mary Gilmore highlighted the struggles and hardships faced by both bush and city dwellers. Henry Lawson and Mary Gilmore were socialists and their politics and commitment to working class causes is evident in their poetry. Lawson's *Faces in the Street* (1900) paints an alternative picture to the popular nineteenth-century bush myth, describing instead the struggle and despair of working class city people during a typical day and night and includes the exhausted workers returning home, the unemployed lingering in the streets and sex workers using the streets for trade:

> They lie, the men who tell us, for reasons of their own,
> That want is here a stranger, and that misery's unknown;
> For where the nearest suburb and the city proper meet
> My window-sill is level with the faces in the street–
>   Drifting past, drifting past,
>   To the beat of weary feet–
> While I sorrow for the owners of those faces in the street.
>
> (Lawson 1900: 26–32)

This is a city of slums, disease and despair and Lawson imagines a time when the workers might reclaim these 'cruel' streets and march together in revolution:

> Then, like a swollen river that has broken bank and wall,
> The human flood came pouring with the red flags over all,
>   And kindled eyes all blazing bright with revolution's heat,
> And flashing swords reflecting rigid faces in the street–
>   Pouring on, pouring on,
>   To a drum's loud threatening beat,
> And the war-hymns and the cheering of the people in the street.
>
> (Lawson 1900: 26–32)

Mary Gilmore's interest in working class politics and the plight of the poor was sparked by the years she spent as a teacher in mining towns (Jose 2009). She was especially interested in how poverty and hardship affected women and this is expressed in *In Poverty and Toil*:

> It's workin' early, workin' late,
> Year in, year out, the same;
> Until we seem but work-machines,
> An' women but in name.
>
> (Gilmore 1953:127)

This is a pessimistic picture as the harsh life is relentless for the women in Gilmore's poems:

> So up, and out to work, my girl,
> We have no time to waste,
> Our lot, the bitter bread of life,
> We eat in bitter haste.
>
> (Gilmore 1953:127)

Poems by Lawson and Gilmore present an important and alternative view of colonial life in Australia – far removed from the romantic, idyllic bush; the descriptions here are based in the real, everyday experience for those near the bottom rung of colonial society (the bottom rung occupied by Aboriginal people).

Although in contemporary Australian society there is a tendency to ignore the poems of hardship from the colonial era in favour of the more romantic bush ballads, it should be noted that these poems were likely to have been read (or accessed) by working class people when they were written. It was not unusual in the nineteenth century for writers from different class backgrounds, from 'mechanics to the governing elite' (Jordan and Pierce 1990: 14) to be published in the same publications and a reasonably diverse community of writers existed, aided by the establishment of Mechanics Arts Institutes which were set up as libraries and learning spaces for working class people (Jordan and Pierce 1990). There was a desire for Australian representation in poetry from 'working men and pioneer women' (Jordan and Pierce 1990: 15) as education in the arts was seen as a method of moral improvement. And Haynes points to the importance of nineteenth-century verse, especially rhymed verse, of the time which had popular appeal due to its ability to 'document history, heroics and current events, tell stories, comment on social issues and satirise' (Haynes 2001: 9). There were exclusions, of course, as Trouillot states, each 'historical narrative is a particular bundle of silences' (1995: 27) and the working class poets included in these forums were most likely Anglo-Celtic – this was a time when the exclusion of Aboriginal people and racism towards ethnic minorities such as the Chinese population were overt.

Carter suggests that changes to this relatively democratic poetry community began in the early 1920s when particular high-profile poets and editors geared their work towards a more formally educated reader in possession of the cultural capital required to appreciate modernist forms of poetry (Carter 1999). And while some small poetry magazines retained their intentions to remain accessible to a wide readership, others began to distance themselves from the 'common reader' and popular forms and turned instead towards experimental work and sophisticated cultural critique (Carter 1999). Such magazines began to dominate the poetry scene and their influence has been lasting, with the trend toward modernist styles remaining which has implications for the availability of spaces sympathetic to working class poetry.

This lack of formal spaces for the publication of working class poetry did not mean that working class people stopped writing, and there were groups of writers and editors committed to the representation and publication of working class voices (Syson 1989). In 1944 a group of socialist writers founded the Realist Writers Group, and a specialist working class publisher, the Australasian Book Society was established in 1952 (Syson 1999). The Communist Party of Australia, the Socialist Party and trade unions encouraged and assisted in the formation of a small number of presses focused on writing by and about workers. These presses such as Current Book Distributors in Sydney and the Australian Student Labour Federation of the

1940s and 1950s, included poetry about miners, rural workers and other working people (Scalmer 1997). By the end of the 1950s many of the established writers had left the Communist Party of Australia due to the presence of McCarthyism and some writers turned completely away from politicised writing. Publications such as the *Realist Writer* and *Overland* moved away from their previous emphasis on working class writing (Scalmer 1997).

However, working class politics continued to be explored in poem and song form and produced by ordinary working people. In *Ratbags and Rabblerousers: a Century of Political Protest, Song and Satire*, Warren Fahey has collected a number of poems and songs written by working class people between 1900 and 2000 and which includes the experiences of hardship during the depression years. *The Depression* was written (and intended to be sung) by a working man, Herb Green:

> I'm only an old relief worker, I haven't got much of a life,
> I do six days work every fortnight, to keep the kids and the wife.
> We never have very much tucker, our blankets are faded and old,
> It's weeks since the kids tasted butter, we shiver all night with the cold.
>
> (Fahey 2000:111)

This worker's voice provides contemporary readers with a view into the past and a context for contemporary working class writers to work from. And despite the disappearance of working class forums such as the *Realist Writer*, working class experiences were still being conveyed through union songs and popular music throughout the 1960s and 1970s. In 1973 Denis Kevans and Seamus Gil wrote *Across the Western Suburbs* which depicted the movement of working class people from inner city Sydney to the outer suburbs due to the sale and development (later gentrification) of traditional working class homes:

> Before I even knew it, we were shifted to Mount Druitt,
> And the planners never gave me any say, boys.
> Now it really makes me weep, I am just at home to sleep,
> For it takes me hours to get to work each day, boys.
>
> What's happened to the pub, our local little pub
> Where we used to have a drink when we were dry, boys?
> Now we can't get in the door for there's carpet on the floor
> And you won't be served a beer without a tie, boys.
>
> (Fahey 2000:248)

Moving into the 1980s and a group of Melbourne writers led by performance poet π.o. created a writing collective and a magazine with the intention of publishing poetry by working people. The magazine was called *925* and π.o. and other members of the collective handed it out for free outside workplaces. The majority of poetry in *925* focused on everyday working life as illustrated in the poem *Shiftwork* by Bonny Henderson:

> Dad's on the midnight shift again,
> DON'T rules: 4 kids,
> endless dumb afternoons having
> a "bit of bloody consideration".
> Dad's asleep; Mum's on patrol.
>
> Dad slept through 3 births,
> 4 first school days, 14 eisteddfods,
> 4 first communions, & when we all
> became soldiers of Christ. Slept
> when peter joined the railways,
> when wal went to Sydney
> hairdressing, when 2 grannies
> & 2 granddads died, when aunty
> poll forgot her hearing aid
> & didn't see the train …
>
> Once I caught him between bed & work,
> a big man, toppled, beer in hand,
> on a chrome & vinyl chair,
>
> & said: Dad, Dad. He turned
> as if whatever propped him up
> had melted, & focused on me:
> Dad! I gotta 100, I gotta 100
> for shorthand. O well, he said,
> do better next time …
>
> (π.o. 1985: 24)

Henderson lets us into the world of the shift worker and in a characteristically working class fashion, uses humour to illustrate the impact of the father's shift work on the whole family. The worker is disassociated from his family and like many working class people who do not have control over work hours his exhaustion means that he is unable to participate fully in life outside work.

According to π.o. (1985) it was a struggle to have this kind of poetry acknowledged by the established literary journals which preferred the more esoteric and language-driven poetry of their middle class contributors. But poets such as π.o. continued to perform their work to diverse audiences at poetry readings in pubs and workplaces and self-published and distributed their work.

After the flurry of organised activity orchestrated by π.o. in the 1980s, there has been a dearth of organised activity from working class writers or publishers. Since then there have been some attempts to create spaces for working class voices such as the small magazine *Red Lamp*; however, this periodical ceased publication in the late 1990s and to date the only press committed to working class writing is Melbourne's Vulgar Press which is a small independent publisher with limited resources. Syson (1997) suggests that the lack of 'sympathetic' publishers and collectives has left working class writers working alone and has meant that working class readers are often unaware that there is writing representing their experiences. But, despite this isolation, working class poets do still tend to operate within similar contexts (Haslett 1999) and this is manifested in the shared characteristics of working class poetry and also in the continuation of themes/stylistic concerns from colonial verse to the present day.

Working class poetic

How can working class poetry be defined? Does working class poetry exist as a body of definable work? It can be argued that working class poetry fills the gaps of representation and creates spaces for the expression of working class life (Lauter 2005) – from the hardships and oppression to the celebration of working class community and culture (Daniels 2005). Working class poetry challenges elitist notions of 'high art' and empowers working class writers and readers and disrupts the comfortable world of privilege. It is often poetry created with a particular aim, to draw attention to the experiences of class and to provide a sense of shared culture (Coles and Zandy 2007). Working class writing is 'marked by its roots in … historical moments' (Coles and Zandy 2007: xxiii) as writers respond to specific historical events. Ultimately it is a collectivist model of writing 'by, about and in the interests of the working class' (Coles and Zandy 2007: xxii). Some working class poetry calls overtly for change and political action, some is linked to socialist ideals (Lauter 2005) and some is created out of a desire for working class life to be acknowledged and understood. But all working class poetry is written with a working class audience in mind.

Working class poetry tends to emerge from direct experience – despite a small number of middle class poets who have displayed certain empathy for working class life – most Australian working class poets come from a working class background. They have been employed in a variety of working class jobs from labouring to clerical work and there are those who have written while still on the job and those who have since left such occupations to take up adult education. These backgrounds create a sense of lived experience which informs the poetry with empathy and authenticity.

I would argue that Australian working class poetry possesses some defining characteristics in both style, form and content and these commonalities can be traced from the early to the contemporary. The poetry is generally written in a direct, accessible way with an emphasis on working class speech patterns and slang (Christopher and Whitson 1999) – the result of which is a natural rhythm (Morley and Worpole 1982) and style that lends itself to be read aloud. This emphasis on working class speech can be seen in the work of colonial poets such as C.J. Dennis who used renditions of working class dialect in his poetry – written phonetically to allow the reader to 'hear' and 'feel' the accent which serves to validate this particular version of English. Wesling (1993) suggests that this kind of rendition challenges the idea of 'standard' English and positions the reader intimately with the poem's narrator. It also serves as a way to record particular versions of working class speech to provide future readers with an understanding of how working class argot may change over time. The devaluing of non-standard English is also felt by writers from other marginalised groups such as Aboriginal and migrant writers and in an untitled poem π.o. (1978: 76) uses a rendition of Greek accented English:

Pita! yoo rayt leta!

the akchell rock hit me was the size of
evrij pilow (apox 40/50lb)
the walls whor saif. w-hay it hepen, i do not know.
thet was up to the pepol abav me.

i was drilling whit my machin.
the rock hit my halmat and giv me conchshn,
and i hev 2 to 3 tayms a wek sever hadaks.

i wen to fissioterapiss, 7 munts
bicoss i was paralaiss
and my lef ensait is very wek.

This poem demonstrates the effects of injuries sustained at work: specifically a construction worker's head injury. Although this particular poem is light in tone, it shows that many workers face daily dangers and risk serious injury. The character in the poem is still suffering months after the accident occurred and serious implications for his future health are suggested, as is the absence of adequate workers' compensation. This poem also presents an innovative style of language as π.o. uses phonetic renditions of a Greek accent, allowing the migrant's voice to be presented and challenging the assumption that poetry should only be written in 'standard English'. The rules of the dominant language are subverted and the poet adapts and reworks the language creating a new hybrid version which rejects the codes of the dominant culture (Corkhill 1994). The language therefore becomes his own. Reclaiming language is an important factor in working class poetry as poets reveal the richness and diversity of their speech and dialect.

If there is a tendency in Australian working class poetry to write using authentic speech patterns, there is also a tendency to avoid the use of metaphor and ambiguous imagery (Lauter 1997). While acknowledging that metaphor is used strategically by some writers faced with a repressive, censoring state power, it can be suggested that in an Australian context, metaphor can be seen as an indulgence to those faced with hardship (Daniels 1995) and is generally favoured by those who can distance themselves from such concerns (Bourdieu 1984). Imagery in working class poetry is therefore more likely to be grounded in the quotidian and generally avoids obscure references to art, philosophy, classical literature, etc. However, some poetry does include references to specific events such as strikes and other collective action. For Hoggart (1973), this can be seen in working class art in general which places an emphasis on everyday life, and Williams points to the success of art that is able to 're-create' such experiences for the reader (1961: 34). Working class poetry is rarely lyrical (Daniels 2005) and poets often favour a clear narrative structure which points to the importance of storytelling in working class culture. Although a writer might fictionalise an event and characters, there is always a sense of the everyday reality of work and life in general. However, if workers are using poetry as a way to 'daydream' through their day, the poetry they produce throws the reader straight back into the reality of that workplace and their daily struggle as can be seen in Justine Williams' *Meatworker* (2003) which considers the position of female abattoir workers in the 1950s:

> So Patsy got the job, X dollars a week in hand
> on the slaughter chain, plus hygiene cap
> that sealed her blazing hair in a white calyx.
> Did her father say, like my neighbour pontificating
> THEY'RE UNFEMININE, I'VE SEEN THE WAY
> THEY FLASH THEIR KNIVES, YOU'D THINK TWICE
> BEFORE YOU SLEPT WITH 'EM. WHY, IN A DUST-UP
> A MAN MIGHT LOSE HIS BALLS. But I found out
> Patsy's father took off with another woman long ago
> and her mother already works in the gut-house.
> Now she'll buy wisps of silk for her white limbs
> and bike tyres for two brothers running wild
> and music that will drown the meat-works din.

> She learns to keep up with the queue of carcasses,
> to wield the sterile knife. One plunge extracts
> the steaming heart, thins arms embrace
> the grey guts and heave them down the chute,
> working like a man for something less reward
> and only equal when the strike is called.
>
> I saw her yesterday, without her cap,
> unexpected as a poppy opening scarlet petals
> in the grey tension of the picket line.
>
> (Williams 2003: 61)

Williams is a Western Australian poet and left-wing radical born in 1914 whose work centres on the rights of women and workers. In *Meat Worker* she highlights the position of women taking traditional masculine roles in the workforce and also points to the solidarity displayed by many workers during periods of industrial action. Arguably a continuing cultural phenomena among working class people.

If 'standard' poetry collections and anthologies contain poems with an emphasis on abstract themes such as 'love' and 'truth' and 'beauty' (Oresick and Coles 1990), then working class poetry tends to focus on work – the daily routine of working class occupations, the struggle to support individuals and families, women's work in the home and the absence of work during periods of unemployment. Generally, this kind of labour is not the subject matter for poetry published in mainstream literary journal, but Syson suggests that the combination of poetry and work offers potential for the creation of inspiring literature (1999–2000).

Australian poets have written about many different types of work. This has included rural work – farm labouring, timber felling, fishing and urban work – factory jobs, trades, retail work, service industries as well as the underground work of sex workers, drug dealing and other criminal activities. Various workplace themes appear; sometimes the writer recreates the repetition of menial tasks (Christopher and Whitson 1999), and sometimes issues of working conditions such as exploitation and injury are highlighted. There is often a sense of 'us and them' as workers fight for better conditions and pay, or despondency at the seeming powerlessness felt by some workers when faced with an unjust work situation. Poems also deal with the human cost of working class jobs – the effect on the body and the effect on family life (especially for shift workers) and the often devastating effects of redundancy and unemployment. But there can also be a celebratory tone as writers convey camaraderie or illustrate the pleasures to be found in doing a job well, regardless of the nature of that job. In *you (pointing), gesture (beard), jigga-jigga*, Cathy Young (2004) describes the grind of factory work in a 1970s Melbourne fruit cannery but also the connections that can be made between workers:

> seven pairs of eyes looked at me
> along and across the peaches belt
> large and juicy fruit halves
> final paring steady congenial pace
> question unimaginable on apricots
> small fruit no talk possible
> fourteen Greek Polish Yugoslav Aussie
> seasonal eyes different tongues
> looked up and smiled
> wicked women of the factories
> laughing knowingly
> at what mothers couldn't tell
> common language of existence
> dreamtimes or
> peace and a good night's sleep
>
> (Young 2004:34)

Here, Young shows how the workers share a common language of experience despite their language and other cultural differences. They find a way to connect and to find some happiness despite the repetitive nature of their work.

Australian working class poetry tends not to deal with abstraction. If abstract notions such as 'beauty' or 'nature' are explored, they are generally made concrete and relate back to direct experience and everyday life. Working class poets are more likely to deal with the effects of poverty on a young couple in love or present a landscape from a timber feller's perspective. This is because it is the people who take centre stage in working class poetry – and the autobiographical content, while based on individual experience, is intended to be understood as collective experience and shared understanding (Zandy 1995). And despite the often harshness of life depicted, there is also space for hope and possibilities (Zandy 1990) as demonstrated by Cathy Young in *When Jenny George Spoke*:

> the clouds sang
> deep bass and contraltos
> filled days and nights
> no longer lonesome.
> I heard the stories and tunes
> dreams and wishes of workers
> tumbling from the guts of her voice
> calling me to dance.
> I waved my washerwoman
> factory shop-girl picker sorter
> packer cleaner arms high
> moved my often bent

squeezed squatted toting body
rhythmically to the beat
my back straight and proud
as the strongest of trees
my voice humming along to her chorus
me and millions of other working women
worth our salt.

(Young 2004: 82)

This poem is a celebration of working class collectivity and shows the inspiration that certain individuals can create when working class people believe someone has their best interests at heart (Jenny George was the president of the Australian Council for Trade Unions 1996–2000). Here, Young also highlights some of the effects of working on the body – she doesn't gloss over the negative effects of such legacies of working life but she does also suggest how working class people can draw strength from each other in collective action. This links to the kind of camaraderie displayed in many working class poems throughout Australian literary history.

Within Australian literary history since European invasion there have been many Aboriginal writers who have written about their particular experiences. Aboriginal poets such as Oodgeroo Noonuccal (writing mainly in the 1960s) have written about the position of Aboriginal people since invasion and others such as Kerry Reed-Gilbert, Alf Taylor, Graeme Dixon and Charmaine Papertalk-Green write about hardship and economic struggle within a racist society. Including Aboriginal poets under the umbrella of working class writing is problematic as it is possible that such a definition denies the specific experiences of Aboriginal oppression since invasion (Syson 1993) and I am aware that my white skin privilege implicates me in the past and present racist treatment of Aboriginal people in Australia. But, having said this, Aboriginal people are over-represented within the working class and their stories of struggle and oppression can be paralleled with that of non-Aboriginal working class poetry. There is a similar tendency towards the use of non-standard English and colloquial speech patterns and certain common themes of everyday hardship and inequality pervade Aboriginal poetry. In *Riches*, Kevin Gilbert (1978) writes from an Aboriginal woman's perspective:

Had one pair of shoes between us
Carried 'em in our hands each day
Three miles to town from our old bag humpy
Dirt floor, open fireplace I turn *green*
At the thought of how hungry we was at times
And we'd take turns to wear the shoes ...

(Gilbert 1978:17–18)

I would suggest that Aboriginal poetry challenges the narrow view of Australian working class culture as only white and Anglo-Celtic.

Because working class poetry is written with different intentions to most bourgeois poetry, it needs to be approached differently and its aims, messages and context of creation need to be considered. Working class poetry, while possessing aesthetic qualities is not often created as art for art's sake and its social function needs to be taken into account. The small sample of Australian working class poetry presented in this chapter shows how working class poetry can reflect and question life, and offers a way to understand those who are marginalised. Poetry can highlight the inequalities and oppression experienced by working class people and can empower those who have had little opportunity to have their stories told. Poetry can be a celebration of identity and culture and can bring together members of a community through shared experiences. It can provide a window into those experiences for those on the outside. Cultural production of any kind is empowering for working class people and the cultural products produced whether in the form of poetry, fiction, film, song, etc. are an important component of working class cultural heritage. Because of the documentary nature of much working class poetry, it provides links to the working class past and allows working class readers to understand how their cultural heritage has been shaped by class. Readers can learn how class impacted on the daily lives of their forebears and see how the legacies of class have persisted or transformed over time. Poems that reveal life on the land or the road as farm labourers or shearers and domestic servants, etc., provide a human aspect to the official histories. The language and storytelling in these earlier poems points to the ways in which cultural formations have occurred as the stories in poems continue to be heard. The twentieth century working class poetry provides a window on life for working class people dealing with world wars, economic depression, immigration and shows how a sense of shared experiences leads to collective understanding. Twenty-first century working class poetry shows that, despite an overall relative improvement in work conditions for working people, class remains a force for oppression and that contemporary experience continues to echo the past. These cultural products allow working class people to trace their history, to understand how their stories have been told and to share experiences and therefore, the importance and significance of working class poetry cannot be underestimated.

Acknowledgments

Sections of this chapter have appeared in different versions in Attfield, Sarah (2009) *Working-Class Voices: the Working-Class Experience in Contemporary Australian Poetry*, Saarbrüken: VDM.

References

Bourdieu, P. (1984) *Distinction: A Social Critique of the Judgment of Taste*, Cambridge: Harvard University Press.

Carter, D. (1999) 'Magazine culture: notes towards a history of Australian periodical publications 1920–70', in A. Bartlett, R. Dixon and C. Lee (eds) *Australian Literature and the Public Sphere: Refereed Proceedings of the 1998 Conference*, QLD: Association for the Study of Australian Literature.

Christopher, R. and Whitson, C. (1999) 'Towards a theory of working-class literature', *NEA Higher Education Journal*, Spring: 71–81.

Coles, N. (1986) 'Democratizing literature: issues in teaching working-class literature', *College English*, 48: 664–80.

Coles, N. and Zandy, J. (eds) (2007) *American Working-Class Literature: an Anthology*, New York: Oxford University Press.

Corkhill, A. R. (1994) *Australian Writing: Ethnic Writers 1945–1991*, Melbourne: Academia Press.

Daniels, J. (1995) 'Troubleshooting: Poetry, the Factory and the University', in J. Zandy (ed.) *Liberating Memory: Our Work and Our Working-Class Consciousness*, New Brunswick: Rutgers UP, pp 86–96.

——(2005) 'Work Poetry and Working-Class Poetry: The Zip Code of the Heart', in S. Linkon and J. Russo (eds) *New Working-Class Studies*, Ithaca: Cornell University Press.

Eagleton, T. (2006) *Criticism and Ideology: a Study in Marxist Literary Theory*, revised edn, New York and London: Verso.

Fahey, W. (2000) *Ratbags and Rabblerousers: a Century of Political Protest, Song and Satire*, NSW: Currency Press.

Gilbert, K. (1978) *People are Legends: Aboriginal Poems*, St. Lucia: Queensland University Press.

Gilmore, M. (1953) 'In poverty and toil', in M. Pizer (ed.) *Freedom on the Wallaby: Poems of the Australian People*, NSW: Pinchgut Press.

Graham, J. (1946) *Blood on the Coal and Other Poems for the People*, Sydney: Current Book Distributors.

Haslett, M. (1999) *Marxist Literary and Cultural Theories*, Basingstoke: Macmillan.

Haynes, J. (2001) *An Australian Heritage of Verse*, Sydney: ABC Books.

Hoggart, R. (1973) *The Uses of Literacy*, Harmondsworth: Penguin.

Inglis Moore, T. (1971) *Social Patterns in Australian Literature*, Sydney: Angus and Robertson.

Jordan, R. and Pierce, P. (eds) (1990) *The Poet's Discovery: Nineteenth Century Australia in Verse*, Victoria: Melbourne University Press.

Jose, N. (ed.) (2009) *Macquarie PEN Anthology of Australian Literature*, NSW: Allen and Unwin.

Lauter, P. (1997) 'Caste, class and canon', in D. P. Herndl and R. Warhol (eds) *Feminisms: An Anthology of Literary Theory and Criticism*, Basingstoke: Macmillan.

——(2005) 'Under construction: working-class poetry', in S. Linkon and J. Russo (eds) *New Working-Class Studies*, Ithaca: Cornell University Press.

Lawson, H. (1900) *In the Days when the World was Wide and Other Verses*, NSW: Angus and Robertson.

McIntosh, D. (2001) 'The shop steward', *Overland*, 165:20.

Morley, D. and Worpole, K. (eds) (1982) *The Republic of Letters*, London: Comedia.

Oresick, P. and Coles, N. (eds) (1990) *Working Classics: Poems on Industrial Life*, Chicago: University of Illinois Press.

π.o. *Panash* (1978) Melbourne: Collective Effort.

——(1985) *Off the Record*, Victoria: Penguin.

Scalmer, S. (1997) 'Imagining class: intellectuals in the 1950s and insights into the present', *Overland* 146:21–25.

Silverman, H. and Fairchild Ruggles, D. (eds) (2007) *Cultural Heritage and Human Rights*, New York: Springer.

Stein, J. (2001) 'Industrial music: contemporary American working-class poetry and Modernism', in J. Zandy (ed.) *What We Hold in Common: An Introduction to Working-Class Studies*, NY: The Feminist Press.

Syson, I. (1989) 'Australian working-class women's writing: a "different manner of apprehension"', unpublished PhD thesis, University of Queensland.

——(1993a) 'The problem was finding the time: working class women's writing in Australasia', *Hecate* 19.2: 65–84.

——(1993b) 'Towards a poetics of working class writing', *Southern Review* 26.1: 876–100.

——(1997) 'Fired from the canon: the sacking of Australian working-class literature,' *Southerly* 57.3: 78–89.

——(1999–2000) '"It just isn't trendy at the moment": thinking about working-class literature through the 1990s', *Tirra Lirra* 10.2: 5–14.

Trouillot, M-R. (1995) *Silencing the Past: Power and the Production of History*, Boston: Beacon Press.

Van Ooij, J. (ed.) (2000) *925: Workers Poetry from Australia 1978–1983*, Melbourne: Collective Effort.

Wesling, D. (1993) 'Mikhail Bakhtin and the social poetics of dialect,' *Papers on Language and Literature*, 29.3: 303–22.

Williams, J. (2003) *My Country, My World*, WA: Lone Hand Press.

Williams, R. (1961) *The Long Revolution*, Westport: Greenwood Press.

Young, C. (2007) *The Yugoslav Women and their Pickled Herrings*, Tasmania: Cornford Press.

Zandy, J. (1990) *Calling Home: Working-Class Women's Writings an Anthology*, New Brunswick: Rutgers University Press.

——(1995) (ed.) *Liberating Memory: Our Work and Our Working-Class Consciousness*, New Brunswick: Rutgers University Press.

Chapter 15

Industrial folk song in our time

Mark Gregory

Imagine a reference system with three million articles, 18 million pages, 300 million edits, 10 million users and 260 languages. Those are the 2009 statistics for Wikipedia, the online encyclopaedia that more than fits the description of shared and collaborative public space. Five years ago, I began to add information to 'industrial folk song' (Wikipedia 2009c) a sub-set of wiki's folk song entry. Since then that article has evolved out of recognition although I can still find traces of my contributions.

Although the industrial revolution (Wikipedia 2009d) began over 200 years ago and songs reporting the effects of it date back to a time when unions (or combinations) were illegal, the use of the term 'industrial folk song' is quite recent. In 1965 folklorist and singer A.L. Lloyd used the term in his entry on Folk Music in the *Encyclopaedia Britannica* (Lloyd 1965). Lloyd had pioneered the collection and study of mining songs in Britain in the early 1950s and published his influential *Come All Ye Bold Miners* (Lloyd 1952). Earlier, in 1944, his *Corn on the Cob: Popular and Traditional Poetry of the USA*, a booklet introducing American ballads and songs to the British public, included a number of industrial folk songs. In the introduction Lloyd wrote:

> Till recently it always seemed there was clash between what was cultured and what was traditional, and it was reckoned that culture would win and the traditional would die out. Now it is not so clear, and it really looks as though there may be a blending of the two kinds. Each has something the other needs. If they do blend together properly, and there is every reason to believe they may, then American poetry, for one thing, will indeed be something for the world to admire.
>
> (Lloyd 1944: 17)

The study of industrial folk song has involved many collectors and folklorists as I will illustrate in this chapter. Collectors often had close relations with union members in the industries they were studying. In 1925 in the United States, the young journalist George Korson began to write down the songs of Pennsylvania coal miners. Often on his field trips he was accompanied by a union delegate who would assist in introducing him to the close-knit mining communities. His original collection was first serialised in the *United Mine Workers Journal* and later published as *Songs and Ballads of the Anthracite Miner* in 1927 (Gillespie 1980). Korson's pioneering work marks a convenient tipping point for folklore studies. Following it, he published other significant collections including *Minstrels of the Mine Patch* (1938) and *Coal Dust on the Fiddle* (1943). Linkages existed too among the collectors themselves and they often worked together, an invaluable contribution to the slowly emerging genre. For example, Ruth Crawford Seeger, mother of folksingers Peggy and Mike Seeger, transcribed the tunes of 13 songs for *Coal Dust on the Fiddle* (Gillespie 1980: 83).

Korson's work was not highly regarded by American folklorists until the New Deal, the sweeping changes made by the Roosevelt administration in its attempts to deal with the 1930s depression. Laws were repealed to unshackle unions and encourage collective bargaining. New economic theories and solutions proposed by scholars such as John Maynard Keynes were taken seriously, as the nation attempted to recover. Folklorists Alan Lomax, Benjamin Botkin and Charles Seeger were employed to oversee important collecting projects. All three were interested in songs emerging from a changing world and the connections these songs had with traditional folk song.

In 1940 Woody Guthrie, Pete Seeger and Alan Lomax worked together on a songbook bringing together the work of some of the great vernacular songwriters of the time including Aunt Molly Jackson, Jim Garland, Sara Ogan Gunning, Big Bill Broonzy, Ella Mae Wiggins, Washboard Sam, Sonny Boy Williamson and of course Woody Guthrie. It was not published until 1966, perhaps a reflection of the decades of 'cold war amnesia' regarding lyrical material associated with the left. Seeger writes about the history of the book:

> Alan Lomax had spent five years putting together a great collection of protest songs collected from farmers, coal miners, textile workers, etc. – men and women mainly in the southern and western states. He gave us big stacks of disks and paper and said, 'Why don't you two finish working all this into a book?' I transcribed the tunes and words; Woody wrote the introductions: friends in New York, Elizabeth Higgins and sculptor Harold Ambellan, let us camp in their studio. Elizabeth saved a carbon copy of the manuscript, *Hard Hitting Songs for Hard Hit People* (I suggested the name). Thanks to her saving a copy it finally did get published in 1966, but in 1940, no luck.
>
> (Seeger, Pete 2009a: 17)

The continuing relevance of the Lomax, Seeger and Guthrie collection was dramatically demonstrated in 2009 when Pete Seeger (approaching his 90th birthday) led the huge audience at President Barack Obama's inauguration concert singing Guthrie's *This Land Is Your Land* complete with the three most political verses that are usually omitted:

> In the squares of the city
> by the shadow of a steeple
> By the relief office
> I saw my people
> As they stood there hungry
> I stood there whispering
> This land made for you and me
>
> A great high wall there
> tried to stop me
> A great big sign there
> said private property
> But on the other side
> it didn't say nothing
> That side was made for you and me
>
> Nobody living
> can ever stop me
> As I go walking
> that freedom highway
> Nobody living
> can make me turn back
> This land was made for you and me

Today's Global Financial Crisis and government attempts to regain economic stability naturally resonate strongly with the New Deal era. According to the *New York Times* obituary for the American folklorist Archie Green who died 28 March 2009 his last project was

> to convince Congress that it should, as in the days of the New Deal and the Works Progress Administration, set aside money for artists, filmmakers, photographers, writers and, yes, folklorists, to document the projects put into motion by the stimulus bill.
>
> (Grimes 2009)

The obituary also makes clear the key role Green played in persuading Congress to create the American Folklife Center at the Library of Congress in 1976.

Green came to folklore from a background as a skilled shipwright and carpenter. His first book, *Only a Miner* (Green 1972), was a study of Korson's work among North American miners. Green proposed the word 'laborlore' to describe the study of songs, sayings, stories, interest in work techniques and union organisation. His last folkloric work was as an editor of the *Big Red Songbook* (Green 2007). This songbook marked the centenary of the Industrial Workers of the World (IWW) *Little Red Songbook,* a compilation of over 250 songs and poems taken from all the editions that had been published.

The connections established between scholars interested in industrial folk song is also demonstrated in the work of Italian oral historian Alessandro Portelli. Like Green, Portelli followed Korson's pioneering work carrying out his own study of songs of the mining communities in Harlan County in the Eastern Kentucky coal fields. In Italy, in his home town of Terni he researched the origins of a particular industrial song, *The Death of Luigi Trastulli*:

> On 17 March 1949, the 21-year-old steelworker Luigi Trastulli was killed by the police during a demonstration against NATO. Sante Carboni, a mechanic, former railroad worker and draftsman, wrote a song about the event.
>
> (Portelli 1990: 181)

Portelli had available a number of sources for the song including the original typewritten text, verses remembered by close friends of Carboni, a letter from Carboni that discusses the song and an interview with Carboni. In his analysis of the song he writes:

> When a song is born, it reflects the moment of its birth, but also much of the history of its creators. It then continues to live and react to history. The geological layers of forms inside Carboni's ballad teach us about history because the song is not merely a description of a historical event, but a summary of the identity of those who were involved in and reacted to it. The song is a synthesis of the event's meaning for those who lived on to sing the tale.
>
> (Portelli 1990: 192)

Describing how Harlan County in the USA and Terni in Italy had gripped his imagination Portelli writes:

> more than anywhere else in my knowledge, these two areas had produced songs in which an advanced modern working-class awareness combined with the integrity of traditional forms of expression.
>
> (Portelli 1990: xiii)

Portelli's discussion of the relationship between oral and written creative material resonates with Lloyd's reflection about a blending of the cultural and the traditional cited earlier in this chapter:

The artists of oral expression create an aesthetics based on the very limitations of their medium, on the interplay of necessary repetition and inevitable change, making a virtue of a necessity ... Devices created by orality to ensure stability and permanence are adopted by written literature to connote fluidity and improvisation ... Ironically, however, writing mimics orality by adopting precisely those devices which orality developed to 'write' itself – with repetition being foremost – thus creating the impression of a written discourse which is struggling with time as if it were oral.

(Portelli 1990: 280)

Folk Song Revival

A pioneering recording project of Alan Lomax brought together folklorists in many countries, including those interested in industrial folk song. In the early 1950s, he left the Cold War hysteria of the USA on a mission to record folk songs in England, Scotland, Ireland, Spain and Italy for the *Columbia World Library of Folk and Primitive Music*. Wherever he went he seemed to act as a catalyst for the emerging revivals of folk music. In Britain, he brought together Ewan MacColl and Lloyd who were later regarded as the founders of a new phase of the UK folk revival. While in England Lomax published his 1960 collection *The Folk Songs of North America*. Peggy Seeger and Shirley Collins were responsible for the music transcriptions while MacColl, Lloyd and the Australian folklorist Edgar Waters are among the list of those Lomax thanks for their work on the collection.

The surge of interest in the folk song revival encouraged MacColl and Lloyd to work together and record LPs of English and Scottish Ballads, Drinking Songs, Sea Shanties, Sporting Songs and Australian Bush Songs. In 1954, MacColl and Peggy Seeger recorded *Shuttle and Cage* for Topic, a landmark first album of British industrial songs (MacColl and Seeger 1957). A booklet of songs with the same title was also published (MacColl 1954). In 1957 Folkways released Pete Seeger's LP *American Industrial Ballads* and, by 1963, Lloyd was collaborating with young singers from the folk revival, including Anne Briggs, Bob Davenport, Ray Fisher, Louis Killen and Matt McGinn, for his influential Topic LP *The Iron Muse: A Panorama of Industrial Folk Music* (Lloyd 1963).

During this period, there was a similar folk revival in Australia, starting with the rediscovery and collection of bush song and poetry. Folklorists like Ron Edwards and Hugh Anderson began publishing songbooks of the newly discovered material (Anderson 1955).

A number of Australian bush songs seemed closer to the industrial songs in their sentiment and outlook than to the old rural ballads, and in many cases, the names of the authors were known. The itinerant bush workers were famous for their strong union organisation, a situation that inspired poet

Henry Lawson to write *Freedom on the Wallaby* and *The Old Rebel Flag* in the 1890s in support of the Queensland shearers' strike. Australia's most famous song, *Waltzing Matilda*, was written by A. B. ('Banjo') Paterson at the close of the shearers' strike and is recognised today as coded support for the shearers' struggle. This apparently rural song, set to a traditional Scottish tune, was in reality an industrial song.

In 1952, the Australian revival was given a theatrical birth through the New Theatre production of *Reedy River* (Diamond 1970), a very popular musical play written by Dick Diamond, Victorian Secretary of Actors Equity, set in the shearers' strike and featuring some of the recently collected bush songs. This was at a time when a conservative government was attacking unions. One of the songs performed in *Reedy River* was *The Ballad of 1891*, a newly written song about the 1891 shearers' strike that has since become a union anthem in Australia. Just as in Britain and the United States, the interest in industrial songs in Australia has been closely related to the folk song revival and to the concerns of the union movement.

Industrial Song and Radio

Radio early on played a considerable role in the dissemination and evolution of industrial folk song. Many of the songs of striking textile workers in the United States in the 1920s were broadcast on local radio (Roscigno and Danaher 2004). In Britain an innovative example of BBC Radio production combined traditional and newly written songs and recordings of interviews with workers in industry, the *Radio Ballads* (Cox 2008). The first Radio Ballad broadcast was *The Ballad of John Axton,* a 1958 collaboration between Ewan MacColl, Peggy Seeger and Charles Parker. Fifty years later in Australia, Seeger described the process developed for writing songs for the eight programmes:

> The big thing about the Radio Ballads was that if you didn't know something about a subject or know it well enough to write about it you went out and you held a microphone in front of somebody and you virtually said 'what's it like to be you? What has your work done to you? What has your life done to you and for you?' And when you ask this in a certain way people open up and they give you words, phrases, breathing patterns, ideas, connections, that you would never ever have yourself. And if you know how to use those to make songs out of them you are on to a winner.
>
> (Seeger 2008)

The international web of synergies and connections around industrial folk song is personified in Peggy Seeger. For example, she had a relationship with Australia even before she visited the country. In the late 1950s she provided instrumental backing for Lloyd's LPs of Australian songs. In 2008 she described those recordings:

> I was thrilled with the new material, I'd never heard it, and of course I stayed at Bert's house when I first went to England. He was very kind to me, I think I stayed at his house for six weeks, I think long by the sell-by date I'm sure! My father (Charles Seeger) gave me an introduction to Bert Lloyd, because he knew him.
>
> My memory was just of enjoying the songs so much, and getting a real respect for the unaccompanied singer.
>
> (Seeger 2008)

Seeger went on to describe her memories of meeting Alan Lomax at that time.

> Alan's house was chaotic! There was Shirley Collins and Alan in one room, myself and Alan's daughter in another, and Alan's ex-wife came to visit with her Spanish partner, and this was a tiny flat in Highgate.
>
> Then there were all the visiting folk singers and Alan's tapes and tape recording all over the pace, a kitchen that two people couldn't be in at once, absolute chaos.
>
> But thrilling absolutely thrilling, being near to Alan was like being near a power house, you were constantly charged by his energy and his interest, his enjoyment.
>
> (Seeger 2008)

Industrial Song and the Internet

Interest in industrial folk song is an international phenomenon and many of its collectors are connected as I have described. The Indian folklorist Kali Dasgupta, who was based in Calcutta, collected hundreds of songs mainly in North-East India, since as a union organiser he came into contact with all kinds of workers.

On a visit to the UK, Dasgupta met MacColl at the request of fellow Indian folklorists:

> We had at that time The Folklore Institute, and the secretary of the Folklore Institute he wrote me a letter that they were going to publish an anthology asking me to contact Ewan MacColl and get a contribution from him. That's why I tried to find Ewan, so I phoned him at his home in Beckenham, Kent.
>
> He said, 'Come along, you'll eat with us' Ewan's practice is that everybody goes to his house. Ewan was very aware and we had a long discussion about Indian politics and he knew quite a lot of people from India, people I also knew. There he said 'You can come to our club'.

> Then, you know in England there are about eighty clubs, then the ball starts rolling. I started getting bookings. And I made so many friends there.
>
> (Dasgupta 2000)

My recordings of Dasgupta in 2000 formed the basis of a website, kalidasgupta.com (Gregory 2009a). The website precipitated emails from friends who had lost touch with the folklorist after he moved back to India. Through these connections it was revealed that Dasgupta had been interviewed by BBC producer Charles Parker and that his singing had also been recorded by the British folksinger Jack Warshaw. After his death in 2005, his wife Rosanne Dasgupta released these recordings on CD. Today there are five CDs with 85 songs sung by Dasgupta and also by Lokosaraswati (Lokosaraswati 2009), the folkloric group he founded and led.

The web has become a significant resource enabling the collection and dissemination of industrial folk songs. The industrial lyrical material I am particularly interested in continues a largely unremarked tradition of 'reports from a changing society'. An example of this is the experimental site, Union Songs, which I constructed in 1997. The primary functions of the Union Songs site are collection, the introduction of new material to the community and accessibility in a public space. The collection has provided me with a regular stream of new (and new to me) material for over a dozen years. Initially my expectation was that songwriters would email songs and poems for the collection site. This expectation was dramatically fulfilled in 1998 when the Easter break saw the attempt by the conservative Howard government to cripple or destroy the Maritime Union of Australia (MUA). The dock company Patrick, owner of half of Australia's ports, organised a military style force of balaclava-wearing armed guards with dogs to clear the ports of MUA members. By the next sitting of Parliament, government ministers were openly boasting, 'mission accomplished'.

Over the next month as community and union campaigns against this action grew, I received over 30 songs and poems that had been written during the lockout and performed at community picket lines and benefit concerts around Australia. This material was uploaded to the web together with mp3 audio files feeding back to the MUA workers and their supporters. These songs and poems later formed the basis of *With These Arms*, a CD commemorating the MUA Centenary that was celebrated four years after the MUA victory over Patrick and the Howard government, This victory, involving the whole labour movement, ultimately led to the ignominious demise of Howard – a Prime Minister who dramatically made history by losing his own seat in the landslide election of 2007.

The functionality of the web and online connectivity can produce remarkable outcomes. In 2004 I received a song by email from US songwriter Frank Manning and added it to the Union Songs web collection together with his email address. The song, *Louis Tikas*, was written about a friend of Manning's grandfather. Tikas, an immigrant from Greece, became a union organiser. He was shot dead by the Colorado National Guard in the 1914 Ludlow Massacre. Late in 2007 Manning sent me an article for the Union Songs site titled 'Look what unionsong has done!'

> I just wanted to shoot you a note about events that came my way after you posted the song *Louis Tikas* on unionsong.com. I've received several e-mails from various countries commenting on the song or asking for information. I've talked on the phone with Americans, I've exchanged Christmas greetings with Italians, and I've met Greeks in person, all because of the Internet and unionsong.com. We are united in our admiration and gratitude for Louis.
>
> Last winter a music producer in Athens contacted me and asked for permission to use the song in March in some dance performances he was working on. His name is Nikos Valkanos, and I was honoured that he included a song I wrote. Shortly thereafter he asked if he could also use it in Athens Festival 2007 in July, and again I was glad to grant permission. People from all over the world attended Athens Festival. I can only guess at how many countries they came from.
>
> This shows the global unity of the workers and their supporters. It is truly cause for optimism.
>
> (Manning 2008)

The potential of the web in relation to the collection of industrial song is far reaching. Searching for non-English material online led me to the website of Tetsuro Tanaka, a Japanese worker who has been picketing daily for more than two decades. His home page is headed 'Never import the corporate fascism of Japan!' (Tanaka 2009a). Tanaka writes songs that he sings on his daily protest. With his permission his work was added to the Union Songs collection. One of the songs he sings at the factory gate is called *The Wind*:

> The wind asks 'Haven't you forgotten?'
> The wind asks, 'Haven't you given up?'
> Your sadness isn't yours alone.
> Your anger isn't yours alone.
> It blows against the wall of history.
> Even if you can't see it now the wind moves the trees.
>
> Let's be the wind.
> Let's live as the wind.
> Over the sea. Over the hate.
>
> Your peaceful mind flies up to the blue sky.
> It blows down the old leaves of oppression.

> The wind is brought by your struggle.
> The wind broadens your compassion.
> It blows enveloping pain and efforts in vain.
> Even if you can't see it now the wind will live again.
>
> (Tanaka 2003)

The sentiment embodied in this Japanese song is very different from the more strident compositions that might be sung at an Australian or British picket. Its inclusion in the Union Songs collection invites comparisons and indeed, analysis. Another of Tanaka's compositions that he plays as hundreds of workers pass through the factory gate each morning is a classical guitar work, *Etude at The Gate*. Tanaka wrote about his long struggle in a web article titled 'Philosophy of Struggle'. It begins:

> Anger and hatred are different. The struggle coming from an anger against an injustice can make people happy. The action came from hatred towards trying to make others unhappy. It has strong power for a short time, but it will gradually destroy you.
>
> When you struggle against a powerful opponent. Trying to defeat and trying not to be defeated are different. Even if the opponent is strong, so you can't defeat him, you cannot be defeated.
>
> (Tanaka 2009b)

Further communication with Tanaka resulted in my partner, filmmaker Maree Delofski, and I working on the feature length documentary *Tanaka-san Will Not Do Callisthenics* which was completed in 2008 and which to date has been screened in Ireland, USA, Japan, Canada and Turkey. The website, tanakafilm.com (Blue Room Productions 2009) has assisted this feature length documentary achieve global reach.

Most recently I have created a blog to collect Australian Railway Songs (Gregory 2009b). This site is a growing repository of songs associated with Australian railways, railway workers and passengers. Former railway worker and union activist Brian Dunnett (Piper and Dunnett 2005) has collected Australian railway songs and poems for more than 30 years. His collection of several hundred items is the largest for any industry to date. In 2009 the blog became a vehicle for the Rail Tram and Bus Union (RTBU) to help promote its song and poetry competition. Like a number of Australian unions the RTBU has a tradition of such competitions, a tradition that is another valuable resource for industrial song catchers. Topics covered in the songs submitted for the RTBU competition include working conditions, closure of railway workshops, waiting for trains, train disasters, the role of the railway in people's lives. Industrial lyrical material continues to be written by men and women of all ages.

The web is also a convenient repository of other works relating to industrial song. My 1970 interview with A.L. Lloyd (dealing with folk songs, industrial songs, the folk revival and other musics) was only recently transcribed for publication, urged on by the fact that 2008 marked the centenary of Lloyd's birth. The transcription quickly found a place on the web in the British online magazine Musical Traditions (Musical Traditions Web Services 2009). In the interview Lloyd described how he viewed the effect of the folk song revival in Britain on the creation of new miners' songs.

> The revival of the creation of miners' songs after 1950 I think is probably connected with the phenomenon the folk song revival itself, that first of all young colliers became acquainted with styles of song concerning trades for example which were an interesting reflection of the life of people working in those trades ... and older colliers too found that that kind of song had a certain prestige. ... when in the early 1960s, the pit (Harrington or Cotia pit) was gradually closed and the workers were gradually transferred, old George Purdon made this song, *Farewell to Cotia*, which is an important song for colliers because it has got sung as a kind of ceremonial song at the farewell parties when a group of colliers, say twenty, are being transferred to the Midland coalfields or South Wales. It's usual for them to have a party and their workmates come and it's quite common now for the song *Farewell to Cotia* to be sung at the end of the party in the same way *Auld Lang Syne* is sung at New Year. So there's a piece of song making in what one can only take as classic folkloric circumstances and assuming the kind of powerful social function that in fact very few classic folk songs had the honor of receiving.
> (Lloyd 1970)

Eight years after that interview, in a chapter in *Folk Music in School*, Lloyd appears to expand the definition of folk song. Citing Matt McGinn's *With Fire and With Sword*, a political song based on a Glasgow children's street song, he wrote:

> ... perhaps this kind of composition is symptomatic of the process by which home-made song, emerging from below, owing little to the establishment culture of the entertainment corporations but much to that unofficial culture of which folk song is a component, begins to move towards a new style, a broader ambience, a more ample perspective. The song, *With fire and with sword*, is here given as transcribed from the singing during a mass meeting of shipyard workers in Glasgow in March 1971. Vietnam and Kent State were in the mind then, but the song reflects an ever-present care, particularly with men whose yards find it easier to get war contracts than peaceful ones. Not folk song? As the folk change, their songs change: it's a truism.
> (Leach and Palmer 1978:28)

In November 2009 an eightieth birthday tribute was held in Sydney for Jack Mundey, a building worker and union leader who in the 1970s became famous in Australia and internationally for helping preserve large historic parts of Sydney from demolition. His union, the Builders Laborers' Federation (BLF), with community support, placed 'Green Bans' on environmentally important areas and on buildings that had special heritage value. The newspapers and politicians of the time scorned the idea that building workers might have a say in the future of the built environment. At the Mundey tribute a number of green ban songs were sung: *Green Bans Forever, City of Green, Monuments* and *Across the Western Suburbs*. *Across the Western Suburbs* was written by Seamus Gill, who was, in the 1970s, a BLF organiser. The song is set to the tune of the Australian bush song *Across the Western Plains,* itself based on the sailors' song *Across the Western Oceans.* An Australian example of 'advanced modern working-class awareness combined with the integrity of traditional forms of expression' noted by Portelli (2009).

> Where is me house, me little terrace house
> It's all gone for profit and for plunder
> For the wreckers of the town just came up and knocked it down
> Now across the Western Suburbs we must wander
>
> Chorus
> Under concrete and glass, Sydney's disappearing fast
> It's all gone for profit and for plunder
> Though we really want to stay they keep driving us away
> Now across the Western Suburbs we must wander
>
> Now I'm living in a box in the west suburban blocks
> And the place is nearly driving me to tears, boys
> Poorly planned and badly built and it's mortgaged to the hilt
> But they say it will be mine in forty years, boys
>
> Now before the city's wrecked these developers must be checked
> For it's plain to see they do not give a bugger
> And we soon will see the day if these bandits have their way
> We will all be driven out past Wagga Wagga

The internet is clearly changing the way all types of music reach an audience. It offers a new kind of collaborative, shared public space, where minority sensibility and taste can vie with the music produced and promoted by the entertainment corporations. Independent recording companies can achieve a global reach as can singers and songwriters. Many of the 260 authors who have allowed me to add their work to the Union Songs collection have their own websites, and my contact with them is largely by email.

Wikipedia has entries for Green Bans (Wikipedia 2009b), the Radio Ballads (2009e) and many of the folklorists I've cited: Charles Seeger and his second wife Ruth Crawford Seeger, Pete Seeger, his sister and brother Peggy and Mike, Alan Lomax and his father John Lomax, George Korson, A.L. Lloyd, Ewan MacColl, Benjamin Botkin, Archie Green and Alessandro Portelli. Peggy Seeger (2009) has her own website and Portelli (2009) his own blog. Pete Seeger (2009b) has a number of appreciation websites and Sing Out! (2009) the magazine he founded back in 1950 has a website too. Birmingham City Council (2009) has a Charles Parker archive as part of its website.

Websites have become, perhaps, a fifth estate in today's world. It seems the virtual world is becoming an important medium for collecting and storing our intangible heritage. Industrial folk songs are an important part of that heritage.

References

Anderson, H. (1955) *Colonial Ballads*, Fern Tree Gully: Rams Skull Press.

Birmingham City Council (2009) *The Charles Parker Archive*. Online. Available at HTTP: <http://birmingham.gov.uk/charlesparkerarchive>, (accessed 30 March 2011).

Blue Room Productions (2009) *Tanaka-san Will Not Do Calisthenics*. Website. Available at HTTP: <http://www.tanakafilm.com/> (accessed 24 September 2009).

Cox, P. (2008) *Set Into Song: Ewan MacColl, Charles Parker, Peggy Seeger, and the Radio Ballads*, London: Labatie Books.

Dasgupta, K. (2000) (Interview with author, 2000).

Diamond, D. (1970) *Reedy River*. Australian theatre workshop, South Yarra, Vic.: Heinemann Educational Australia.

Gillespie, A. K. (1980) *Folklorist of the Coal Fields: George Korson's Life and Work*, University Park: Pennsylvania State University Press.

Green, A., Roediger, D., Rosemont, F. and Salerno, S. (eds) (2007) *The Big Red Songbook*, Chicago: Charles H. Kerr Publishing Co.

Green, A. (1972) *Only a Miner; Studies in Recorded Coal-Mining Songs, Music in American Life*, Urbana: University of Illinois Press.

Gregory, M. (2009a) *Kali Dasgupta*. Website. Available HTTP: <http://kalidasgupta.com/> (accessed 24 September 2009).

——(2009b) Australian Railway Song. Website. Available at HTTP: <http://railwaysongs.blogspot.com/> (accessed 24 September 2009).

Grimes, W. (2009) 'Archie Green, 91, Union Activist and Folklorist, Dies', Online article. Available HTTP: <http://www.nytimes.com/2009/03/29/books/29green.html> (accessed 24 September 2009).

Keynes, J. M. (2009) 'An open letter to President Roosevelt'. Online. Available HTTP: <http://newdeal.feri.org/misc/keynes2.htm> (accessed 24 November 2009).

Korson, G. G. (1927) *Songs and Ballads of the Anthracite Miner; a Seam of Folk-lore Which Once Ran Through Life in the Hard Coal Fields of Pennsylvania*, New York: F.H. Hitchcock.

——(1938) *Minstrels of the Mine Patch; Songs and Stories of the Anthracite Industry*, Philadelphia: University of Pennsylvania Press.

——(1943) *Coal Dust on the Fiddle; Songs and Stories of the Bituminous Industry*, Philadelphia: University of Pennsylvania Press.
——(1949) *Pennsylvania Songs and Legends*, Philadelphia: University of Pennsylvania Press.
Leach, R. and Palmer, R. (1978) *Folk Music in School* Resources of music. Cambridge: Cambridge University Press.
Lloyd, A. L. (1944) *Corn on the Cob: Popular and Traditional Poetry of the USA*, London: Fore Publications.
——(1952) *Come All Ye Bold Miners (Ballads and Songs of the Coalfield)*, London: Lawrence and Wishart.
——(1963) *The Iron Muse A Panorama of Industrial Folk Music*, LP, London: Topic Records.
——(1965) 'Folk Music', *Encyclopaedia Britannica, Vol. 9*, Chicago: Encyclopaedia Britannica, pp. 522–26.
——(1967) *Folk Song in England*, London: Lawrence and Wishart.
——(1970) Interview with author, 20 September 1970. Online. Available at HTTP: <http://mustrad.org.uk/articles/lloyd.htm> (accessed 24 September 2009).
Lokosaraswati (2009) 'Lokosaraswati', Website. Available at HTTP: <http://lokosaraswati.blogspot.com/> (accessed 25 September 2009).
Lomax, Alan (1960) *Folk Songs of North America*, New York: Doubleday.
MacColl, E. (1954). *The Shuttle and Cage: Industrial Folk-Ballads*, London: Workers' Music Association.
MacColl, E. and Seeger, P. (1957) *Shuttle and Cage*, LP, London: Topic Records.
Manning, F. (2008). 'Look what unionsong has done!' Online posting. Available HTTP: <http://unionsong.com/reviews/manning/index.html> (accessed 2 November 2009).
Musical Traditions Web Services (2009) *Musical Traditions*. Website. Available at HTTP: <http://mustrad.org.uk/> (accessed 24 September 2009).
Piper, A. and Dunnett, B. (2005) *Train Whistle Blowing: Celebrating 150 years of Australian Railways and the Culture it has Inspired*, Armidale, N.S.W.: University of New England.
Portelli, A. (1990) *The Death of Luigi Trastulli, and Other Stories: Form and meaning in oral history*, SUNY series in oral and public history, Albany, NY: State University of New York Press.
——(2009) 'Alessandro Portelli', Website. Available at HTTP: <http://alessandroportelli.blogspot.com/> (accessed 30 March 2011).
Roscigno, V. J. and Danaher, W. F. (2004) *The Voice of Southern Labor: Radio, Music, and Textile Strikes, 1929–1934*, Minneapolis: University of Minnesota Press.
Seeger, P., Fleming, J. and Scott, I. (1998) *The Peggy Seeger Songbook: Warts and All: Forty Years of Songmaking*, New York: Oak Publications.
Seeger, Peggy (2008) Interview, Late Night Live, ABC Radio, March 2008.
——(2009) *Peggy Seeger – Folksinger, Songmaker, Activist*. Website. Available at HTTP: <http://www.peggyseeger.com/> (accessed 24 September 2009).
Seeger, Pete (1957) *American Industrial Ballads*, LP, Washington DC: Folkways Records.
——(2009a) *Where Have all the Flowers Gone: A Singalong Memoir*, New York: A Sing Out! Publication.
——(2009b) *Pete Seeger Appreciation Page*, Website. Available at HTTP: <http://www.peteseeger.net/> (accessed 24 September 2009).
Sing Out! (2009) Website. Available at HTTP: <http://www.singout.org/> (accessed 24 September 2009).
Tanaka, T. (2003) 'the Wind', Song Lyrics. Available at HTTP: <http://unionsong.com/u223.html> (accessed 25 September 2009).

——(2009a) 'Never import the corporate fascism of Japan!' Online posting. Available at HTTP: <http://www.din.or.jp/~okidentt/eigohome.htm> (accessed 25 September 2009).
——(2009b) 'Philosophy of Struggle'. Online article. Available at HTTP: <http://unionsong.com/reviews/philosophy.html> (accessed 24 September 2009).
Wikipedia (2009a) Website. Available HTTP: <http://wikipedia.org/> (accessed 24 September 2009).
——(2009b) *Green Ban*, Online. Available *HTTP:* <http://en.wikipedia.org/wiki/Green_ban> (accessed 8 November 2009).
——(2009c) *Industrial Folk Song*. Online. Available HTTP: <http://en.wikipedia.org/wiki/Industrial_folk_song> (accessed 24 September 2009).
——(2009d) *Industrial Revolution*. Online. Available HTTP: <http://en.wikipedia.org/wiki/Industrial_Revolution> (accessed 24 September 2009).
——(2009e) *Radio Ballad*. Online. Available HTTP: <http://en.wikipedia.org/wiki/Radio-ballad> (accessed 24 September 2009).
——(2009f) Website. Online. Available HTTP: <http://en.wikipedia.org/wiki/Main_Page> (accessed 24 September 2009).

Part IV

Case Studies in Commemoration, Remembrance and Forgetting

Chapter 16

'The world's most perfect town' reconsidered

Negotiating class, labour and heritage in the Pullman community of Chicago

Jane Eva Baxter and Andrew H. Bullen

Every year, thousands of tourists flock to Chicago's far south side to experience the four block neighbourhood of Pullman. Some come to see the architectural remains of the intentional community developed by George M. Pullman to house his workers and his state-of-the-art factory: a major attraction of Chicago's 1893 World's Fair and the place dubbed 'The World's Most Perfect Town' for 14 consecutive years during its heyday. Others come to view the places associated with the influential labour strike of 1894, when Pullman factory workers received a cut in wages without a decrease in rent for their company housing and compelled Eugene Debs and the American Railway Union to sympathise with their cause bringing rail traffic to a standstill and reform to company towns.[1]

When visitors come to Pullman they tour the Hotel Florence and factory building, view the local historical museum, peruse outdoor signage, attend organised events and participate in tours. The community groups and organisations that host these events and staff these attractions are largely grass roots and are comprised of community members who have resided in Pullman for different lengths of time. Different waves of residents have unique connections to the place, and the neighbourhood is a space that is imbued with meaning around class and labour for both visitors and residents alike. This work focuses on how ideas about class, labour and heritage are negotiated between the visiting audiences interested in events of national and international importance and the resident guides who view Pullman's history as local and/or family history.

Then and now: visiting the world's most perfect town

During the last two decades of the nineteenth century, visitors to the Chicago area had a new destination they could add to their itinerary. Located some five miles south from the downtown area on the Illinois Central Railroad was the town of Pullman. The town of Pullman was the vision of industrialist George M. Pullman who wanted to build a model company town around his Pullman Palace Car Factory. Pullman hired architect Solon Beman and landscape architect Nathan Barrett to actualise his vision. The result was a company town that was in every way 'state of the art'.

The town of Pullman was most easily reached by rail, and when disembarking at the Pullman train depot, visitors could see the factory whose façade was dominated by the large clock tower of the administration building and the artificial lake, Lake Vista, in the foreground (Figure 16.1). Behind the administration building was the impressive water tower, some nine storeys high, and the formidable Corliss steam engine that brought power to the Pullman factory after its display at the 1876 Centenary Exhibition in Philadelphia. Panning to the right was the baroque façade of the Hotel Florence: its wide open porches leading to 65 rooms in three different class categories and every amenity a weary traveller might desire. Just a bit further south was the Arcade, a majestic structure that held a library, theatre, bank and shops all housed in opulence and style.

Behind this trifecta of public architecture were the homes of the factory employees: from managers to unskilled workers all had a place in this community. The homes were the physical manifestation of Pullman's ideals. Every home was considered to be on the cutting edge of technology and very current in style, providing safe, healthy and refined living for all community members. Executives of varying types, skilled workers and unskilled workers were all to occupy different types of housing; the finest of which was around the parklands and public spaces of the hotel and arcade and the most humble at the margins of the community.

Figure 16.1 Pullman Panorama circa 1885. This photograph shows the remote and almost rural setting of the Pullman Community when it was still an area detached from the city of Chicago. This view is looking east and shows the factory works to the left, and on the opposite side of the unpaved road the Hotel Florence, the Arcade and the Greenstone Church. Several of the more central executive and skilled worker homes can also be glimpsed between the hotel and arcade structures. (Photo courtesy of the Industrial Heritage Archives Collection, Pullman State Historic Site).

This elaborate design was part of a conscious effort to elevate the moral and social conditions of the working class. Providing workers with 'ideal' living conditions would not only make them better workers, but better members of society as well. Visitors came in large numbers and with great curiosity to marvel at Pullman's visionary experiment and to see if there were lessons that could be learned and adapted for other working class communities. Public attention was lavished on the community, so much so that in 1882 it became necessary to place the industrial areas off limits as the hundreds of daily visitors were disrupting the work at the factory (*Chicago Tribune* 1882). The town was featured in international publications, perhaps most famously in Richard Ely's 1885 article in *Harper's Magazine* that detailed the 'social experiment' of Pullman, and in 1887 the *London Times* reported the visit of an Englishman to Pullman who stated, 'No place in the United States has attracted more attention or has been more closely watched' (Buder 1967: 93). Cattle cars brought throngs of visitors to the town as a side excursion of the 1893 Columbian Exhibition. Clearly, this progressive community had captured the world's imagination in its earliest years.

This earlier era of social reform and paternal capitalism came to an abrupt end with the now famed labour strike of 1894. As the American economy entered into a recession known as the panic of 1893, George Pullman had to make choices about how to manage his company's finances. He decided to continue to pay his investors a 6 per cent return despite the downturn, and cut his workers' wages to make this strategy possible. Workers' wages were cut, but the rent they paid to the Pullman Company for their neighbourhood homes was not reduced, thereby putting workers in a position of fiscal hardship. Approximately 3000 employees of the Pullman Palace Car Company went on a wildcat strike, and were able to gain the attention and sympathies of the American Railway Workers' Union, whose members refused to operate trains carrying Pullman cars. The Union and the Pullman workers subsequently became embroiled in what *The New York Times* described as 'a struggle between the greatest and most important labor organization and the entire railroad capital', an action which involved some 250,000 workers in 27 states at its peak (Papke 1999: 35–37). The railroad stoppage made the Pullman strike an issue of national importance, and resulted in President Grover Cleveland dispatching Federal Troops to the town (a decision that cost him his re-election to the presidency) and the Supreme Court ultimately ruling on the conditions that caused the strike. The Pullman Company was forced to divest from the town and workers were able to purchase the houses in the community and gain autonomy over their homes. This decision set a major precedent in United States labour law, and the Pullman community's reputation was no longer as a perfect community of the Gilded Age, but rather as a site of a major victory for the American working class and collective worker action.

Today, visitors still flock by car or via the same rail line that carried visitors over 100 years ago to the Pullman community to tour the remains of the nineteenth-century company town. The town still stands about 95 per cent intact as a small enclave in the highly developed landscape of Chicago's south side (Figure 16.2). While Pullman is within the city limits of Chicago, Pullman is at the edge of the city and is still a deliberate destination for visitors. A great many visitors come as part of organised tours. School groups are quite common as are teacher training outings, but just as often tours are from community groups, labour organisations, or retirement communities coming to experience a bit of local history. Estimates of annual visitors range from 10,000–30,000 for any given year, a wide span reflecting the many people who come independently to Pullman to stroll through the streets and peer over the fence at the factory.[2] Others come to town for organised events such as House Tour or Labor Day festivities, both long-held traditions in the community.

The social experiment and progressive community that attracted so many visitors in the late nineteenth century is long defunct, and the interests that drive contemporary tourism to Pullman are far different. While impossible to ascertain systematically the motivations for visiting Pullman, questioning

Figure 16.2 Visiting Pullman in 2009. Bike riders line up for the Annual Labor Day Bike Ride through the industrial landscapes of south Chicago and northwest Indiana, while others explore the veranda of the Hotel Florence and read surrounding signage. Events like these are one of the many ways the community opens itself up to outside visitors so they can engage with the local history of Pullman. (Photo courtesy of the Bertha Ludlam Library, Pullman State Historic Site).

tour group members offers a glimpse as to why people come to Pullman. Members of 46 tour groups (between 14–45 individuals per group) from 2007–9 were verbally prompted to tell their guide what they knew about the Pullman community.[3] There was the occasional railway fan, a few people who had read the *Devil and the White City*,[4] some were students of architecture, and a few were interested in seeing where relatives had worked and lived in the past. Of those who chose to respond to the prompt, 'the labor strike' was the most common response, with an estimated 90 per cent of respondents citing the strike as their point of reference for the community.

The contemporary understanding of Pullman as a site of labour unrest and victory has eclipsed its earlier history as a model company town, and has focused visitor's interests towards issues of class, labour and injustice. This refashioning of Pullman comes not from the strike itself, which at the time was quite a powerful and poignant event, but rather more likely, from the way Pullman has been treated by historians. School textbooks that teach history are most often event focused, and entire labour movements become focused on events such as the Pullman Strike, the Haymarket Riot or the Ludlow Massacre, which become emblematic of working class history as a whole (Fallace 2008; Cobble and Kessler-Harris 1993). Popular and scholarly histories about Pullman either emphasise the injustices inherent in the system of paternal capitalism enacted by Pullman, or use the strike as a launching point to discuss labour struggles and unrest in the community (Hirsch 2003, Papke 1999, Smith 1996). Contemporary visitors most often define Pullman, therefore, as a site rich in working class history, particularly from the perspective of oppressive management systems, labour unrest and strikes: a view fuelled by the source materials available to the general public.

Venues and opportunities to experience Pullman's heritage

Regardless of individual motivations, visitors to Pullman have a variety of largely informal options for engaging with local history and heritage. The four square blocks of tree-lined streets that comprise Pullman are an active neighbourhood, but the area's city, state and national landmark status has helped to keep the structural façades true to their nineteenth-century appearance. Many visitors come simply to stroll along the streets and admire the neighbourhood; a strategy used by default for many who come outside the normal operating hours of the local interpretive centre.

Efforts at interpreting the neighbourhood for visitors are well described as grass roots, relying mostly on local community members to fund interpretive exhibits and to staff attractions as part-time staff or volunteers. There are few attempts to use heritage for profit in Pullman despite the numbers of visitors. There are no book stores, gift shops, or souvenir shops and only one of the open sites charges an admission. Most of the offerings made by the community to its visitors are free, and are more a statement of pride in local heritage than an opportunity for economic gain. There are four main opportunities for visitors to experience Pullman history during a visit to the community.

Interpretive signage and informal viewing

A variety of open air signage has been placed in the areas around the factory, hotel and arcade building. These placards are sponsored by the Pullman Civic Organisation and have been funded both through general membership funds and special funds set up in memory of former residents. These signs are well patronised by visitors who are viewing the community at their own pace, and visitors can be seen reading the signage on a daily basis.

Historic Pullman Foundation Visitors' Centre

The most consistent and easily recognisable portal for visitors coming to Pullman is the Visitors' Centre operated by the Historic Pullman Foundation (HPF), which sits on the former arcade building site in a mid-twentieth century American Legion Hall. The HPF is open six days a week from 9:00 to 3:00 and features an introductory film and a variety of exhibits about the town. The HPF also offers neighbourhood walking tours with local residents as guides. They are the only organisation that maintains a website targeted at those visiting Pullman. They do charge admission to the Visitors' Centre and have a few items for sale.

Hotel Florence and Pullman State Historic Site

The State of Illinois owns the Hotel Florence and the remaining acreage around the administration and factory building and operates it as the Pullman State Historic Site (PSHS). The site is officially a 'closed' site, but volunteers from the local community staff the hotel and offer self-guided tour opportunities for visitors seven days a week from 11:00–03:00 pm from May to October. Over a hundred organised tour groups also tour the hotel and/or factory each year and are lead on tours by staff members or volunteer docents from the community.

Organised tours and events

The town of Pullman has many social organisations for its residents, but it also hosts events to which the outside community is actively invited. Most prominent among these is the House Tour, which occurs annually in October. Ten different residents donate the use of their homes for the weekend and visitors can tour a variety of historic homes under the guidance of local community volunteers. Groups in town also sell foodstuffs and crafts and bands play in the park. The ticket price for the event is split into two uses. The first half supports the next year's event and the second half goes into a lottery to fund matching grants for homeowners making historically accurate improvements to their homes. Other events, such as the Labor Day bike ride and picnic, have their own long standing tradition and allow people to celebrate the holiday in Pullman and bike through the industrial heritage areas in Northwest Indiana and south Chicago.

This dedication to the preservation and presentation of Pullman's heritage by local residents represents significant investments in their time and treasure. Most of the venues experiencing the heritage of Pullman are completely reliant on volunteer time and funding from local individuals. The highly local nature of heritage interpretation at Pullman is in notable contrast to other prominent nineteenth-century industrial communities, particularly Lowell, Massachusetts, where the National Park Service runs museums and tours and local businesses operate around the historic site to provide services for visiting guests (National Park Service).

Heritage and working class histories of Pullman

The Pullman community offers a unique perspective on working class history, where presentations of heritage are presented by the local community with very little assistance, training, or content filtering by external organisations. Many of Pullman's residents are descendants of those workers who bought their homes from the Pullman Company in the 1890s, others have returned to a neighbourhood that holds a place in their family history, and still others have moved to a historic neighbourhood because of a belief and interest in history and preservation. The selection of how to portray Pullman as the 'World's Most Perfect Town', as the site of a labour strike of national significance, or as something else gives interesting insights into a working class neighbourhood in the waning days of industry. So, how do the residents of Pullman interpret their neighbourhood for visitors?

The two venues that are open for tours and self-guided visitation are the HPF Visitors' Centre and the PSHS Hotel Florence and factory. Presentations of heritage were evaluated by visiting each venue and taking in the exhibits, attending a tour lead by a volunteer at each site, and in the case of the PSHS viewing the volunteer training materials available for docents. No comparable materials were available from the Visitors' Centre. Public signage was also viewed and the texts and images analysed.

Recreating 'The World's Most Perfect Town'

The HPF Visitors' Centre, while in a vintage 1950s era building, holds exhibits that are similar to offerings found at local historical societies and house museums across America (Kammen 1996). Interpretive signage is limited and various cases, installations and wall displays contain objects and images of neighbourhood and company history. A large section of displays are dedicated to 'The World's Most Perfect Town'. Large photos of the prominent buildings of the town: Factory, Arcade and Hotel as well as artefacts from the hotel are a large portion of the display. Many images of families with their homes in more recent times are also a common theme. The largest category of displayed materials is items from the Pullman Company itself, particularly decorative items from the interior of Pullman cars such as china, playing cards, washcloths and drapery panels. There is no signage interpreting these materials.

One case contains information regarding the labour strike and includes a small placard outlining the history of the strike, three nineteenth-century photographs of Pullman factory workers, two photographs of striking railroad workers, a poster commemorating an anniversary exhibition of the strike, several older publications of strike testimonies and various unlabelled pins and ribbons, presumably from unions. This exhibit takes up less than 5 per cent of the exhibits space in the museum.

The film and its viewing space take up approximately one-third of the museum, and the film is the first stop for all visitors to the Centre. The film presents an overview of the town's history with an emphasis on the town's architecture and original plan, and a few insights into the problems that led up to the strike and the general discontent of workers who lived in Pullman. Arguably, however, the film's focus is on the preservation of the community by local residents in more recent times. Acquisitions and renovations of properties, the founding of community organisations, the various levels of landmark status the neighbourhood enjoys, and the events of the community are an important part of the film's storyline.

The tour that was attended for this project was one of the free tours offered the first Sunday of each summer month, and the tone of the tour mimicked that of the movie. An emphasis on the original town and architecture and efforts made by current residents to restore homes to the nineteenth-century heyday of Pullman were central aspects of this tour. The lives of people who lived in the homes during the Pullman era and the dynamics of the community including the strike were topics left largely unmentioned.

The signage around the community sponsored by the PCO also tends to the theme of 'The World's Most Perfect Town' and appears to be primarily designed to fill in the gaps of the original town plan, by providing maps, images and descriptions of the important parts of the 1881 design that have been lost to history. Placards are devoted to the Arcade Building (demolished in the 1920s) and provide visitors with a chance to see the structure in photos while standing at a vantage point that would have overlooked the actual structure in its day. The other signs provide the same perspective for the old train depot and Lake Vista that were lost when the railroad beds were raised above grade and new roads were put in for automobile traffic.

The complexities of living in 'The World's Most Perfect Town'

Visiting the Hotel Florence and attending a tour of the property with a docent there was a very different experience from the HPF offerings. The tour at the Hotel began with the docent proclaiming, 'I stand here before you in the lobby of the Hotel Florence, a place where my grandfather, a Pullman factory worker, would never have been allowed to stand.' The description of the hotel as a place for wealthy visitors of the Pullman Company and not a place where workers would have been allowed was the vantage point through which visitors gained an understanding of the place. This theme is emphasised in the docent training manual, and the docents are encouraged to teach guests about the Hotel in relation to the working residents of the town. While the Hotel was in no way the centre of working class life in Pullman, the tour and exhibits at the hotel focus on the gender and class-based organisation of the hotel itself, underscoring the types of social differences that were present in the nineteenth-century community.

The factory tour, too, spoke of the class dynamics and conditions of labour that shaped the operations of the site throughout its history, from its nineteenth-century origins to the twentieth century when the factories were converted into service for the Second World War. Aspects of the landscape, like the separate entrances for the administrators and factory workers, and the location where the strike began are aspects of the tour, as are the more technological and mechanical aspects of the factory and details of its restoration.

The displays and docent training manuals that encourage discussions of class and gender that become manifest in the tours offered by volunteers from the local community were developed by the local staff at the PSHS. The site is officially operated by the Illinois Historic Preservation Agency, a state agency, but the site is officially 'closed' despite being host to thousands of guests each year. All efforts at interpretation are generated by local staff, two of whom are Pullman residents, and no funding is made available for displays or the development of tour materials. While the site is a state site, the interpretation is completely local, with no input or oversight from the state.

A single interpretive sign is located on the grounds of the Hotel Florence, and the tenor of this sign is unique among those in Pullman. The sign marks the 'Memorial Rose and Herb Garden' placed on the location of the National Guard encampment for the soldiers dispatched to Pullman during the strike of 1894. The garden was officially dedicated in 2000 to commemorate the strike, and the garden restoration and the associated signage were funded by individuals and families in Pullman who are enumerated on the plaque. The inscription on the signage details the history of the strike and the formation of the garden, but the introductory paragraph contains a quote by George Pullman himself, that by its very invocation in the context of the inscription debunks the myth of 'The World's Most Perfect Town'. Pullman is quoted as saying, that his town would have 'a refining influence [on the workers]' and that 'With such surroundings and with such regard with the needs of the body as well as the soul ... the disturbing conditions of strikes and other troubles that periodically convulse the world of labor would not need be feared here.'

Contextualising contemporary heritage interpretations: the dynamics of Pullman in the later twentieth century

Because these attempts in the interpretation and presentation of Pullman heritage come from the local community, it is useful to understand these current public offerings in the context of more recent community history. The origin of these community groups, the contexts of their formation, and the decisions made about heritage all play out in the contemporary landscape of signs, museums, tours and events experienced by visitors to the community.

The Pullman neighbourhood in 1960 was almost entirely white, primarily Italian and mostly working class employed in local factories. Residents of the neighbourhood were faced with a rapidly changing world as Chicago was losing its smokestack industries that had sustained its far south-side economies for 100 years. Cars and aeroplanes were making heavy inroads into the very industry that had created the neighbourhood, passenger car manufacturing and support. And, of course, the demographic makeup of the population in the region and throughout Chicago was changing.

In 1957, expanded and modernised port facilities opened at Calumet Harbour. These facilities were intended to support the recently opened St. Lawrence Seaway and to be the main port for the city of Chicago. The Roseland-South End Chamber of Commerce saw this as an enormous opportunity. The Chamber of Commerce viewed the port as a vehicle for regional growth, much as the soon-to-be expanded O'Hare Airport was causing a number of motels, warehouses, forwarding and shipping agencies, manufacturing facilities and restaurants to be opened at a record pace around its perimeter.

The Chamber of Commerce hired the consulting engineering firm of Burda and Van Scheltema to make a survey of the Roseland and Pullman areas. The 20-page report proposed the demolition of the Pullman neighbourhood for the purposes of creating an industrial estate. This report was picked up by two local papers and ran as headline news on 9 February 1960. A month later, on 10 March 1960, more than 600 Pullman residents met at the Greenstone Methodist church to discuss the report and to decide how to respond to it. Led by the late Arnold Bader, the community decided to fight the proposal (Avignone 1980).

Bader had flyers printed and distributed to every home in Pullman. These flyers, begun as leaflets announcing meetings and updates, became the *Pullman Flyer*, a monthly community newspaper still in print. The structure of the Pullman Civic Organization (PCO), still used today, was set up at that time

(Pullman Civic Organization 1960a) and by May 1960, a bylaws committee meeting had created the first set of bylaws.

Reaction to the rather alarming urban renewal zeal exhibited by the Chamber of Commerce was understandably emotional. The lead article of the *Flyer* stated:

> With the acquisition of land for this industrial park, nothing has been mentioned about its boundaries. What are they? Is Pullman included as it was in the 'original survey'? Will this 'progress' be at our expense? Who can answer these questions?'
>
> (Pullman Civic Organization 1960)

Themes that have shaped the Pullman experience since 1960 for both good and ill can therefore be said to have surfaced right from the beginning: A strong sense of *us* and *them*, a reliance on strong personalities for leadership and guidance, reliance on outside agencies for improvement and top-down, hierarchical management. These themes emerge in Avignone's unpublished November 1980 article, which described the March 1960 Greenstone Church meeting thus:

> Pullman residents were fearful for the future of their community and their homes. They knew that the South End Chamber of Commerce was a billion dollar organization composed of the industries, merchants and professional people in and surrounding Roseland and Pullman. Some of the residents were afraid that the fight would be in vain as they were giants and we were just ordinary working or retired people in Pullman.
>
> (Avignone 1980:1)

Ultimately, the survey and the activities of the Chamber of Commerce came to nothing. The planned industrial estates never materialised to the west of Calumet Harbour and north of 115th street. The Calumet Expressway, now known as the Bishop Ford Expressway, was linked to the Dan Ryan Expressway in 1962 and train and ship traffic gradually gave way to overland truck traffic, eroding the need to expand the port facilities.

In less than four years, a group of strong leaders had arisen who believed that Pullman's path to redevelopment could best be met by striving to bring the town back to the lost state of harmony and perfection of the 1881 model city. These leaders were educated and persuasive. Driving the overall agenda of the nascent Pullman Civic Organization, education about Pullman in general became a primary focus. The January 1964 issue of the *Pullman Flyer* writes that the February 1964 meeting of the PCO 'will consist of Pullman Night – Mr. George Doty (n.b.) – a descendant of one of the first chroniclers of the Town of Pullman, Duane Doty (Doty [1890?]) will talk on 'Pullman of Yesteryear' (Pullman Civic Organization 1964a).

Almost from the beginning, the PCO worked to combat 'urban blight'. As written in the September 1964 *Pullman Flyer*, 'Pullman, right now, is a marginal housing area. We can improve our appearance and grow, or we can deteriorate further, and be the subject for urban renewal.' Committees formed right away to begin fighting what was seen as 'many violations to civil and moral law in Pullman' (Pullman Civic Organization 1964b: 3). Committees included Community Improvement, Safety and Protection, and the Noise, Odor and Smoke Abatement committees.

Much of the PCO's influence has stemmed from such powerful committees staffed by neighbourhood leaders with strong personalities. One of the most important was the Beman Committee founded in 1968 and still extant and influential today. As envisioned by its founder, John Erstman, it was intended to 'make Pullman a Historic Town' (Avignone 1979: 1), meaning to seek external recognition of the historic neighbourhood and 'get landmark status for Pullman'. The committee began to document architectural details about the historic fabric of the town and (if need be) prevent residents from altering the historic characteristics of their property. The committee worked tirelessly for landmark status, getting first a state designation of 23 August 1970, then national status on 28 February 1971 and finally getting city status on 16 October 1972 (City of Chicago Landmarks Commission 2003).

This last designation was the most important for the purposes of preserving the fabric of the neighbourhood, as the City could enforce zoning laws using the heightened strictures of the landmark designation. The same theme of *us* and *them* was used to rally support for the city designation:

> Who is against it, then? Take a look at the record. The owners of the stock exchange and the owners of the train station in the Loop designed by Beman are two examples. The reason? Both of the[m] were to be torn down to make more money for developers and speculators.
> (Pullman Civic Organization 1972: 1)

Important for the Beman Committee was the external recognition and validation that the status would bring, 'Landmark status would also be an honor and official recognition for everyone in Pullman' (Pullman Civic Organization 1972: 1). External recognition and validation were also achieved through tours for groups, which eventually were revamped on 12 October 1974 into a series of annual house tours and are still extant. The importance of these now annual house tours cannot be overstated. They have become the primary vehicle for the formal presentation of the vision of Pullman as a model community as well as the primary contact opportunity that the outside world has with the Pullman neighbourhood.

The spirit that guided the Beman Committee at that time was one of accepting an almost holy mission, one of returning to the *World's Most Perfect Town*. As Avignone wrote about the demise of so many local restaurants, theatres, factories and other facets of Calumet area life, 'Only the town of Pullman is here as an example to the world to never give up when things look hopeless' (Avignone 1984: 1). A local paper, the *Calumet Index,* noted that 'Pullman is not like other communities. Elsewhere it might be thought that new is better, but in Pullman progress means preserving the past' (*Calumet Index* 1974). Further in the article, Avignone was quoted: 'It's a hidden spirit that you can't feel or touch, which Pullman left here when he passed on' (*Calumet Index* 1974: 3). The article states the tangible benefits of this spirit: 'The Pullman spirit rippling thru [sic] the neighbourhood coalesces into some tangible benefits, such as the absence of fear, littered streets and aloofness, which are thought to be the trademark of Chicago' (*Calumet Index* 1974: 3).

Nowhere can this spirit better be seen than in the creation of the Historic Pullman Foundation, an entity set up as an non-profit 501(c)(3) fundraising and education foundation and still in existence. A natural outgrowth of the Beman Committee, the HPF was created in 1972. Tellingly, the title of a section in a self-published history of the HPF describing the creation of the HPF clearly illustrates the missionary zeal behind the founding of the HPF: 'A Commitment Accepted: A New Chapter in Pullman's History' (The Historic Pullman Foundation 1992: 2). A wire story article about changes in Pullman profiles Pat and Mike Shymanski as officers of the HPF:

> A fast-moving world has left the Shymanskis not quite sure what they believe outside of the limits of their family, home and community ... Things have happened so fast in the past 15 years, Mrs. Shymanski said. 'When is it all going to slow down? It's moving so fast. It gives you a sense of helplessness, that things are out of control, moving under their own power, and no one's in charge, and no one seems to care.'
> (St Petersburg Times 1976: 8).

The same article, also printed in the *Arkansas Gazette*, adds a paragraph not included in the *St. Petersburg Times*. After 'no one seems to care' Shymanski then adds: 'No one seems to care, so why should I? That's why Mike and I believe in Pullman, by simply helping to restore it and making it a nice place to live, it'll be our contribution, not only to our two children, but to our country as well' (*Arkansas Gazette* 1976: 10B).

The HPF, almost from the beginning, took on a strong preservation role, acquiring a Masonic Lodge/boarding house property. The property became the meeting room for the PCO and still functions as a meeting room and offices for the HPF. Financial support for the group came from membership fees and from generous donations of Florence Lowden Miller, granddaughter of George Pullman (The Historic Pullman Foundation 1992: 2). In 1974, it acquired the then recently burned Market Hall, intending to restore it to at least some semblance of a viable commercial structure. Faced with possible loss and degradation of the signature significant property in the neighbourhood, the Hotel Florence, the HPF worked to acquire the property in 1975.

The HPF has always faced a shortage of monies needed to restore and maintain the massively expensive and complicated 1881 Beman commercial structures. Faced with overwhelming costs in running and restoring the Hotel Florence, which had suffered from serious neglect for more than 50 years, the HPF worked with the State of Illinois and with the newly formed Illinois Historic Preservation Agency (IHPA) for the state to acquire and manage the Factory site and the Hotel Florence in 1991. The site is now collectively known as the Pullman State Historic Site (PSHS).

For the first eight years of state ownership, the properties languished as the IHPA struggled to finance their restoration and ascertain what to do with a site requiring so many different types of stabilisation and repair. In December 1998, a vagrant living in the deserted factory complex deliberately set the south wing and main tower on fire; the resulting destruction rallied the neighbourhood to pressure the state to save the site and restore it. The state responded quickly, perhaps prodded into action by the international press attention. The IHPA created two permanent staff positions, a site supervisor and a curator, and, due to federal monies, restored much of the fire damage to the factory, stabilised the Hotel Florence, and began a restoration for the Hotel Florence interior.

The Hotel Florence has always acted as a community centre. The Pullman State Historic Site staff members have upheld that tradition, creating community events, hosting community groups and conducting educational programmes. Much effort has been devoted to digitising historical artefacts and images, and maintaining a professional-level reference and research library.

Conclusions: contemporary communities and working class histories

Class has been an integral part of the Pullman story from its inception as a model town designed to better the working classes, to its role as the epicentre of an important event in labour history, and later as one of many working class neighbourhoods on Chicago's industrial south side. The ways in which class has been materialised and memorialised by the twentieth-century residents of Pullman give insights into the class consciousness of a working class community in the waning days of local industry. Pullman is similar to communities in North Carolina and Yarmouth, UK, that have been the subject of recent inquiry regarding people's relationships to heritage and history in communities that have lost their major industrial base of employment (Watson 2007, Wedgewood 2009). Wedgewood identifies these working class communities as having strong 'emotional' ties with their landscape and architecture (Wedgewood 2009: 283). Reasons for this attachment stem from the multi-generational residence in a single neighbourhood creating deep personal and family histories with particular spaces, and the fact that working class families are likely to have earned their living from the land (place) or from employment in a physical landmark such as a factory or mine (Wedgewood 2009: 284). These emotional connections to place become particularly acute when these communities enter into a decline and are condemned by others as deteriorating spaces. Criticisms of place become criticisms of community residents as well.

This strong attachment to place combined with external perceptions of decline and deterioration make heritage and history of very real importance in working class communities (Wedgewood 2009: 295). Heritage, while often selective and celebratory, becomes an important part of the future in the eyes of residents, and local efforts at preserving local history are a vital means of sharing the meanings of local places across generations. Presenting history to those outside the community also is a vital strategy for community preservation as outside interest and recognition may bring much needed resources into the community.

When Pullman residents in the 1960s took up the gauntlet to save their neighbourhood, class played an integral role in their strategies, and many of these 'emotional' ties and resulting strategies in preservation and promotion are evidenced in their story. The first were attempts to elevate the standing and importance of the neighbourhood in broader arenas. Residents chose to emphasise the original nineteenth-century design and plan of the town in a conscious attempt to revive the 'World's Most Perfect Town' and to portray Pullman as a 'model community'. Efforts to seek external recognition for the town under these rubrics were paired with conscious and deliberate steps to organise internally and to clean up their neighbourhood so as not to be part of the widespread 'urban blight' on the south side. The choice to downplay the importance of Pullman in labour movements and to emphasise its Gilded Age history was a conscious appeal and an effective strategy for gaining outside recognition while retaining local control over the destiny of the preservation and presentation of the community. Today, the exhibits, tours and signage that are born of this legacy still reflect the tendency to downplay the working class heritage of the community while emphasising the original model town as its source of historical and touristic interest.

It is hard to argue that the arrival of the IHPA shepherded in a new set of sensibilities about class that resulted in new types of neighbourhood interpretation, particularly as most of the staff and all of the volunteers are still Pullman residents. The treatment of class and labour at the hotel and factory and on the Rose Garden placard are much more in the forefront, and are actively balanced with interpretations of Pullman's Gilded Age. It is more likely that the success of earlier efforts by community organisations to raise the profile of Pullman as a site of historic importance have created a space that enables different stories about the town to be explored in the presentation of local heritage. These stories of class struggles, labour unrest and the everyday life of ordinary families align the presentation of the town's nineteenth-century history with its twentieth-century legacy as a vibrant and tenacious working class community. These stories also resonate with the external understandings of Pullman as an important site in labour history that still fascinates national and international audiences and brings them to this small community on Chicago's South Side.

Notes

1 The history of the town of Pullman has been researched extensively, and such a large history can only be given cursory treatment here. The most enduring history of record is Stanley Buder's 1967 work *Pullman: An Experiment in Industrial Order and Community Planning 1880–1930*, New York: Oxford University Press. Many other works are widely available through major publishers and book distributors.
2 These estimates are informal and are based on tallies kept of visitors who come to the Pullman State Historic Site, the Historic Pullman Foundation Visitor's Centre, and from ticket sales for annual House Tour Events.
3 This was an informal survey conducted by Jane Baxter over a two-year period. Tours were of the factory site, or of the town itself. Groups included: three labour history groups, one regional conference tour, one union group, nine groups of school teachers, three high school/junior high school classes, 22 groups of university students and seven groups from local senior organisations or retirement homes.
4 Derek Larson's *Devil in the White City: Murder, Magic, and Madness at the Fair that Changed America* (New York: Vintage Press 2004) is a very popular account of the 1893 Chicago World's Fair that includes references to the Pullman Community.

References

Arkansas Gazette (1976) 'Newcomers awaken Pullman to new urban vitality', 25 July, p.10B.
Avignone, M. (1979) miscellaneous notes on Pullman, unpublished.
——(1980) history of the Pullman Civic Organization, unpublished notes.
——(1984) 'First walking tour of historic Pullman scheduled for May 6', *Fra Noi*, April, p.21.
Buder, S. (1967) *Pullman: An Experiment in Industrial Order and Community Planning 1880–1930*, New York: Oxford University Press.
Calumet Index (1960) 'Update on redevelopment plans', 29 June.
——(1974) 'Pullman not like most communities', 3 November, p.12.
Chicago Tribune (1882) 'Visitors to Pullman overwhelm factory works', 12 April, p.3.
City of Chicago Landmarks Commission. (2003) 'Chicago Landmarks', Online. Available HTTP: < http://www.cityofchicago.org/Landmarks/P/PullmanDistrict.html> (accessed 21 September 2009).
Cobbie, D. S. and Kessler-Harris, A. (1993) 'The new labor history in American history textbooks', *Journal of American History*, 79:1534–45.
Doty, D. ([1890?]) 'Doty's Article on Calumet region', Online. Available HTTP: <http://www.pullman-museum.org/cgibin/pvm/mainRecordDisplayXML.pl?recordid=12671> (accessed 21September 2009).
Ely, R. T. (1885) 'Pullman: a social study', *Harper's Magazine*, 70:452–66.
Fallace, T. (2008) 'Did the social studies really replace history in American secondary schools?', *Teachers College Record*, 110: 2245–70.

Hirsch, S. E. (2003) *After the Strike: A Century of Labor Struggle at Pullman*, Champagne: University of Illinois Press.

Historic Pullman Foundation (1992) *Historic Pullman Foundation: The First Ten Years*, Chicago: Historic Pullman Foundation.

Kammen, C. (ed.) (1996) *The Pursuit of Local History: Readings on Theory and Practice*, Walnut Creek, CA: Alta Mira Press.

National Park Service (2009) Lowell National Park. Online. HTTP: <http://www.nps.gov/lowe/index.htm> (accessed August 2009).

Papke, D. R. (1999) *The Pullman Case: The Clash of Labor and Capital in Industrial America*, Lawrence: University of Kansas Press.

Pullman Civic Organization (1960) 'minutes of the Pullman Civic Organization', *The Pullman Flyer*, June, p.1.

——(1964a) *The Pullman Flyer*, January, p.1.

——(1964b) *The Pullman Flyer*, October, p.1.

Pullman Civic Organization. (1972) 'City landmark status', *The Pullman Flyer,* January, p.3.

Smith, C. (1996) *Urban Disorder and the Shape of Belief: The Great Chicago Fire, the Haymarket Bomb and the Model Town of Pullman*, Chicago: University of Chicago Press.

St. Petersburg Times (1976) 'Newcomers awaken Pullman to new urban vitality', 25 July, p.8.

Watson, S. (2007) 'History museums, community identity, and a sense of place', in S.K. Knell, S. McLeod and S. Watson (eds), *Museum Revolutions: How Museums Change and Are Changed*, London: Routledge: 160–72.

Wedgwood, T. (2009) 'History in two dimensions or three?: Working class responses to history', *International Journal of Heritage Studies*, 15(4):277–97.

Chapter 17

Tolpuddle, Burston and Levellers
The making of radical and national heritages at English labour movement festivals

Hilda Kean

Every July the Tolpuddle Martyrs' festival is celebrated at a small Dorset village near Dorchester. Thousands of trade unionists regularly converge on the village to commemorate the six local agricultural labourers from Tolpuddle who were deported to New South Wales and Tasmania in the Spring of 1834. The men had been seeking to form a union to resist a reduction in their weekly wages. They had not taken part in strike action. Nor had they participated in the so-called Captain Swing riots in agricultural areas in the early 1830s in which, as Hobsbawm and Rudé have calculated, some 252 were sentenced to death,19 actually executed and 505 sentenced to deportation and 644 imprisoned (Hobsbawm and Rudé 1973: 224). Since the Combination Acts outlawing unions had been rescinded the agricultural labourers had broken no law in forming a union. However, they were convicted of swearing an oath, reputedly under the village sycamore tree, as part of the proceedings of a friendly society. They were prosecuted under the Mutiny Act of 1797 passed to prevent sedition, although, as John Rule has noted, 'there was no question of the six having any such intent' (Rule 1986: 311). In March 1834, a London meeting of some 10,000 people was organised by the Grand National Consolidated Trade Union. It also subsequently organised a demonstration for their release, not in Dorset, but in London, at Islington's Copenhagen Fields on 21 April 1834. As a result of various campaigns the six men received a free pardon in 1836: George Loveless returned to London in June 1837 and the others to Plymouth on March 17th 1838, some four years after the trial. On Easter Monday 1838 a procession was held to welcome their return, again in London (TUC 1934).

A July date plays no part in the chronology of events, yet this is when the festival is held. It is the moment of defeat that is the focus. The place where this act of remembrance is performed is not the place of labour movement strength in London where demonstrations were held for their pardon, but weakness, Tolpuddle.[1]

This summer labour movement festival is not unique. In Norfolk at the tiny village of Burston, near Diss, a September event commemorates the 'longest strike in history'. Christian socialist Annie Higdon had been employed with her husband Tom to run the village school in 1911. Having organised the local agricultural workers, Tom Higdon topped the poll for the parish council, defeating the vicar, who was also the school manager. In April 1914 the couple were dismissed reputedly for caning a child (which was a common practice of the time). Mrs Higdon denied this. The couple were supported by parents and also by the schoolchildren, who went on strike in their support. At the time the case was seen by the local agricultural workers' union, and unions nationally, as an example of persecution by the local hierarchy against trade unionists. As Tom Higdon wrote at the time, 'There is not a principle or practice of Truth or True Rebellion, of Common or Individual Justice, of Personal or Political Liberty, of Trade Unionism or Socialism, which is not involved in this fight' (Higdon in Burston strike n.d.). Children marched around the village in support.

Funded by donations from the trade union and labour movement nationally, a new alternative school was established by the Higdons on the village green in 1917 with the foundation stone being laid by the future leader of the Labour Party, George Lansbury. Around the outside of the building donations were recorded from a wide range of organisations and individuals: the Watford Labour Church, Hendreladis Lodge of the South Wales Miners' Federation, City of London Independent Labour Party and Mr Cullen from St Kilda in Victoria, Australia. It continued as a school until 1939 shortly after Tom Higdon's death. In 1949 the school became an educational charity administered by trustees.

This 25-year timescale has led the Burston school strike to be characterised as 'the longest strike in history' (Burston n.d.; Page 1984). Despite ongoing efforts, the Higdons were never reinstated in their former posts (Edwards 1974). This focus of the festival, created in the 1980s, is on the village green, where the former school building continues to stand. Such a village location has been seen as a significant place, as a 'portion of England left over after the squire and parson have cast lots for the remainder' (Casey 1915 in Griffiths 2007: 27). The event always includes a march around the village (which replicates the march of striking children in 1914).

The third festival I will consider, Levellers' Day, is held in Burford, a town of just over 1,000 residents in Oxfordshire in May. The modern Burford, represented in parliament by Prime Minister David Cameron, was recently defined by the business magazine *Forbes* as one of the most idyllic places to live in Europe.[2] The festival also commemorates a political defeat of the radical Levellers during the English Civil War more than 350 years ago. Leveller leaders had led mutinies in the Army during the civil war and had been arrested and imprisoned: Burford was seen as a final stand. The Burford mutiny followed on from the defeat of radical ideas at the Putney debates in 1647. There had also been mutinies when men who refused to volunteer for service in Ireland were demobilised without payment of arrears. However, on previous occasions the generals had not executed mutineers

(Hill 1975: 109). According to Christopher Hill, here the defeat of 'the more extreme radical' activists resulted in a 'total rout' (Hill 1985: 17). On 17th May 1649 Cornet Thompson and Corporals Church and Perkins were executed in Burford churchyard (Hill 1975: 70).

On one Saturday in May, in the local church, gardens and streets, people from outside the town construct a different character to the conservative norm, marching around the town with banners, hearing radical speeches and placing wreathes in the churchyard.

Heritage and class

Public awareness of history is shaped by factors that demand critical examination (Wright 2009: xv). To understand the nature of these occasions we need to consider not simply their 'political' content but the form and location of such constructions. It has been argued that people view heritage through a 'whole series of lenses' including religion, ethnicity, gender, wealth, personal history and class (Graham and Howard 2008: 2). As Howard has noted, class is a major factor in creating heritage values, often being seen as cultural capital to be acquired specifically to increase class or status (Howard 2003: 215).

Recently, West has explored aspects of class and heritage, within a framework of material heritage that is usually created inside museums. For her, working class heritage is seen primarily within a framework of industrial heritage or working class housing since, she contends, 'class relations themselves are no longer in the foreground of our sense of personal or national politics' (West 2010: 273). Assuming that heritage is centred on material culture and suggesting that 'people in poverty' owned 'fewer possessions' to enable them to create particular heritages, West argues that the enduring representations of 'the working classes and the destitute are their workplaces and housing' (West 2010: 274). This approach emphasises the way in which material aspects of an industrial past can be presented by professional historians, rather than the way in which people themselves engage with, and construct, their own interpretations of the past. Such an approach de-emphasises people's own explorations of the past and of making history (Kean and Ashton 2009; Kean 2010). It devalues experience, particularly the experience of those outside academia. As Samuel spelt out in *Theatres of Memory*, history is not the prerogative of the historian but 'a social form of knowledge; the work in any given instance, of a thousand different hands' (1994: 8).

West's approach is rather different to the emphasis that Laurajane Smith has placed on working class people creating their own meaning within museums. As she analyses it critically, the Authorized Heritage Discourse constructs heritage as something that is engaged with passively, it is not an active process of experience (Smith 2006: 31). In her study of the creation of heritage in the former mining town of Castleford, Smith noted that working class residents used heritage actively to make and re-make their own identity

(Smith 2006: 273). In similar vein, as Jon Newman found when curating an exhibition on the photographs of Harry Jacobs, visitors, mainly working class African-Caribbean visitors, created their own meanings on the material displayed. Visitors to the Brixton exhibition appended post-it notes to the images to give more information about the subjects who had been anonymised in Jacobs' archive (Newman 2009). In such ways working class people become particular makers of history (Moore 1994: 169). Taking the idea of contested meaning further and drawing on both the work of Laurajane Smith and Raphael Samuel, Iain Robertson has analysed the construction of memorials in the Scottish island of Lewis. Here different, small, communities have created, as Roberston defines it, 'heritage from below' (Robertson 2008: 145–48).

Tolpuddle, Burston and Levellers are all festivals in which working class radical organisations and individuals have attempted to create their own commemorative heritage separate from the frameworks constructed by academic or professional historians. Although seeking to remember a particular sort of past, the participants might also be seen to 'reconnect with pasts from which generational and socio-economic change has left them feeling disconnected' (Stanton 2009: 69). These autonomously organised events are examples of working class people attempting, as James Green has put it, 'to get their history into their own hands' (Green 2000: 81). The attempts to create a memory of a radical past within the nation have also resulted in the creation of memories of the commemorative events themselves as part of a radical political culture.

Physical location and commemoration in the landscape

The festivals deliberately focus on places seen as important because of actions which occurred there in the past (Hayden 1997). Accordingly, a part of the process is to imagine and engage with a past to enable present and future political action. As Malraux described it: ' the cultural heritage is not made up of the works that men (sic) must respect, but of those only that can help them to live. Our heritage is made up of all the voices that can answer our questions … ' (Malraux in Wright 2009: xi).

The events are situated in rural localities that might be seen as being more typical of dominant heritage sites than labour movement sites of memory. John Urry, for example, has analysed the ways in which rural landscapes have become a 'very attractive object of the tourist gaze' (Urry 2002: 87). Only certain types of countryside, however, are 'attractive' to the tourist. From this landscape are excluded farm machinery, labourers, tractors, dead and diseased animals, concrete farm buildings and nuclear power stations (2002: 88). What is required by the tourist is a sense of timelessness. However, a different sense of time is being created in these festivals, one of moments that cross time.

Although May Day demonstrations may still be a feature of London political-cultural life (Kean 2003), it is mainly in the countryside or localities outside conurbations that important labour movement festivals occur.[3] This is surprising in some ways since, 'Throughout its history the Labour Party has been firmly associated with the urban environment' (Griffiths 2007: 3) yet, as Griffiths has argued, within the Labour Party the idea of Merrie England, a 'self consciously historical vision was pervasive' (2007: 26–7). Excluded from such lyrical landscapes are notions of political organisation that these labour festivals seek to reinsert into a locality, albeit for a day every year. These commemorations are anachronistic and 'out of place'.

Aspects of material culture associated with the events being commemorated in these sites have changed over time – and are still contested. The former alternative school building at Burston was converted into a community hall, and in the 1990s refurbished as a small museum. Outside there are plaques indicating the name of organisations, including trade unions, that donated to the school suggesting a solidity to this past. Inside, however, hang two different ways of framing this event. At one end is a print of Daniel in the lion's den, recalling, amongst other things, the Non-Conformist adage 'Dare to be a Daniel, dare to stand alone'. Near the door is a written plaque offering – as a form of reconciliation – an apology for the way in which the vicar had unjustly accused Mrs Higdon of hitting a child. Underneath is a small coda, recording that two long-standing residents wished to disassociate themselves from such a statement. This suggests that the Burston school strike past is as part of the present for some local residents as it is for the annual visitors.

The six memorial cottages at Tolpuddle, built in 1934 under the consultancy of Raymond Unwin, the architect responsible for Letchworth, were intended for elderly trade unionists, with attention paid to interior design for those with mobility problems (Citrine n.d.). However, these structures were never just homes. They were built to symbolise the labour movement as evidenced by being floodlit for two hours a night 'so no one travelling along the main road to Dorchester could fail to be impressed by the standard which trade unionism had set for agricultural housing' (Griffiths 2007: 294–95). Recent suggestions that one of the cottages be rented out as a holiday let have proved controversial, with one angry resident being reported as saying, 'It flies in the face of the story of the Tolpuddle martyrs and shows the TUC is as money-grabbing as everyone else' (Morris 2009).

The physical commemorative landscape of Tolpuddle is neither settled nor timeless. A new gravestone was designed by Eric Gill for the grave of James Hammett, the only 'martyr' to die in England (TUC 1934b).[4] A plaque adjacent to a sycamore tree grown 'from a seedling from the original tree' (under which the labourers swore their oath) was planted by the TUC general secretary in 1984, Len Murray. Another plaque by the tree celebrated the Queen's golden jubilee in 2002 giving it designated status as 'The Tolpuddle martyrs tree'. Now incorporated within a national heritage the plaque declares the tree to be 'one of fifty great British trees in recognition of its place in the national heritage'.

In the 1990s in Burford, within the churchyard itself, was erected a plaque recording the three shot Levellers. This, like the Tolpuddle museum and cottages, is a permanent simple memorial. The only information given is the names of the three soldiers who were executed and the date and the words 'To the memory of three Levellers'. It is a memorial 'erected by those, and for those, who already have this knowledge', of why such a memorial is appropriate (Hargreaves 2005: 3). Although the words suggest 'insider knowledge', in its form of memorialisation, a plaque on the wall of a church, it is also part of a Protestant commemoration of the dead and thus can be understood more broadly as a site of remembrance event by those not sharing specific knowledge of the Levellers' thoughts or actions.

The creation of such structures at these different physical sites serves to make a particular permanent physical presence within a recognised *national* landscape of historical commemoration. As such, the otherwise ephemeral spectacle created by outsiders on one day a year is embedded in the locality, contesting the dominant narrative throughout the rest of the year.

Moments and continuity: suffering and defeat

All three festivals emphasise, in different ways, 'moments' out of the ordinary. Implicit is a concept of history as change and rupture rather than continuity. While it may be the case that, as Francois Hartog has argued, heritage is never 'nourished by continuity' (Wright 2009: xix) nevertheless a sense of continuity is provided through the nature of the commemorative event itself. The festivals provide an annual opportunity to remember the past for the present, often a present that has lost an earlier sense of the future (Wright xviii), implied by the hope embedded in past militant actions. The events being remembered are seen as extraordinary and they are moments of defeat or long suffering in a political cause, not success. These are not held in merely rural locations that summon up established ideas of Englishness but those in which a trade union and labour movement presence has not been easily established (Griffiths 2007: 8). The events are exceptions both in the events being remembered *and* in their place of enactment. The histories being created are not those in keeping with the dominant Conservative politics of the localities. Accordingly, a sense of empathy with past 'martyrs' is facilitated: in this sense the past and the present elide. The events are organised by bodies, such as the TUC (Trades Union Congress), based outside the immediate locality, that – albeit for one day in the year – contest the dominant political discourse.[5]

In his positive analysis of commemorative people's history in the United States, James Green has argued that although such history may be criticised as 'nostalgic celebrations' nevertheless, he continues, 'We can return to our lives in the present with a better set of maps about where we want to go in the future. We can return with a more grounded moral critique of what appear to be the inevitable forces of progress' (Green 2000: 119). This possible disjuncture between political experience and cultural activity has been analysed in respect of the miners during the 1984–85 strike. Describing the return to work after the defeat of the year long strike 'with banners of the departed ... called upon to give the miners an imaginary strength' Samuel characterised this as 'mobilis[ing] the old world to redress the balance of the new. As catharsis it enabled the miners to celebrate in ceremonial form, and on a very public stage, the victory which in real life had been cruelly denied them' (Samuel 1986: 6). Taking this argument further, more recently Alessandro Portelli has criticised both Italian popular culture and political and academic culture as having difficulty seeing workers 'as individuals, rather than as symbols'. 'Whatever we think', he continues, 'of the historical role of workers as a class today, workers as individual people are still very much in existence ... the worker's political plight is also deeply personal ... they exist even when proletarian revolution is no longer imminent' (Portelli 2005: 58). In the labour movement annual festivals we see people creating pasts needed for their own present and one which, in different ways, sustains them emotionally, as well as politically, in the present.

Radical pasts with a connection to the present, however these pasts might be defined over the years, are being explicitly promoted. They are occasions constructed to provide those who attend with images from the past that, as Walter Benjamin put it, threaten to disappear irretrievably if they are not seized upon in the present (Benjamin 1940: 247). Although the locations have memories ascribed to them, the nature of social memory is such that it is 'continuously productive rather than merely confined within demarcated sites' (Graham and Howard 2008: 7). A flyer distributed to promote Levellers' Day 2009 described such festivals as a 'family of events', 'Together they create a focus for working people, socialists and the trade union and labour movement to come together and gain inspiration to carry forward their struggles into the future' (Levellers 2009). There is a clear and explicit relationship spelt out between the past and the present although what is constructed from the past changes over time. Neither Levellers' Day nor Tolpuddle have – obviously – a direct living connection with the original protagonists. However, at Burston there existed until relatively recently a 'living link' with the events being commemorated. Writing what is now the standard history of the strike in 1974, Bertram Edwards, a schoolteacher from Hitchin, tracked down the then elderly former schoolchildren to include their accounts in his writing (Nevitt 1992: 93). The film of the strike broadcast on BBC 2 in 1985 also caught the last of this living connection. So did the interview in the same year in the *Morning Star* with Tom Potter, taught by Mrs Higdon in the 1920s (and who had been in the Communist Party since 1941, chair of the parish council and secretary of the local agricultural workers union) (Burston file, TUC: n.d.). Accordingly, some 'authority' in the creation of this history was established by these links with people who themselves had experienced the events being commemorated at first hand. But 'authority' is also achieved through the very act of attendance at the festivals, of bearing an annual witness to the past.

Some motifs in the festivals have a continuous life: the commemorators celebrate narratives of martyrdom and suffering almost in a religious sense. These are stories of injustice: deportation, execution, long-term unemployment. They are consciously melodramatic in that the protagonists are depicted as standing alone against the odds and sticking to their beliefs through various vicissitudes.[6] Fortitude is praised as a success. This religious, protestant, theme of suffering in a just cause is also complemented by the ritualistic forms adopted during the commemorations. In this sense it is not dissimilar to the characterisation of the 1984 –85 miners' strike eliding Protestantism and politics as 'an act of faith in their leader, faith in the union, faith in themselves' (Samuel 1986: 29–31). Moreover, it is a narrative not dissonant with national motifs unrelated to radical themes. Some commemorations include the laying of wreaths, for example, on James Hammett's grave in Tolpuddle or at the plaque on the side of the church in Burford. All include a demonstration around the locality in which the events occurred, almost as a sign of bearing witness to having attended: latter day examples of standing up and being counted. While the character of the demonstrations, accompanied by banners, takes the form of a radical political event, in some ways these rituals themselves are not distinct from national commemorations such as Remembrance Sunday in November.

Reinventing trade union, Methodist and Liberal pasts: Tolpuddle

Although a sense of timelessness is created at these three events, the spectacle is being repeatedly reinvented. As Meghan O'Brien Backhouse has explored in her work on re-enactors, collective identity is reiterated by means of cultural performances such as traditions, objectified in material goods and by imbuing the natural and built landscapes with commemorative meanings (O'Brien Backhouse 2009: 118). But, as she acknowledges, although it may appear that symbols have remained the same as the years pass, the original meanings have changed (2009: 199). Labour movement commemoration of its own history was not an invention of the mid-twentieth century. In both their press and banners the Chartists recalled earlier radical histories. They drew on the writings of Shelley and Byron for inspiration, employing epithets such as 'He who would be free himself must strike the blow.' In turn, these forms were adapted and re-fashioned in the early twentieth century by the women's Suffrage movement, who both drew on similar works to those of the Chartists and also referred back to John Hampden's civil war slogan

'Taxation without representation is tyranny' (Kean 2005). In the later nineteenth century May Day was invented as a socialist, as opposed to an agricultural, event at a time of extraordinary growth and expansion of the labour and socialist movements in numerous countries. Significantly it was associated with the 'symbolism of spring'. In the same way that festivals occur in the summer months replicating village shows, so too was the rural year appropriated for a radical cause (Hobsbawm 1983: 283–86 in Green 2000: 106).

Tolpuddle was first discussed as a *national* labour movement commemoration nearly a century after the events themselves. For some years the Agricultural Workers' Union had held a yearly event commemorating the death of the martyrs (TUC 1932: 263). At the TUC annual congress in 1932, a motion was proposed by Clynes of the General and Municipal Workers Union and James of the Agricultural Workers Union. It recorded its 'deep appreciation of the service rendered by the Tolpuddle Martyrs to Trade Unionism and Humanity ... ' and instructed the general council to arrange for a national demonstration 'in keeping with the character and devotion of these pioneer stalwarts'. In speaking to the unanimously carried motion, Clynes referred to the men as 'arraigned, sentenced, punished and banished. But their spirit was not killed, and as they returned they were honoured' (TUC 1932: 262). Clynes placed the rationale for the commemoration firmly in the present where 'there is fresh the recollection of betrayal, of men who recently deserted our cause' (1932: 263). Here the TUC saw itself as maintaining the labour movement cause against the 'traitor' Ramsay MacDonald who had formed the national government. They thus become identified with the martyrs of the past through their own experience of betrayal in the present. The TUC commissioned and published 30,000 books, as well as a pictorial brochure souvenir (TUC 1935: 199), that provided a history for that particular time with the imprimatur of Fabian historians Sidney and Beatrice Webb, praising the 'gentle innocence of the victims' and arguing for a strong party in the House of Commons to prevent a repetition of the repression of 1834 (TUC 1934: xiv-xiv). The president of the TUC, Andrew Conley, also situated the labourers against the abolition of trade unionism by 'armed force' in some countries that had instituted dictatorships, although no specific reference was made to any particular country or fascism as such (TUC 1934: xii).[7]

The 1934 volume was reissued by the TUC in 1999, two years after the election of a Labour Government, without any change in the text. There was a new introduction by John Monks, the general secretary, who suggested that, 'Some stories rise about their place in history. They do so not by chance but because they have a timeless quality and because their significance seizes the imagination of succeeding generations' (TUC 1999: n.p.). Despite this notion of timelessness and continuity, he chose to make modern comparisons with the Tolpuddle labourers. Highlighted were the workers at GCHQ (Government Communications Headquarters) who had regained trade union rights under the Labour Government, removed by the former Conservative Government, some 13 years on. The 'story' then became not a timeless narrative but one of a current moment. It was also specifically linked to a *Labour* Government. The story of respectability that had helped the Tolpuddle labourers be feted in both 1834 and 1934 was again privileged. Moreover, the decision not to commission a new work on the Tolpuddle martyrs – cost aside – had the effect of making more stable and settled the past 'icons' to which current trade unionists might relate. This re-visiting of an early trade union commemoration also suggested that this had always been an exclusively labour movement commemoration.

However, the national labour commemoration in 1934 was not the first public commemoration of the labourers. If the TUC's decision was largely concerned with present morale (Griffiths 1997: 151), the appropriation of the labourers fulfilled the same function in the early years of the twentieth century for the Wesleyan Methodists. Four of the labourers were Methodists (Marlow 1974: 12–18) and George Loveless had been a Methodist local preacher, arguing in his 1837 pamphlet 'The Victims of Whiggery' that he was 'from principle, a Dissenter, and by some in Tolpuddle it is considered as the sin of witchcraft'. This was a view upheld by the *Morning Chronicle* at the time that declared that the poor Methodists were being assailed in the country villages of the south and west of England (Robinson 1999: 5). Wesleyan Methodism, the main branch of Methodism at that time, could boast some 358,000 members in 1850 rising to over 450,000 in 1900, but between 1906 and 1912 the Methodist movement was in a continued decline (Wearmouth 1957: 46–47). When Wesleyan Methodists formed a memorial committee and issued a pamphlet seeking support for the building of two cottages and the creation of two scholarships to Ruskin College, Oxford, in honour of the Tolpuddle labourers, the apparent rationale was to emphasise and promote the role of Methodism. 'Since three of the men were Wesleyan Methodist local preachers, it is only natural that Wesleyan Methodists should be specially interested in the story of their struggles and sufferings', declared the organising committee (Memorial Committee, n.d.: 9). Any memorial should commemorate their suffering both 'in the course of economic freedom but also for the sake of their religious convictions' (Memorial Committee, n.d.: 9). Although the fund raising attempts were not successful, a memorial arch was erected in front of the 1860s Methodist chapel and unveiled by Labour MP and future Labour party general secretary Arthur Henderson, who was also a Methodist, in 1912 (Robinson 1999: 11).

Different religious services were conducted on the memorial weekend: Arthur Henderson spoke in Dorchester Methodist church and local preachers addressed an open-air meeting at the tree where the oath had been taken (*Methodist Recorder* 1934). Former Liberal prime minister Lloyd George laid a wreath at the Methodist memorial archway, and was presented to the only surviving son of James Hammett. In Lloyd George's speech to the west Dorset Liberal association, he acknowledged that the Whigs were responsible for the prosecution of the labourers, but also argued that the radicals were responsible for their release. The martyrs had become Liberal icons too: what Liberalism needed now was the spirit of the old reformers (*Scotsman* 9 July 1934).

This appropriation by Liberals, trade unionists and Methodists is not as strange as it might appear for the labourers certainly fitted nineteenth-century concepts of respectability. While they had ostensibly broken a law, they were not the machine breakers of the southern counties, nor the Luddites of Nottingham and Derby, or those who would be involved in the Newport uprising of 1839 (Hobsbawm and Rudé 1973). They were not the first trade unionists, although they are at risk of being reinvented as such.[8] However, they were seen as worthy of incorporation within particular concepts of trade unionism that has sought to position itself as a key protagonist within the life of the *nation*. Spectacles, plays, tableaux and processions at the first 1934 festival elided the Tolpuddle martyr events with those of 'rural' history such as mummers, going to the fair and child workers of 1834. Several of the events did not have a distinctive labour movement perspective. There was, for instance, a fruit, flowers and vegetable show (with a special prize for that presented by a trade unionist in Dorchester); bands played the 'Teddy bears picnic' and tunes from the light opera *The Gondoliers*. There were sports: football, cycling, walking and lawn tennis (TUC 1934b). Such ephemeral activities – including the nature of the speeches, for example – have changed over the years but the Tolpuddle 'martyrs' are still being employed for different purposes at different moments. For instance, they have been invoked by Age Concern as 'the inspiration for a team of older peoples [sic] campaigners in Dorchester' (Age Concern 2008) or as 'simply [making] a stand for what was right' (Flett 2007).

The English Civil War: shop stewards and Christianity

Levellers' day was established over 300 years after the events at Burford. It originated from the Workers' Education Association (WEA) Oxford Industrial Branch, the motto of which was 'Knowledge is Power'. This particular branch was set up in 1972, with the aim of taking the movement back to its working class labour movement roots. It was largely initiated by tutor organisers and university extramural tutors, who had felt that those most in need of further adult education were not taking advantage of the subsidised WEA classes (Levellers 1976: 4). In 1975, a Levellers' sub–committee was established and organised a wreath laying in 1975 attended by 80 people including local trade unionists. 'As an industrial branch member remarked, "those soldier delegates – the "agitators" – were the first shop stewards!"' (Levellers 1976: 4). One of the early organisers, Dudley Edwards, explained on Radio Oxford at the time, 'We are hoping it will become an annual event and gradually grow in importance like the Tolpuddle Martyrs' (Ayers 2009: 42).

Although it has grown, unsurprisingly there has been local opposition to the commemoration from the first events in the 1970s (Ayers 2009: 43). More recently, a local historian has both debunked the idea that Burford was the site of an important event (Moody 1999: 3) and the politics of the commemoration as 'an attempt to find English roots for a political theory that does indeed fit uneasily in the English scene' (1999: 40). More surprisingly, although the English Civil War Society (ECWS), a re-enactment society, aims to bring history alive, the ECWS has chosen not to participate in Levellers' days as it is apparently a 'non-political' organisation'(!) (Ayers 2009: 51).

There had been popular interest in the Levellers during the 1940s. Both in the Army Bureau of Current Affairs and in Labour Party propaganda the civil war – and the position of the Levellers – was employed to different ends. In *Why not trust the Tories* (1944), Nye Bevan concluded with an account of the Putney debates and the radical position of the Levellers. He argued that Cromwell had feared, that 'If they who have no goods and chattels make the laws equally with them that hath they will make laws to take away the property of them that hath all' (Bevan 'Celticus' 1944: 88–89). This was also realised today, he said, by the Tories: what was needed now was the wisdom of Thomas Rainbro whose views had been defeated at Putney: 'Either poverty must use democracy to destroy the power of property, or property in fear of poverty will destroy democracy' (1944: 88–89).

Certainly, Cromwell was also invoked during the Second World War by the organisers of education within the British Army, the Army Bureau of Current Affairs, 'Cromwell's army ... spent a considerable part of its time in discussing topics very similar to those that are being considered with such vigour in the second world war.' Even the Levellers' petition to Parliament was mentioned (Hawkins and Brimble 1947: 158). However, as Martin Lawn wryly comments, 'But while the Cromwellian army of the soldier–citizen was certainly created from above, the discussion remarked upon such as that of the Levellers, took place in spite of the "generals"!' (Lawn 1989: 117). There was also a specific connection between such wartime discussions and the Burford commemorations. Alan Hicks, who had taken part in a military mutiny in Bavaria in late 1944 and 1945, had been interested in the Levellers as mutineers and later became involved in the Oxford campaign joining forces with Dudley Edwards, an Oxford trade unionist.[9] Moreover, the politics of the Cold War period in the late 1940s also led to Dudley Edwards first drafting his pamphlet 'The last stand of the Levellers', in response, he said, to the mass media portrayal of communism as 'everything that was alien to the "true spirit" of the British nation' and a 'purely foreign importation' (Edwards 1978: preface). When the pamphlet was reissued in 1978, Edwards introduced this later edition as a challenge to the concept of national heritage. Contesting the past and creating different focuses for heritage were conscious acts of the organisers. As Edwards maintained, 'When these words "Our national heritage" are used by the representatives of capitalist society, the aim is to blot out that other heritage – the heritage of the common people' (Edwards 1978: preface). The pamphlet was also intended as an antidote to 'official historians' who 'have buried such incidents as the battle of Burford under great files of dry as dust manuscripts' (1978: preface). Edwards argued that 'most of the political ideas' the Levellers had fought for had been realised although 'economic emancipation is yet to be achieved' (Edwards 1978: 16). Continuity with the past was created, he continued, by the modern working class movement, 'and the Marxist wing of the movement in particular' who are 'the true heirs to this great tradition of militant struggle against the exploiting classes' (Edwards 1978: 20).

The narrative of the 1970s Levellers was seen as part of a commemoration of people 'hidden from history', the phrase often used by contemporary radical historians. Until the organisation of Levellers' day the scratched name on the Burford font 'Anthony Sedley prisoner 1649' had been 'the only inscription to commemorate the last stand of the Levellers' (Edwards 1978: 16). Speaking on Oxford local radio in 1976, one of the organisers, Alan Hicks, situated the executions at Burford within the framework of the Putney debates, 'Debates were held at Putney to decide how England should be run after the [civil] war was over. They were forced to watch the executions in order to intimidate them, this was the first democratic experiment in elections' (Radio Oxford 1976). In a pamphlet of 1976 based on a talk given at Levellers' Day, Tony Benn, the leading left wing Labour MP, invoked the Levellers for the present, suggesting that they would have much to say on a variety of issues from the huge accumulation of financial power to the recall and replacement of parliamentary candidates (Levellers 1976: 14). The introductory statement from the Oxford WEA industrial branch also gave a contemporary focus. The rationale of the booklet was pedagogical, they said, in that it was to 'show the kind of thing that industrial branches like ours may do to provide for the education and enjoyment of members' (Levellers 1976: 4). The continuity with the past was made even more forcefully when Benn argued that, given 'the power of their ideas to move us even today, in what sense can we say that they are *not* here?' (Levellers 1976: 15). Those who attend the May celebrations are assumed to acknowledge the Levellers' political importance and share sympathy, in some way, with their ideals. Both a group identity is being created in the present and inspiration gained from the former suffering of those who died for their cause. Those simply attending the lecture at Burford as part of the commemoration were themselves the very heirs of the Levellers. This was not an act of returning to a distant past but creating a particular sort of living present. This theme continues into the twenty-first century. Some sense of identity is being created with those who have previously attended or spoken at Levellers' Day. There is a 'remembrance' of the distant past but also of the more hopeful 1970s, when the commemorative day was established.

Conclusion

Tolpuddle, Burston and Levellers' Day continue to be presented by their respective organisers as part of a working class, radical history of resistance in difficult times. The celebrations are self-created, autonomous from state control. However, they do not take place in a cultural vacuum. The people and events being remembered may be radical but they are also part of a national trope of religious dissent and fortitude against adversity which owes more in its narrative construct to *Pilgrim's Progress* than the writings of Marx. The permanent forms of remembrance in the landscape: plaques, buildings, gravestones help to establish radical ideas as a part of the nation's heritage, using established forms. The annual gatherings also have another function, of renewing the political hope and emotional strength of the participants.

Acknowledgements

Thanks to Chris Coates: the TUC librarian, Robert Ayers, Dee Daly, Hannah Jones, Ken Jones and participants at the Robert Tressell Festival 2007 at which an earlier version of this chapter was presented.

Notes

1 An exception has been the 'Tolpuddle King's Cross Commemoration festival' held in April 2009 to celebrate the London demonstration in Copenhagen Fields in April 1834.
2 Laura Williamson: 'The tiny Oxfordshire town named on Forbes list of Most Idyllic Places gears up for influx of Americans' 17th April 2009 http://www.dailymail.co.uk/travel/article-1170519/Burford-tiny-Oxfordshire-town-named-Most-Idyllic-Places-planet.html#ixzz0OMAlGRRu
3 See also, the Durham miners' gala and the Robert Tressell festival in Hastings, Daley (2009); Mellor and Stephenson (2005); Wray (this volume).
4 For a time the other martyrs had settled in Greensted and High Laver, two villages in the Chipping Ongar area of Essex, but emigrated to Canada where they died.
5 At March 2011 Richard Bacon was Conservative MP for South Norfolk and the local district councillor covering Burston is also a Conservative. The representative on Dorset council for the area including Tolpuddle is also Conservative. Oliver Letwin is Conservative MP for West Dorset, the constituency for Tolpuddle.
6 This is also the case for the Robert Tressell festival.
7 There were also other commemorative labour movement pamphlets from this period, including Hunt, A. (1934); Brookes, H. (1929), Citrine, W. (1934); *Vox of Labour's Northern Voice* (1931).
8 For example, 'The draconian penalty provoked public outrage and the first great mass trade union protest'. *Morning Star,* Saturday 14 July 2007.
9 The ashes of Hicks are now interred in Burford churchyard where Tony Benn, one of the first speakers at Levellers' Day has also told organisers, 'he too would like his ashes scattered' (*Witney Gazette* 22 May 2007 as quoted in Ayers, 2009: 4).

References

Age Concern (2008) *Age Concern Weekly Lottery News Leaflet*, February.
Ayers, R. (2009) 'Bullet holes and blue plaques: Traces of the Civil War, revolution and rebellion in Oxford and the surrounding area', unpublished dissertation, Ruskin College, Oxford.
Flett, K. (2007) 'A history of resistance', *Morning Star: The Star at RISE*, 14 July 2007.
Benjamin, W. (1940) 'Theses on the philosophy of history', in Arendt, H. (ed.) *Illuminations*, London: Fontana, 1992.
Benn, T. (1976) *The Levellers and the English Democratic Tradition*, Nottingham: Russell Press.
Bevan, N. (Celticus) (1944) *Why Not Trust the Tories?*, London: Victor Gollancz.
Brookes, H. (1929) 'Six heroes in chains: A true tale of sacrifice retold', Poole: Looker.
Burston file (n.d.) Cuttings file, LA 639 in TUC archive.
Burston Strike school trustees, (n.d., ca. 1980s) 'The Burston strike school: The story of the longest strike in history', Trustees of Burston strike school.
Citrine, W. (1934) 'TUC cottages Tolpuddle: A memorial to brave men', London: TUC.
Daly, D. (2006), 'Raising the banners: Socialist and Trade Union festivals as a way of creating the public history of the Left in Britain', unpublished MA portfolio, Ruskin College, Oxford.
Edwards, B. (1974) *The Burston School Strike*, London: Lawrence and Wishart.
Edwards, D. (1978) *The Last stand of the Levellers*, Nottingham: Spokesman.
Graham, B. and Howard, P. (2008) *The Ashgate Research Companion to Heritage and Identity*, Aldershot: Ashgate.
Green, J. (2000) *Taking History to Heart, The Power of the Past in Building Social Movements*, Amherst: University of Massachusetts Press.
Griffiths, C. (1997) 'Remembering Tolpuddle: Rural history and commemoration in the inter-War labour movement', *History Workshop Journal*, 44: 145–69.
——(2007) *Labour and the Countryside*, Oxford: Oxford University Press.
Hargreaves, M. (2005) 'The Burford Leveller memorial plaque. A proper memorial with more than one meaning?', unpublished MA portfolio, Ruskin College, Oxford.
Hawkins, T. H. and Brimble, L.J.F. (1947) *Adult Education: The record of the British army*, London: Macmillan.
Hayden, D. (1997) *The Power of place: Urban landscapes as public history*, Cambridge, Massachusetts: MIT Press.
Hill, C. (1975) *The World Turned Upside Down: Radical Ideas During the English Revolution*, Harmondsworth: Penguin.
——(1985) *The Experience of Defeat: Milton and Some Contemporaries*, Harmondsworth: Penguin.
Hobsbawm, E. (1983) 'Mass-producing traditions: Europe, 1870 – 1914', in Hobsbawm, E. and Ranger T. (eds) *The Invention of Tradition*, Cambridge: Cambridge University Press: 283–86.
Hobsbawm, E. and Rudé, G. (1973) *Captain Swing*, Harmondsworth: Penguin.
Howard, P. (2003) *Heritage: Management, Interpretation, Identity*, London: Continuum.
Hunt, A. (1934) *Class against class, Tolpuddle and to-day*, London: Martin Laurence.
Jones, P. (2002) 'The Tolpuddle Martyrs museum and related sites', *Labour History Review* 67(2): 221–28.
Kean, H. (2003) 'The transformation of political and cultural space', in J. Kerr and A. Gibbon (eds) *London: from Punk to Blair*, London: Reaktion Books: 148–56.
——(2005) 'Public History and Popular Memory: issues in the commemoration of the British militant suffrage campaign', *Women's History Review*, 14 (3 and 4): 581–602.

—— (2010) 'People, historians and public history: De-mystifying the process of history making', in *The Public Historian*, Vol 32: 3, August: 25–38.
Kean, H. and Ashton, P. (2009) 'Introduction' to P. Ashton and H. Kean (eds) *People and their Pasts: Public History Today*, Basingstoke: Palgrave Macmillan.
Lawn, M. (1989) 'The British way and purpose: The spirit of the age in curriculum history', *Journal of Curriculum Studies*, 21(2), March–April: 113–28.
Levellers (1976) Preface to Tony Benn 'The Levellers and the English Democratic tradition', Nottingham: Russell Press.
Levellers Day Committee (2009) Flyer for Levellers Day, 16 May 2009, Oxfordshire: Levellers Day Committee.
Levellers Day (2009) Website. HTTP available at: <http://www.levellers.org.uk/levellersdayhistory.htm> (accessed 20 September 2009).
Malraux, A. (1936) 'Our cultural heritage', *Left Review,* 2(1), July, as quoted in P. Wright, (2009) *On Living in Another Country*, Oxford: Oxford University Press.
Marlow, J. (1974) *The Tolpuddle Martyrs*, St.Albans: Panther.
Mellor, M. and Stephenson, C. (2005) 'The Durham miners' gala and the spirit of community', *Community Development Journal*, 40:3, July:343–51.
Memorial Committee (n.d., 1900s) *The Tolpuddle Martyrs*, Weymouth: Warden and Co.
Methodist Recorder (1934) Press cuttings in Tolpuddle Arrangements file, HD 6664, TUC library.
Moody, R. (1999) 'Burford, the Civil War, and the Levellers', 2nd edn, Burford: Hindsight.
Moore, K. (1992) 'Labour history in museums: development and direction', in S. Pearce (ed.) *Museums and the Appropriation of Culture*, London: The Athlone Press.
Morris, S. (2009) 'Tolpuddle martyrs cottage is no holiday home for the rich, say villagers', *Guardian*, 18 June, Online Posting. Available HTTP: <http://www.guardian.co.uk/uk/2009/jun/18/tolpuddle-martyrs-cottages-tuc> (accessed 3 April 2010).
Nevitt, R. (1992) *The Burston School Strike*, Oxford: OUP.
Newman, J. (2009) 'Harry Jacobs: The studio photographer and the visual archive', in P. Ashton and H. Kean (eds) *People and Their Pasts,* Basingstoke: Palgrave Macmillan.
O'Brien Backhouse, M. (2009) 'Re-enacting the Wars of the Roses: history and Identity', in P. Ashton and H. Kean (eds) *People and their Pasts,* Basingstoke: Palgrave Macmillan.
Page, W. (1984), 'The longest strike in history', Diss: Wilf Page.
Portelli, A. (2005) '"This mill won't run no more": oral history and deindustrialization' in J. Russo and S. Linkon (2005) (eds) *New Working Class Studies*, Ithaca: Cornell University Press.
Radio Oxford (1976) 'Seven days at Radio Oxford ', broadcast 25 April 1976. Tape held in Oxfordshire local studies library, Oxford, transcript available in appendix of R. Ayers (2009) 'Bullet holes and blue plaques: Traces of the Civil War.
Robertson, I. (2008) 'Heritage from below: class, social protest and resistance', in B. Graham and P. Howard (2008) *The Ashgate Research Companion to Heritage and Identity*, Aldershot: Ashgate.
Robinson, D. M., (1999) *Report on the Former Methodist Chapel at Tolpuddle, Dorset*, unpublished report of English Heritage, accessed in TUC library.
Rule, J. (1986) *The Labouring Classes in Early Industrial England 1750–1850*, Harlow: Longman.
Samuel, R. (1986) Introduction to R. Samuel, B. Bloomfield, G. Boanas (eds) *The Enemy Within. Pit villages and the miners' strike of 1984–5*, London: Routledge, and Kegan Paul.

——(1994) *Theatres of Memory*, London: Verso.
Scotsman (9 July 1934) Souvenirs Cuttings file, HD 6664, TUC library.
Smith, L. (2006) *Uses of Heritage*, London: Routledge.
Stanton, C. (2009) 'The past as a public good: the US National Park Service and "cultural repair" in post-industrial places', in P. Ashton and H. Kean (eds) *People and Their Pasts*, Basingstoke: Palgrave Macmillan.
Trades Union Congress (1932) *Annual Report*, London: TUC.
——(1934a) *The Book of the Martyrs of Tolpuddle 1834–1934*, London: TUC.
——(1934b) Commemorative booklet and programme, Dorsetshire labourers' centenary, London: TUC.
——(1935) *Annual Report*, London: TUC.
——(1999) *The Book of the martyrs of Tolpuddle 1834–1934*, with new introduction by John Monks London: TUC.
Urry, J. (2001) *The tourist gaze*, 2nd edn, London: Sage.
Vox of Labour's Northern Voice (1931) *Transported for Trades Unionism: The story of the six Dorset labourers*, Manchester: Coop Printing Society.
Wearmouth, R. F. (1957) *The Social and Political Influence of Methodism in the Twentieth Century*, London: Epworth.
West, S. (2010), 'Heritage and class' in R. Harrison (ed.) *Understanding the Politics of Heritage*, Manchester: Manchester University Press (with Open University).
Wright, P. (2009) *On Living in an Old Country*, 2nd edn, Oxford: Oxford University Press.

Chapter 18

Working class heritage without the working class
An ethnography on gentrification in Ciutat (Mallorca)

Marc Morell

> ... in order to compensate the degradation that threatens an urban landscape, neighbourhoods are classed as safeguarded sectors. But this compensation, already partial from its very origin, can be emptied of its substance because the statutory schemes of safeguarded sectors produce a privileged space of *economic valorisation*: investors acquire the properties which are then renovated, rented or sold at prices that are, by and large, above the ones from before the classification, the operation ends in the departure of present populations and a profound breakdown of the previous life milieu. In this case, conservation is reduced to a pure façade materiality that serves as a support for, thanks to an injection of capital, new territorial hierarchies and social segregations
> (Guillaume 1980: 166, his emphasis).[1]

> If you pay attention to these [street] names, all of them bearing a profound Palmesan resonance,[2] you will realise that these are names that remind us about the working man, that remind us of the hands of the person, a being that earns a living offering a tireless effort to the community. In this sense, all of this old Palma is a museum of itself, but watch out, this is a living museum, a museum of who once were the men that built it, lived it and laboured it slogging their guts out.
> (Joan Bonet,[3] referring to Es Barri. Extract of the manifesto he wrote on occasion of the demonstration 'Rehabilitation is not destruction' that took place against renewal in 1991)

Working class as an idealised image

In July 2010, I attended a talk that took place in a newly opened bar, in a building that once housed the oldest business in Es Barri and in Ciutat: Ca la Seu.[4] Ca la Seu closed down two years ago, but for over almost 500 years, one could buy products made out of wicker, esparto grass and rope there. They even manufactured some of these products. Its name derives from the shop's provision of all sorts of manufactures to the Cathedral.[5] However, most of these artefacts are now either no longer in use, or far too expensive when locally produced. The elderly Monserrat family, which had owned Ca la Seu for most of its business life, gave up the business since there was not a new generation to take over the running of the shop.

The new bar, one out of the 27 bars to be found in Es Barri (there are 11 more bars to open in the coming year), has maintained a great deal of the crafts character of the old business, with esparto baskets and wicker objects hanging from its walls and ceiling, which grants a certain aura of history to the bar. The talk was given by a historian, who for the last two decades has committed himself to organising guided tours around the island, including the Historic Centre of Ciutat (hereafter Centre). This historian-guide is also responsible for a good deal of the Centre's historic recovery. With an audience mostly composed of people past their 50s, citizens from across the city, captive spectators hungry for the history of the Centre and the odd resident belonging to the local neighbours' association, the historian extolled the guild past of the neighbourhood, which came to an end in the middle third of the nineteenth century. While those present consumed beers and refreshments, he named one by one the streets that still bear the name of the extinct guilds, and of the many economic activities that had taken place there. Just as an example, one of the several names Es Barri bears is that of Sa Gerreria (The Pottery). No wonder, as Bonet's quote reminds us at the beginning of this chapter, this part of the city was the one that hosted both the organised pre-industrial labour and most of the proto-industrial and trading activities.[6]

The historian romanticised these names, often ignoring the harsh social reality the exploitation of the working class entailed. Indeed, the ode of the historian forgot to mention the pseudo-proletarian past of the neighbourhood, a hideout for the working class movements of the island from the mid-nineteenth century until the beginning of the Spanish Civil War in 1936. He only mentioned en passant its red-light district, he never spoke of the vigorous neighbours' opposition to the implementation of the harsh regeneration schemes that took place between 1989 and 2004, and he never mentioned the exceptionally few manual workers remaining in the neighbourhood. To sum up, the purpose of the talk was to transmit a bland stereotyped image, a de-historised version of the past, that would amuse his host, the bar owner, and his audience, apparently solely interested in respectively selling drinks and gaining pleasure out of the aesthetics and history of the place; and not at all in the recent miseries that had shaped Es Barri, and certainly wished to avoid the class implications of these travails.

On heritagisation and gentrification

No doubt, in the heavily touristified context of the Balearic Islands, the politics of heritage plays a key role in the production of places that aim to attract visitors and capital. The logic of this production, the revaluing of space, is driven by the expectation of surplus-value. It is in this context of conservation and development that the centre of the capital city of the Balearics will soon become an 'Asset of Cultural Interest', under the legal form of a Historic Site (*Diari de Balears*, 23rd June 2010), and that the *Serra de Tramuntana*, the Majorcan Northern mountain range and the biggest of the archipelago, is a candidate to become a Cultural Landscape of UNESCO's World Heritage List.

Indeed, UNESCO's World Heritage process is an example of how heritage intervention happens above the local state realms. Other examples of this suprastate intervention can also be found in the Euromed Heritage programmes financed by the European Union. In short, in its making, heritage incorporates and involves places, peoples and social practices of varied kinds, who hold a particular idea of culture, one that encapsulates the disparate paraphernalia that can become, and be used, as heritage. As we will see, these incorporations and involvements make heritage a highly ambivalent matter (Breglia 2006).

Guillaume's introductory quote, coming from an economist, is priceless, so to speak. Even though the publication date of *La politique du patrimoine*, is 1980, and despite the toing and froing that has taken place since in the relation between home ownership and class formation,[7] its content is still amazingly relevant, not least because of the current expansion of heritage-based initiatives related to the territorial hierarchies and social segregations he mentions.

This expansion of heritage has two facets. On the one hand, *nouveau* heritage does not any longer solely rely on the enactment of physical places and things, but now also considers intangibles (UNESCO 2003). Interestingly, as we will see, this global move towards incorporating the incorporeal, immaterial and moveable into the world of heritage is replicated on the local and regional scales either in the form of popular and traditional culture, or in embodying living memory, such as the one Bonet reminds us of in the introductory quote. In fact, memory, be it in the form of oral history or other kind of accounts, works as a means of building up a heritage which may well be representative of those who never owned the means of production, nor the sites of production, nor the produced products; and even those who never thought of themselves as being traditional nor popular. On the other hand, this expansion brings about issues of inclusiveness and control, since there is an increasing recognition of 'other' heritage discourses, subaltern to the discourses and actions that come from 'above'. Furthermore, there are also attempts to understand as heritage the uses, experiences, emotions and material representations that heritage arouses, and even the dissonance they bear and the contestation they trigger (Smith 2006).

This new focus on intangibility and inclusiveness proves the need for exploring the social environment for new resources, in order to exploit them as heritage. I refer to this process of making heritage as 'heritagisation'. It has been argued that heritagisation is a cultural practice that not only involves identifying and selecting new cultural heritage, but also legitimising this very same cultural practice (Bendix 2009). On another level of analysis, it has been qualified as the presentism of the past, in which the fleeting present soon becomes a purged past (Hartog 2003).

Nowadays, heritagisation plunges into the quotidian lives of citizens, becoming itself quotidian, and in a way presenting itself in more or less democratised and popularised forms, thanks to the feigned inclusion of those who had been previously excluded. Hewison (1987) already referred to the politics of heritage as a place of conflict, triggered by the imposition of a nonexistent past onto the working class. Hewison's view, often tagged as rather pessimistic, was strongly critiqued by Samuel (1994), who had a more optimistic view of how the working class actually engages in making its own heritage, and rejected the fact that heritage is an instrument originating exclusively from the accommodated classes (something Hewison pointed out). Although Samuel's outlook on the possibilities of the popularisation, democratisation and empowering of heritage is definitely encouraging and inspiring, since it allows us to look towards a more research and emancipating horizon in the heritage field, and he therefore offers a guideline for superseding the current mode of production; my research has admittedly not encountered such a solid trend. While working class traditions have managed to seize their own 'heritage moments' they have, as we will see, been co-opted into statist projects or into the market whirl of real estate.

There are many examples of this, but I think the most striking one is when heritage is used as a mere cultural resource that detaches memories from their context, and perpetuates the memory of a past in a stabilised manner (Rautenberg 2003). Nevertheless, this perpetual stabilisation is not exempt from conflict, which is particularly blatant when dealing with working class history. In fact, one could argue that this conflict appears when there are attempts to impose what I have come to call 'de-memory', that is, the eviction of memory through the 'politics of and for oblivion':

> [m]onumentalising policies are truly of and for a fib memory. A great makeup operation that converts memory into a parody based on replica and simulacrum, evocation of nonexistent spaces that contrast with the proliferation of de-memorised spaces, mass meaning losses in the name of a belittled and fraudulent pseudo-memory. Notwithstanding … , those policies of memory undertaken by the authorities are usually, in true, policies of and for oblivion.
>
> (Delgado 2007: 106).

Broadly speaking, the process described by Guillaume is known as gentrification.[8] In any case, a variant of it based on heritage as a spearhead of the image the city planning schemes attempt to project, while de-memorising through the 'politics of and for oblivion'. The canonical and foundational definition of gentrification comes from British urban sociology, and involves the middle class colonisation of working class neighbourhoods and the removal of a working class presence (Glass 1964). In the last four decades geography has been, by and large, the discipline that has most extensively re-worked the concept. This has meant a shift in how gentrification is now explained, by placing emphasis on the shaping of the urban environment via the logic of capital accumulation (Smith 1996), ultimately managed by the capitalist class, or by highlighting the importance of the arrival of higher income newcomers, bearers of critical values of cultural politics in the search of location distinction (Ley 1996).

Guillaume (1980) is not the only one that has linked gentrification and heritagisation. Many authors working with the issue of gentrification have signalled its bondage to heritage, at the least with questions related to historic preservation, social preservation and authenticity (for example, Zukin 1987, 2010; Lees *et al.* 2008; Brown-Saracino 2009),[9] as well as several levels of middle class consumption and taste (for example, Jager 1986; Ley 1996; Shaw 2005). The very same social anthropological literature dealing with gentrification establishes a direct connection between the heritagisation of space, and the diverse readings of the process that are to be found. In any case, it shows a major interest in the never passive role the gentrified play in the explanation of gentrification (for example, Herzfeld 2009; Morell 2009; Franquesa 2010).

This text aims to elucidate the presence of the class issue in the field of identity and in cultural policies (Smith 2000) by linking heritagisation to gentrification. Thus, in order to explain the heritagisation of the working class, I opt for investigating gentrification as a class strategy (for example, Smith and LeFaivre 1984; Dávila 2004; Ruben and Maskovsky 2008). As Lefebvre has already argued, 'the working class has been subjected to manipulations in the spatial field, since there is a politics of space that is more and more active, more and more conscious and deliberate' (1976: 152). I am therefore interested in seeing to what extent the politics of space explains the politics of heritage so to finally understand where the deep de-structuration announced by Guillaume (1980) leads us.

Pau, the carpenter, and Es Barri, the neighbourhood

What used to be the old café *Granja La Suiza* now hosts a carpenter's workshop, presumably one of the last of its kind in Es Barri, and perhaps the whole Centre of Ciutat. Outside the workshop, a sign reads: 'Working in the neighbourhood since 1940'. Inside, fine sawdust clouds the entire environment. Old pictures of the family trade, press cuttings, posters of the *Barcelona Futbol Club* and the *Atlètic de Balears* teams, and a girly calendar cling to the wall, as if trying to escape the piercing noise of the circular-saw that finds its way into every nook and cranny. Leaning on his carpenter's bench Pau actively labours, engrossed in sawing up a wooden plank. He has work for their main client, an insurance company that covers the whole island. He and his brother, both of them self-employed and in their mid-sixties, combine this work with serving customers, from across the city and beyond, that come either to order woodwork and the like or to have their old objects repaired.

'We have followed the tradition', says Pau. When the Spanish Civil War (1936–39) came to an end, his forefathers came to live in Es Barri and opened a carpenters' workshop specialised in repairing 'whatever got broken in the time of the war'. Pau does not need to make an effort to recall his family past. He vividly remembers the tragic circumstances that drove their family to leave their town, Sóller, in the *Serra de Tramuntana* (now candidate to become a World Heritage Site), and open the carpentry in Ciutat. As soon as the National rebellion was announced against the Republic (and Majorca fell immediately in the National territory), his grandfather, a carpenter for hire, was, ironically, imprisoned in Ca'n Mir, an old wood warehouse near the Centre of Ciutat. The reason was that until then he had been politically active, to the point of actually leading the local Socialist group of Sóller. Meanwhile, Pau's father, at the early age of seventeen, was compulsorily sent to the frontline in Burgos (in the mainland) to 'shoot against the Republicans'.

When the war came to an end father and grandfather left Sóller forever, and took their families to the capital city, where they founded the carpentry. Pau was born and grew up in the post-war period, in a silent and silenced manual workers' tradition soaked in left-wing political values,[10] between the workshop and the neighbourhood. When the time came, he became an apprentice in the family business. Pau eventually moved out of Es Barri, towards the nearby new developments in the mid-1960s, when he got married, his wife being from Es Barri too. However, he maintained, together with his brother, the rent subrogation of the workshop their father had left them.[11]

In the mid-1960s, the 'great transformation of the Balearic economy', tourism, was well on its way: 'it was no longer to be the conventional products of the countryside or the urban workshops that would favour the change; it was the *foreigner industry*' (Manera and Garau-Taberner 2009, original emphasis). Along with tourism urbanisation accelerated. A clear example of this is the city-development scheme of 1963, which allowed the exponential growth of Ciutat (Ruiz Viñals 2000: 112). In 1964 there was a kind of a reaction. The Centre became 'historic', as it was declared a 'Historic-Artistic Zone'.

This protection zone was aimed at conserving the historic charms of the built environment from any further development than that allowed by the scheme of 1963. In the words of the former head of the heritage department in the city council, now a member of the board of the Association of Neighbours of Es Barri,[12] such a nomination did not protect the whole of the Centre from social degradation and constructive predation.[13] In fact, as the municipal archaeologist put forward when referring to the particularities and commonalities of the different geographical cuttings of the Centre, at a public meeting organised by a conservation association (ARCA, of which I will soon briefly refer to) back in 2003, the problem was that:

Of course, after the law of 1985 these divisions do not exist and the whole of it is declared 'Collection of Historic Buildings', but at first it was divided into different levels of protection. This led to, uh, some quite serious interventions taking place, while other areas were conserved, almost frozen. I mean that they continued to restore some as if they were a drawing, especially the neighbourhood of the Cathedral and all that, and on the other hand, there was very rapid degradation ... Well, not that fast, slow but very powerful in other places of the city, such as the ones that obviously are the origin of the special plans [renewal schemes]: Puig de Sant Pere, Sa Calatrava and Sa Gerreria. What happened, to my understanding, is that because of both the declaration of Collection of Historic Buildings and the General Plan of 1943, these areas remained, from a certain moment, out of planning; that is to say, building work could not take place because the provision was for the complete demolition of the area. From then on the lack of maintenance caused the degradation of the buildings, the failure to incorporate new services, and the abandonment of these buildings or their occupation by people with increasingly lesser purchasing power or by immigrant groups because the owners did not have any way of acting on the building.

Thus, the Historic-Artistic Zone (a continuation of the Collection of Historic Buildings of 1943 mentioned by the municipal archaeologist) contributed to, on the one hand, the touristification of the monumental core; and, on the other, the filtering down of its immediate margins.[14] The poly-functional city-development scheme that followed (Ajuntament de Palma 1973 and 1974) reaffirmed the situation. With time, the monumental core (itself a celebration of the dominant classes, not only of the past but also of the present) and its commercial boulevards became the most usable and visible space of the city. Meanwhile, Es Barri, abandoned by most of its old-time residents, who looked for housing in the new city and jobs in the tourism industry, and newly inhabited by an impoverished working class, fell into decay, together with other neighbourhoods at the margins.

Es Barri got poorer and poorer. Prostitution, already long present in the area, expanded, working conditions for the women degraded, whilst drug trafficking and the social problems linked to it became common. Es Barri fell into decay, together with other neighbourhoods at the margins of the Centre, to the extent that the press sensationalised this situation, and formed public opinion on the matter by referring to Es Barri as a 'human dunghill' and 'Palma's Harlem' (*Diari de Balears*, 5th February 1985). In 1985, six years after the establishment of the first democratic elections after the full of the francoist regime, the City Council of Ciutat approved a new general development scheme for the city that proposed four special renewal schemes for protecting and renewing the built heritage of the margins, one of which fully affected Es Barri, then known under the name of Sindicat (Ajuntament de Palma 1985).

Renewal appeared inextricably linked to heritage. Thus, among the aims of these future renewal schemes, there was 'the conservation or the protection of values and relevant features that concur in the territory, such as the conservation and the valorisation of heritage' (Ajuntament de Palma 1985: 11). Interestingly, the schemes also demanded 'a complete study of the social and economic consequences of its [the renewal's] execution and the adoption of measures for guaranteeing the defence of the affected population' (Ajuntament de Palma 1985: 13). The support for such measures became the political cornerstones of two distinctive urban movements.

In 1987, a group of young intellectuals, academics and civil servants founded the Association for the Revitalisation of Old Centres (ARCA), with the clear aim of fostering those conservation and protection values included in the 1985 development scheme. In the words of ARCA's secretary, in those days the aim was to transform the concepts of 'decrepit and seedy' into 'old and recoverable', whereas now it is about making of the Centre a place inhabited with 'new life' (*Diario de Mallorca*, 28th February 2004). Thus 'revitalisation' was understood as bringing life back to the Centre by revaluing its built heritage.[15] The other urban movement, the Federation of Associations of Neighbours of Palma (FAVP), was a much older one, a key player in democratising society from below, at a time when the dictatorial regime of Franco, one in which political parties and trade unions not belonging to the 'National Movement' were banned, was still at work. After a time FAVP took charge of defending 'the affected population' of Es Barri, and in 1991 founded an association of neighbours for the area of Es Barri – the association was given the name of Canamunt.

In 1991,[16] both ARCA and FAVP-Canamunt encouraged the participation of the neighbours, either by organising the opposition to the 1989 partial renewal scheme proposal of Sindicat under the slogan 'rehabilitation is not destruction', since the partial scheme adopted an intervention incompatible with the preservationist aims of the general scheme of 1985, or by getting involved in the revision of a second proposal that appeared at the beginning of the 1990s. This later proposal, which was finally approved in 1995 under the name of Special Plan of Protection and Inner Reform of Sa Gerreria, was delayed due to political bargaining for almost six years. The aims of this last partial renewal scheme were many (Ajuntament de Palma 1995: 42) and despite the fact that ARCA's and FAVP's views and positions influenced the final text, their involvement is self-evident, it ought to be said that these entities were horrified to see what the outcome of it all was.

The first aim was that of maintaining the urban morphology and of the architectonic typologies fundamental to the neighbourhood. Although these architectonic typologies were varied in nature, ranging from the odd lordly building and small medieval arcades, to a row of popular housing built in the eighteenth century, what everyone had in mind were the remnants of the old potteries, and especially their chimneys, their most visible feature. The entities of the so-called civil society of Ciutat clearly aimed at making heritage of the industrial built environment the heritage of capital rather than of the working class. However, as Bonet's quote reminds us, the most precious legacy of the working class is its labour and its struggle.

The second aim was that of substituting the degraded urban fabric to generate rehabilitation and revitalisation of the neighbourhood. This particular strategy was aimed at getting rid of what a good deal of the population in Ciutat viewed as the 'underclass', made up of drug addicts, drug traffickers, sexual labourers, Spanish and Portuguese Roma communities. These people did not fit well with the recovery programme of what was thought to be the working class heritage the chimneys represented. Nevertheless, they had been the necessary link for devaluing land for the gentrification that came later.

The third aim insisted in guaranteeing the conservation and the protection of Sa Gerreria (The Pottery version of Es Barri) and the maintenance in the neighbourhood of the original population, overall preserving their rights. By 'original population', these organisations had in mind the remaining and still living old population who had worked in the workshops Es Barri once supported. This aim clearly separated out those who were seen to be of working class pedigree from the feared and heterogeneous population that had been filling in the degraded built environment.

The fourth aim was the arrangement and regulation of non-residential activities, combining them with measures leading to the erasure of the existing degradation. That is, fighting crime and drug trafficking, as well as hiding, rather than eradicating, prostitution. The final aim, and one that would prove to be incompatible with the increased protection of Es Barri, was the arrangement and the hierarchisation of the street layout.

Thus, revitalisation appeared as both conservation and erasure. Both organisations reacted very differently. Whereas ARCA celebrated the chimney revival, it objected to the street realignment that meant the demolition of many buildings just for the sake of making them match a more rigid street grid. As for the FAVP-Canamunt, they opposed this harsh division of the population into desirable and non-desirable elements, since they suspected that what lay behind this was a gentrification process based on expelling the so-called 'underclass' and awaiting the death of the elderly 'originals' (it has to be said that most of this old population was not born in Es Barri, but elsewhere in the island or even the mainland).

Pau, who had always been socially active in the neighbourhood's life, soon became a member of Canamunt. Although his main concern was that of the future of the family workshop, he did not hesitate at all in helping to recover, organise and participate in the fiestas of Canamunt, in an effort to recreate the ancient guild and parish fiestas he remembered from when he was a child. The fiestas of Canamunt were part of a wider strategy of the neighbours' movement, that sought to fill with pride people that sooner or later would witness renewal and their own displacement. There is no doubt whatsoever that the fiestas were central in this strategy of uniting the different groups that made up Es Barri, and it did so by both bringing people together through the experience of the fiestas and community narrative of resistance and camaraderie, regardless of whatever divisions the renewal scheme was interested in fostering. Along with this, and in consonance with the conservationist efforts of ARCA, the chimneys of the old potteries were repeatedly exploited, and soon became the logo of the association of neighbours. It was in such ways that not so much the rootedness of the population, but rather more their unity in outrage, was expressed before the advent of the partial renewal scheme.

At first, renewal appeared surrounded by an amicable atmosphere. 'Where there was a house there will be a house, where there was a business there will be a business, where there was a workshop there will be a workshop', recalls Pau. However, this rhetoric soon ended, and gentrification appeared in its true colours. Works began in 1998 only after the arrival of EU funds from the URBAN Community Initiative (from now on Urban),[17] and after the writing of a new general development scheme that literally encouraged gentrification in terms of social mix:

> measures for encouraging the installation of mid-high population strata, which together with the already housed social population, will produce the mix the Historic Centre once enjoyed, one that made it socially alive.... There is consequently the need for more dynamism and management agility, in order to lead the rehabilitation of the Historic Centre to safe harbour.
>
> (Ajuntament de Palma 1998: 80)

Thus, 'management agility' would be measured in terms of the magnitude of the gentrification in Es Barri. Five years later a local poet, long associated with the social squatting initiatives in the neighbourhood, put it:

> The roofs collapse in their houses forbidden to the indigent, abandoned doors bricked up with bricks and farce. Hungry diggers feeding on the charm of the paving while speculating scaffoldings touch up the paint of what was a rent within everybody's reasonable reach, at the end of the day, cheap, leaving the whole of our Old Centre a shitty colour. *Socorro!* The racist Court grows and expels the gipsy chord, expels the whores, imprisons the dealer, evicts the old shoemaker, the pensioner widow, myself, the neighbour and the friend, the baker, the barber, the innkeeper, the tobacconist, the cats, the dogs, the bicycles and the tale of the dairymaid, because since yesterday, the sun in the neighbourhood, is only for those who can pay for it.
>
> (López 2003, adaptation of own co-translation)[18]

Indeed, land in the neighbourhood would be for those who could afford it. There would be new houses and businesses where old houses and businesses stood, but there would also be new inhabitants and manual workers where the old inhabitants and manual workers had been. In short, in 1999, Pau and his brother, fed up with the neighbours' organisation in its associative form, left behind their old workshop, for which they received a ridiculous compensation.

While most of the manual-work workshops such as Pau's were disappearing, the Urban Community Initiative Programme for Es Barri aimed at boosting arts and crafts by implementing a crafts and restoration training centre and a crafts' boulevard (*Passeig per l'Artesania*, from now on PA), that would link to a newly created tourist circuit. This tourist circuit was aimed at both foreigners and local citizens. Until then, the stigma of the previously mentioned illicit activities of the Barrio Xino (prostitution and drug trafficking) acted as a daring frontier. The call for the involvement of citizens in the circuit for locals addressed the breaking of this closure by revaluing its humble, yet decent, crafts' past. The PA was built from scratch on bulldozed land not far from where Pau's old workshop stood. The inhabitants were uprooted and sent to other sites of the city, not necessarily in the Centre, and new inhabitants, who had been displaced from a high-rise block of flats at the waterfront that had been demolished, moved in to the brand new apartments.

The idea was to link the present PA with the past of the humble classes – never referred to as the working class – in a very narrow vision of what artisanship was about, and increasingly focused on the tertiarisation of Es Barri. In 1996, the Office of Work Insertion for Groups with Difficulties, of the municipal social services, had established contact with people working at the Municipal Housing Office. At the time, the Municipal Housing Office was putting together a bid for the Urban Community Initiative Programme. A mixed team of social workers, architects and lawyers submitted a first draft that was rejected, but they were encouraged to improve their submission for future bids.

The proposal that finally got through in 1997 included a set of economic and social measures to tackle training and employment, as well as economic incentives. The team came up with the idea of supporting crafts, because, as they viewed it, Es Barri had been a crafts neighbourhood in the past, and crafts were now understood as the adaptation of the crafts industry to the new current situation of production, new technologies and commercialisation. Language is important. Note that this is not about 'manual workers' but 'artisans'. However, most, if not all, the workshops Es Barri bustled with in the past were manual-working ones. The process by which manual work, or a certain manual work, became artisanship is not a trivial issue, and neither is the fact that much manual work, such as that of Pau's carpentry, is not considered to be artisanship.

From the very beginning, the PA was conceived of as a space to develop local commerce. The idea was to offer premises to craftspeople through a public tendering procedure (theoretically below market price). Those with an interest had to present both a craft production and a business plan. If selected the local craftspeople had to make an initial investment to establish the business they would run on the premises. In 2001, after four years of construction works and preparations, the PA was launched. Initially 15 workshop businesses settled in, but soon the craftspeople abandoned the site, as they could not sustain their businesses. A local newspaper headline announced that: 'One of them leaves after losing more than the €42,000 she invested – She claims that only distributors remain in the PA' (*El Mundo-El Día de Baleares*, 17th December 2002).

According to the head of the PA development, problems occurred because the PA was an isolated space in the middle of a neighbourhood in the making. This neighbourhood also carried the stigma of the illicit activities that were still taking place. Moreover, it was argued that the products were not attractive enough to pull in either tourists or locals as customers, and that the craftspeople were lacking a clear marketing strategy. They were accused of waiting for the clientele to turn up 'naturally', or be brought to them 'artificially' by the municipal authorities. Nevertheless, despite it being an empty space, the PA continued to argue that it would soon become the leading edge of a revitalisation that acknowledged a past of the neighbourhood, no matter how imagined it might be.

In 2006, the Town Hall resuscitated the PA. It counter-attacked by establishing new admission conditions, by awarding new contracts and by modernising the corporate image of the PA and the new businesses that clustered around it. Documentation and interpretation centres were provided, and a historical walk was designed, guiding tourists around the places where trades that had disappeared were carried out, and telling the story of its past as a centre of artisanship and even, as the '1st industrial neighbourhood of Ciutat'. All in all, the past of Es Barri was now to be viewed as part of what the Balearic Law understood as 'immaterial ethnologic heritage', or 'popular and traditional culture', that is:

> the set of cultural manifestations, either material or immaterial, such as music and musical instruments, dances, attires, fiestas, customs, *techniques and trades*, gastronomy and games, sports, ritual or religious dances, representations, literary creations, as well as all those activities that bear a traditional character and that either are or have been popular.
> (Govern de les Illes Balears 2002: 4947–48, my emphasis)

However, opportunities for searching for traditions of a popular character, subaltern to the current ones, were totally wasted. In any case, the Interpretation Centre musified and froze the humble manual-working past of Es

Barri in the form of dioramas, and interviews with the disappeared bearers of a 'lost tradition' on state-of-the-art audiovisual equipment. The sweetened version of the past involved in these representations of techniques and trades of manual workers glossed over whatever harsh daily conditions and class-consciousness there may have been, and merely focused on the technical features of crafting, and did so with many nostalgic references. The museum project of the Interpretation Centre limited itself to outlining the specific features of 'artisanship', with nostalgic references to the disappearance of these jobs and never referred to the resilience of labour in terms such as those of Bonet.

The Interpretation Centre delved into stereotyped forms of technological knowledge, and the romanticised past of what had been left behind in the road to modernisation. Thus, nothing was said of the social reality in which the displayed artisan models lived in, and it said less about the strife many existing manual workers experienced, in terms of not only their direct working conditions and their demands for better wages, but also in their struggle to remain in place. It is important to note, as Kirk (2007) and Shackel (2009) argue in the British and American contexts respectively, data about working class lives and experiences can be retrieved from the past that offer a nuanced account of what working class culture is about.

Artisanship, let alone manual work, was to be purged and elevated to heritage without a single reference to the hardships and struggles of the working class (a concept not even mentioned). The interpretation centre shallowly dealt with the social and labour changes effecting manual work, which were inherent in the booming of tourism in the 1960s, rather than profoundly examining the causes of the disappearance of the 'old jobs'. Not one word mentioned the class substitution the neighbourhood was undergoing, although there were several references to the 'recovery' of the past that came along with the 'revitalisation' of Es Barri. Of course, whatever the recovery, it was always so sanitised that even mentioning the Francoist repression people like Pau's forefathers suffered would be considered an anathema, if not a clear threat to the immediate ancestor of the current political Spanish system, a challenge to the status quo achieved with the so-called democratic transition.

In 2002, after struggling to find a solution with the authorities and the developer who had acquired the property where the old workshop stood, Pau and his brother contacted the owner of La Granja Suiza, an old retired woman who had left the property without leasing it for several years. She knew the carpenters well, was fond of them, and thus helped them out with a low rent. Since the facilities met carpentry workshop regulations, the lease was soon approved and Pau and his brother remained in the neighbourhood, although they abhorred what had been going on with what Pau referred to as the 'elite of manual work', artisanship, of the PA, a one-minute walk from where their new workshop stands.

In 2009, the PA definitively abandoned its artisan crusade, and went for a creative new economy based on what are still vacillating efforts for implementing cultural services, design industries and new technologies. No doubt, this transformation responds to the changes in residential makers and use of the neighbourhood, in which the working class of the potteries and other workshops have been substituted, along with the Barrio Xino, by workers specialising in leisure activities, culture and IT.

Conclusions

The link between gentrification and heritagisation suggests that the latter may involve as much of a class relation as the former. Thus, a close examination of gentrification becomes useful in heritagisation analysis. It does so because, at first, the making of built heritage that leads to gentrification seems to be about the economic revalorisation of space. In fact, by looking at how heritage (whatever the heritage) is made and how it expands, we gain an insight on how deeply gentrification disrupts the lives of working class people.

This chapter has dealt with the working class experience in a neighbourhood, the gentrification of which has recently been imbued with an expanding heritage practice. I here use 'class experience' in clear reference to the classic, but still terribly valid, writings of Thompson, for whom class formation is 'experience of determination and the "handling" of this in conscious ways' (Thompson 1978: 106). Thompson's understanding of class consciousness is in terms of process, as a 'relationship', a 'social and cultural formation' which always involves people against other people (Thompson 1965). In short, class is understood as being peopled. By exploring the class experience gentrification entails I hope to have shed some light on the class experience of heritagisation.

Heritage is a political arena in which, under some not always precise rules and limits, constant struggles take place between development and preservation. This struggle, although it does not actually take into consideration social class as a subject for social transformation, does involve it in its everyday becoming. That is to say, heritage is no other than an ideological field in which a non-explicit class-struggle takes place, one that mostly has to do with organisations and collectives that have abandoned the question of class, and that get tangled up with the city planning and legal vocabulary that neutralises other realities such as segregation and population de-structuration, so linked to the hierarchisation of places and realms in the politics of heritage.

On the one hand, the politics of heritage appears as the crudest expression of class struggle in the working class habitat, understood as its milieu of residence and neighbourliness. To the more classical class struggle (which takes place between workers and capitalists) it is not only necessary to add the land-owner class, as one might assume from Katznelson (1992: 109), but also the issue of the formation of the middle classes, with regards to their relation to their gentrifying action (Butler 1997, and Butler and Robson 2003). On the other hand, and returning to the earlier quote of Guillaume, the politics of heritage assists in the production of a privileged space for economic valuation. At the end of the day, the 'injection of capital' that privileges a space for the 'economic valuing' is, above all, a political action, just as political as the establishment of 'classification' criteria, and the will to support the 'new hierarchies of the territory and social segregations'.

Thus, economic 'injection of capital' is only a partial account, since heritage 'compensation' comes to be, and thus the revalorisation and gentrification via heritage, political. On its attempts for positively discriminating for degradation the political decisively intervenes in the 'economic revalorisation'. Indeed, politics of gentrification appears most crudely in new forms of class struggle, that take shape around several topics, including heritage. Evictions take place following the rhythm of the heritage reorganisation of space.

As we have seen, pressures do not just come from capital and the state. We ought to note, and not treat with contempt, the shift towards an interest in heritage that has taken place in the very same urban social movements that, not that long ago, advocated an oppositional organisation to urban policies on the basis of the issue of social classes. The example of the neighbours' movement is a clear one in this sense, followed at a distance by the ficklenesses of the heritage phenomenon. While the first project (that represented by FAVP-Canamunt) has stopped advocating a profound transformation of society, the second one (represented by ARCA) never considered it.

The heritagisation of Es Barri has acquired a working class aftertaste, while at the same time contributing to its gentrification, and therefore to sanitisation, of whatever presence of the working class that is left. The working class has commonly entered the realm of heritage as a 'heritage of the working class', one displayed by the capitalist class in such a purified manner that it strips the working class of its social being and aims at its oblivion, rather than a 'heritage *of* the working class', one controlled by the working class. Both ways of linking the working class to heritage pose the prickly question of who is the actual working class, and what working class past should be represented.

For instance, in the Western European contemporary context of our cities, the working class is certainly many-sided with regards to origins, identities, cultural practices and so on. It is not at all clear if there is the possibility of, let alone the will for, bringing together the working class heritage of people and the working class heritage of place, since the latter is generally related via kinship to a fair deal of the current so-called 'new middle classes'. Interestingly, as Smith (2006) reveals, heritage consumption seems to be a middle class thing to do. Therefore, it is not at all crazy to think, to a certain extent, of heritage consumption by middle classes as not only consuming their own ancestry but actually producing it.

I will leave the thorny issue of the abuse of the middle class terminology for another occasion. Here, I only want to express my concern with the fact that 'middle class' has become an all-encompassing term, that may well involve an actually existing working class that is camouflaged in the 'middle' and in the realm of 'consumption', another way of actually understanding production. Related to this issue, there is that of merely focusing on class as an outcome of unequal distribution (Strangleman 2008: 16). Clearly, class is inextricably related to production and to the ownership of its means, as I have tried to portray with a concrete case study on the production of space (Lefebvre 1991). Or to put it in other words, class is the relation between those who create surplus and those who appropriate it (Leeds 1994).

Class has not died, it is alive and kicking! Therefore, making heritage of it is something that has to be handled with extreme care. 'Heritage of the working class' offers an account of class struggle and attempts to redefine the working class by placing it in actual and metaphorical display cabinets, while subduing the spaces where it has a lively present. Such a view on who is heritagised has much in common with who is gentrified. Thus, while Pau and his brother were left to struggle in the search for a place where they could work once evicted, an avatar of their family past was being set up as heritage. As for a 'heritage *of* the working class', this seems to be utopian at the moment. For the one thing heritage has been for a long time is a bourgeois affair, and therefore the softened heritage versions of the working class the PA offers, and for the other, if there were to be a 'heritage *of* the working class', what would this look like and would it be satisfied with just the intangible memory of the hardship of labour? Would it be fair to reify as past a living practice? What faction of the working class would control this heritage? Gentrification, as a key process in the class formation within the sphere of social reproduction, would use what new means of cultural technology to fill in the emptiness left by heritage, now indeed *of* the working class? A 'heritage *of* the working class' is something pretty much impossible if not an oxymoron. *Nouveau* heritage forms, backed upon the expanding uses of authorized heritage discourses, respond to a strategy of working class memory-taming, if not erasure, and, most importantly, to the eviction of the very same presence of whatever might be left of the working class in the capitalist seizing of the historic city.

Acknowledgements

I want to thank the *Programa de Beques Doctorals* (*Direcció General de Recerca – Govern de les Illes Balears*) for funding most of my research; and especially Laurajane Smith, Paul Shackel and Gary Campbell for encouraging me to publish the present text, for language editing, and for giving me the advice I required. Manuel Delgado (Universitat de Barcelona), Alejandro Miquel (Universitat de les Illes Balers) and Camilla Lewis (University of Manchester) provided insightful comments. Finally, I am grateful to Eleanor Lobb for proofreading the English of the original draft.

Notes

1 All translations of transcripts and quotations are my own.
2 *Palmesà*, translated here as Palmesan, is the name given to the inhabitants of the city of Palma, also known as Ciutat.
3 Joan Bonet was a well-known local journalist, writer, painter and sculptor, born in Es Barri, and father to the most well-known Majorcan singer of the Catalan *Cançó* (a protest song movement that promoted the values of the so-called democratic transition – democracy for all, amnesty for political prisoners and devolution of statutory rights – in the vernacular language of the Catalan-speaking territories of Spain).
4 The official name for Ciutat is Palma, also known as Palma de Mallorca. However, I choose Ciutat (City) not only because of its everyday use, admittedly, but nevertheless far from inconsiderable, nor because of its relation to the rest of the island of Majorca, the *Part Forana*, that is, the countryside, but because of the political connotations it bears: as a space for public debate, civil rights claims and citizen action. A citizenship of which I am certainly sceptical about, see Alain (2006), given the form and content it takes; showing, whichever way you look at it, that its operational range for social transformation is fairly short in comparison to the political subjects linked to the class issue. Es Barri (The Neighbourhood) is often referred to by other names too (Sa Gerreria, Sindicat, Barri Xino, Canamunt ...); each of which indicates different boundaries and social contents. This means that depending on which term one uses the size of the neighbourhood will vary, ranging from the 8 hectares of Sa Gerreria (The Pottery) to the 20 of Canamunt. Whatever the name and size, it is clear that Es Barri was once the industrial and working class neighbourhood par excellence of Ciutat (Escartín 2003).
5 'La Seu' means Cathedral, as in religious seat, and 'Ca' means house, place or landed property. Ca la Seu implies something like 'the place linked to the Cathedral'.
6 It ought to be noted that the industrialisation of Majorca was far from being a factory-driven one; it was mostly forged in family workshops and the guild system (Escartín 2001).
7 López and Rodríguez (2010, 467–76) point out that the process of deproletariatisation via home ownership of the last decades has reversed. We now find ourselves in the vast process of proletariatisation of the middle classes in which ownership is still present, but mainly in the form of debt.
8 For a fairly complete, although excessively geographic, handbook that deals with the history, debates and research on the issue of gentrification, see Lees, Slater and Wyly (2008).
9 Although I do not fully share the Brown-Saracino's sociological thesis (2009), I do celebrate the problem she presents under the term 'social preservation', that is, the desire many gentrifiers have for maintaining in their place several population groups that are under the threat of gentrification.
10 Without a doubt, the manual self-employed workers that inhabited, and still inhabit, Es Barri are part of the working class. Having said this, I am aware that nowadays Balearic Islands manual workers are a minority compared to those who work in tourism and building activities.
11 *Associacions de Veïns* literally mean Neighbours' Associations. The reader will have noticed that I sometimes use the word 'resident' and I sometimes use that of 'neighbour'. It may be argued, and with reason, that 'resident' might be a better word. However, the Catalan *veí* (neighbour) is more than the Catalan *resident* (literally resident). It not only also implicates people who work but do not reside in a given neighbourhood, but also stretches the capacity of the individual as a mere resident since it stresses a relational, social, dimension by bringing into action the presumably positive qualities of neighbourliness

(such as knowing each other, mutual assistance, etc.). In this sense, the term 'resident' can be misleading since it only focuses in the actual physical space of residence without considering its social dimensions.
12 This was such a cheap rent that it was matchless: 60€ per month in 2000. This workshop, though, was different from the current one. The nearby area where the old workshop stood no longer exists. It is now the site for a major built-from-scratch and trendy-looking apartment development.
13 Something that the Asset of Cultural Interest will seem to protect, under the heritage figure of the Historic Site.
14 Filtering refers to the process through which the housing stock becomes inhabited by classes with a lesser purchase power than the previous inhabitants. In the process, buildings age and deteriorate, which eventually favours the support for renewal and gentrification.
15 It is not at all trivial the fact that the proposal of a partial renewal scheme for Es Barri appeared at the precise moment in which the press dealt most incisively with the issue of the Barri Xino (the red-light district), the neighbourhood of drugs and prostitution.
16 As we are seeing, the contradiction stems from the fact that cultural revitalisation entails, inevitably, an economic revitalisation.
17 The European funds the URBAN Community Initiative 1994–99 brought to Es Barri were €7,630,000. This represented 50 per cent of the cost of a strategy that included: infrastructural and environmental improvements, the promotion of new economic activities, the social integration of residents, and the promotion of training and education (<http://ec.europa.eu/regional_policy/urban2/urban/initiative/src/frame1.htm>, accessed 29th October 2009).
18 Co-translation of Franquesa and Morell available at: <http://www.medvoices.org/pages/showresource.aspx?id=2646&lang=0> (accessed 14th October 2009).

References

Ajuntament de Palma (1973 and 1974) *Ordenanzas Municipales Sobre el uso del Suelo y Edificaciones en Palma de Mallorca,* Palma de Mallorca: Excmo. Ayuntamiento de Palma de Mallorca.
—— (1985) *Plan General de Ordenación. Normas urbanísticas*, Palma: Ayuntamiento de Palma.
—— (1995) *Sa Gerreria. Pla de Protecció i Reforma Interior*, Palma: Excm. Ajuntament de Palma.
—— (1998) *Revisió del Pla General d'Ordenació Urbana, Text Refós*, Palma: Gerència d'Urbanisme, Ajuntament de Palma.
Alain, C. (2006), '?El impase ciudadanista. Contribución a una crítica del ciudadanismo?', at bsquero.net/textos/el-impasse-ciudadanista-contribucion-una-critica-del-ciudadanismo (accessed 17 December 2009).
Bendix, R. (2009) 'Heritage between economy and politics. An assessment from the perspective of cultural anthropology', in l. Smith and N. Akagawa (eds.) *Intangible Heritage,* London: Routledge.
Breglia, L. (2006) *Monumental Ambivalence: The Politics of Heritage*, Austin: University of Texas Press.
Brown-Saracino, J. (2009) *A neighborhood that Never Changes. Gentrification, Social Preservation, and the Search for Authenticity*, Chicago: University of Chicago Press.
Butler, T. (1997) *Gentrification and the Middle Classes*, Ashgate: Aldershot.
Butler, T. and Robson, G. (2003) *London Calling. The Middle Classes and the Re-Making of Inner-London*, Oxford: Berg.
Dávila, A. (2004) *Barrio Dreams. Puerto Ricans, Latinos and the Neoliberal City*, Berkeley: University of California Press.
Delgado, M. (2007) *La Ciudad Mentirosa. Fraude y Miseria del Modelo Barcelon*, Madrid: La Piqueta.

Escartín, J.M. (2001) *La Ciutat Amuntegada. Indústria del Calçat, Desenvolupament Urbà i Condicions de Vida en la Palma Contemporània (1840–1940)*, Palma: Documenta Balear.
——(2003) ' "La ciutat esvaïda" o destruïda?', *Última Hora*, 28th June.
Franquesa, J. (2010) *Sa Calatrava Mon Amour. Etnografia d'un Barri Atrapat en la Geografia del Capital*, Palma: Documenta Balear.
Glass, R. (1964) 'Introduction. Aspects of change', in Centre for Urban Studies (ed.) *London: Aspects of change*, London: MacGibbon and Kee.
Govern de les Illes Balears (2002) 'Llei 1/2002 de 19 de Març, de Cultura Popular i Tradicional', *Butlletí Oficial de les Illes Balears*, 38: 4947–49.
Guillaume, M. (1980) *La Politique du Patrimoine*, Paris: Éditions Galilée.
Hartog, F. (2003) *Régimes d'Historicité: Présentisme et Expérience du Temps*, Paris: Éditions du Seuil.
Herzfeld, M. (2009) *Evicted from Eternity. The Restructuring of Modern Rome*, Chicago: The University of Chicago Press.
Hewison, R. (1987) *The Heritage Industry: Britain in a Climate of Decline*, London: Meltuen London Ltd.
Jager, M. (1986) 'Class definition and the aesthetic of gentrification: Victoriana in Melbourne', in N. Smith and P. Williams (eds.) *Gentrification of the City*, Boston: Unwin Hyman.
Katznelson, I. (1993) *Marxism and the City*, Oxford: Oxford University Press.
Kirk, J. (2007) *Class, Culture, and Social Change. On the Trail of the Working Class*, Houndmills: Palgrave MacMillan.
Leeds, A. (1994) 'Classes in the social order', in A. Leeds and R. Sanjek (eds) *Cities, Classes, and the Social Order*, Ithaca: Cornell University Press.
Lees, L., Slater, T. and Wyly, E. (2008) *Gentrification*, New York: Routledge.
Lefebvre, H. (1976 [1974]) 'La clase obrera y el espacio', in *Espacio y Política. El Derecho a la Ciudad II*, Barcelona: Ediciones Península.
——(1991 [1974]) *The Production of Space*, Oxford: Basil Blackwell.
Ley, D. (1996) *The New Middle Class and the Remaking of the Central City*, Oxford: Oxford University Press.
López, I. and Rodríguez, E. (2010) *Fin de Ciclo. Financiarización, Territorio y Sociedad de Propietarios en la onda Larga del Capitalismo Hispano (1959–2010)*, Madrid: Traficantes de Sueños.
López, V. C. (2003) 'La flor y muerte de un barrio', *Rakia*. Palma: Ediciones Desesperadas.
Manera, C. and Garau-Taberner, J. (2009) 'The transformation of the economic model of the Balearic Islands. The pioneers of mass tourism', in L. Segreto, C. Manera, and M. Pohl (eds.) *Europe at the Seaside: The Economic History of Mass Tourism in the Mediterranean*, Oxford: Berghahn.
Morell, M. (2009) '*Fent barri*: heritage tourism policy and neighbourhood scaling in Ciutat de Mallorca', *Etnográfica*, 13(2): 343–72.
Rautenberg, M. (2003) *La Rupture Patrimoniale*, Grenoble: À la Croisée.
Ruben, M. and Maskovsky, J. (2008) 'The homeland archipelago: Neoliberal urban governance after September 11', *Critique of Anthropology*, 28(2): 199–217.
Ruiz Viñals, C. (2000) *L'urbanisme de la ciutat de Palma*, Palma: Editorial El Far.
Samuel, R. (1994) *Theatres of Memory. Volume 1: Past and Present in Contemporary Culture*. London: Verso.
Shackel, P. A. (2009) *The Archaeology of American Labor and Working Class Life*, Gainesville: The University Press of Florida.
Shaw, W. (2005) 'Heritage and gentrification. Remembering 'the good old days' in postcolonial Sydney', in R. Atkinson and G. Bridge (eds.) *Gentrification in a Global Context. The New Urban Colonialism*, London: Routledge.

Smith, L. (2006) *Uses of Heritage*, London: Routledge.
Smith, N. (1996) *The New Urban Frontier. Gentrification and the Revanchist City*, London: Routledge.
——(2000) 'What happened to class?', *Environment and Planning A*, 32(6): 1011–32.
Smith, N. and LeFaivre, M. (1984) 'A class analysis of gentrification', in J.J. Palen and B. London (eds.) *Gentrification, Displacement and Neighborhood Revitalization,* Albany: State University of New York Press.
Strangleman, T. (2008) 'Sociology, social class and new working class studies', *Antipode,* 40(1): 15–19.
Thompson, E.P. (1965 [1963]) *The Making of the English Working Class*, London: Victor Gollancz.
——(1978) 'The poverty of theory or an orrery of errors', in *The Poverty of Theory and Other Essays*, London: Merlin Press.
UNESCO (2003) *Convention for the Safeguarding of Cultural Intangible Heritage.*
Zukin, S. (1987) 'Gentrification: culture and capital in the urban core', *Annual Review of Sociology*, 13: 129–47.
——(2010) *Naked City. The Death and Life of Authentic Urban Places*, Oxford: Oxford University Press.

Index

Aboriginal poetry 216, 227–28
Aboriginal people 219, 223, 227–28
Actors Equity 236
activist 4, 7, 8, 24, 28, 39, 42–43, 58–59, 61, 63–64, 66, 91, 93, 95, 99, 102, 106, 110–11, 137–38, 197, 205, 240, 265
American Federation of Labor (A F of L) 35, 39
American Folklife Center 233
American Railway Workers Union 249, 251
Ashton, Paul xi, 268, 281
archaeology 5, 7, 53, 62–65, 119, 125; as emancipator 63–65
Army Bureau of Current Affairs, Britain 277
Artisanship 293–96
Arts and Humanities Reserach Council, UK (AHRC) 25–29
Association for the Revitalisation of Old Centres, ARCA 288–89, 290–92, 297
Authorized Heritage Discourse (AHD) 2, 4–5, 8–9, 25, 70, 85, 87, 88–89, 96, 101, 268, 298; see also discourse

Beamish Open Air Museum 106, 114–15, 116, 136, 142, 179, 272, 280
Benjamin, Walter 19–20, 21, 32
Big Red Songbook 234, 243
Blackball Museum 138
Blair, Tony 76, 92, 209
Branting, Hjalmar 185–86
Bragg, Billy 196, 209–10, 212
British Broadcasting Commission (BBC) xii, 25–29, 32–2, 236, 238, 272
British National Party 78
Builders Labourers' Federation (BLF) 242
Burns, Robert 205, 211

Capital 5, 6, 32, 38, 40, 50, 120, 142, 183, 200, 251, 283, 284, 287, 291, 297
Capitalism 6, 32, 43, 44, 47, 53, 81, 137, 251, 253
Carpenter, Edward 193–94, 200, 201–4, 206, 209, 211, 214
Castleford 7–8, 24–25, 31, 85–102
Castleford Community Learning Centre 94
Castleford Heritage Trust 91–92, 95–96, 97, 98–100
Carlyle, Thomas 199–200, 212
Channel 4, UK 24–25, 31, 33, 99
Chartism 199–200
Chicago 6, 11, 34–50, 37, 40, 49, 204, 209, 210, 249–55, 250, 252, 258, 261–64
Chicago Historical Society (CHS) 42
Chicago Police Department (CPD) 42, 49, 49
city planning 286, 296
civil society 71, 73–74, 291
civil war: American 39, 53, 120, 132, 205; English 193, 196, 197, 202, 205, 267, 273, 276–79; Spanish 284, 288
class 1–4, 7, 13, 20–21, 50, 63, 69–73, 75, 78, 81, 85, 87, 107, 109, 111, 116–17, 119–20, 127–28, 130, 131, 138, 140, 147, 149, 183, 200, 216–17, 228, 249–50, 253, 257, 262–64, 268, 272, 284–85 295–96, 298; analysis 71, 81; chav culture 73; consciousness 20, 185–86, 193, 295–96, 262; conflict, 2–3, 52–53, 78, 120, 123, 126–29, 131; decline of class as a term of analysis 20–21; ethnicity 13, 72, 81; gender 3, 7, 20, 66, 78, 94–95, 140, 153–54, 175, 180–81, 257, 268; identity 6, 12, 20, 72, 106, 188, 120, 268–69, 287;

304 Index

inequality 88; moral imperative 100; politics 20, 89, 179, 183, 187–88, 218, 220; race 3, 5–7, 9, 20, 72–74, 131, 165, 167; solidarity 1, 40; struggle 2, 53–54, 78, 89, 137, 296, 297–98; whiteness 6, 70, 72–75, 81; *see also* middle class, ruling class, underclass, working class
classless society 52
Cooleemee Historical Association 124–26, 131–32
Colorado National Guard 239
Community Party: American 42, Australia 216, 219–20; Britain 272
Communist Party of Great Britain's Historians Group 20
community 1, 3, 7–8, 12, 23–24, 25, 35, 64–65, 69, 70, 74, 78–79, 85, 106–7, 119–21, 124–26, 129–32, 140–42, 161–63, 166, 170, 193, 219, 238, 242, 253–55, 256–57, 262–63, 270, 283, 292–93; activism 23, 59, 61, 64, 85, 91, 106, 238, 258–59; arts 138; business 46; curation 24, 65, 95–96, 106–7, 126, 138, 249, 262–63; driven research 8, 64; engagement 63; farming 76; heritage 1, 5, 8, 13, 29, 70–71 100, 258–63; identity 70, 72, 74, 78–79, 86–87, 90–91, 95, 97, 106, 216, 228; immigrant 35, 77–80; industrial 11, 85, 90, 255; memory 79, 91, 112, 131, 133, 192; mining 19–31, 65–85, 92–102, 107–17, 137; model 249–53, 255, 257, 260–61, 263; post-industrial 5, 23, 25, 111, 117; pride and self-esteem 24, 86–90, 97–98, 119, 126; studies 72–73, 81; white 69, 81; working class 1, 2, 4–5, 7, 13, 75, 85, 89, 93–94, 102, 222, 251, 262–64; values 98–99, 101
commemoration 1, 4, 5–7, 10–12, 24, 28, 40, 50, 61, 64, 131, 192, 194, 200, 204, 208, 269–71, 273–75, 277–78
company town 55, 249–50, 252–53
Cortonwood Colliery 21
critical heritage studies 4, 9; *see also* heritage studies
cultural capital 219, 268
cultural loss 173

Danielsson, Axel 185, 190
deindustrialization 87, 24, 30, 85, 90–91
Delgado, Manuel 286, 298, 300

democratization of history 132–33
Depression, the Great 122–24, 127–28, 138, 166, 220, 232
Derrida, Jacques 20, 32
discourse 5, 7, 12, 13, 21, 25, 61, 69–70, 72, 75, 86–88, 100, 139, 188, 235, 271, 285; historical discourse 52–53; heritage as discourse 12, 86–89, 100; of heritage 72, 75, 85, 87–89, 99–100, 182, 285; *see also* Authorized Heritage Discourse; of nostalgia 3; of social exclusion 74; of whiteness 70
Durham Miners Association 108–9, 110, 115
Durham Miners' Gala 23, 99, 110–14, *113*, 117, 279

East London 72, 76
Edwards, Dudley 276–78, 280
emotional degeneration 90
emotional regeneration 23, 99
emotions 3, 71, 74, 87–88, 90–91, 111, 124, 149, 154, 259, 262–63, 272, 279
Employment Contracts Act, New Zealand, 136
Engel, George 37, 38
Engels, Friedrich 198, 200
Englishness 6, 80, 271
Es Barri, Sa Gerreria 283–84, 287–96, 299–300.
Ethnicity 13, 72, 81
exclusion 4–5, 10–11, 22–23, 74–75, 131, 216, 219, 286

Fairclough, Norman 87, 103
Faue, E. 119–20, 133
Federation of Organized Trades and Labor Unions 35
Federation of Associations of Neighbours' of Palma (FAVP) 290, 291, 297
festivals 1, 11, 12; Athens 239; Burston 267, 269–73; Castleford 24, 96–98; Cooleemee Historical Association 124; Es Barri (fiesta) 292; Levellers' Day 267, 269–73, 276; Po-Boy 160, 163, 165, 168, 170–74, 175, 176; Tolpuddle 266, 269–76
Fielden, Samuel 36–38
Fink, L. 127, 130, 133
Fischer, Adolph 36–38
Folkways Records 235
Franquesa, Jaume 287, 300, 301

Index

Fraser, Nancy 13, 14, 88–89, 101–3, 182–83, 190
Fraser, Ronald 147, 152, 158
Fusion Project (AHRC/BBC) 25–29

gender 3, 7, 20, 66, 78, 94–95, 140, 153–54, 175, 180–81, 257, 268
gentrification 12, 220, 284–87, 291–92, 296–98, 299, 300
Gilbert, Kevin 227, 229
Gilmore, Mary 217–18, 229
Glasier, J, Bruce 194–95, 198, 202, 210, 214
Gramsci, Antonio 3, 7, 64, 67, 140
Green, Archie 233–34, 243
Green Bans 242–43
Green, Herb 220
Green, James 35, 36, 39, 51, 269, 271–72, 274, 280
Guillaume, M. 283, 285, 286–87, 297, 301
Guillory, John 182, 184, 189, 190
Guthrie, Woody 232–33

Hall, Stuart 181–82, 190
Hamper, Ben 150; 158
Hatfield-McCoy feud 54
Hatfield, Sid (Sheriff) assassination 55–56
Haymarket Riot 34–38, 37, 46–48, 48, 49, 50, 253
Henderson, Bonny 221
heritage 1–5, 21, 26, 30–31, 50, 69–75, 80–81, 85–89, 95–96, 101–2, 106, 139–40, 147, 151, 156–58, 205, 216–17, 268–69, 271, 294, 296–98; as a cultural process 88–89, 100, 200; as a discourse 5, 7, 12, 70, 85–89, 100; archive 26–28; authenticity 8; Authorized Heritage Discourse 2, 4–5, 8–9, 25, 70, 85, 87, 88–89, 96, 101, 268, 298; beliefs 179; community 1, 5, 8, 13, 29, 70–71 100, 258–63; critical heritage studies 4, 9; digital 10; dissonant 2, 86, 91; folk 6; from below 3; and gentrification 12, 284–87, 296; heritage making 91, 101; identity 10, 12, 179, 182–83; industrial 2, 6, 9, 21, 26, 30, 96, 250, 255, 262–63, 268, 291; intangible 4–5, 8–10, 12, 24, 86, 101, 158, 179, 189, 192; 200, 208, 216, 243, 285, 294; literary 178–82, 202; management 187, 198; material heritage/culture 1, 8–9, 19, 64, 86, 89, 96, 101, 156, 157, 158, 189, 268–69, 270, 273, 284, 285, 294; memory 28, 71, 75, 78; musical 200–202, 208; national 5, 80, 182, 184, 187, 188, 270–71, 277–78, 279; performing 209; poetic 207, 217; theme park 141; regeneration 25, 99, 290
heritage industry 141
heritage industry critique 2–3
heritage studies 9, 13, 21, 70, 178, 183, 188; see also critical heritage studies
heritage tourism 12, 65, 253–54
Herrington Miners Banner Partnership 8, 106–7, 110, 111–12, 114–16
Hewison, Robert 2–3, 14, 31, 86, 87, 101, 103, 139, 143, 286
Hickey, Pat 137
Higdon, Annie and Tom 266–67, 270, 272
Hill, Joe 102, 196–97, 208, 215
History Workshops, Ruskin College 20

identity 1, 4, 7, 10, 12, 61, 70–72, 74–76, 78–80, 88–89, 101,106, 109, 110, 112, 119, 123, 125, 130, 152, 156, 180–81, 187–88, 228, 234, 278, 287; British 74; class 6, 12, 20, 72, 106, 188, 120, 268–69, 287; collective 23, 111, 179, 273, 278; community 70, 72, 74, 78–79, 86–87, 90–91, 95, 97, 106, 216; English 69–70, 72, 74–75, 80–81; heritage 9–10, 179, 182–83, 187–88; historical 28, 124; occupational/organizational 107–8, 109, 100, 111–12, 116–17, 156; national 69–70, 72, 73, 86–87; politics 10, 88–89, 130, 140, 182–83; Tornedalian 180; working class 20, 73, 85
ideology 72, 136, 139, 142, 202, 211, 216
inclusion 4–5, 13, 69, 75, 187, 217, 286
inequality 1–2, 71, 81, 88, 227
industrial buildings 24, 90
industrial sites 2
industrial revolution 2, 34, 53, 77, 157, 231
Industrial Workers of the World (IWW) 137, 139, 196, 207–8, 234
intangible heritage 4–5, 8–10, 12, 24, 86, 101, 158, 179, 189, 192; 200, 208, 216, 243, 285, 294
International Labour and Working Class History 3
Internationale 198, 212
Illinois Historical Society (ILHS) 42–43, 44
International Working Peoples Association 35
Internet 10, 132, 163, 171, 237–43

Index

John Brown 39
John Brown's Body 201, 202, 205
Jackson, Aunt Molly 232
Jay, Martin 149; 158
Jennings, Humphrey 157–58, 159
Johnson, Eyvind 184, 186–87
Jerusalem 198, 204

Kean, Hilda 268, 270, 274, 280–81
Kevans, Denis 220
Kershaw, Baz 139, 143
Keynes, John Maynard 232, 244
Korson, George 231–32, 233–34, 243, 244
Knights of Labor 35

Labour: activists 42, 93; and capital 5, 6, 35, 200; child 123; conflict 52–66, 253, 263–64, 291; church movement 201; heritage 42, 120, 249; history 6, 11, 13, 20, 42, 50, 65, 119, 120, 128, 139, 157, 161, 173, 262, 264; labourism 30; leaders 39, 50, 149; martyrs 6, 11, 34, 39–43, *41*, 45, 46, 50, 122, 210, 266, 270, 271, 274–75, 276, 277; memory 34, 50; movement 6, 7, 11–12, 23, 34–35, 38–40, 42–44. 48, 52–53, 56, 184–87, 193, 201, 203, 206–7, 238, 252–53, 263, 266–67, 269, 270, 271–72, 273–75, 276; organized 2, 46, 50; organizations 35, 44, 138, 219–20, 46, 124, 192; process 2; repressive policies 55; white 75
Labor Day 61–62, 252, *252*, 255
Labour Party: British 73–74, 78, 92–93, 94, 99, 102, 204, 209, 267, 270, 274–75, 277; Independent 193, 194, 203, 210, 267; New Zealand 136, 138
lay historians 119, 123–24, 126–27, 132–33
Lawson, Henry 197, 217–18, 229, 236
Levellers' 267, 271, 277–78
Levellers' Day 267, 272, 276–79
literary heritage 9, 178–87
Lingg, Louis 37–38
Linkon, Sherry 3, 14, 15, 90, 103, 117, 118
Lloyd, A.L. 231, 234–35, 237, 241, 243, 244
Lomax, Alan 232, 235, 237, 243, 244
Lomax, John 243
Lowenthal, David 2, 11, 12, 14, 21, 31, 33, 86, 103, 179, 183, 190
Ludlow Massacre 52, 239, 253

McCormick, Cyrus 36, 39, 50
masculinity 94–95

Marshall, T. H. 156, 159
Martinson, Harry 184, 187
Marx, Karl 19–20, 31, 33, 183, 279
Marxist perspectives 63, 127, 140, 183, 278
Mathews, Race 190, 193, 194, 196–98, 208, 210, 215
Maritime Union of Australia (MUA) 238
Maryland, my Maryland 205
May Day 6, 35, 39, 42, 43, 50, 137, 203, 210, 270, 274
media 22, 25–26, 29, 32, 50, 72, 79, 115, 138, 164, 168–69, 170, 172, 173, 277; attacks on mining communities 22
memory 3, 26, 29, 61, 87, 89, 91, 97, 117, 119, 122–23, 125, 126–27, 129–33, 149, 151, 157, 192, 196, 269, 285–86, 298; class 7, 81, 298; collective 31, 111, 117, 202; community 79, 91, 112, 131, 133, 192; forgetting 10–12; heritage 28, 71, 75, 78; historical 34; identity 74; industrial 80; making 2, 101; popular 23, 29, 202; public 34, 38, 39–40, 42, 46, 48–50, 170; remembering 4–6, 9, 12–13, 19, 24, 30, 85, 95, 99, 202; sites 269; social memory 69–81, 91, 181, 272
Methodism 275
Methodists 258, 273–76
Michaels, Walter Benn 182–83, 190
middle class 12–13, 72, 138, 169, 175, 199, 200, 222, 287, 297–98
militarization 56–57
miners, coal 6–7, 21–33, 25–31, 52–53, 55–56, 60, 62, 64–65, 95, 106, 108–9, 111, 114–16, 128–29, 137–38, 149, 220, 213–2, 233, 241, 267, 272; 1984–85 strike (UK) 5, 21–31, 29, 85, 90–94, 97, 106, 109–10, 111, 114, 116, 272, 273; aftermath 22, 90–91
mining; communities 19–31, 65–85, 92–102, 107–17, 137; industry 22, 98, 114; *see also* unions
moral imperative 1–2, 13
Morris, William 194–95, 201, 202, 205, 209, 210
Multiculturalism 6, 69, 74–75, 77, 81
museums 2–3, 4, 5, 11, 13, 64, 65, 87, 96, 106, 115–16, 119, 124–26, 128, 131, 138–39, 141, 187, 210, 250, 255–56, 258, 268, 270, 271, 283, 295; house 125, 131, 252, 254, 255–56, 260
Mundey, Jack 242

National Register of Historic Places (US) 53, 59
National Union of Mineworkers (NUM) (UK) 91, 21–22, 91, 108;
Neebe, Oscar 37–38, 40
Neighbourhood; see *working class*
neo-liberalism 21, 136, 138, 139, 142
New Deal 232–33
New Left 20, 148
New Left Review 147, 151
New Working Class Studies 3–4, 13
Newman, Jon 269, 281
Nora, Pierre 192, 212
Nostalgia 1, 2–3, 24, 77, 86, 130, 172

Obama, Barack 232–33
Open Archives Project (AHRC/BBC) 25–29
Orwell, George 193, 213
oral history 120, 122, 125–26, 129–30, 131–32, 147–48, 152–53, 161–64, 285

Paris Commune 197, 204
Parsons, Albert 35–38, 40, 43
Parsons, Lucy 39–40, 42, 43
Passeig per l'Artesania (PA) 293–96, 298
Paterson, A.B. (Banjo) 236
π.o. (Pi O) 221–22, 223, 230
Protectors of Chicago 46–49, 47, 48, 49,
Plummer, Ken 148, 159
politics of recognition 10, 88–89, 101, 178, 181–83, 187–88
Portelli, Alessando 120, 127, 128–29, 131–32, 148, 159
preservation 7, 9, 10, 59, 64–65, 119, 123, 125–26, 131, 158, 165, 174, 182, 255–56, 257, 261–63, 287, 290, 296
Pullman Palace Car Factory 249–50

race 3, 5–7, 9, 20, 72–74, 131, 165, 167
racialized language 167
racism 130–31, 219
Rail Tram and Bus Union (RTBU) 240
reconciliation 2, 23, 30, 44, 270
Red Flag 203–10
Red Scare 38–39, 40, 50
regeneration 24–25, 78, 99, 284
remembering 4, 5–6, 9, 12–13, 19, 24, 30, 38–40, 85, 95, 99, 202
Robertson, Iain 3, 15, 269, 281
Rooke, Phill 139, 142
Rumley, J. 120, 123–24, 127–31

Rumley, L. 123–24, 126, 129, 131–32
Ruskin College xi, 20, 275
ruling class 71, 186;
Russo, John 3–4, 14, 15, 90, 103, 117, 118, 117,
Rydberg, Viktor 185–86

Samuel, Raphael 3, 15, 20, 21, 29, 31, 33, 87, 104, 148, 157, 159, 268–69, 272–73, 281, 286, 301
Sayer, Andrew 1, 10, 15, 71, 73, 82, 85, 89, 102, 104
Syson, Ian 216, 219, 222, 225, 227, 230
Seeger, Charles 232, 237, 243
Seeger, Mike 232, 243,
Seeger, Peggy 235, 236–37, 243, 244
Seeger, Pete 123, 196, 232–33, 235, 243, 244–45
Seeger, Ruth Crawford 232, 243
Serra de Tramuntana 284–85, 288
Schwab, Michael 35, 37–38, 40
segregation 130–31, 283, 296–97
Semple, Bob 137
Shackel, Paul A. 3, 10, 15, 52, 63, 67–68, 295, 301,
Shuttle and Cage 235,
social inclusion; *see* inclusion
social exclusion; *see* exclusion
socialist international 39
Society for the Study of Labour History 20
solidarity 1, 23, 40, 46, 52, 60, 73, 108–10, 137, 140, 185, 225
songs 1, 10, 39, 119, 122, 140, 149, 166, 175, 183, 192–215, 216, 220, 228, 231–43, 300
Smith, Laurajane 2, 3, 4, 8, 15, 24, 25, 33, 52, 63, 68, 70, 82, 86–87, 88–89, 96–97, 104, 180, 182, 188–89, 190–91, 200, 213, 268–69, 282, 285, 297, 301
Spies, August 35–38, 39
Springsteen, Bruce 196
Stanley, Liz 148, 153, 157–58, 159
Strangleman, Tim 3, 15, 88, 90, 98, 104, 151, 159, 298, 302
strike: Blackball strike 137; Blair Mountain 6–7, 52–66, 54; Burston School Strike 266–67, 270, 272; General Strike (UK) 52; General Strike (US) 122–23, 127–28; General Textile Strike (US) 128; Haymarket 6, 52, 34–50, 210, 253; London Dockers' Strike 204; Loray Mill 122; Maritime strike (NZ) 208; miners'

strike, 1984–85 (UK) 5, 21–31, 29, 85, 90–94, 97, 106, 109–10, 111, 114, 116, 272, 273; New Orleans Railway Workers 161–62, 163, 166–67, 171–72; Pullman Factory Workers 11, 249–51; 253, 255–57; Rand Miner's Strike, Johannesburg 207; Shearers' Strike (Australia) 197, 236
Strindberg, August 185–86, 189

Taksa, Lucy 87–88, 103, 104, 120, 126, 130, 134
Tannenbaum 205, 208
Textile Heritage Initiative 125–26
Textile Unions (US) 122–23, 127–28
Thatcher, Charles 195
Thatcher, Margaret 21, 24, 85, 90–91, 92, 110, 112
Theriault, Reg 149–50, 159
Thompson, E.P. 20, 33
Tolpuddle Martyrs 11, 266, 270, 273, 274–77
tourism *see* heritage tourism
trade unions 7–8, 11, 28, 42, 44, 46, 53, 55, 56, 58–60, 61–62, 64, 66, 78, 91–102, 106, 108–10, 117, 122–23, 124, 136–38, 140, 161, 164, 167, 172–73, 196–97, 207, 219, 231–32, 234, 235–36, 256, 266–67, 270, 272–73, 274–76, 290; Agricultural Workers Union (UK) 274; American Federation of Labor (A F of L) 35, 39; American Railway Workers Union 249, 251; Australian Council of Trade Unions 227; Builders Labours Federation (BLF) 242; Banners 96, 105, 110–15; 137, 140, 273; Durham Miners Association 108–9, 110, 115; Federation of Organized Trades and Labor Unions (US) 35; General and Municipal Workers Union (UK) 274; Grand National Consolidated Trade Union (UK) 266; legacies 85, 95; Maritime Union of Australia (MUA) 238; National Union of Mineworkers (NUM) (UK) 91, 21–22, 91, 108; Rail Tram and Bus Union (Australia) 240; Shearers' Union (Australia) 197; Textile Unions (US) 122–23, 127–28; Trade Union Congress (TUC) 266, 270, 271, 273–75, 276; Union of Democratic Mineworkers 21–22; United Mine Workers (UMW) (US) 55–56, 58, 60, 61–62
Trade Union Congress (TUC) 266, 270, 271, 273–75, 276

UNESCO 2, 8, 87, 101, 285
underclass 73, 291
unemployment 23, 90, 111, 116, 225–26, 273

Waldheim Cemetery 39, 43
Waltzing Matilda 236
Webb, Paddy 137
White Cockade, The 204–5, 207–9, 211
Whiteness 6, 70, 72–75, 81
Wikipedia 231, 243
Williams, Justine 224–25, 230
Williamson, B. 107–10, 116–17, 118
Wobblies 137, 196
working class 1, 19–20, 30, 40, 63, 65, 69, 72–73, 88, 101, 116, 120, 123, 126, 130, 139–40, 150, 161, 169, 172,178, 183–85, 188, 193, 199, 216–17, 225, 227, 251, 252, 257–58, 262, 276, 278, 279, 283–84, 286, 289, 291, 293, 297–98; and archaeology 63; communities 1, 2, 4–5, 7, 13, 75, 85, 89, 93–94, 102, 222, 251, 262–64; consciousness 20, 185–86, 193, 295–96, 262; culture 1, 58, 107–10, 137, 142, 150, 154, 217, 222, 224, 228, 295; culture, mocking and appropriation of 1, 168–70; dialect 163, 168–69, 170, 223–24; history 1–2, 20–21, 87, 147, 161, 171, 173, 217, 253, 255, 286; identity 20, 73, 85; idealised image 283–84; museums 3, 138, 187, 210; neighbourhoods 24, 35, 167, 255, 262, 286–87, 295–96; people 1–2, 13, 20, 40, 147, 149, 151, 156, 172–73,184, 217, 227–28, 225, 220–21, 268–69, 296; town 78, 100, 168; women 72, 90, 94–95, 169, 170, 225, 227, 289
women 95, 121, 139, 167, 218–19, 225, 226, 227, 232, 289; class 72, 90, 94–95, 169, 170, 225, 227, 289; in film 29, 32; literature 180–81; miners' strike, UK 94–95; suffrage movement 273; Women Against Pit Closures 28; Women's Liberation Federation 193, 210, 214;

Women and Suffrage Campaign Song Book 193, 210, 214
Workers' Education Association (WEA) 276, 278
Worklab 3
World Heritage Convention 8
World Heritage List 2, 86, 285
World Heritage site 288

Wright, Patrick 2–3, 16, 21, 31, 33, 86, 87, 101, 105, 268, 269, 271, 282

Young, Cathy 225–27, 230
Youngstown 117

Zandy, Janet 217, 222, 226, 229, 230